Additional Praise for

"In this refreshingly serious book, New Testament scholar and theologian Tommy Givens emancipates the usurped rallying cry 'we the people' from its ecclesially and nationally institutionalized violence to an innovative mode of discursive power by emplotting peoplehood internal to God's gratuitous election of Israel. Givens has marshaled a startling array of sources, faculties, and commitments toward a relentlessly perspicacious review of theopolitics that is first frightening and then emboldening."

Jonathan Tran, Baylor University

"*We the People* is a dangerous title tempting the reader to think they know the 'we' before reading this extraordinary book. However, through the argument Givens develops, we come to a chastened understanding of the 'we.' He does so by giving us fresh eyes to see how the 'we' that refers to the American 'we' can make us less than God's people. This is a demanding but very important book."

Stanley Hauerwas, Gilbert T. Rowe Professor Emeritus of Divinity and Law, Duke University

"In this provocative book, Tommy Givens exposes and challenges the dangerous theological roots and deadly consequences of modern 'peoplehood' and its expression in nation-states. In critical conversation with Yoder, Barth, and N. T. Wright, he calls on Christians to recognize the election of Israel and its incarnation in

Jesus as the foundation of a peaceable Christian identity and witness. His biblical and theological arguments deserve a wide hearing and careful engagement."

Michael J. Gorman, St. Mary's Seminary & University, Baltimore

We the People

We the People

Israel and the Catholicity of Jesus

Tommy Givens

Fortress Press
Minneapolis

WE THE PEOPLE

Israel and the Catholicity of Jesus

Cover design: Laurie Ingram

Cover image: Hermitage, St. Petersburg, Russia / The Bridgeman Art Library

Library of Congress Cataloging-in-Publication Data is available

Print ISBN: 978-1-4514-7203-5

eBook ISBN: 978-1-4514-8445-8

The paper used in this publication meets the minimum requirements of American National Standard for Information Sciences — Permanence of Paper for Printed Library Materials, ANSI Z329.48-1984.

Manufactured in the U.S.A.

This book was produced using PressBooks.com, and PDF rendering was done by PrinceXML.

To the honor of my parents, Tom and Sharon Givens

Contents

Acknowledgments

A project like this book has a way of impressing upon you what you owe to others. My wife, Kim, has endured the frustrating slowness of its progress through countless stages, remaining a constant companion and even an admirer. My chin has usually been up because of her. Our children, Anna, Isaiah, Amaya, and Judah, know this book primarily as what has kept their dad up late for most of their lives and what has sometimes vied with them for my attention. They have helped me keep my feet on the ground as I have read, thought, and written, often in eleven-minute intervals between their visits to my desk. Somehow they seem to have avoided bitterness toward my work for the most part, and I am grateful for their resilience and for the times they have rightly insisted that there were more important things for me to do.

My years at Duke Divinity School were some of the richest in learning of my life, both with professors and fellow students. The germ of the dissertation on which this book is based sprouted in a seminar on the Gospel of Matthew with Richard Hays in 2007. After several stimulating seminars in modern philosophical theology and coaching for preliminary exams, Stanley Hauerwas guided me patiently through the writing, chapter by chapter, welcoming me for spontaneous conversation throughout as he has famously done for many others. While Stanley was the one who introduced me to Barth in the currents of modern philosophy, it was J. Kameron Carter who helped me to see the significance of Barth's theology in the context of Christian colonialism and the formation of the West. J.'s lectures on Christology were truly inspiring, and if there is any articulateness in this book's treatment of race, I owe it primarily to him. Along the way at Duke, I had the good fortune to meet Peter Ochs. Besides (and through) training me in the practice of Scriptural Reasoning, Peter has been my teacher in hermeneutics, theology, and Bible. His influence is subtle but ubiquitous in this book, and I am grateful for it. Kavin Rowe's New Testament Theology seminar was among the best courses I took in the ThD program at Duke, artfully integrating biblical studies and theology with uncommon acumen. He joined these other four to make a dream dissertation committee.

In 2007 Joel Marcus taught a witty and historically rich seminar in Early Christianity and Judaism, which diligently brought me nearer to an intricate ancient landscape that has been characteristically oversimplified. Paul Griffiths cut incisively into my patterns of thought on countless occasions, not least in a theology and ethics colloquium in which I presented an early draft of my dissertation proposal in 2009. His insightful remark that evening that "'Israel' is a term of theological art" has since remained at the forefront of my mind; I hope this book does it a measure of justice. And finally, Douglas Campbell, who graciously allowed me to audit more than one of his courses on Paul and tolerated me as a research assistant, shared expert knowledge and experience with me in class, in colloquiae, and in his home over way too many cups of tea one weekend while we worked furiously on the Greek in his fine and epic volume, *The Deliverance of God*.

Some of the most impressive people I befriended while at Duke were fellow students. I don't know how many courses I took with

Nathan Eubank in addition to the Matthew seminar with Richard Hays, but he always upped my game and made our learning together a joy. Matthew Whelan and Natalie Carnes couldn't make the colloquium where I presented a draft of my dissertation proposal, so they graciously invited me to lunch a day or two later and shared their thoughts with me. That was but a token of their earnest friendship, intellectual and otherwise, that I have known since my first years at Duke; I hope the future holds substantial time together for our friendship to grow. God looked kindly upon me when placing me in a doctoral carrel next to Andrew Thompson and Jeff Conklin-Miller on the fourth floor of Perkins Library. While I was writing the initial chapters of this book, they listened generously to my random attempts to piece the argument together and, as they had before and have since, warmed the long, air-conditioned days with their friendship and especially with their laughter. Daniel Weiss was a student at the University of Virginia whom I met through the Duke-UVA Colloquium. Our intellectual interests overlap extensively, and I thank him for his instructive comments on early drafts of the first two chapters. My closest companion at Duke was Sameer Yadav. Our friendship goes way back, and what I have learned in conversation with him over the years runs deep in this book and in my life. Thank you, Sameer.

I have written most of this book while teaching New Testament and Christian Ethics at Fuller Theological Seminary since 2010. I thank the New Testament Department, the Latino Center, and the seminary administration for helping me to prioritize the completion of this work during some demanding years in my life. I am also grateful for the stimulus that my colleagues and students have added to my thinking and for the editorial assistance of Hannah Kelley and Brian Hohmeier. Glen Stassen, of blessed memory, indulged me in tireless dialogue on the issues of this book as well as other matters in

Christian ethics. He also took the time to read the entire manuscript several drafts ago and to send me lengthy comments by e-mail.

It turns out that the years of writing this book have also been the years of my parents' dying of particularly difficult diseases. They supported me proudly and unswervingly to the very end, even as I sometimes wrote by their bedsides. I feel some sadness that they did not live to see the publication of what understandably remained to them a mystifying collection of words. The reader might guess that the argument of this book is opposed to much of the Christian formation I received under my parents' influence, but I hope the substance of the argument conveys that I gratefully owe to my parents more than I could ever oppose. I suspect my mom rivals many of the saints in the amount of prayer she offered to God for her oldest son, from well before the time I was born, and she was, of course, too proud of me to imagine that I was very wrong about anything. While just as proud, my dad knew better. The gifted Baptist preacher of my local church from my days in the womb forward and Little League baseball umpire extraordinaire, he has left an impression on my life and this book that I can scarcely estimate, even as the voice of which my own is a discordant echo. Perhaps a few words that he wrote me years ago, when troubled by my politically charged learning from the likes of John Howard Yoder and N. T. Wright, capture his presence in the words of this book: "I'll always love you more than I disagree with you." May this book honor my parents.

I grew up in a church full of people who loved my dad deeply. One of them was the trenchant Bonnie Ryan, who, seeing the end of her long life approaching, generously funded my studies at Duke simply for her love of my father. She died not long before I finished, but because of her, my family and I are carrying a much smaller financial debt than we would have. In fact, I may not have finished without her help, so I am delighted to mention her here with thankfulness.

The demands of research and writing over the past several years have impressed upon me my debts to many others as well. But writing this book as I was losing my parents made some of those gifts seem beyond measure. The culture of Fuller Seminary breathed comfort into my life through a long and agonizing season of loss. The people and pastor of Knox Presbyterian Church did the same. And besides the affection and gritty intimacy of my wife, Kim, I wish to acknowledge the steadfastness of my life-long friends Matt Kelly and Jonny Eveleth. They have faithfully accompanied me in grief, in work, and in remembrance.

Introduction

Giorgio Agamben writes,

> In the Bible, the concept of a "people" is . . . divided between *am* and *goy* (plural *goyim*). *Am* is Israel, the elected people, with whom Yahweh formed a *berit*, a pact; the goyim are the other peoples. The Septuagint translates *am* with *laos* and *goyim* with *ethnē*. (A fundamental chapter in the semantic history of the term "people" thus begins here and should be traced up to the contemporary usage of the adjective *ethnic* in the syntagma *ethnic conflict*.)[1]

Peoples have not always been what peoples now are. Peoplehood has a history. With the rise of the nation-state in recent centuries, "the people" has emerged as the most determinative form of human community. And as Agamben indicates, this ideological emergence is part of a biblical history and discourse.

By "most determinative" I mean the primary basis for killing. What or who belongs to the people of reference in the form of the modern nation-state must be protected and is the measure of life. What or who threatens the people of reference is killable and is the measure of death. The differentiation underlying modern peoplehood, therefore, is not simply a matter of who is killed and who is protected. It is the

---

1. Giorgio Agamben, *The Time That Remains: A Commentary on the Letter to the Romans*, trans. Patricia Dailey (Stanford, CA: Stanford University Press, 2005), 47, emphasis his.

measure of life and death. It is a matter of which lives are nourished and which lives are passed over, if not actively starved or hunted down, both across the border of the body politic and throughout its teeming complex. In fact, the differentiation I am describing *is* the border of which territorial borders are only derivative, a distinction that constitutes and polices "we the people." Thus, to belong to the people of reference, that is, to be citizen, is to enjoy certain "rights." To belong to some other people is to enjoy such "rights" more conditionally, depending on what it implies for the people of reference. Then there is the plight of those nation-stateless persons, who don't belong to any people at all.

But there are citizens and then there are citizens, just as there are immigrants and then there are immigrants. It is harder for some citizens to go to a good school than it is for others, just as it is easier for the same citizens to go to jail. It is much more difficult to immigrate to the United States from Latin America or Africa than from Western or Northern Europe. Thus, the political difference that constitutes "the people" as distinct from others ramifies both internally and externally, exposing the operation of at least one, more fundamental difference, which Agamben identifies above with the term "ethnic." Yet, however occult the "ethnic" constitution of "the people," peoplehood has come to be the decisive imaginary for negotiating human difference in modernity, that is, for negotiating the difference between life and death, from military and police violence, to the contours of political economy, to the most mundane interaction among neighbors.

All this seems remote from the Bible. But it is among the aims of this book to show that it is not, that the modern drama of peoplehood is, as Agamben observes above, a biblical development. In chapter 3, I demonstrate that modern peoplehood has been a colonialist and countercolonialist Protestant appropriation of the one true God's election of Israel according to the Bible. As Christendom broke up in the colonialist scramble for dominance and Christian aristocracies sought antimonarchical bases of political order, Euro-American projects of peoplehood competed with one another to be the new and true Israel, and resistance movements in their colonies often mimicked them in opposition to colonial rule. Thus, the Christian supersessionism at work in Christendom leading up to modernity provided a key language, conceptuality, and optic for the imagination of modern peoplehood and the production of peoples. Modern political order has therefore been made with a development of Christian supersessionism—the declared displacement of an old Israel by a new Israel, and it is with that development that it remains burdened.

As Protestantism grew more protestant, the category of religion emerged, and it did so as a problem.[2] Accordingly, with religion appeared something supposedly nonreligious and less problematic, culled from the disintegrating structures of Christendom: what is now known as "we the people." Distilled from "the people of God," this modern, "nonreligious" peoplehood became more determinative than what was conceived as "religious association," as evidenced by the readiness with which persons and communities of the same religious association have exploited and killed one another in the name of their respective "peoples." Meanwhile, religion became the small province of sentimentality, personal piety, and the afterlife, to put matters rather cynically. Supposedly distinct from politics, modern religion has been understood to shape the material existence of "the people" only obliquely. Nevertheless, a particular understanding of the election of Israel remains the operative basis of modern peoplehood.[3]

2. See Charles Taylor, *A Secular Age* (Cambridge, MA: Belknap Press of Harvard University Press, 2007).

The modern distinction between religion and politics was anticipated by a premodern fissure in Christian theological ethics, dividing the calling of Christians into two: one determined by the episcopal structures of the church, the other by the monarchical structures of territorial governance, both imagined and operated by Christians. With the modern progression of this fissure, Christians are supposed to live one way as religious beings and another as political beings. In the realm of the personal and the soul, Christians are to be guided by the light of Jesus. In the realm of the political and the body, Christians must follow other, more realistic lights, Scripture ready and waiting to offer support.[4] Thus, Christianity has been able to prop up a most violent political existence with its putative prioritization of the spiritual over the material.

John Howard Yoder responded to the modern dualism of religion and politics by theologically debunking the distinction. He argued that to be Christian is to be called to follow Jesus politically *as a people*; the church is a political community in its own right. The church can therefore not allow any peoplehood other than its own to determine the way it lives. This is to follow the nonviolent politics of Jesus rather than the violent politics of Constantinian and other gentile orders of community, not least the modern peoplehood of the nation-state.

Yoder did not overlook the connection between Constantinian political order and Christian understandings of "Israel," although he did not perceive some of its most important ramifications. He recognized that the New Testament has been particularly vulnerable to distortion insofar as Jesus has been shorn from the people of Israel,

---

3. Cf. "All significant concepts of the modern theory of the state are secularized theological concepts." (Carl Schmitt, *Political Theology: Four Chapters on the Concept of Sovereignty*, trans. George Schwab [Chicago: The University of Chicago Press, 1985], 36).

4. John Howard Yoder, *The Original Revolution: Essays on Christian Pacifism* (Scottdale, PA: Herald Press, 1971), 125–39.

that is, as he has ceased to be known as a Jew. The nonviolent politics of Jesus that is innocent of the false dichotomy of religion and politics is, Yoder argues, simply the Jewish way to live. Constantinian Christianity is therefore precisely that "Christian" existence that has refused to be Jewish.

While Yoder's compelling Christian account of peoplehood goes a long way toward articulating a politics faithful to the God of Israel—and that is my reason for choosing him as a principal interlocutor—I argue in this book that his account cannot adequately subvert and resist the violence of the modern imaginary and discourse of peoplehood. Instead, it plays into some of its central tendencies. Yoder argues that the true people of God are those faithful to the love of God revealed in Torah and finally in Jesus the Messiah. Those who are not, those who refuse this Jewish way of life, do not count as the people of God in any meaningful sense. This understanding of the constitution of the people, I submit, is inadequate to the witness of Scripture and captive to the modern discourse of peoplehood.

According to the Bible, the people of the one true God, which is always Israel, is not self-constituted. It is not constituted by Israel's faithfulness to the exclusion of its unfaithfulness, but by God's faithfully holding Israelite faithfulness and unfaithfulness together with hope and forgiveness. The people of Israel is constituted, in other words, by God's election, which is fulfilled in the Messiah who is the elect one. Moreover, it is precisely God's election that makes Israel a people of peace and a peacemaking people.[5]

This last claim of course flies in the face of superficial readings of the Bible and recent understandings of election, a notion at once repugnant and ubiquitous in modernity. The idea that God has

---

5. Because of the oneness of the people of God, I have usually treated "the people" as a collective singular noun calling for singular verbs and singular demonstrative pronouns, despite the awkwardness of this mode of expression.

chosen only one people to be God's people seems the essence of unfairness and a recipe for violent aggression with impunity, hardly the basis of peace. Yet, at the same time, nothing is deemed more sacrosanct than the existence of the people of the modern nation-state, and this sacrosanctity by definition attends the political order of "our" people and not the enemy's. Thus, the same claim that a certain people is sacrosanct by something tantamount to God's election is both despised and worshiped: despised when abstract, conventionally religious, or made by enemies; worshiped when embodied as "we the people."

For understandable reasons, then, Yoder virtually ignores God's election of Israel in an effort to describe a nonviolent, Judeo-Christian peoplehood accountable to God's revelation in Torah and Jesus. But in so doing he neglects two important considerations: 1) the situation of his account in the streams of the modern discourse of peoplehood, and 2) the key christological reality of Jesus' solidarity with the people of God in its sin. This solidarity, rather than Jesus' supposedly disowning the violent, "false" members of God's people, makes the cross the culmination of God's election of Israel and the way to the resurrection of the dead for the whole world by the Spirit, that is, the way to peace. Thus, Jesus' solidarity with all of God's chosen people even in its sin,[6] what I call *the catholicity of Jesus* as the elect one, has dramatic implications for the politics of the Christian life, particularly as the church lives in the divisive currents of modern peoplehood.

Neglecting the catholicity of Jesus and the modern discourse of peoplehood in which his account operates, Yoder has appropriated in ethical terms the modern Western imaginary of political difference, which is predicated on a certain supersessionist concept of God's

---

6. This solidarity is itself God's electing, as Karl Barth argues (see chapter 4 below).

election of Israel. According to this imaginary a people is purely and timelessly itself by its own (voluntary) agency and vis-à-vis other peoples. It is endowed with criteria and/or processes for discerning and policing its totalized political self, of which its representatives (or at least some of them) enjoy a complete view. In other words, the people is deemed able to decide who is and who is not the people, who belongs and who does not, who must be preserved and who can be disowned (e.g., killed). Thus, Yoder has refused one form of modern self-election for another, and any self-election opposes God's unconditional and irrevocable election of Israel as it is narrated and observed in Christian Scripture.

The concern of this book as a whole, then, is to provide a Christian account of what it means to be the people of God amidst the warring "peoples" of our time, particularly as peoplehood is determined by the election of Israel and revealed in Christ. In providing such an account, I aim not to relativize the Christian nonviolence of Yoder's understanding but to deepen it in pursuit of peace. The election of Israel cannot be reduced to Israel's self-understanding, written out of the story of the people of God, or conceived as an unfortunate liability to be outgrown. It is a matter of God's own activity and is basic to the testimony of the Bible and to the way things are. According to Scripture, the election of Israel is the revelation of the one God and as such the way of the oneness of creation.

While the entire book can be understood as an appreciative revision of Yoder's Christian account of peoplehood, his account will be the focus of only the first chapter, "The Gospel of a People." I wish not to offer a cheap critique of Yoder but one that builds patiently on his insight, which I find deeply compelling. Accordingly, in the first chapter, I offer an exposition of Yoder's account of the politics of the Christian life and his analysis of the anti-Jewish way in which the Christian church has tended to articulate its story, its self, and the gospel. Chapter 2, "The Jewishness of Christian Peoplehood: Yoder's Misstep," then offers a consideration of the theological program of Yoder's account and an initial critique in light of God's election of Israel, followed by an adumbration of the arguments of subsequent chapters in relation to the modern discourse of peoplehood. Throughout the book, I engage Yoder not only as an influential Christian voice but a compelling representative of the modern tendency to "decide" between who is the true people and who is not, a tendency that has littered the talk of Christians and non-Christians alike for some time.

Chapter 3, "'Israel' and the Modern Discourse of Peoplehood," may have surprised the reader without this introduction. I did not plan to write it when mapping out the dissertation on which this book is based. But after engaging Yoder's account of peoplehood, I was impressed with what I perceived as his debt to modern ways of imagining "the people" and wondered about the contours and dimensions of that imaginary. I had no idea that "Israel," much less the election of Israel, had provided such a crucial trope in the modern discourse of peoplehood. As I awakened to that fact, I realized that the scope of my and the reader's concern with that modern discourse must range far beyond Yoder's debt to it and that an analysis of it deserved an entire chapter. I also determined that this analysis should follow my treatment of Yoder so that the reader has an idea of the sort of theological account that it exposes as problematic. This runs the risk of convoluting the argument of the book as a whole, but I think it is worth the risk. The reader is advised to consider my exposition of Yoder's account not as a simple commendation but a sympathetic restatement of a representative understanding of peoplehood with a view to the constructive criticism and alternative developed in chapters 2–7. If the reader finds herself persuaded by Yoder's account as I present it in chapter 1, I shall have done my job.

The election of Israel, it turns out, lies deep in the grammar of the modern discourse of peoplehood, so that we need to better understand the theopolitical air that Yoder and the rest of us in Western modernity have been breathing. Drawing on political philosophers such as Étienne Balibar and Americanist Sacvan Bercovitch, I have found myself making staggering claims in chapter 3 about the function of Christian supersessionist understandings of the election of Israel in the colonialist construction of what is now known as race and its modern child of nationalism. Ignoring the Christian theological contribution to these colonialist developments cripples (among other things) attempts to articulate both Christian resistance and alternatives to the violence of modern peoplehood. Thus, in the third chapter, I offer the reader a summary analysis of the modern discourse of peoplehood, focusing on its Jewish foil and its fictive ethnicity of "new Israel." I then illustrate and extend my analysis in the terrain of particularly influential modern projects of peoplehood, lingering long over the case of the People of the United States. My rationale for that is that the People of the United States constitutes perhaps the most compelling illustration of the claims of my analysis and has been the most powerful political discursive machine of peoplehood for some time. It is the peoplehood that the church must confront, especially in the United States, and it likely claims most of my readers as its own.

The claims of chapter 3 raise the stakes significantly for the Christian question of what it means to be the people of the God of Israel, placing the question at the heart of the geopolitical forces that have shaped the modern world, one horrific ramification of which was the Shoah. In the course of my research for this book, I soon learned that these stakes were not lost on Karl Barth. When envisioning the book, I had planned to turn to Barth simply as a corrective to Yoder and the wide tendency he represents. But after completing chapter 3, I found that Barth's account of the election of the community in *CD* 2/2 has implications much more substantial and far-reaching than I had anticipated. That account is therefore the subject of chapter 4, "The Politics of the Election of Israel: Help from Karl Barth."

Chapter 4 and its complement, chapter 5, "The History of the Election of Israel in the Flesh: God's Story of Hope," illustrates the approach of the entire book, namely, to address the urgent theopolitical question of peoplehood rather than merely rehearse the views of secondary writers. I am concerned not only to criticize others but also to offer somewhat developed alternatives. Just as I exposit Yoder's Christian account of peoplehood and then begin to build critically upon it in chapters 1–3, so, in chapters 4–5, I exposit Barth's account of peoplehood and then develop a derivative account of my own that attempts to draw on Barth's insights and address his shortcomings.

Barth is my other chief interlocutor besides Yoder because he rightly makes God's election of Israel central to both the self-revelation of God and what it means to be the people of God while confronting head-on the violence of anti-Jewish, modern peoplehood. Barth shows that the people of God does not choose its own existence (against Yoder) and is not a natural phenomenon. But while Barth's account helpfully provides a sort of idealist grammar of election, it falls prey to some of the modernist tendencies evident in Yoder (and some of the other dangers of philosophical idealism). Specifically, it cannot name or tell the historical course of the electing activity of God in the flesh that constitutes Israel as the people of God. It can offer only formal christological poles that are supposedly always pulling Israel's existence dialectically toward its fullness in Christ. This is impatient with the contingency and moral ambiguity of Israel in the flesh and promotes corresponding political impatience. Barth is unable to answer the question that must be answered, namely, "Who is Israel according to God's election in the flesh?"

The question, "Who is the people of God?" has typically invited not the telling of a history in the flesh but the construction of a border between a true and false people of God or between a natural and adopted people of God. Constructing such borders is precisely that—our construction, an imposition that attempts to resolve the ambiguity of the flesh of the people. It is not a way forward through the modern discourse of peoplehood but a way of remaining captive to its vicious cycles. Whereas Yoder does not perceive this, Barth does perceive it and begins to address it. But I contend that he cannot finally overcome this tendency. So, in chapter 5, I move beyond Barth to give an answer to the question, "Who is Israel according to God's election in the flesh?" In doing so, I dispose of what has become a standard answer to that (or a similar) question in many quarters, one which is really no answer at all and an accretion of the modern discourse of peoplehood, namely, that Israel proper is ethnic Israel.

My consideration of biblical texts in chapter 5 is limited to the Tanakh/Old Testament. My intent in doing so is not to claim that one must read the Tanakh independently of or theologically prior to the New Testament. That cannot be done and should not be attempted by Christians. But it is the eclipse of the witness of the Tanakh by the prejudice of certain poor readings of the New Testament that has allowed Christians to draw a border between a true and false people of God and to relativize the flesh of Israel and therefore of Jesus. So while my consideration of certain texts from the Tanakh anticipates my readings of Matthew and Romans in chapters 6 and 7, I have postponed those New Testament readings in hopes that they be adequately disciplined by patient consideration of the Law and the Prophets as presented in chapter 5. Thus, in chapter 5, I articulate God's election of Israel according to the Tanakh as a living, ongoing historical activity of God from before the foundation of the world rather than a dead decree enclosed in a God alien to time. My account exposes the canonical texture of Israel in the flesh ignored by well-established readings of the New Testament (and of the Old in light of the New) on the question of the identity of the people of God, showing how these modern exegetical developments have been rushed along by the modern discourse of peoplehood.

I might have begun the whole book with chapters 6 and 7, respectively "The Election of Israel according to the First Gospel" and "The Election of Israel according to the First Letter." This is where all the key theopolitical moves of the constructive argument are made. I might have made the naïve claim to draw the argument of the book directly from such a close reading of biblical texts. But such claims ignore the living situation of biblical exegesis, and more importantly, the role of biblical scholarship itself in the production of the modern discourse of peoplehood and its corresponding geopolitical developments. Were I to begin the book with the content of chapters 6 and 7, I fear that the reader would not appreciate what biblical exegesis is up against and would expect an approach to exegesis that is itself theopolitically problematic. I hope that my saving it for the last two chapters as the substantiation and development of the preceding argument, especially of chapters 4–5, enables the reader to perceive the care that the subject matter of chapter 3 has forced me to exercise when reading the New Testament. The order of the chapters, therefore, may not be systematically material to the argument of the book. It reflects to some extent the course of my own learning, even though I of course began with working understandings of the biblical texts in question. But the order of the chapters also strikes me as a fitting presentation given my concern 1) to build primarily and critically on Yoder and Barth in that order, 2) to engage the modern discourse of peoplehood as a biblically determined discourse, and 3) to stake my claims finally on the words of Scripture.

1

The Gospel of a People

When the Jerusalem temple police arrested some of Jesus' spokesmen for the second time, the spokesmen offered a defense of their dissidence. They said that God had made Jesus "ruler and savior to give repentance and forgiveness of sins to Israel" (Acts 5:31). In response, Jerusalem's governing council

> was infuriated and moved to impose the death penalty. But someone in the council stood up. It was a Pharisee named Gamaliel, a teacher of the law who was held in honor by all the people. He ordered that the men [Jesus' spokesmen] be placed outside for a moment, and he addressed them [the rest of the council]:
>
> "Men of Israel, be careful in what you are about to do with these men. For in recent days Theudas emerged, claiming to be someone important, and a number of men joined him, some four hundred. But he was put to death, and as many as were won over by him were disbanded and came to nothing. After him, Judas the Galilean emerged in the days of the census and drew a company of people away under him. He too was destroyed and as many as were won over by him were scattered. And so, in the case now before us, I say to you, leave these men alone and release them. Because if this movement or this work be merely of

human beings, it will be destroyed. But if it is of God, you will not be able to destroy them, and you may well be found God-fighters."

And they were persuaded by him. (Acts 5:33–39)[1]

Rabbi Gamaliel sees that the community of Jesus' disciples is a politically subversive movement within Israel. It lays claim to Israel's legacy. It is not a merely religious or spiritual movement. It is on the order of the political revolutions attempted by Theudas and Judas the Galilean,[2] although the Jesus movement has, by contrast, refused to marshal a violent militia. And yet, this understanding of the Jesus movement leads Rabbi Gamaliel to defy the decision of the rest of the council, which has already condemned this latest uprising and moved to kill Jesus' detained spokesmen. He questions the council's authority to undertake the dissolution of Jesus' community by violence or even to police it to the margins of Israel. He apparently cannot discard the possibility that God has commissioned the revolution of Jesus for Israel. His understanding of Israel is, we might say, too catholic to simply outlaw this dissident voice. It must be met with patience.

There is ostensibly nothing that Jesus or his spokesmen have said or done that immediately disqualifies their claim to witness to Israel's promised future. That God has raised one man from the dead ahead of the many God will yet raise is not in itself out of the question. That many of Jerusalem's authorities had colluded to crucify this same one whom God has now allegedly raised to be Lord for the sake of Israel is not impossible, however offensive it is to Jerusalem's governing council. Instead of ruling their testimony out of court, Rabbi Gamaliel claims that the truth of the witness of Jesus' spokesmen can be judged—and this is crucial—*only with time*. God

---

1. All biblical quotations in this chapter are my translations unless otherwise noted.
2. Cf. Josephus's account of these revolutionary figures (*Jewish War*, 2:117–118; *Jewish Antiquities*, 18:1–8; 20:97).

has shown in past cases like those of Theudas and Judas the Galilean that God's providence can be trusted to deal by various means with Israelite movements that threaten Israel's integrity and faithfulness, if that is what Jesus' movement turns out to have been. The activity of God exceeds Israel's authorities and so must be waited upon instead of fictitiously (legally) co-opted or preempted, as Israel continues to wander through time, with its God both leading and following. To pronounce the final judgment of death independently of how Jesus' community develops in time, in relation to both the rest of Israel and gentile powers, is to usurp God's judgment rather than to witness to it. It is to undermine the very integrity and faithfulness of Israel that such a pronouncement would profess to protect. This is the wisdom of Rabbi Gamaliel, "a Pharisee and teacher of the law who was held in honor by all the people."

Our modern sensibilities would like to describe Rabbi Gamaliel's wisdom as "religious tolerance" or even "commitment to the political process," neither of which is a bad idea. But that is not what Rabbi Gamaliel is displaying. He is witnessing to something much deeper at work in the life of the people of Israel, the politics of which refuses to separate judgment from the flow of time or to imagine God's saving activity independently of the course of Israel through history. Rabbi Gamaliel refuses time-less criteria. The politics to which he bears witness is not generic, however. Its historical provenance and concrete development on the earth are not incidental or secondary to what this politics is, as a mere species of a general political genus would be. It is not merely a "model" to be appropriated by this community or that; its human context of application is not undetermined. In short, it is not the politics of just any history or of just any people but of the concrete, ongoing history and people of Israel, its extended drama as a political community. It is a politics that grows out of God's election of Israel such that it proceeds with the patient confidence that Israel is held together in the flesh by something more powerful than anything it can do to ensure its own continuity, integrity, and future as a people.

Of course, this understanding of Israel's election presumes that election operates with a particular ethical force. The force of Israel's election for Rabbi Gamaliel is not to justify whatever self-defense Israel (through the Sanhedrin authority) sees fit to undertake, such that Israel is entitled to do anything to preserve itself (e.g., put Jesus' spokesmen to death). Quite the opposite: God's election means that Israel does not fully know the self it would seek to defend or preserve. Israel must struggle to further find itself in time. That is not to say that Israel has no continuous self, no particular identity, for it has grown from an irreplaceable past that reverberates into the present and must be reckoned with rather than forsaken. But God's electing Israel makes it an eschatologically oriented people, a people that must wait upon God for its promised future. That is not easy for its people or its authorities to remember, especially when they are suffering or facing mortal danger. That is when God's election can be perverted into political self-assertion, as it apparently was by much of Jerusalem's council in Acts 5. Thus, the irrevocable and unfolding nature of God's election of Israel saddles its authorities and the rest of its people with ominous temptations (e.g., Jer. 7:4-11; Matt. 21:12-14).

But as Rabbi Gamaliel seems to understand it, God's election empowers Israel to expose itself to risks that are typically unthinkable for other peoples. Death does not hold the same power over the elect people that it does over others. As a result, a given generation of the people of Israel can confront threats like Theudas, Judas the Galilean, and Jesus in a way that inspires political life rather than the closure induced by violence. To this death-enduring life, and thus life-giving death, Rabbi Gamaliel bears witness, and this life-giving death reaches full disclosure in the cross and resurrection of Jesus. The

New Testament describes Jesus as God's elect one. Yet, being God's chosen did not move Jesus to live as if his own life were sacred and to be defended unconditionally. That is the way of the kingdoms of the world (John 18:36). As the elect one, Jesus "came not to be served but to serve and to give his life as a ransom for many" (Mark 10:45).

Perhaps I'm reading too much into Rabbi Gamaliel's speech. If only he'd known what those spokesmen of Jesus would go on to do! They would galvanize a movement of immeasurable historical power that would often spurn his wisdom, claiming in various ways to know Israel's self fully and intuitively, and to embody it exclusively. In many cases it would obey the spirit possessing Jerusalem's council in Acts 5 before Rabbi Gamaliel's speech and turn its guns on non-Christian Jews like him. The path of its theological reasoning would eventually help make room, as it turns out, for modern ideologies that have configured the Jews as the enemy of the state, a community to be eradicated by unspeakable atrocities. Perhaps Rabbi Gamaliel was not, after all, the voice of deep theological wisdom I have made him out to be. Maybe he was simply a shortsighted pragmatist who thought he knew a needless political quagmire when he saw one. Or perhaps he is a character concocted by a Christian writer simply to vindicate Jews of Gamaliel's ilk and make Christians look even better. We shall have to wait and see in what follows.

In order to consider the sort of political existence that is election by the God of Israel, I will first clarify with the help of John Howard Yoder how the Christian life is that of a people and what this life has to do with God's chosen people Israel. At the end of chapter 2, I will ask what Yoder might make of the politics of Rabbi Gamaliel. In the meantime, I intend to show how peoplehood is central to Yoder's account of the politics of the Christian life and how the Christian peoplehood he describes must be understood as also Jewish. I will then turn in the next chapter to criticize Yoder's account of Judeo-

Christian peoplehood for its neglect of the election of Israel and its implicit claim that the people of the God of Israel is self-constituting, that is, that it consists only in communities and members who make good on their claim to be the people of God (i.e., by being faithful). In so doing, I will be laying the groundwork for a constructive account of how the people of the God of Israel is not self-constituting but constituted by God, who disciplines unfaithfulness by holding the faithful and unfaithful together as one people.[3] The term for this ongoing activity of God is "election," and I contend that attending to it deals with Yoder's inadequacies in a way that is consonant with his own program of peace. In the course of these opening two chapters, then, I hope to crystallize the central question of everything that follows: How does the election of the people of Israel determine what it means to be Christian? My concern in formulating this question with Yoder's help and then going on to address it is not primarily theoretical, though theoretical reform is indeed a subsidiary concern. My primary concern is the way that Christian collective self-understanding informs the way that Christians live, not least our willingness to kill and our corresponding, internal hostility. The violence we direct against our enemies cannot be separated from the violence within the Christian community.

Situating John Howard Yoder's Quest for Peoplehood

For all of his insistence that he was merely reporting and synthesizing the findings of others, Yoder's *The Politics of Jesus* has proven to be a watershed. With a historically sensitive reading of the Gospel of Luke, Paul's letters, and other New Testament writings, he substantiated the audacious claim that "The ministry and claims of

---

3. This is not to imply that Israel is passive in its constitution over time. My constructive account in this and the following chapters will attempt to articulate how Israel's agency is related to its constitution by the God of Israel.

Jesus are best understood as presenting . . . one particular social-political-ethical option."[4] Yoder thus debunked the standard assumption that Jesus was of primarily religious or personal significance and only derivatively of social, political, or ethical import. Instead, Jesus' nonviolent way of living, which was his way of dying, constituted a certain political way of being, as attested by the political shape of early Christian communities. This is not simply a possible construal of the historical person Jesus; it is, Yoder argued, how Jesus is presented in the New Testament, which claims not to dream up a compelling character but to treat of the Jewish man of flesh and blood who was crucified under Pontius Pilate. Only this distinctively political life, then, according to Yoder, can be the basis of sound claims about the person and work of Christ and what it means to be Christian.

Claims about Jesus that downplay the political way he lived are either not historically truthful or inconsistent with the Christian confession of the incarnation. They minimize or distort the political shape of the Jesus presented in the New Testament, or imply that the political shape of Jesus' flesh was only the shell of a more substantive reality, perhaps a "spiritual" one. Therefore, to accommodate Jesus to a political ethic of self-preservation and "responsibility" in the name of some more determinative truth *about* Jesus (e.g., a "religious" or "spiritual" truth), as much of the church has in fact done through its history, is a christological mistake. It is to deny that Jesus, in the political fullness of his flesh, was God's decisive revelation; it is to be guided, instead, by some ethical norm other than Jesus as presented in Scripture, by "other lights."[5] The christological stakes are thus significant, for "if Jesus is human but not normative, is this not the

4. John Howard Yoder, *The Politics of Jesus: Vicit agnus noster*, rev. ed. (Grand Rapids, MI: William B. Eerdmans, 1994 [1972]), 11.
5. John Howard Yoder, *The Original Revolution: Essays on Christian Pacifism* (Scottdale, PA: Herald, 1971), 125–39.

ancient ebionitic heresy? If he be somehow authoritative but not in his humanness, is this not a new gnosticism?"[6]

This means that Rudolph Bultmann and Billy Graham are both wrong about the gospel. They are not wrong because they present Jesus as liberating human selves from anxiety, guilt, confusion, immorality, or eternal punishment. Jesus may be said to do that. They are wrong because that sort of liberation is not the gospel. It is not what Jesus is about according to the New Testament. To make such personal liberation the subject of Jesus' life is therefore to narrow our gaze considerably and finally to betray him. It is to regard Jesus' flesh as only an apparition and to relocate the drama of his life from history to an individualized human experience that owes little to Jesus and is only incidentally in time.[7]

The Politics of Jesus is thus concerned with overcoming deeply entrenched personalist understandings of Jesus and the resulting Constantinian reduction of Christianity to a "religion." Such personalist understandings wrongly imagine that individual persons are more fundamental than the groups of which they are a part, that human groups are no more than the sum of the persons that compose them, and that Jesus therefore relates to individual persons more determinatively than he does to communities or social structures. We must, it is thought, choose between the personal and the political and

6. Yoder, *The Politics of Jesus*, 10. *The Politics of Jesus* is thus fundamentally a work in Christology, although this is often overlooked because history is seldom deemed the proper theatre of Christology. Rather, it is assumed that Christology is a discourse about natures that is not determined by any historical contingency. For Yoder, one cannot study divinity or humanness apart from how God and human beings have unfolded in time. The way Jesus lived, then, constitutes who God is and who humanity is. Concepts of divinity or humanness condition but cannot predetermine historical consideration of who Jesus is. Cf. John Howard Yoder, *The Royal Priesthood: Essays Eschatological and Ecumenical*, ed. Michael G. Cartwright (Scottdale, PA: Herald, 1998), 95 and Dietrich Bonhoeffer, *Christ the Center* (New York: Harper & Row, 1978), 31.

7. Yoder, *The Original Revolution*, 31–32; John Howard Yoder, *For the Nations: Essays Evangelical and Public* (Grand Rapids, MI: William B. Eerdmans, 1997), 82; Yoder, *The Royal Priesthood*, 73.

prioritize the former. The Jesus we are left with is one who steered clear of the contaminating mess of politics and busied himself with the more important task of restoring individual souls. This Jesus has proven very useful for the religious justification of violence, as Jesus' nonviolence in the body becomes insignificant and he is taken to constitute some good worth killing for (e.g., killing to preserve the political order in which persons can be "saved from their sins").

Personalist understandings of Jesus are possible, Yoder suggests, only if we forget that Jesus was a Jew. However unwittingly, such understandings are anti- or at least a-Jewish. The Jewish way of life from which Jesus hailed—the Jewish way of life of the Hebrew prophets—knows nothing of a personalist flight from the political.[8] Thus, Yoder frames the *The Politics of Jesus* as a defense of a *messianic* ethic.[9] He shows that a much more historically and theologically sensitive reading results if, instead of stripping Jesus of his Jewishness and reducing his proper domain to "the heart," we recognize him as fully incarnate and active in the common, brutal struggle known as the political, that fray where peoples are forged in the heat of mutual opposition and cooperation.

But what *The Politics of Jesus* has to do with peoplehood may remain unclear. For some, the question of peoplehood is secondary to politics in general and the politics of Jesus in particular. Few would deny that politics involves human community, but community has come to be a generic concept that is distinguishable from the political itself, as community is often understood as only a component or circumstance of the political (which is in turn more about "issues" and "structures"). And peoplehood—a more ambitious and exclusive concept than community—is sometimes deemed the preemption of good politics, at least of the innocent sort that Jesus supposedly

8. Yoder, *The Politics of Jesus*, 108–9.
9. Ch. 1 is entitled, "The Possibility of a Messianic Ethic."

embodied. The politics of Jesus may be about peace, justice, and love, but none of these is determined in relation to any peoplehood, it is thought. Not so, says Yoder. To the justification of violence in the name of preserving or enhancing "the people," Jesus does not respond with a politics that avoids peoplehood. He answers violent peoplehood with a peoplehood of his own: a nonviolent one. That Christians can think that politics is about something other than peoplehood is yet another anti- or a-Jewish habit that we must unlearn if we are to reckon with Jesus. The politics of Jesus, according to Yoder, simply consists in making a people:

> God's promises of righteousness to be brought to the nations through His servant Israel were from year to year reiterated, reinforced, clarified, even though the likelihood that the Israelites would become the instrument of their fulfillment seemed less and less evident. These were promises, Christians believe, Jesus came to keep. Jesus did again what God had done in calling Abraham or Moses or Gideon or Samuel: He gathered His people around His word and His will. Jesus created around Himself a society like no other society mankind has ever seen:
>
> 1. This was a voluntary society: you could not be born into it. You could come into it only by repenting and freely pledging allegiance to its king. It was a society with no second generation members.
> 2. It was a society which, counter to all precedent, was mixed in its composition. It was mixed racially, with both Jews and gentiles; mixed religiously, with fanatical keepers of the law and advocates of liberty from all forms; with both radical monotheists and others just in the process of disentangling their minds from idolatry; mixed economically, with members both rich and poor.
> 3. When He called His society together Jesus gave its members a new way of life to live. He gave them a new way to deal with offenders—by forgiving them. He gave them a new way to deal with violence—by suffering. He gave them a new way to deal with money—by sharing it. He gave them a new way to deal with problems of leadership—by drawing upon the gift of every member, even the most humble. He gave them a new way to deal with a corrupt society—by building a new order, not smashing the

old. He gave them a new pattern of relationships between man and woman, between parent and child, between master and slave, in which was made concrete a radical new vision of what it means to be a human person. He gave them a new attitude toward the state and toward the "enemy nation."[10]

Jesus did not bring to faithful Israel any corrected ritual or any new theories about the being of God. He brought them a new peoplehood and a new way of living together. The very existence of such a group is itself a deep social change. Its very presence was such a threat that He had to be crucified. But such a group is not only by its existence a novelty on the social scene; if it lives faithfully, it is also the most powerful tool of social change.[11]

We will return to the Jewishness of the politics of Jesus below. For now, let us clarify Yoder's claim that Jesus did not embody or teach an ethic of which a people is merely the context, support, or epiphenomenon. He did not constitute a political imperative that can be safely appropriated by any people or applied willy-nilly within any existing social or political structure, vocational office, or "situation." Jesus is not such an abstraction in search of concretion. To understand the politics of Jesus in this way mistakes Yoder's wild claims for something much more tame, something happy to regard the relevance of Jesus as predetermined by independently existing social structures (e.g., family, country), that is, defined contexts that we take to be universal or foundational to human existence. It is to accommodate Jesus to some structure supposedly more fundamental than he is, to overlook that Jesus confronts all social structures, calling into question (and revealing) even what it means to be human.

10. Yoder, *The Original Revolution*, 28–29. Also in Yoder, *For the Nations*, 175–76. In ch. 2, I will consider Yoder's claim that Second Temple Jewish society was a voluntary one, as it controversially implies that one was not born a Jew but chose to be Jewish.
11. Yoder, *The Original Revolution*, 31. In other contexts Yoder does not conflate "society" and peoplehood as he does here (e.g., Yoder, *The Politics of Jesus*, 37, 106, 155, 189, 247). In view in what I have quoted is the most determinative form of human association. His usual term for that form of community is "people."

Refusing such accommodation, Yoder insists that the politics of Jesus simply was the formation of a people. Jesus' life, death, and resurrection generated a particular, concrete people, one that was unique vis-à-vis other peoples and has persisted to the present. The particularity of this people does not consist in arbitrary relation to Jesus by virtue of its beliefs about Jesus or its institutional continuity since Jesus. Its particularity consists in the way its collective life is in fact patterned after Jesus, obedient to his commands. Thus, Jesus announced and enacted a "new peoplehood"[12] constituted by practices of mutual self-giving, whose touchstone is the love of enemies and whose social economy moves from cross to resurrection. The cross to bear is not just any burden the Christian finds herself beset by, as common English usage would have it, but the raised standard of this people's costly, nonviolent political ethos, "its own deviant set of values and its coherent way of incarnating them."[13] The peoplehood of Jesus thus consists in a collective perseverance in the nonviolent political life that Jesus revealed to the world, refusing any peoplehood constituted by the violent subjugation of enemies, be they internal or external. Exposing the violent foundation of other political constitutions (whatever their claims to be founded on "justice" or "freedom") by deviant counterexample draws persecution, and so the Christian life is one of taking up a cross as Jesus did.

But some may still think that Yoder's account of the people inaugurated by Jesus is one among many commendable political options. That might be the case only if God did not raise Jesus from the dead, only if Jesus is just one among many lords. If God did raise Jesus from the dead, however—disclosing the goal of history right in the middle of it—then the people gathered by Jesus is the one people

12. Yoder, *The Original Revolution*, 24.
13. Ibid., 28.

that serves the Lord of all lords. This people attests that the way of the cross is the way to resurrection and, therefore, the direction of history. Being patterned after Jesus, it does not claim merely to witness to a good way of doing things. In forgiving, suffering, and sharing as Jesus did, it claims to witness to what it means to be human and to the historical arc of all creation. Following Jesus *is* its claim to the truth. Yoder thus contends not only that Jesus formed a particular people but that this people is one of historic and cosmic distinction, as Jesus is "King of kings and Lord of lords" (Rev. 19:16).[14]

In *The Politics of Jesus*, when moving from the life of Jesus as portrayed by Luke to the New Testament communities that knew Jesus as the resurrected Lord, Yoder continues his case against the personalist domestication of Jesus. If personalist assumptions have induced readings of the Gospels that understand Jesus to be concerned primarily with the restoration of individual souls, they have done the same to readings of the rest of the New Testament, aided by the disregard of the Gospel narratives. To counter these readings and to demonstrate the political continuity between Jesus and the early Christian movement, as well as the political relevance of Jesus today, Yoder offers an account of "the powers." He draws this account primarily from Pauline letters with the help of Hendrik Berkhof.[15]

The powers are created but corruptible metaphysical forces or structures that allow for the *relative* integrity and intelligibility of human existence within God's unfolding creation. We see the work of the powers in "the dimensions of cohesiveness and purposefulness which hold together human affairs."[16] They course through time and

14. John Howard Yoder, *The Royal Priesthood*, 73–75. Cf. Yoder, *The Politics of Jesus*, 154.

15. Hendrik Berkhof, *Christ and the Powers*, trans. John Howard Yoder (Scottdale, PA: Herald, 1977).

16. John Howard Yoder, *The Christian Witness to the State*, 2d ed. (Scottdale, PA: Herald, 1964, 2002), 8.

space such that there is a "patternedness"[17] to society, a social fabric. Human life therefore depends on the powers and cannot dispense with them. The ubiquity and immanence of the powers are such that their "totality is overwhelmingly broad," making them difficult to describe concretely.[18] They mediate such staples of life as law and language and thus the *limited* but crucial regularity, predictability, and generalizability that characterize the order by which humanity exists and moves. For example, the powers allow human communities to name and restrict "crimes" or "status" across diverse contexts by the institution of a legal code. Likewise, the powers inspire language with a life of its own, such that verbal communication can be intelligible even if speakers and hearers have no personal knowledge of one another. Law and language thus illustrate how human beings are held together and moved by bonds that precede and regulate the activity of any one person or even of the sum of any number of persons (including all their mental activity). The powers help us name how the sociopolitical whole is more than the sum of the parts. They underlie "the patterns or regularities that transcend or precede or condition the individual phenomena we can immediately perceive."[19] As such, the powers are pervasive in the constitution of any social fabric and key to understanding the politics of Jesus and the people he inaugurated. In fact, "it would not be too much to claim that the Pauline cosmology of the powers represents an alternative to the dominant ('Thomist') vision of 'natural law' as a more biblical way systematically to relate Christ and creation."[20]

17. Yoder, *The Politics of Jesus*, 138.
18. Ibid., 143. "We have here [in Berkhof's account] an inclusive vision of religious structures (especially the religious undergirdings of stable ancient and primitive societies), intellectual structures (-ologies and -isms), moral structures (codes and customs), political structures (the tyrant, the market, the school, the courts, race, and nation)" (142–43).
19. Ibid.
20. Ibid., 159.

The corruption or rebellion of the powers consists in their claims to autonomy or sovereignty, their refusal to convey God's rule and their correlative assertion of their own unity.[21] Thus, the legal constitution of a particular political order tends to absolutize itself as nonnegotiable or somehow entitled to persist. Likewise, certain language has been associated by various generalizing tendencies with the particular histories of human groups or their relatively common physical traits such that they are essentialized as races. The reach of the powers is so overwhelming that human communities have come to relate to them as autonomous principles or deities and thereby the bases of "nature" or "necessity," especially as these latter are thought to justify and empower human political agency. This is how the powers acquire an "ideological function," assigning to a particular family or political community or economic system or piece of land or human experience a "thread of meaning which is more important than individual persons, their lives and well-being, because it in itself determines wherein their well-being consists."[22] The result, in a word, is violence. By virtue of the powers' rebellion, human communities order themselves internally and in relation to one another such that there is some well-being to be pursued at the price of dominating, even destroying, both member persons and other communities. According to Yoder, the death and resurrection of Jesus reveal decisively that such well-being is a lie, the product of false generalizations, universals, or absolutes that are informed by corrupted powers.

The powers—which includes talk of angels and demons in the New Testament—are therefore not a dispensable feature of an outdated religious cosmology. Yoder points to the "patiently

---

21. Such claims are contingent because the powers are part of creation but weren't/aren't created as rebellious.
22. Yoder, *The Politics of Jesus*, 229.

growing scholarly consensus" that, at least in the Pauline conception of the powers, "we have to do with an alternative political cosmology or philosophy of history, neither sacral imperial order nor 'national liberation,' but a universe being reordered by the Word of the resurrection."[23] Political criticism, therefore, does not need to be added to the New Testament or to a naïve early Christianity as if it were not already there. More importantly for Yoder, the reality of the powers precludes attempts to minimize or even deny Jesus' relevance to the political and philosophical challenges of power and structure in the interest of a supposedly more fundamental relation between Jesus and other persons (e.g., a "spiritual" relation). Persons are always conditioned by powers that bind them to one another, a fact that is not lost on the New Testament but rather is basic to its presentation of Jesus and his community of disciples.

As with political cosmology, so with history. Jesus' relation to persons cannot be abstracted from the situation and constitution of persons in time. It cannot be articulated at the price of relativizing the complex ways in which the powers shape the course of history and therefore the persons that are formed by it. The radical personalism that characterizes so much of the modern Western world, which Yoder diagnoses as anti-Jewish, as we will soon see, wrongly imagines that we can understand Jesus and our personal reality only if we free him and ourselves from history. Yoder's quotation of Bultmann says it all:

> Unlike the prophets' preaching, His [Jesus'] preaching is directed not primarily to the people as a whole, but to individuals. . . . Thus Jesus in His thought of God—and of man in light of this thought—'dehistoricized' God and man. . . . [Jesus] released the relation between God and man from its previous ties to history.[24]

---

23. Yoder, *For the Nations*, 87.

Yoder has no interest in denying the reality of persons in their uniqueness or the significance of Jesus for each person. But he refuses to reify with Bultmann the abstraction of persons constituted independently of one another as "individuals." Such individuals simply do not exist; they are the mythologization of actual persons into timeless, supposedly identical entities (i.e., human units) that are fundamentally unconnected to one another, unmediated by the social bonds that have brought them into existence and continuously form them over time. There is therefore no individual personal reality that is not already mediated by the corruptible powers that bind human beings to one another. This puts the question of the Christian life back where it belongs according to the New Testament: in history, in the struggle we call politics. "Tradition tells us to choose between respect for persons and participation in the movement of history; Jesus refuses because the movement of history is personal."[25]

How, then, did Jesus overcome the corruptible powers that, in history, make peoples out of persons and persons out of peoples? How did Jesus subdue the powers so that they serve rather than oppose God's good purpose for humanity? Jesus overcame the powers as they operated in the political forces of his time by accepting the subjection to the powers that is the nature of human existence but resisting to the death their false autonomy. He resisted the claims of fellow Jewish authorities to final righteousness by preaching and incorporating a

---

24. Yoder, *The Politics of Jesus*, 135n1. Yoder quotes from Rudolph Bultmann, *Theology of the New Testament*, trans. Kendrick Grobel, 2 vols. (New York: Scribner, 1951), 25. A few pages earlier, Yoder has noted the same thought in Carl Henry (128).

25. Yoder, *The Politics of Jesus*, 109. Yoder is thus concerned with Jesus and other persons "in time" because they should not be understood as constituted otherwise. The manifold details that come together in time to conceive persons and form them over the course of their lives are not incidental to but constitutive of who persons are. These details should not be minimized in a (usually violent) rush to generalize about persons or their groupings. Taking such details seriously discloses the political nature of personal reality and the powers that operate in the formation of communities and their members *as* history. To say that Yoder is concerned with Jesus and other persons "in time" is to say that Yoder refuses to describe Jesus or his relation to other persons apart from this personal/interpersonal movement of history.

greater righteousness. He resisted the universality of the *Pax Romana* by embodying in his social relations a more universal political order of peace. He resisted the absoluteness of death—the power that in fact limited the righteousness of Judean Jewish authorities and the universal "peace" of Rome—by his resurrection. Jesus did not succumb to the fear of death, even death on a cross, and his resistance finally exposed the false moral pretentions of those who opposed him, those who profaned a Jewish holy day and violated Roman law in order to kill him and preserve themselves. Their politics was thus shown to be incoherent—not autonomous or sovereign but finally arbitrary and imposed by force. By contrast, Jesus refused violence, that is, he refused to cheapen the well-being of his friends or his enemies with any falsely generalized good, truth, or imperative, including that of his own life. Thus Jesus broke the power of the powers. He "unmasked" the powers as false gods, "disarming" them by taking away their weapon of illusion, "their ability to convince us that they were divine regents of the world, ultimate certainty and ultimate direction, ultimate happiness and the ultimate duty for small, dependent humanity."[26]

> His cross is a victory, the confirmation that he was free from the rebellious pretensions of the creaturely condition. Differing from Adam, Lucifer, and all the Powers, Jesus did "not consider being equal with God as a thing to be seized" (Phil. 2:6). . . . Here we have for the first time to do with someone who is not the slave of any power, of any law or custom, community or institution, value or theory. . . . Thus it is his death that provides his victory: "Wherefore God has exalted him highly, and given him the name which is above every name . . . that every tongue might confess that Jesus Christ is Lord" (2:9-11).[27]

26. Ibid., 147, a quotation of Berkhof.
27. Ibid.

The people constituted by the power of the cross and resurrection, then, is the people that refuses the violence of illusory, noneschatological absolutes, including their own well-being at the expense of others' well-being. The resurrection of Jesus reveals the lie of that choice, as eschatological *shalom* comes not by overpowering enemies but by loving them, even to the death.

> In the Pauline witness Jesus is confessed as foundationally relevant to the political realm—not only in the biographical sense [i.e., Yoder's preceding reading of Luke's presentation of Jesus' life], but in the cosmological sense that "cross and resurrection" designates not only a few days' events in first-century Jerusalem but the shape of the cosmos.[28]

This shape of the cosmos is the "rule" or pattern of the political community of Jesus, the basis of its peoplehood. It does not maintain its existence or integrity as other peoples do. It does not live by destroying human threats, by rendering human lives instrumental to its aims, whether these aims be enshrined in a legal code or a supposedly manifest destiny. Jesus' victory over the powers creates a people that can, by the Spirit of his resurrection, recognize the false pretenses of violence. This people flourishes as such to the extent that it confronts violence with love. It does not necessarily flourish by growing in numbers or apparent stability. In fact, it has often deteriorated by increasing its population and institutional establishment at the expense of faithfulness to the nonviolent way of Jesus, while it has thrived through suffering loss. The way that Jesus lived, died, and was raised is thus the measure of its peoplehood. There is simply nothing more determinative of who or what it is as a people than that.

A people that flourishes by confronting violence with love as Jesus did, while still living by the powers, must continuously fix its gaze

---

28. Ibid., 160.

upon Jesus and be guided by his Spirit. Its life depends on ongoing discernment and concrete enactment, for it has not been given an infallible institution of faithfulness or a reliable theory of love. That is why the people constituted by Jesus is *itself* hermeneutical. It constantly calls itself into question instead of regarding itself as a given that would justify preservation or expansion. In the concrete circumstances in which it finds itself gathered, it continually reconsiders Scripture's witness to the people it is called to be, that is, it continually rediscovers itself, as its peoplehood is a hermeneutical process inspired by the Spirit.

> What we find at the heart of our tradition is not some proposition, scriptural or promulgated or otherwise, which we hold to be authoritative and to be exempted from the relativity of hermeneutical debate by virtue of its inspiredness. What we find at the origin is already the process of reaching back to the origins, to the earliest memories of the event itself, confident that the testimony, however intimately integrated with the belief of the witnesses, is not a wax nose, and will serve to illuminate and to adjudicate our present path.[29]

The people assembles regularly to discern and enact who it is in response to concrete challenges. In making decisions as to its next steps, every member must be allowed to address the assembly (i.e., "church"), and the integrity of the process is contingent upon the inclusion of both weak and dissenting voices.[30] Likewise, it comes together as a body in a meal whose shape is Jesus' death, which is

---

29. Yoder, *The Priestly Kingdom*, 70. Just a few paragraphs previously, Yoder offers the following description of the tradition of a people. "Far from being an ongoing growth like a tree (or a family tree), the wholesome growth of a tradition is like a vine: a story of constant interruption of organic growth in favor of pruning and a new chance for the roots. This renewed appeal to origins is not primitivism, not an effort to recapture some pristine purity. It is rather a 'looping back,' a glance over the shoulder to enable a midcourse correction. . . . The effect of pruning is not to harm the vine, but to provoke new growth out of the old wood nearer to the ground, to decrease the loss of food and time along the sap's path from roots to fruit, and to make the grapes easier to pick."
30. Yoder, *The Priestly Kingdom*, 23.

to say, a meal of self-giving mutuality that typifies wider economic sharing.[31] The peoplehood of Christians is about being a people patterned after Jesus rather than ruled by some other norm or by the general currents of wherever it lives; but the authority of that pattern visibly arises from the people by the Spirit rather than from an elite class by historic institution or a charismatic ruler of "spiritual" credentials.[32] Nothing is more urgent than the integrity of this formative process of peoplehood, for in it is embodied the nonviolent, patient way of Jesus, whose Spirit overcomes the rebellious powers and binds the people together, leading it to clear consensus or urging it to wait. The corrupt powers continue to tempt the community to embody an order predicated on self-preservation and the correlative destruction of enemies. But this people witnesses to Jesus' victory over the powers by showing that it is possible to live, and to live well, without resorting to violence.

The foregoing exposition suggests that Yoder does not offer a complete *theory* of peoplehood or of the Christian life, one that could then become the rule of Christian communities. Instead, he argues with readings of the New Testament that the Christian life is most basically the ongoing political life of a people and that its peoplehood comprises a particular set of open-ended practices faithful to Jesus. The shape that the people takes through those practices cannot be determined a priori, as the practices themselves must be allowed to determine the shape of the people.[33]

---

31. Yoder, *For the Nations*, 31–32; John Howard Yoder, *Body Politics: Five Practices of the Christian Community before the Watching World* (Nashville, TN: Discipleship Resources, 1992), 14–27.
32. Yoder, *The Priestly Kingdom*, 15–45; Yoder, *For the Nations*, 44, 83.
33. For an account of how such practices can work, see John Howard Yoder, *Body Politics*.

Yoder's Turn to the Jews

Because of Yoder's concern that the Christian life be governed by Jesus instead of something else, he sometimes leaves the reader with the impression that the people he describes effectively began with Jesus (e.g., his various appeals to the "newness" of Jesus and his community).[34] But as I mentioned above, Yoder's account of peoplehood may be characterized as an attempt to recover the Jewishness of Jesus and of Christianity. He claims that the people of God did not cease to be Jewish with Jesus or Paul but with Constantine, and that it is the dejudaization of Christianity that relocates the drama of the faith from history to the heart, from politics to souls. The claim to surpass Judaism, to have broken out of its fleshly bonds by coming into possession of a more intimate, personal knowledge of the God of Israel—knowledge purified of historical and political contingency—has constituted a betrayal of Christianity. Consequently, Yoder attempts to exhibit the New Testament's claim *to* Judaism rather than to overcoming Judaism and implies that much of the church's history has been a fall *from* Judaism rather than its "fulfillment."[35] He is therefore adamant about the continuity between ancient Judaism and the Christianity that arose from it.

> The work of God is the calling of a people, whether in the Old Covenant or the New.[36]

> Peoplehood is a gift, not a given, in the former covenant no less than in the latter. That nation's survival is not assured (to use Isaiah's vocabulary) by horses or chariots but by faith.[37]

34. Yoder, *The Original Revolution*, 28–31; Yoder, *The Politics of Jesus*, 219; Yoder, *The Royal Priesthood*, 73; John Howard Yoder, *For the Nations*, 41, 175–77.

35. "The 'Fall' of Christianity consisted in the loss of certain elements of the Jewish heritage." See John Howard Yoder, *The Jewish-Christian Schism Revisited*, ed. Michael G. Cartwright and Peter Ochs (Grand Rapids, MI: William B. Eerdmans, 2003), 121. Hereafter *JCSR*.

36. Yoder, *The Royal Priesthood*, 74.

37. Yoder, *For the Nations*, 86.

> From Genesis to Apocalypse, the meaning of history had been carried
> by the people of God as people, as community.[38]

The inability to observe the continuity between the Testaments, between the history of the people of God before Jesus and the history of that same people after Jesus, made room for the personalism that has trumped the nonviolent politics of Jesus through so much of Christianity's history. Yoder suggests that peoplehood will elude Christian communities so long as they understand Christianity to consist in the surpassing or replacement of Judaism, to say nothing of essentializing the Christian life as that which is *not* Jewish. There is simply no Christian peoplehood that is not the peoplehood of Israel.

Having clarified Yoder's claim that peoplehood is fundamental to the Christian life, we come to the central question of this and every subsequent chapter: How does the people of Israel determine what it means to be Christian? As a theological question, this is at once a historical and a political question. It is to ask how the politics of Jesus was constituted by his relation to his people and how that relation determines the shape of the Christian church. In the remainder of this chapter, I will offer a critical consideration of Yoder's account of the relation between the Christian life of the New Testament and the Jewish life from which it sprung, focusing on his *The Jewish-Christian Schism Revisited.*[39] I will then take up his account of "the parting of the ways" and scrutinize his tendency to play a "true" form of Judaism off against a "false" one. Let us begin with one of Yoder's most systematic answers to our central question:

38. Yoder, *The Priestly Kingdom,* 138.
39. My reading of this collection is deeply indebted to the insightful introduction, commentary, and conclusion of the editors, Michael Cartwright and Peter Ochs. I have not been able to dialogue extensively with them in the body of this chapter because its central question is somewhat wider than that of the editorial commentary on Yoder's collection of essays on the Jewish-Christian schism. My aim is to situate the claims of the collection in relation to Yoder's other work on the politics of the Christian life (especially his *The Politics of Jesus*) and to focus theologically on the question of peoplehood.

From the ancient Hebrews through the later prophets up to Jesus there was real historical movement, real "progress"; but the focus of this progress was not a changing of ethical codes but rather in an increasingly precise definition of peoplehood. The identification of the people of Israel with the state of Israel was progressively loosened by all of the events and prophecies[40] of the Old Testament. It was loosened in a positive way by the development of an increasing vision for the concern of Yahweh for *all* peoples and by the promise of a time when *all* peoples would come to Jerusalem to learn the law; it was loosened as well in a negative direction by the development of a concept of the faithful remnant, no longer assuming that Israel as a geographical and ethnic body would be usable for Yahweh's purposes. These two changes [i.e., positive and negative loosening] in turn altered the relevance of the prohibition of killing.[41]

Yoder describes an account like the above as "how the Christian can own the Israelite history, in such a way as to see the gospel as an organic prolongation of the original early Israelite experience and vision, rather than as a rejection or reversal."[42]

Abraham did not try to guarantee the future of his people because he trusted God to provide for it per God's covenant promise. Against all appearances—even against the apparent consequences of his obedience to God's commands (e.g., to sacrifice Isaac) and the prospect that he would see next to nothing of God's promise fulfilled before dying—Abraham obeyed and believed. This faith of Abraham, according to Yoder, was the seed of the covenant people who would come to define its boundaries less and less by geography or ethnicity and more and more by costly obedience to the universal, nonviolent purpose of God.[43] The people of Israel thus determines the Christian life to be the progressing continuation of the political life of that

---

40. Yoder does not mean "prophecies" primarily as "predictions" but as the prophetic calls for covenant justice, which bore threats of judgment and/or promises of salvation.

41. Yoder, *The Original Revolution*, 101, emphasis his. I have standardized Yoder's transliteration of the Tetragrammaton in this and all other quotations.

42. Yoder, *The Politics of Jesus*, 87.

43. Yoder, *The Original Revolution*, 85–104.

people in the way of Jesus. With this "historical progress" definition of peoplehood, Yoder has already deprived the church of its conventional foil of "Judaism," for Christianity simply continued the developing faith of Judaism; it did not supplant it or change course.

But for a long time, Yoder thought that Judaism did not reach the universal love of nonviolence along this trajectory until Jesus. Then he discovered that Christian historiography had claimed for Jesus what was apparently characteristic of Judaism long before Jesus' time.

"Not until I had been studying for decades in the field of *Christian* pacifism did I discover to what extent Christian pacifist convictions had been foreshadowed in the Jewish experience of Jews since Jeremiah. This is one of the gaps in my own education for which I least can forgive my teachers."[44] It is this "gap" that Yoder is addressing in *The Jewish-Christian Schism Revisited* (hereafter *JCSR*). One might otherwise surmise that the essay collection is concerned primarily with contemporary Jewish-Christian dialogue. To be sure, Yoder is addressing and engaging in that dialogue in the various essays, which first circulated with a preface entitled "What Needs to Change in the Jewish-Christian Dialogue and Why." But what needs to change, according to Yoder, is precisely what counts as "Judaism" and "Christianity." Yoder's revisionist (or "radical-reformation") historiography of ancient Jewry and the split within it that eventually produced "Judaism" and "Christianity" therefore serves a more fundamental theological-ethical program. This is borne out in his various turns, some more veiled than others, from historiography to normative statements about what constitutes the right way to serve the God of Israel, the way to be a holy people.

---

44. John Howard Yoder, *Nevertheless: Varieties and Shortcomings of Religious Pacifism* (Scottdale, PA: Herald Press, 1992), 122, emphasis his. This telling remark comes in a footnote added in the 1992 edition of the original 1971 publication. In fact, Yoder added a whole section entitled "The Pacifism of Rabbinic Monotheism" to the 1992 edition (122–25).

Unlike *The Politics of Jesus,* there is no systematic or linear argument to *JCSR,* but its central claim seems to be that Christianity is Jewish. Christians cannot be the people they are called to be without being Jewish, to say nothing of trying to be *not* Jewish; the church grew less faithful to Jesus to the extent that it departed from the ethos of the Jewish people. As this implies, for Yoder ancient Jewry came to be, at bottom, not ethnic or religious, but political and ethical.[45] While elsewhere Yoder insists on Jesus' Jewishness by pointing to the locus of Abraham or "the prophets' line" or even the YHWH war tradition as variously anticipating the politics of Jesus,[46] in *JCSR* Yoder does something different. He attempts to paint a historical picture of the Jewish way of life that Jesus directly inherited—the "type" of life that it was—such that what Jesus did was not to abrogate or modify it but to reinforce and deepen it. The typological correspondence between the politics of Jesus and those earlier loci remained somewhat thin historically in Yoder's earlier works. But in *JCSR,* while his approach remains typological (i.e., a considerable strand of Second Temple Judaism and the politics of Jesus are presented as belonging to the same political type), Yoder predicates the correspondence also on substantial historical continuity. Jesus and early Christianity simply extended the way of life developed under exilic prophets like Jeremiah and quite common to the Jewish community of Jesus' time.

> The "Judaism" which survived after the last Zealot defeat in 135 [CE] assumed the same stance which Jewry everywhere else but in Palestine had already been taking since Jeremiah, namely "seeking the peace of the city where they had been sent" (Jer. 29:4-7). The Jewish settlers in Babylon (and in all the other cities to which they were scattered of which we know less) accepted "not being in charge," not as a lesser-evil

45. That these are construed as alternatives is questionable and will be considered critically below in chapters 2 and 3.
46. Yoder, *The Original Revolution,* 58, 85–104; Yoder, *The Politics of Jesus,* 76–89.

strategy of mere survival, nor as a mere tactic, but as their mission. That experience created the culturally unique traits which define "Judaism" and thereby Christianity in turn:

- the phenomenon of the synagogue; a decentralized, self-sustaining, non-sacerdotal community life form capable of operating on its own wherever there are ten households.

- the phenomenon of Torah; a text around the reading and exposition of which the community is defined. This text is at once narrative and legal.

- the phenomenon of the rabbinate; a non-sacerdotal, non-hierarchical, non-violent leadership elite whose power is not civil but intellectual, validated by their identification with Torah.

Each of these marks was sociologically innovative. Each was indispensable to define Jewish identity outside of Palestine and to make it viable. Each had its Palestinian counterparts, but the home of each was in the diaspora. Each of them guaranteed that while "quietist" and "pacifist" in the sense defined above,[47] this community would be neither silent nor powerless. Cumulatively they made of Jewry an effective missionary people all across the Middle East, not ending their outreach completely even when the Christians, with the same ethos and polity, took over that role.[48]

47. The previous definition to which Yoder refers is this: "If you begin thinking, as in our culture we usually do, with the assumption that it is our moral responsibility to administer the course of human events, then the position I have been asked to describe may be designated as "quietism." If the assumptions are further specified to provide that we normally have a duty to enforce upon others, by military means, our conception of the desirable direction of events, then the position I describe may be called "pacifism." Yet both of these characterizations, which figure in our programme title, presuppose a framing of the moral question which is already tilted. Therefore the more functional or formal phrase in my title "not being in charge", is more fitting" (*JCSR*, 168).

48. Ibid., 170–71. In giving his picture of ancient Judaism, including what was to become rabbinic Judaism, Yoder cites, at different points, conversations with or the work of Steven S. Schwarzchild, Charles Primus, Jacob Neusner, David Novak, H. J. Schoeps, Elija Benamozegh, Ephraim Urbach, Everett Gendler, Daniel Smith-Christopher, Robert Wilken, and Reuven Kimelman. Yoder goes on to say on 171, "There is wide recognition that the Christians of the first two centuries were pacifist, or at least that their most articulate teachers of whom we have record were. The historians debate about whether this was univocally the case, and the ethicists debate about whether, if it was, it should be normative for later Christians. Yet in all of that voluminous debate, neither party takes account of the fact that the ethos of the early Christians was a direct prolongation and fulfilment of the ethos of Jewry. . . . Jesus' impact in the first century added more and deeper authentically Jewish reasons, or reinforced and further

The force of this historical claim of Yoder's is that what Jesus constituted, that is, the political life to which Christians are called, simply continued the trajectory of diasporic Jewry and thus is thoroughly Jewish. Jesus was not an anomaly but the historical culmination of the Jewish nomos. To those who balk at this claim to the extent that the Christian life owes something to Paul, the apostle to the gentiles, Yoder dedicates chapter 3, entitled "Paul the Judaizer." "Far from being the great Hellenizer of an originally Jewish message, Paul is rather the great Judaizer of Hellenistic culture."[49] In various Hellenistic urban centers around the Mediterranean, Paul was building up and in some cases founding communities of a people of the above Jewish traits.

Christianity did not remain Jewish in continuity with Paul's political vision, however. Yoder agrees with the early Protestant consensus that the church had suffered a "Fall" long before the Reformation.[50] But the "Fall" of Christianity, whenever it took place in the half millennium following the apostles, was a loss of Jewishness:

> The first dimensions of the loss to become visible are precisely those traits of early Christianity tied to the Jewishness of the gospel. . . . [The Christian] faith became an ahistorical moral monotheism, with no particular peoplehood and no defences against acculturation, no ability to discern the line between mission and syncretism.[51]

validated the already expressed Jewish reasons, for the already established ethos of not being in charge and not considering any local state structure to be the primary bearer of the movement of history." Cf. a similar remark on 191.

49. Ibid., 95.

50. I add the scare quotes to "Fall" because the concept wrongly assumes that the church was at some point upright or unfallen. That the church has been more faithful at some times than others does not imply that there was ever a "Fall" of the church, especially when the function of claiming such a "Fall" is to justify ecclesial divorce and violent revolution. It is better to understand the "Fall" as singular and initerable, diffuse in created existence, and assumed in redemption rather than escaped or erased (e.g., 2 Cor. 5:21; Col. 1:24).

51. Yoder, JCSR, 107. Yoder claims that the precise location in time of this "Fall" or "Great Apostasy" (not before the sixth century according to the Magisterial reformers and much earlier according to radical reformers) is immaterial to his argument that it was a "Fall" from Judaism.

Yoder's historical claim is at once an ethical one. He insists that the ethos of the Christian life as we find it in the New Testament is Jewish and, correlatively, that Christian communities have been unfaithful—disobedient to the Word that speaks through both scriptural Testaments—to the extent that they have lived a non- or anti-Jewish life.

But let us further develop the main contours of Yoder's historical sketch of the Jews of the Second Temple period so that we may feel the force of his claim (and understand what he means by "Jewish"). In his sketch, we may discern four basic elements: cosmopolitanism, ethos of halakah, scriptural authority, and nonviolence. With each of these, Yoder attempts to hammer a nail in the coffin of the theory that early Christianity constituted an abrupt shift from Judaism such that Judaism and Christianity are fundamentally different. His agenda for Christian ethics is especially evident in his frequent comparisons of post–586 BCE Judaism and radical Protestant Christianity.[52] And, as we will see, Yoder's historical contention serves a wider, theological understanding of history, which we will examine following the exposition of the four aforementioned elements.

1. The Cosmopolitanism of Pre-Christian Judaism

First, Christianity has often been understood to have remedied Jewish parochialism with cosmopolitan vision. The Jewish people have always lived within the limits of flesh, while Christianity reaches to the ends of the world by the spirit, Christians have claimed. This, Yoder insists, is historically wrong. Neither Jesus nor Paul

---

52. Especially in ch. 4, "The Jewishness of the Free Church Vision," and ch. 5, "The Forms of a Possible Obedience." The latter continues an argument thematic to Yoder's writings, namely, that, against Reinhold Niebuhr, the nonviolent ethic of the New Testament is not an impossible ideal but the realistic calling of Christian discipleship. It is realistic or possible because it is not bent on "winning" politically but on living and dying faithfully, by the light of the victory of Jesus' cross and resurrection.

brought universal vision to Judaism because Jeremiah already had. Under him and other diasporic authorities, Jewry had already become cosmopolitan.

> When Christianity became the established religion of Caesar's realm, it seemed to those who were at home in that imperial culture that "the whole world" had been taken over for Christ. Yet on the world scale the Roman Empire, although enormous, was a province. It excluded known civilizations to the north and south and east, including (older and more developed) civilizations to the south and east where Jews had been living for centuries, and Christians for generations. The Jewish world vision was *in lived experience* wider than was the Roman Empire. . . . Likewise the way in which monotheism demanded detachment from civil religion was a safeguard of a wider world-view than the imperial one. . . . We have been thinking so long of Jews as being in the ghetto and of Rome as being the whole world, that it takes a special mental effort to be able to come to terms with the fact that it was really the other way around.[53]

Instead of universalizing a provincial Judaism, then, Christianity came in time to be the provincialization of universal Judaism in the name of Jesus. Postapostolic Christian apologists and philosophers would claim, over against Judaism, to encompass the world by demonstrating that Christian "belief" perfects the universal logos of humanity and by invoking the Platonic transcendence of one God who is "spiritually" or sacramentally accessible to all through Christ. This ironically allowed Christianity to draw its own boundaries on grounds other than the way Jesus lived and to locate truth within those boundaries. But Judaism, including most of early Christianity, refused the illusion of an intellectual or spiritual shortcut to the universal via the purity of Platonic transcendence, true belief, or the completeness of sacramental ritual. Jewish knowledge of the cosmos was material and practical—and thus more substantial, unfolding

---

53. Yoder, *JCSR*, 73, emphasis his.

rather than "perfect"—through a common way of life across wide geographic and cultural dispersion. "The Most High God . . . does not accentuate transcendence in the interest of Platonism or ritualism, but in the interest of relativizing our claims to locate him on our own turf and make him the enemy of our enemies."[54] Jewish transcendence was therefore more in touch with the world than dejudaized Christianity. It was not about two levels of reality—a higher, atemporal, and nonmaterial one that is known purely only to insiders and is more determinative than the lower, temporal, material one to which the rest of the world is confined. Instead,

> the Hebraic view considers transcendence much less purely. That which is not yet "earthly" is not "ethereal" but "to come". The dualism points toward new possibilities for this world [rather than escape from this world], toward promises which both condemn and redeem [instead of justifying and/or abandoning the present order].[55]

Christianity's a- or anti-Jewish reach for the universal ironically rendered it theologically and ethically parochial. Its inability to imagine the limits of its intellectual vision impoverished its engagement with material difference and undermined its capacity for ongoing reform, which depends upon

> some experiential base for the awareness of "otherness". This is what Christians largely lost when they settled into provincial establishment. They lost it in terms of social base by becoming imperially provincial; that freed them to lose it intellectually by becoming theologically provincial. What Christians borrowed from Plotinus through Augustine, and from Cicero through Ambrose, nailed shut the door which Justin had begun to close.[56]

54. Ibid., 163.
55. Ibid., 164.
56. Ibid., 81.

By contrast, Judaism sustained a more truly cosmopolitan vision and has continued to do so up to modern times. "Every foreign land can be home: every homeland is foreign.[57] World awareness is not (as for most of us in monolingual middle America) an educational privilege. It is identity."[58]

Still, one desideratum for Jewish cosmopolitanism remains, namely, the conditions of membership. Surely Christianity opened to the world the doors that Judaism kept closed. Surely it overcame the insularity of the flesh characteristic of all pre- and non-Christian communities and epitomized by Judaism. Did Christianity not welcome into the people of God gentiles for whom Jewish peoplehood had no room? Once again, this claim is historically wrong, says Yoder. "The calling of Israel was always to be a mouthpiece for proclaiming the Lordship of YHWH. Beginning with the break-up of the state structures in the land of Israel, this had already begun to include inviting significant numbers of people of non-Jewish birth into the fellowship and the lifestyle of the covenant."[59] Christians have read an ethnic or analogous exclusivism

---

57. Curiously, this is precisely the claim of the *Epistle to Diognetus* regarding Christians (6:5), the Platonic tendencies of which are widely recognized. Yoder does not give Plato enough credit, in my view.

58. Yoder, *JCSR*, 79. For the record, Yoder thinks "cosmopolitan" a term "too snooty" for the "authentic sense of world culture" he is attributing to diasporic Jewry (79). Cf. 244: "It is only when they have left their homeland and maintained an identity elsewhere that the 'Judaeans' (named for their tribal background or their homeland) became 'the Jews'. The worthy successors of those founders are heroes of costly obedience [like Joseph, Daniel, and Esther]. It would be superficial to see these accounts [of Joseph, Daniel, and Esther] as merely demonstrative of individual virtue. They define a distinctive understanding of the nature of God. A distinctive understanding of the nature of obedience as disobeying the authorities defines God as sovereign above and if need be against the kings of the world, rather than as the 'religious' undergirder of things as they are. Since this is the case, it should be no surprise that on down through history, people who know that about God would be different from their neighbours, and would make problems for their rulers. Thus being out of place or out of phase will then be one of the marks of their identity. This is what has been going on in Jewish life, for now nigh on twenty six hundred years."

59. Ibid., 152.

into ancient Judaism that was not only not there but is contradicted by pre- and post-Christian, Jewish proselytism.

> Although we remember that Jesus once spoke of Jews crossing land and sea to make proselytes [Mt. 23:15], we have generally underestimated the extent to which the Jewish culture of the time was self-conscious and aggressive about propagating the faith.[60]

> The rejection not only of pagan cult but also of every way of putting their own YHWH/Lord in the same frame of reference with pagan deities, even not speaking the divine NAME as others would, was tied for the Jews in Babylon with the proclamation of his sovereignty over creation and history. . . . That anti-idolatry message is not bad but good news. It can free its hearers from slavery to the powers that crush their lives. Many Gentiles watching the Jewish culture saw it that way, so that long before Christian beginnings, standard ways had been found to welcome "God-fearers" on the edge or even in the middle of the synagogue.[61]

> Jeremian/Babylonian Jewry was already bicultural, bilingual, long before "Paul" came on the scene. It was already making proselytes (of all degrees from the "God-fearers" staying on the edge of the synagogue to full integration through baptism and circumcision) long before Paul came along.[62]

---

60. Ibid., 96. Note that Jesus is addressing Pharisees in Matt. 23:15, the very group read by Christians to be ethnocentric, close-minded, etc.
61. Ibid., 195, caps his. I have standardized Yoder's spelling of "God-fearers" in this and other quotations.
62. Ibid., 33. This is also a claim of Marcel Simon's now classic *Verus Israel: A Study of the Relations between Christians and Jews in the Roman Empire (AD 135–425)*, trans. H. McKeating, Littman Library of Jewish Civilization (Oxford: Oxford University Press, 1986). Marcel Simon's picture of Second Temple and rabbinic Judaism is quite similar to Yoder's. Nevertheless, whether Second Temple Judaism was engaged in proselytism has been a matter of dispute in recent decades. While Yoder clearly sides with those who say that it was so engaged, his argument would be upset only if it were the case that Jewish communities refused to Judaize gentiles under any circumstances. It matters not whether proselytes were actively sought or simply allowed. Nor is Yoder committed to the rather late (though pre-Christian), technical concept of "proselyte"; his argument is committed only to the fact that gentile-born persons could participate in "the fellowship and lifestyle of the covenant" before Christianity (*JCSR*, 152). On the ancient history of Jewish proselytism, see Louis H. Feldman, *Jew and Gentile in the Ancient World: Attitudes and Interactions from Alexander to Justinian* (Princeton: Princeton University Press, 1993).

Paul did not break any new ground, then, by welcoming gentiles into the covenant people.

> Paul simply puts two and two together. We recognize in Jesus the inbreaking of the messianic age. It is actually happening on a greater scale than before, that Gentiles who hear about Jesus come to the messianic synagogues. Conclusion: the will of God for our age is the active ingathering of Gentiles into a new kind of body.[63]

Paul's opponents did not disapprove of welcoming gentiles into the covenant people, only the terms on which Paul did so.[64] Insofar as it had long been possible for persons of non-Jewish birth to become Jewish by certain practices of initiation, or even simply by absorption through intermarriage across generations, ancient Judaism did not impose any genetic closure upon Jewish peoplehood. This is not to deny that Judaism maintained a certain "ethnic" stability. It is to say that the Jewish community was not "ethnically pure" and that ethnicity—here understood as "genetic purity"—was not some ground floor of Jewish identity.[65]

> Certainly Jewry has an ethnic definition, because a Jew is normally a child of a Jewish mother, yet by virtue of their success in proselytizing, to which already Jesus referred, and because of their voluntary and involuntary mobility, there was probably less genetic purity among Jews than among most other ethnic groups.[66]

The question, then, is not the possibility of membership for persons of non-Jewish birth—the possibility of *becoming* Jewish is presupposed

---

63. Yoder, *JCSR*, 96.
64. Ibid., 49. Nor were Paul's terms antinomian and his opponents' legalistic. The terms of each contender, according to Yoder, were nomic.
65. While disputed by others, this is a point made strongly by Jacob Neusner in, e.g., *Making God's Word Work: A Guide to the Mishnah* (New York: Continuum International, 2004), 63–99. Nevertheless, Neusner does not agree with Yoder's unjustified and polemical inference from the nonethnic, ethical constitution of Jewishness that its constitution was voluntary.
66. Yoder, *JCSR*, 58. I have corrected a typo in this quotation to avoid confusion. The published text reads, "Certainly Jewry has an ethic [*sic*] definition."

by the fact of proselytes and of some intermarriage—but the practical terms on which such membership was regulated. This brings us to the second element of Yoder's picture of ancient Judaism—an ethos of halakah. But before taking that up, let us briefly summarize what Yoder has attempted with the first element of cosmopolitanism. He has attempted to debunk the standard Christian claim that the difference between Judaism and Christianity is that Judaism is particular and Christianity is universal. That claim is historically wrong and undermines the peoplehood of the Christian life insofar as the people of God is a covenant people and therefore not ethnically but ethically exclusive and particular. But that ethical particularity is cosmopolitan *in practice,* open to all who would commit themselves to it, and responsive to diverse contexts across the known world. Yoder simply does not accept the universality of Christian "knowledge" or "belief," which rendered Christianity not universal but imperial, with no good news for the world. What witnesses to true, peaceful universality is the presence of one people in widely different contexts of the world with a practical way of life that meaningfully engages those contexts in hopeful openness, while refusing to assimilate them by violence.[67]

2. The Ethos of Halakah of Pre-Christian Judaism

With the second element of his picture of ancient Judaism, an ethos of halakah, Yoder makes a claim about what Jewishness was at its most basic. What made the Jewish people what it was over time was a constellation of concrete practices that were possible anywhere and stable across a wide diversity of contexts. These were practices of nonconformity with the idolatrous world around them. Yet, in conjunction with the first element above, Yoder contends that this

67. In this connection, Yoder claims that this "Jeremianic Model" of diasporic peoplehood "is bigger than [Jeffrey] Stout's *Fragestellung*" (ibid., 192–96).

ethical particularity was not the rival to Jewish cosmopolitanism but its partner.

> Although there is plenty of material, and plenty of freedom, with which thinkers over the centuries can develop Jewish philosophical systems (cosmological, mystical, linguistic, scientific), the ground floor of identity is the common life itself, the walk, *halakah*, and the shared remembering of the story behind it.[68]

> The Jews, wherever they went, although adapting more or less to the outside shape of the host society, retained their Sabbath and (many) their *kashrut*, thus reminding themselves that they are not fully at home anywhere, at the same time that their family story-telling and their visits from cousins reminded them of all the other places where God's people are also living.[69]

> The readiness to be atypical, to be non-conformed . . . is strengthened by one further turn of the argument in which Jewish thought had already taken the path which Jesus followed further, and which later rabbis took still further. This is the preference for the concrete case. *Halakah*, the tradition about specific behaviour, is clarified and codified sooner and more firmly than the *aggadah*, the vision of things in a world under God which makes such behaviour reasonable. The concrete shape of the culture of faithfulness is more crucial to a people's commonality of commitment than is the piety with which it is filled out, kept alive, personalized, and explained to outsiders. Imperatives like "go the second mile" or "first be reconciled with your brother" or "swear not at all", or reality readings like "whoever marries a divorced woman commits adultery" or "if you do not forgive others God will not forgive you" are more trans-culturally translatable, and more foundational in defining a community's identity, than the more abstract "first principles" from which academics would like to say they are "derived". We moderns would like first to say something formal like "so act that your behaviour could be a rule for everyone". Then we would like to say something substantial but broad like "the nature of marriage is . . . " or "every person has a right to . . . " Only a few logical steps later would we

---

68. Ibid., 187, emphasis his. I have standardized the transliteration of "halakah" in this and all other quotations.
69. Ibid., 110.

then be willing to get down to specific duties and decisions. Jesus, Jewry, and the minority churches do it the other way. They first name representative acts that are imperative or excluded. This is *halakah*. Then *aggadah*, "spirituality", considers why such judgements make good sense.[70]

To be Jewish after Jeremiah, then, was to engage in certain concrete practices,[71] which were continually shaped, regulated, and nourished through reading, singing, and studying Scripture in synagogue fellowship. These practices of Jewishness, and the story of the past that they anchored, are, broadly speaking, what gentiles took up as their own when they became Jewish. They are, according to Yoder, what made the Jewish people, and early Christians as part of that people, what it was, as displayed in the Sermon on the Mount. "The ethic of truth-telling which needs no oath, of enemy love which needs no sword, of jubilee sharing which needs no treasures, *is a Jewish ethic*. There is nothing platonic, nothing gnostic, nothing Persian about it. The ethic of the Sermon on the Mount is nothing but Jewish."[72]

The practical constitution of the Jewish people defied the hierarchical and sacerdotal structures devised by other communities and eventually by Christianity. "There was not power authorized to impose uniformity, and if there had been, its focus would have been *halakic*, i.e. concerned with behaviour, not with ritual, doctrine or piety."[73] This practical constitution proved more effective than ritual,

70. Ibid., 74–75. In a footnote (n14) to this paragraph, Yoder remarks, "The oriental catholic churches from the third century to the fifth continued to shape their moral life in terms like these" (88).

71. Elsewhere, Yoder also mentions practices of circumcision, endogamy, and rabbinic and family networking. Sometimes Yoder notes that the "networking" was economic or commercial (ibid., 79, 187).

72. Ibid., 140, emphasis his. Critics will rightly note that the Sermon on the Mount lacks casuistry about quintessentially Jewish practices such as Sabbath and circumcision. I suspect Yoder would not make too much of the lacunae and resist the implication that only halakah that addresses such practices qualifies as such. He might also point to the subtle and not-so-subtle ways that the Gospel of Matthew deals with those topics elsewhere (e.g., Matthew 12 and 15).

doctrine, or piety in resisting provincialization, promoting unity, and breathing distinctive life into a people that endured the rise and fall of one gentile empire after another—on the whole a more faithful witness to the peaceful oneness of the God of Israel. The Christianity of the New Testament, if we should call it that, simply continued this trajectory of a halakic ethos. Later Christianity, by contrast, would come to locate the ground floor of Christian identity in beliefs to be adopted and defended, institutional allegiance, and personal transformation. Yoder has no interest in denying the importance of beliefs, institutions, or personal piety per se.[74] But he contends that basing Christianity on them was and is illusory. The political deficiency and instability of defining Christianity this way came, in time, to relativize the human life that Jesus lived and the concrete commands of Scripture; it came to commend authoritarian structures for enforcing religious uniformity in the name of political integrity. These ecclesiastical structures, rather than the practicing people, came in turn to be "the Church," an institution thus founded on dejudaization. Magisterial Protestantism did not disrupt this tendency and in some ways aggravated it.

> This concern for ethos was often held against the Anabaptists, the Quakers, and the Wesleyans by other Protestants who accused them of a relapse into either Catholic or Jewish works religion. That is of course simply to rephrase the question . . . whether the call of Torah may legitimately be blunted by the concern for justification, or by religiousness, or by speculative theology.[75]

73. Ibid., 48. Here Yoder is describing the "rabbinic" authority that coalesced at Yavneh, though it is clear he takes that authority to be simply illustrative of what constituted Jewish authority both before and after Yavneh in the Jewish Diaspora.
74. For example, Yoder opposes "cynical claims that group identity has very little to do with actual beliefs" (ibid., 112).
75. Ibid., 140.

With this second element of an ethos of halakah, Yoder attempts to unsettle typically Christian ways of reducing Judaism to something whose limits Jesus and Christianity overcame. Jewry was not in fact an ethnicity or an institutional structure or a religious system of personal justification. It was a people who lived in a certain, concretely identifiable way. Yoder is especially concerned to unseat the common conviction that Judaism is a religion of works-righteousness while Christianity is a religion of faith.[76] He claims, instead, that Jewry was a people characterized by particular works of righteousness, as was the Christian part of that people for some time. Any dispute was over which works, and was negotiated, as it had been for centuries, under the authority of Scripture. Christianity lost this Jewishness not by its confession that Jesus is Messiah or by welcoming gentiles committed to Jesus' Jewish halakah but by privileging theological speculation over concrete obedience to scriptural commands. The primacy of sacred theory rendered Scripture supposedly cryptic, in need of an elite of exegetes instead of patient, interconnected local processes (themselves implicit in and authorized by Scripture).[77] It allowed Christianity to imagine and appropriate the question of how politically to enforce both the uniformity of foundational beliefs and the material circumstances deemed necessary for personal and sacramental piety, which in turn became the new locus of salvation. The church thereby lost the diasporic Jewish life, which had forsaken political sovereignty (i.e., being "in charge") in order to remain practically and politically faithful.

76. Several of Yoder's essays in *JCSR* seem to have anticipated E. P. Sanders's conclusions about late Second Temple Judaism in *Paul and Palestinian Judaism: A Comparison of Patterns of Religion* (Philadelphia: Fortress Press, 1977). Yoder's reading of the New Testament (especially Paul) in relation to those conclusions is quite different, however.
77. Yoder, *The Politics of Jesus*, 170; Yoder, *JCSR*, 109.

3. The Primacy of Scripture in Pre-Christian Judaism

An ethos of halakah was, as stated above, developed under scriptural authority (i.e., Torah), which is the third element of Yoder's picture of ancient Judaism. Of course, no one would deny that the authority of Scripture was elemental to ancient Judaism or to Christianity. The question is what sort of authority Scripture had.[78] The polemical edge of Yoder's account comes with the political function of Scripture. His claim is that there was no political authority *effectively* more "transcendent" (or "central") than the scriptural text as it was read by dispersed local communities in network with one another. "The primary vehicle of identity definition is a text which can be copied, and can be read anywhere. Decentralization and fidelity are therefore not [mutually opposing] alternatives, as they are with any religious forms which need a priesthood or a temple."[79] The transgenerational integrity of diasporic Jewish authority lay not in a priestly class or a central sacred edifice. The primary, tangible manifestation of transcendent authority was the book of Scripture. "Torah is a word permanently from above us," its authority never controlled by other channels or distant regulators of revelation.[80]

> The Temple was to be replaced not by another Temple but by a house of prayer, a synagogue, a gathering of believers around the scrolls of Scripture. . . . What Scriptures mean in the life of a community is that people can gather around the physically tangible representation of the fact that they are not taking orders from contemporary authorities alone. In this sense a book represents transcendence, far more than does an ecstatic utterance or a voice from heaven or from the tomb, or an ancient ritual.[81]

78. Also relevant are the questions of which scriptures counted as canonical and how canonical Scripture acquired its authority. Yoder does not take up these questions in his account of diasporic Jewish life.

79. Yoder, *JCSR*, 187. Yoder says little about the significance of "oral Torah." Where he does mention it, he suggests that it was not an esoteric source of authority (ibid., 73).

80. Ibid., 110.

In time, Christianity lost this Jewish correlation of decentralization and fidelity. Even if Scripture retained a formal authority, Christianity came, Yoder claims, to predicate fidelity on centralization.

> Catholic Christianity had the book too, but a screen of clergy and ritual, including a confident explanation of why the book did not have final authority, since it needed the teaching church to make it clear, kept the message of the ancient text from contributing to the Roman Catholic present more than a rubber-stamp function.[82]

Christianity veered from the Jewish way when it turned to episcopacy and clergy for stability.

> [Early] "Christians" modified the synagogue pattern but only slightly by their [particular] openness to non-Jews, and by their love feast; the lay, book-centered, locally managed format of the synagogue remained. When the synagogue polity came later to be overshadowed among Christians by sacerdotalism and episcopacy, that represented a fall back into the pre-Jeremian patterns of Hellenistic paganism.[83]

Faithful Christian continuation of Jewish scriptural authority looked more like this: "Interpreted by the community which its very proclamation in the Spirit creates, the Scripture itself legitimates and empowers a new apostolicity, accredited as such not by juridical succession but by consonance of method and message."[84] The "consonance of method and message" is finally that of the proclamation of the cross, which precludes imposing obedience by force and takes the costly risk of trusting God to hold the people together through its faithful practices as guided by Scripture.

---

81. Ibid., 78.
82. Ibid., 109.
83. Ibid., 201n48.
84. Ibid., 138.

With this third element of scriptural authority, Yoder is not trying to expose the Jewish straw man of Christian self-definition as he was with the first two elements. Instead, he is attempting to expose the way that the institutional displacement of scriptural authority by later Christianity has been read into ancient Judaism. In other words, he is not again criticizing the way that Christian historiography has rendered ancient Judaism as the foil of Christianity but the way that it has assumed that ancient Judaism was the parent regime of established Christianity and therefore a hierarchical, centralized institution. This assumption has deafened Christianity to an important dimension of the Jewish witness and allowed Christianity to reduce the Jewish people of antiquity (or today) to a religion called "Judaism," wherein scriptural texts functioned as they later did for hierarchical Christianity. Instead, the scriptural text constituted a particular kind of public, locally intelligible, political authority that remained over every Jewish institution and whose enactment was entrusted to the locally gathered people. Such scriptural authority kept the Jewish people from introducing structures that could replace the reading people itself or systematically enforce obedience on pain of violence. This brings us to the fourth element of Yoder's picture of the Jewish people that predated and included early Christianity—nonviolence.

4. The Nonviolence of Pre-Christian Judaism

In articulating the nonviolence of diasporic Judaism, its most important element for Yoder, we must at certain points clarify his vocabulary, as his polemical choice of words is sometimes confusing. He will often use "voluntary" or even "choice" to describe summarily the diasporic Jewish political constitution, sending various semantic signals that distract from the force of his claims, which I will try to spell out. As we have already seen, Yoder insists that diasporic Jews did not understand the loss of territorial sovereignty as a blip to be quickly remedied by reconquest and reconstitution of the Israelite kingdom. On the contrary, "with Jeremiah God abandoned kingship as a vehicle of his people's identity."[85]

> The move to Babylon was not a two-generation parenthesis, after which the Davidic or Solomonic project was supposed to take up again where it had left off. It was rather the beginning, under a firm fresh prophetic mandate, of a new phase of the Mosaic project.[86]

> To be scattered is not a hiatus, after which normality will resume. From Jeremiah's time on . . . dispersion shall be the calling of the Jewish faith community.[87]

As a territorial kingdom, the people of Israel had been identified decisively by a limited geographic space and the circumstances of birth, claims Yoder, not by the way the community actually lived. Thus, territorial sovereignty had predetermined ethics, and, with the practically unconditional imperative of maintaining control, it promoted obedience to a legal code by coercion. Once born an Israelite, one could not choose not to be Israelite; Israelites could not disobey their law except on pain of constitutional violence, insofar as authorities were committed to territorial sovereignty. When it was no longer imperative to control geographic borders, however, Jews no longer "had to obey." The people persisted amidst a larger crowd only because its members did obey, even though they didn't have to. Yoder notes that even the persistence of circumcision did not undermine such a "voluntary" political community.

> When it was challenged by reformation radicals, infant baptism was defended by the reformers on the grounds that it was the modern equivalent of Jewish circumcision; i.e., a ritual of birth, not choice.

85. Ibid., 71.
86. Ibid., 184.
87. Ibid., 183. Here Yoder gives a sympathetic gloss of what he takes to be "the message" of Stephen Zweig's play, *See How They Go with Their Face to the Sun.*

On the other hand, to be Jewish after Jeremiah often included some element of freedom. Not only were Gentiles able to join the synagogue community; children of Jewish parents could also lose themselves in the crowd. Sometimes in fact the surrounding pressure exerted on Jews a positive pressure to abjure; thus Jewish identity persisted because it was voluntary.[88]

Thus, by "voluntary" Yoder does not mean that all diasporic Jews were fully "aware" of what they were doing in being Jews. He means that in order to be Jewish in exile, communities could not simply float along in the wider cultural currents of a territorial society, as Yoder supposes the people of Israel could do when it was a geographically defined kingdom. They had to "choose" to be different, often at great cost. Otherwise, they would simply be assimilated by surrounding gentile societies.[89] This clarifies one of the principal traits of ancient Judaism that Yoder indicates in the description with which we began above: "The phenomenon of the rabbinate: a non-sacerdotal, non-hierarchical, non-violent leadership elite whose power is not civil but intellectual, validated by their identification with the Torah."[90] The experience of exile thus proved deeply formative for Judaism, as it witnessed its ability to remain an ethically distinct political community—a holy people—without territorial control. In fact, as Jews beheld the failures of various Jewish attempts to reconstitute a violent central authority (e.g., the Maccabean initiative), they came to see that such authority was not only unnecessary for covenant faithfulness but inimical to it. This is what living in exile under prophetic guidance like that of Jeremiah and Ezekiel produced.[91]

88. *JCSR*, 155.
89. Yoder does not finally break free from a modern notion of identity that is rooted in individual subjectivity, however, as "voluntary" connotes. "Infant baptism is not wrong because a baby cannot have a born-again experience, but because only an adult can enter a covenant" (ibid., 126). I will address this problem below.
90. Ibid., 171.
91. Ibid., 79–80.

> For most of the centuries of Jewish survival, the definition of leadership proceeded by the slow, non-violent, dialogical "competition" of the rabbis for the respect of their pupils, and by the decentralized "congregationalistic" networking of local synagogues, whereby *any* ten heads of family can establish a gathering under no one's outside governance. No central archive, no central government, no permanent turf.[92]

With the element of nonviolence, then, Yoder is not identifying any explicit, synthetically articulated commitment. That is not a Jewish way of doing ethics and thus the wrong thing to expect.[93] Instead, he is identifying both diasporic Judaism's refusal of violent modes of authority and the alternative political power of its halakic casuistry as a dispersed people (as well as naming its renunciation of military force). He quotes Steven Schwarzchild for insider corroboration of his assessment: "No one can speak for Judaism. On the other hand, I believe, on the basis of intense, lifelong, and professional study, that pacifism is the most authentic interpretation of classical Judaism."[94] Yoder is not committed to pinpointing the time at which "nonviolence" became elemental to Judaism.[95] He is committed only to this claim: by the time of Jesus, and especially from the middle of the second century BCE, Jewry was widely and firmly committed to nonviolent modes of authority and to being a distinct, peaceful people dispersed in a violent world.[96] The point is that Jesus and early Christianity simply continued along a stable Jewish trajectory of nonviolence. Accordingly, in chapter 2 of *JCSR*, "Jesus the Jewish Pacifist," Yoder argues that Jesus' pacifism was neither a religious flight from Jewish politics nor a departure from the common

---

92. Ibid., 114, emphasis his.
93. Ibid., 82.
94. Ibid., 95.
95. Ibid., 183.
96. The failure of the Maccabean venture was thus an important confirmation of the direction of the people, that is, the direction the people was moving (ibid., 71).

commitments of his people. Rather, it was the political continuation—the fulfillment—of what had long characterized Israel in exile.

> Jesus prolonged the critical stance which previous centuries of Jewish experience had already rehearsed.[97]

> It is one of the marks of our culture's anti-Judaic heritage that the pacifism of the early Christians is routinely understood as having taken off from scratch from a few words, or a few deeds, of Jesus, when as a matter of fact it was part of the common Jewish legacy which Jesus and the apostles shared with their non-messianic contemporaries like Jochanan ben Zakkai.[98]

In a brief reading of Israel's history before Jesus—from the establishment of the covenant and Israel's early "holy wars," through the Deuteronomistic History, into exile under prophetic authorities like Isaiah and Jeremiah—Yoder tracks the continuity of the nonviolent politics that came to characterize diasporic Jews. He sums it up as a trust in the God of Israel that precluded making their own "political/military" arrangements. Judaism had thus developed a political ethic of nonviolent suffering, as seen in the Suffering Servant of Isaiah 40–53, which Jesus then connected more tightly to the people's redemption.[99] Jesus came to fulfill the Torah as conveyed by this ethic, which constitutes a background that brings some of the color of New Testament "faith" into much bolder relief.

> Both affirmative interpreters of the Sermon on the Mount, like Tolstoy, and critical ones, like Reinhold Niebuhr, have pointed out that love toward the enemy in 5.43ff is parallel to the renunciation of laying up treasures toward one's future security in 6.19-25. Both assume that trust

97. Ibid.
98. Ibid., 170. Jochanan ben Zakkai, perhaps a pupil of the great rabbi Hillel, was an anti-Sadducean sage who opposed the Jewish war against Rome of 66–70 CE and called for peace. He seems to have been an important figure in the postwar renewal of Judaism.
99. Ibid., 71. Ezra and Nehemiah are somewhat ambiguous in Yoder's reading (see note below).

in God's saving intervention makes obedience "realistic". Such trust is what Hebrews 11 calls "faith", and sees as being rooted and perfected in the sacrifice of Jesus.[100]

Given its pre-Christian stability, it is no surprise that the trajectory of nonviolence continued after Jesus in Judaism and in early Christianity within it (i.e., Christianity of both the circumcised and uncircumcised). "When the year 70 sealed the abandonment of visions of national restoration, Jochanan ben Zakkai firmed up the non-violence of the remaining rabbinic leadership and their acceptance of diaspora as a base of Jewish identity."[101] The only established exception to nonviolent structures of authority was perhaps the Sanhedrin, which applied its coercive measures only to Jews. "Everywhere else, and in Palestine after 70, the only authority which Jewish community leaders had over any individual was under the conditions of the voluntarily consenting sub-culture."[102]

> Rabbinic Judaism is thus the way of life, which makes sense of exile as the way it is going to have to be. The rabbis in Galilee after 135, and the House of Assembly later established at Usha, needed the support of the Babylonians to resume their work, and continued to draw their leaders from there.[103] We can say that "Rabbinic Judaism" begins *c.* 200 (redaction of the *Mishna*, 135 (defeat of Bar Kochba)), or 70 (loss of the Temple) or still earlier (foundation of the school of Hillel?), depending

---

100. Ibid., 74.
101. Ibid., 152. Yoder seems to be referring to the role of Jochanan ben Zakkai in Yavneh and primarily Palestinian Jewish leadership. He apparently overlooks at this juncture the relatively speedy reconstitution of the anti-Roman war effort that culminated in the Bar Kokhba revolt (132–135 CE).
102. Ibid., 33. Before and after 70 CE, the authority of Pharisaical leaders "depended on the voluntary loyalty of their disciples. In no sense were they like bishops, nor was the greatest among them like an archbishop. There was the constituted authority of the Sanhedrin, indisputable at the point of having arranged with the Romans to have charge of the management of the Temple, but—partly for that very reason—not enjoying the respect or the adhesion of all the population" (ibid., 48).
103. Part of Yoder's point here is that the prestigious Babylonian sages were important authorities on faithful Jewish life *as a dispersed people*.

on the variables we consider important, but the way of life which the rabbis define has been going since 586 B.C.[104]

To support his historical claim that rabbinic Judaism inherited and continued a stable trajectory of political nonviolence, Yoder offers a summary account of the nonviolence characteristic of talmudic Judaism, as well as its continuation in modern Jewish life.[105] That Jewry (especially in Palestine) could endure the Maccabean, Zealot, and Bar Kokhba revolts, not only unshaken but with renewed vigor, attests a well-rooted constitution that was alternative to territorial kingdom.

> What happened in the years after 70 and again finally after 135 was not the creation of a new system, either social or intellectual, to make diaspora existence (including its non-violence) acceptable as acquiescence to an unavoidable loss of power. What happened was rather the demise of the other views that had been contenders. The communities bearing those other visions had had some strength until they were swept away.[106]

104. Yoder, *JCSR*, 77.
105. Ibid., 82–84, for which he cites the assistance of Steven Schwarzchild, Everett Gendler, and Daniel Smith-Christopher (ibid., 89n17). Yoder also articulates how a good deal of Zionism arose in accordance with this tradition rather than in opposition to it, and how the modern Israeli state, in seeking to be like other nations, constitutes a refusal of the Jewish vision. He cites a number of diverse Jewish authorities whose similar opposition to military Zionism is more trustworthy than his own. Thus the hope of return to the promised land did not belie the nonviolent trajectory of exilic Judaism, because dispersed Jews insisted that living in the land was not an absolute imperative and would have to be different than it had been in the past. It could not be allowed to compromise covenant faithfulness and was entrusted to God's sovereignty rather than Jewish might (ibid., 85). Accordingly, Yoder does not take nonviolence to exclude landedness, only to condition habitation in a homeland. He offers the landed political constitution of Pennsylvania under William Penn as an illustration (John Howard Yoder, *Christian Attitudes to War, Peace, and Revolution*, ed. Theodore J. Koontz and Andy Alexis-Baker (Grand Rapids, MI: Brazos Press, 2009), 240–52. If faithfulness is indeed imperative, a landed administration will be ready to relinquish territorial control if it cannot maintain it faithfully.
106. Yoder, *JCSR*, 79–80. Yoder's reading is ambivalent with respect to Ezra and Nehemiah. On the one hand, there was no attempt at kingship or political independence under their influence. Gentile sovereignty was accepted such that "the Jeremianic shift" colored Jewish life even back in the land of Israel (ibid., 188, cf. 71, 79, 162). On the other hand, they were "deviations from the Jeremiah line since each of them reconstituted a cult and a polity as a branch of the pagan imperial government" (ibid., 194, cf. 170). That they ultimately failed to endure suggests that they were wrong (ibid., 162, 170, 193).

Thus, with respect to the various Jewish currents in which Jesus and Paul swam, Yoder does not wish to proffer his account as "normative Judaism" over other Jewish patterns of life, at least not explicitly. He recognizes that none of the diverse, often competitive groups of Jews can be understood as more normative than others amidst the political turmoil of their time. Yet, he notes that certain ways of being Jewish proved unsustainable (e.g., Sadducean and Zealot ways). What was left, particularly for Palestinian Jewry, promoted a nonviolent, voluntary political existence, one "without the Temple and without the turf."

> This meant structuring a confessing community on non-geographical grounds, an identity that could be voluntarily sustained by a minority of people scattered in lands under other sovereignties. There were two groups who did this successfully, as [Jacob] Neusner[107] says it. There were the messianists, later called Christians, and there were the rabbis. Both of these movements were Jewish. Neither was more Jewish that [sic] the other, although the "Christian" side of the tension had been crystallized earlier.[108] They had almost the same moral traditions, almost the same social structures. They differed from one another only about one very Jewish but also very theological question, namely on whether the presence of the Messianic Age should be conceived of as future or also already as present. The Jews who affirmed the messianic quality of their age (something only Jews could do), by confessing Jesus as risen, were *no less* Jewish than those who rejected that confession (or who may have lived in some region of the Dispersion where they had not yet heard the report). They did not differ about whether to accept Gentiles into their membership, although with time differences developed about how to regulate that openness and how many people would take advantage of it.[109]

---

107. Perhaps a reference to Jacob Neusner, *Method and Meaning in Ancient Judaism* (Missoula: Scholars Press, 1979) or to Jacob Neusner, William Scott Green, and Eernst S. Frerichs, eds., *Judaism and Their Messiahs* (Cambridge: Cambridge University Press, 1987).

108. Cf. Yoder, *JCSR*, 60. Daniel Boyarin also claims that Christianity crystallized before (rabbinic) Judaism in *Borderlines: The Partition of Judaeo-Christianity* (Philadelphia: University of Pennsylvania Press, 2004).

When did Christianity become "less" Jewish then? When it metamorphosed into the religion of the Roman Empire. Yoder frequently notes the wide recognition that the Christians of the first two centuries CE were pacifist.[110] But given the legacy of pre-Christian Judaism, early Christian pacifism was not new and was much thicker than often assumed. It was not a matter of a few isolated words of Jesus or the personal ethical commitment of Christian intellectuals. It was a full-fledged, already-pervasive diasporic political vision that began to corrode among Christian communities the less Jewish they became and the more they accommodated Greco-Roman, imperial structures of power. Thus, "It was in the process of becoming non-Jewish that Christianity also became non-pacifist."[111] According to Yoder, the Jewish political vision of early Christianity would not be substantially recovered by Christians until the Protestant Reformation and then only by minority, radical reformation communities.[112] They would also recover the voluntary ecclesiology of the early church, according to which the political community does not seize members through birth but patiently awaits an adult commitment. This continued the pre- and post-Christian diasporic Jewish way of allowing children to "get lost in the crowd" instead of compelling their membership. By virtue of

109. Yoder, *JCSR*, 49, emphasis his. Yoder's use of "normative" can be confusing or even seem contradictory. At times he is clearly opposed to any claim to a "normative" Judaism. But then he seems to offer a "normative" account of his own, according to which some ways were less Jewish than others. What Yoder is opposed to is any account of ancient Judaism that was institutionally or centrally authorized. But he is not opposed to accounts that 1) attempt to reckon with the shape in which ancient Jewry actually came to exist, and 2) identify the Jewish voices that were the most insightful about that shape (cf. ibid., 121).

110. E.g., ibid., 88, 191. Note also that Yoder's critique of pacifist figures like Justin Martyr above illustrates his awareness that the dejudaization of Christianity was more complex than a departure from political nonviolence and was under way well before Constantine.

111. Ibid., 72.

112. Nevertheless, Yoder cites as a precursor the evangelical poverty of the twelfth century, the "center" of which became the Franciscans and the "left" of which the Waldensians. He also notes the Czech reform of the fifteenth century and allows that the church has never been totally bereft of political faithfulness (ibid., 134, 141–42).

correspondence in an ethical typology, then, post-Christian Judaism counts as a "peace church," and radical reformation ecclesiology is "Jewish."[113] Given its faithfulness to the nonviolence of the incarnation, Judaism hardly qualifies as *not* Christian. Instead, we should know "Judaism as a non-non-Christian religion."[114]

The Jewishness of Early Christianity: Yoder's Account of the Parting of the Ways

In articulating the nonviolent shape of ancient (and later) Judaism, Yoder is concerned primarily with the historical and political inadequacy of predominant (anti-Jewish) Christian self-understandings and practice, especially as these claim Jesus or the New Testament for their basis.[115] By ignoring the Jewish nonviolence that Jesus and early Christianity deepened, later Christians have concocted a spurious first century "Jewish" foil and misunderstood what Jesus and Paul were up to. They were not moving away from Judaism to something less political and more spiritual, much less leaving behind the people of Israel. They were enacting the next chapter of the people of Israel, the dawning messianic age. By placing Jesus and early Christianity within his revisionist account of diasporic Jewry, Yoder shifts the gravity of the question of Christianity's relation to Judaism and therefore of what Christianity is. In so doing, he suggests a different picture of "the

---

113. Ibid., 75–87, 139–42. Cf. 125: "This epistemological assumption of the radical reformation is found as well in the young Luther and the young Zwingli; it is a congregational epistemology. The Word of God is heard in the assembly, known by the unity brought about when the Word is heard. . . . The mark of the Spirit's presence is the gift of unity which reaches beyond the previously present opinions."
114. This is the title of ch. 7 of *JCSR*.
115. Where Christians have recognized Jesus' nonviolence, they have typically regarded it as not political and precisely what set Jesus apart from Judaism, even what led to his murder. The trumped-up foil here is the notorious "Jewish" demand for an earthly kingdom rather than the "spiritual" one that Jesus was supposedly about (Yoder, *JCSR*, 69–70).

parting of the ways," one whose main contours have been confirmed by recent historians with concerns quite different from Yoder's.[116]

The gravity shift comes with Yoder's focus, not principally on the isolated "beliefs" or "ethnic identity" of historical subjects (which facilitate spurious, timeless distinctions of identity), but on "ethical substance," that is, the way historical subjects lived, their patterns of social behavior. This is not a hermeneutic that Yoder imposes on ancient communities but one that he discerns in their own self-understandings (as we have seen above in their halakic constitution) and one with theological rationale, to which we will shortly turn.

> For something like eighty years after Pentecost the (non-messianic) synagogues were not closed to messianic believers, and the "churches" (i.e. messianic synagogues) did not break communion with the rest of Jewry. . . . As far as ethical substance was concerned, this meant that non-messianic Jewish people would act in exactly the same way as the Christians of the same time.[117]

> The ethos of the early Christians was a direct prolongation and fulfilment of the ethos of Jewry.[118]

Christians have often assumed there was an immediate "break of communion" only because they have anachronistically imagined two distinct systems of religious belief and later (Christian) hierarchical structures to impose them. But Yoder insists that first century CE Jewry was no such system and had long refused such structures of authority. "There was never a 'split' at the top, in any way analogous to the later actions of the patriarchs of Rome and Constantinople,

---

116. Yoder offers three summary revisions to the Christian story of the Jewish-Christian schism: 1) There was no such thing as normative Judaism in the first century CE; 2) neither Jesus, nor Paul, nor the apostolic communities rejected normative Judaism; and 3) the Jews did not reject Christianity (ibid., 46–52). Among the works that have confirmed Yoder's account of the parting of the ways is that of Boyarin, *Borderlines*.

117. Yoder, *JCSR*, 152. Yoder is describing not only Jewish Christians but also non-Jewish Christians.

118. Ibid., 171.

or Rome and Canterbury, excommunicating each other, since at that time there existed no such 'top' on either side."[119] Christian historiography has also tended to imagine the split in terms of Jewish ethnocentrism, but, as Yoder has pointed out, Judaism did not impose ethnic closure upon its people but had long been open to the participation of non-Jews and even the full Judaization of persons born to gentile parents. Nor can the split be ascribed to Jewish legalism and Christian impartiality, since Christian communities imposed requirements for initiation and ongoing membership just as Jewish communities did. It is simply the case that, in time, those requirements became quite different. The parting of the ways can therefore not be attributed to the fact of Christianity's openness to the full participation of those who had been gentile. Accordingly, Yoder says this about the early Christian mission to gentiles: "What Jesus did was simply more of the same. The communities that confessed in him the coming of the Messianic age were simply more free and aggressive in doing in the gentile cities what the synagogues had already been doing."[120] Two distinct paths, "Christianity" and "Judaism," "could develop only after the [Jewish] renunciation of openness to the Gentiles, which in turn can only have made sense when Christians had gone overboard in identification with Gentiles."[121] Yoder does not deny that Paul and others like him played a role in this bifurcation. Local Jewish authorities were generally tolerant of "looseness in the application of halakic detail," but "they could not tolerate . . . the way Paul and his kind made a normative case for such looseness, not by keeping the rules less carefully himself

---

119. Ibid., 117. Cf. 53: "Likewise the Christian interpretation of there having been a 'synod' or 'council' at Yavneh to settle upon the canon of the Hebrew Scriptures must be abandoned."
120. Ibid., 152.
121. Ibid., 155. Elsewhere Yoder makes clear that he does not blame one side or the other for the divergence. We should also note that post-Christian Judaism does not seem ever to have totally closed the door to proselytism.

. . . but by teaching that messianic Jews could and in fact should eat with Gentiles who (for their part) would not have to keep the rules."[122] Nevertheless, early Christians like Paul were subject to internal discipline, not treated as gentiles or apostates.[123] And when a local Jewish community was divided over Paul's message and practice, the "messianicly believing" part that resulted from the division remained a synagogue. While the differences between "messianicly believing" and "non-messianic" currents were certainly significant, they were not more fundamental than differences within each current nor the unity of the whole. Thus,

> the total social stream in which these divisions operated—and within which people saw one another as fellow-believers worthy of debating with, worthy of dividing from over issues of truth that both cared about—was still the wider stream of missionizing Judaic culture which *both* the non-messianic rabbis and the messianic *didascaloi* and prophets and elders were trying to lead.[124]

Yoder claims that clear fences were not raised between Christian and non-Christian kinds of synagogue for "two or three more generations at least" after Paul, once "some Gentile minorities started to take the Church away from the Jews."[125] Through this dejudaization of the church, Christianity lost its vision of God's worldwide rule and its "readiness to live in the diaspora style of the Suffering Servant."[126]

---

122. Ibid., 33. Given Yoder's understanding of the political-economic implications of "table fellowship" or "the meal," we should not trivialize what he describes as intramural disputes over how meals were to proceed and who could participate. The meal is a crucial site of far-reaching political economic vision.

123. Ibid., 51.

124. Ibid., 61, emphasis his.

125. Ibid., 152. "Here too (in the post-Kochba diaspora) most 'Christians' were Jews and the 'Christian' community was part of the Jewish community" (59).

126. Ibid. Yoder is aware that this reading of "the parting of the ways" is one-sided, and so he adds to this "Jewish" side of the story a reading of the gradual bifurcation from the "Christian" side (ibid., 152–55). It highlights that Jewish rejection of Christian christological claims came after Jewish authorities discouraged full communion with Christians for other reasons, a decrease

Instead of considering the historical-ethical continuity from Second Temple Judaism through Jesus and early Christianity, the church has, for the most part, assumed a post- and anti-Jewish framework within which to read the New Testament and understand itself. According to Yoder, the result has been a truncation of—even a deafness to—the Old Testament witness, a thinning of the New Testament's nonviolent political vision in favor of something else supposedly more urgent, and a religious program divergent from being the holy people of the God of Israel. Within this anti-Jewish framework, composed primarily of religious "beliefs," "Christianity" and "Judaism" are "systems, existing primordially in a 'normative' form."[127] They are read back into Christian origins so that already in the early centuries, and even when reading the New Testament, "Christians" and "Jews" are understood as two separate "religious" communities existing over against each other.[128] This misreading of the past has deteriorated the peoplehood of the Christian church, since, as a historically sensitive reading of the New Testament attests according to Yoder, Christian peoplehood is not a departure from but simply a continuation of that of diasporic Jewry. The dejudaization of Christian ecclesiology pulled ethics and doctrine apart and gave primacy to the latter. It allowed Christian communities to constitute themselves in political terms that are territorial and violent, even if "orthodox," resulting in a history rife with Christian imperialism and revolutionary and civil war.

in Jewish missionary openness and increase in ethnic self-understanding in response to the Christianization of the empire, and a narrowing of the definition of the role and person of Messiah in response to Christian claims about Jesus. Modern Jewish statecraft, he claims, is the most recent, prominent response to and imitation of Christian forms of dominance. Nevertheless, earlier Yoder has claimed that Judaism has never settled for understanding itself as an ethnicity (110).

127. Ibid., 69.
128. The New Testament of course says very little about "Christians" (only in Acts 11:26; 26:28; 1 Pet. 4:16) and nothing about "religion."

By contrast, Yoder's historicist approach (displayed in the four elements exposited above) identifies ethical continuities that a creedal or institutional lens overlooks or even censors. In *The Politics of Jesus*, he describes the nonviolent "messianic ethic" of Jesus and early Christianity with historically sensitive readings of the New Testament. What he describes is not a program for personal salvation that is politically unrealistic but the realistic life of a people that collectively embodies God's saving peace. In *JCSR*, Yoder attempts to strengthen that historical and exegetical argument by showing how the politics of Jesus continued an ethos that had long characterized the dispersed people of Israel. Jesus and early Christianity did not spring from nowhere or immediately from heaven; nor did they depart from the Israelite Scriptures they had inherited. Thus, Yoder describes diasporic Jewry in a way that seems to make his picture of Jesus and early Christianity truer to their historical setting. It also seems to increase the burden of proof for those who would minimize the nonviolence of the New Testament or subordinate the peoplehood of Israel to some other religious or political imperative. Such imperatives have arisen only as the church has constructed a foil of "Judaism," while, according to Yoder, the Jews have by and large been more faithful to Jesus than the Christian church has.

To our central question of how the people of Israel determines what it means to be Christian, then, Yoder answers that the people of Israel progressively embodied the ethos whereby God brings peace to the world, and faithful Christianity has never ceased to be Israel. The history of Israel is a process of ethical discipline, that is, political formation. God has never abandoned this historical process, and Jesus came to fulfill it. There is therefore no faithful Christianity outside this process, for Christianity lives only in and through it. Those who have persistently refused this discipline of peoplehood throughout its history ceased, on Yoder's understanding, to count as part of the covenant people, for the people is holy as God is holy. To participate in this holy people by being disciples of Jesus is what it means to be Christian, and Scripture bears normative witness to the development of this people. The peaceable life of this faithful people is the revelation of the one God, the God of Israel, in the world.[129]

Yoder's account of Second Temple Jewry and the Jewish-Christian schism is of course controversial, as can be illustrated briefly here. Some features of it seem to bear up under scrutiny. Few would dispute that the Jewish community of the Second Temple Period was widely dispersed and maintained impressive vitality without territorial sovereignty or highly centralized structures of authority. That Israel's Scriptures provided the central and common authority for Jewish life, as Yoder asserts, is difficult to deny, even if matters were more complex than he suggests. Jewish communities were indeed open to proselytes well before Jesus or Paul came along.[130] Augustine famously notes the astonishment with which Seneca observed how Jewish numbers swelled with proselytes: "The customs of that most accursed nation have gained such strength that they have

---

129. This discipline of peoplehood did not leave non-Christian Jews behind as non-Jewish Christian communities began to diverge from non-Christian Jewish communities. On the contrary, as non-Jewish Christian communities began to diverge from non-Christian Jewish communities, especially by the medieval period, it was the Jews who continued the ethic of Jesus most faithfully. "Judaism successfully kept its identity without ever using the sword; it kept its community solidarity without possessing national sovereignty. In other words, medieval Judaism demonstrated the sociological viability of the ethic of Jesus. In terms of actual ethical performance, Judaism represents the most important medieval sect living the ethic of Jesus under Christendom. Jews were granted exemption from becoming 'Christian' because of the racism and anti-Judaism of official Christianity. Their story thereby demonstrates inadvertently that the way to be a Christian sectarian minority is to live without the sword. . . . It was the identity of a nonviolent community under the cross," (Yoder, *Christian Attitudes to War, Peace, and Revolution*, 140).

130. See Louis H. Feldman, *Jew and Gentile in the Ancient World: Attitudes and Interactions from Alexander to Justinian* (Princeton: Princeton University Press, 1993). Cf. Matt. 23:15. See also Shaye Cohen, *Beginnings of Jewishness: Boundaries, Varieties, Uncertainties* (Berkeley: University of California Press, 1999), 109–39. Against Cohen, Yoder suggests that Israel was *more than* ethnic, i.e., "religious" in Cohen's sense, well before the second century BCE.

been now received in all lands; the conquered have given laws to the conquerors."[131] Perhaps Ignatius of Antioch is illustrative of the wider trends Yoder has identified as well—particularly the halakic nature of Jewish identity—when he warns early Christians against "Judaism." He is not concerned with "Jewish" beliefs or ethnocentrism but with the function of particular practices of circumcision and Sabbath.[132] The inability of later generations to place early disputes between Christians of various kinds and non-Christian Jews within a wider pagan culture may have encouraged them to distort the proportions of those disputes and to ignore their common ground in the wider pagan world. As mentioned above, many historians have confirmed Yoder's contention that Judaism and Christianity did not become distinct until well into the second century, if not later. Chrysostom was certainly preaching to Christians who were still resisting divergence from Judaism in his *Homilies against the Jews* at the end of the fourth century CE. Finally, Josephus offers an interesting corroboration of Yoder's account if, when he calls upon the besieged inhabitants of Jerusalem to obey the nonviolence commanded by Jewish history, he evinces an ethos pervasive among Jews of his time.[133]

Other features of Yoder's account are less convincing, however. The Gospels do not seem to portray Jesus as one who is simply deepening or reinforcing a mainstream Jewish ethos. Even his own disciples are rather horrified at Jesus' nonviolence, apparently

---

131. From the quotation of *De superstitione*, in Augustine, *Civ.* 6:11: Sceleratissimae gentis consuetudo conualuit, ut per omnes iam terras recepta sit; uicti uictoribus leges dederunt.

132. *Magn.* 8:1–10:3; *Phld.* 6:1. Cf. Gal. 1:13 where "Judaism" does not seem to mean the ways of all Jews but the way of life that characterized a certain movement among Jews.

133. *The Jewish War*, 5:375–419. 5:390 summarizes the claim of the speech: "To speak summarily, there is not one case in which our ancestors had any success with weapons or, trusting God, failed to succeed without them. When they stayed home, they prevailed as pleased the Judge. But when they fought, they were always ruined" (translation mine). Note that Josephus's theological appeal to history comes after the failure of his more pragmatic advice to the besieged inhabitants of Jerusalem.

unenlightened by the Jeremianic tradition that Yoder presents as typical. His death seems to have been initially perceived more as a disappointment than a fulfillment, leaving behind a numerically insignificant following in its immediate aftermath. In short, Jesus seems to have "rattled the foundations" of his people somewhat more than Yoder suggests. Isn't there significantly more to Christian nonviolence than the refusal to seek territorial sovereignty and the kind of authority structures characteristic of diasporic Jewry? How can Yoder pronounce that "with Jeremiah God abandoned kingship as a vehicle of his people's identity"?[134] Describing diasporic Jewry as "nonviolent" seems to owe more to the foil of "Constantinian" Christianity than to a contextually sensitive, historical consideration of the diasporic Jewish ethos.

Nor does Yoder's insistence on the Jewishness of Christianity sit well with Pauline claims like, "For you who were baptized into Christ have put on Christ. There is not Jew or Greek . . . for you are all one in Christ Jesus" (Gal. 3:27-28). The difference between becoming Christian by messianic baptism and becoming Jewish by proselytism was apparently more substantial than Yoder recognizes. Jesus was arguably not just "more of the same" for Israel, as his resurrection meant quite fundamental and epic change. Moreover, something other than faithful halakah apparently constituted Israel, for Paul seems to deny that there is any immediate correlation between holiness or being Israel and faithfulness (Rom. 11:15-16). Finally, Yoder likely underestimates the early effect of the *Birkat-ha-minim*, even if he is right to deny any centralized anathema.[135]

But these critical, illustrative questions do little more than graze the surface rather randomly of an extremely complex history that is

---

134. Yoder, *JCSR*, 71.
135. Ibid., 52–58, though note 116. See Joel Marcus, "*Birkat-Ha-Minim* Revisited," *NTS* 55 (2009): 523–51.

disputed at virtually every point and that Yoder has portrayed with rather suspicious generalizations. Yoder has attempted, as a professed amateur, to revise the main contours of the standard account so as to make more visible an ethical alternative of peoplehood long eclipsed by a poor reading of the Jewish life in which Christianity emerged and to unmask the conditions of the eventual split. But this invites us to clarify what is ethically at stake for Yoder (and others) in the Christian reading of both its Jewish past and the Jewish-Christian schism. How does the quality of such historiography impinge upon the way Christians should live, not least in their relations with non-Christian Jews? Why is it important to get the story right? How truthful or useful can *generalizations* about the Jewish and Christian past be? What can history ever tell us about what it means to be the people of Israel or to be Christian? To consider these critical questions, we turn in the next chapter to the theological program of Yoder's revisionist historiography and the crucial matter he has virtually ignored: the election of Israel.

2

The Jewishness of Christian Peoplehood

Yoder's Misstep

Few would dispute that historiography is always conducted (or avoided) within a political matrix that determines not only its content but also its function. There is, in a word, a politics to historiography. As we have seen in chapter 1, in Yoder's own revisionist account of the Jewish-Christian schism, he aims to expose the unfaithful (anti-Jewish) politics of the traditional Christian account and to outline a more faithful way forward, whether in historiography, Jewish-Christian relations, or, more broadly, the way that Christian communities live. He thus makes no secret of the theopolitical aims of his own account. In this chapter, I will scrutinize those aims and the way they impinge on Yoder's historiography. I have much sympathy for Yoder's account and its aims, and I will clarify some of the ways in which I think they are sound. Nevertheless, my principal objective in this chapter is to expose, in a way that implicates the reader, a fundamental problem with Yoder's Christian understanding of peoplehood and the whole imaginary of peoplehood that it represents. Stated summarily, the problem is this: "the people" is understood to constitute itself by its own faithfulness, and it therefore polices itself (including the imagination of its past) according to regnant standards of faithfulness, thereby disowning the unfaithful and repudiating God's election. In Yoder's case, these regnant standards of faithfulness are conceived explicitly in terms of "Jewishness." In light of this problem, it is no accident that Yoder's revisionist historiography virtually ignores Scripture's witness to God's election of Israel nor that modern peoplehood has been a sweeping distortion of that election.

The Theological Program of Yoder's Historical Turn to the Jews

In chapter 1 of *The Jewish-Christian Schism Revisited*, "It Did Not Have to Be," after an initial foray into "the historical sociology of the Christian-Jewish relationship," Yoder says explicitly that "the ultimate intention of this study is theological, interpreting the notion of 'theology' especially in the ethical and pastoral modes."[1] As the chapter title suggests, Yoder's revisionist historiography aims to show that the emergence of the Jesus movement among the Jews of the first century CE did not have to effect a bifurcation of Jewry into "Christianity" and "Judaism." Christianity did not have to be non-Jewish. The subtext of this claim, as Yoder bears it out, seems to be that Christianity *should not* have become non-Jewish and, if faithful to the New Testament, is *not* non-Jewish.[2]

The Jewish-Christian schism is illustrative of what Yoder insists is always the case, namely, that history never had to come out the way it did, nor does the past dictate the present or future. The

---

1. John Howard Yoder, *The Jewish-Christian Schism Revisited*, ed. Michael G. Cartwright and Peter Ochs (Grand Rapids, MI: William B. Eerdmans, 2003), 62. Hereafter *JCSR*.
2. "Jewish" in the sense of ch. 1 above, of course.

present remains open to radical transformation. Historians fail to be true to the past if they present any of its developments as inevitable. Good historiography will always respect the contingency of human action and circumstance. What has happened can therefore never be reduced to what is "natural," nor can it be exhaustively accounted for by any subsequent "explanation." Yoder offers two warrants for this contention, both oriented to the case of the Jewish-Christian schism. First, "we do violence to the depth and density of the story if . . . we box the actors of the first century into our wisdom about their children's fate in the second."[3] In other words, such historical determinism is untruthful to the time and persons it treats. It leads historians to "look in earlier texts for explanations of the later polarizations."[4] One example of this would be "explaining" the Jewish-Christian schism with the early Christian practice of welcoming gentiles into Israel upon their baptism into Messiah Jesus. Another would be to read the "Jews" of the New Testament as an ethnic designation.[5]

The second warrant for Yoder's approach to history as "open" is that sin does not have to be. Where there was sin, there was more to the story. There was no step along the way that sealed the outcome of a later stage. To say that the story had to turn

---

3. Yoder, *JCSR*, 44.

4. Ibid., 46. As he argues here with respect to historiography, so Yoder argues elsewhere with respect to ethical theory. The justification of violence notoriously appeals to a mythical mechanism for the effectiveness of violence. It dismisses the cases in which violence has clearly not been effective and "explains" good results with violent causes. Advocates of nonviolence have at times succumbed to the same mechanistic logic, whereby they "explain" good results with nonviolent causes. Yoder opposes such "explanation" in both historiography and ethics. Instead, he advocates christological hope that refuses to turn persons into abstract objects or mythologize the contingency of history into a mechanism (John Howard Yoder, *Christian Attitudes to War, Peace, and Revolution*, ed. Theodore J. Koontz and Andy Alexis-Baker [Grand Rapids, MI: Brazos, 2009], 353–68, esp. 360–62 and 364–67).

5. Ethnically imagined identity tends to impose closure on a historically and materially open community. It also fails to subject to historical scrutiny the contingent conditions that availed for procreation and collective memory across generations.

out as less than God's best implies that God is bound by sin or has bound people to sin. Yoder opposes reading the past that way. He is committed to both divine and human freedom, and he also finds that Scripture encourages trust in God's capacity to bring about the unexpectedly good *from* a disappointing past. A repentant and hopeful historiography will therefore not censor what "could have been." While refusing to lie about the past, it also "refuses to let 'the way things are' have the last word."[6] This is not a historical quest for what was not there but what was there and has not been adequately remembered. Which voices have been suppressed? Which historical details do not fit conventional accounts? What other forces were at work? What resources went unexhausted in the developments that took place? Though it may seem quixotic to those committed to the way things have turned out, this historical method is in fact more rigorous and realistic than one that imposes later closure on earlier moments. It can even offer a prophetic corrective.[7]

Yoder is after this prophetic corrective or critical vision with the revisionist historiography of *JCSR*. The driving ethical question seems to be twofold. First, how has the Christian church persisted in a way of life and self-understanding that, in a crucial earlier period, fomented what was not God's peace, namely, the Jewish-Christian schism? As we might expect, that way of life and self-understanding are not incidental to the church's standard way of telling the story of that earlier period ("the old accounts still control us"[8]), and so faithfully revising the standard story[9] can improve the church's living and self-understanding. The tendency in Christian historiography has been to justify and reinforce the basics of the ongoing schism,

---

6. Yoder, *JCSR*, 44.
7. Peter Ochs calls this "depth historiography" (ibid., 39).
8. Ibid., 61.
9. E.g., by pointing to the historical tenuousness of "beliefs" and the corresponding Christian invention of "Judaism" or to the provincial nature of Christian claims to universal reason.

even if it is recognized as not ideal or deemed impermanent based on an indefinitely suspended eschatological act of God. But "perhaps the purpose of those living that story then, or the purpose of God in letting it happen, was not to explain (or even dictate) a later tragic division, but perhaps even to offer some other option."[10] Yoder is after a historiography that is more searching than that of the standard account, one that is, as noted above, repentant and hopeful. Its mode of historiography is nonviolent insofar as it refuses to impose the cost of conflict on the opposing side (here ancient non-Christian Jews).

The second part of the driving ethical question of *JCSR* is, what other Christian option(s) emerge from a more searching historiography of ancient Judaism and the Jewish-Christian schism? The idea is not to concoct, with theological interest, something that was not there. It is to ask, with theological interest, if the historical gaze shaped by a later imagination has distorted the picture of that past such that something that was in fact there became invisible. It would not be theologically compelling for Yoder if a particular political option is merely literary or wasn't really there. Thus, the option that Yoder commends as having really been there, as we have seen, is a Christian peoplehood that is Jewish in the historical terms he adduces, messianicly open to making Jews of gentiles, and not exclusive of non-Christian Jews. This is an Israelite peoplehood that has not pronounced non-Christian Jews excluded from Israel, nor does it engage in the violence that this exclusion implies.[11] This ecclesiological option cannot be theoretically excluded or deemed structurally impossible because it once existed. It does not finally

---

10. Ibid., 47.
11. Cf. John Howard Yoder, *The Original Revolution: Essays on Christian Pacifism* [Scottdale, PA: Herald, 1971], 180n7: "The testimony of the apostles is not that Israel is displaced but rather that Israel is restored or rediscovered in a new form which takes Gentiles into the covenant." Later, in *JCSR* as noted in ch. 1 above, Yoder suggests that there was nothing fundamentally new about the Christian way of taking gentiles into the covenant.

matter how pervasive it was, although it seems more compelling if it was in fact pervasive and subsequently suppressed. What matters is that it was there and that revisiting the Christian departure from it might lead Christians "to redefine ourselves, i.e., to repent."[12]

The church's past is obviously full of shortcomings that should be addressed with a similarly theological historiography, but the Jewish-Christian schism is a particularly urgent subject. It has of course been fundamental to Christian self-understanding, and the Shoah calls for the gravest Christian attention to the church's anti-Judaism. In addition to these inducements, Yoder points to a possibility for radical reform from within the current church. The *Jewish* criticism of Christianity, which has been at work in its own distinctive, non-Christian existence, resonates eerily with that of certain dissident voices *within* Christianity, particularly those of what Yoder calls reformation or renewal movements.[13] Both they and the Jews accepted deadly minority status vis-à-vis the Christian establishment, although Jews have done so for much longer and at much greater peril. Studying the story of the Jewish community and the criticism it has addressed to Christianity through the ancient schism (and ever since) may therefore enhance the critical power offered by radical Christian renewal movements and nourish needed Christian reform from within the church.[14] As we have seen above, Yoder presents this reform as the restoration of the church's peoplehood.

---

12. Yoder, *JCSR*, 62.
13. "When Jews describe what they reject in Christianity, the list of unacceptable elements will include the linkage of religion with an oppressive political and social system, uncritical assimilation to pagan styles of culture and morality, centralization and sacralization of the man Jesus as competitor for the glory of God. Movements of reformation and renewal within western Christendom—Anabaptists and Friends among them—had some of the same complaints" (ibid., 46).
14. Ibid., 61, 111–12. On 112, Yoder calls for more than the enhancement of the free church witness: "Whether the impact be commonality or dialogue, confession of guilt or joy in reconciliation and common witness, to restore the recognition of the sister communion [i.e., Jewry] might just call Christians back to their roots as the free church minorities in the West have been failing to do."

Yoder also contends that the conventional reading of the Jewish-Christian schism does not reflect the ethical shape of the Jewish and Christian communities today. He observes that what it means to be Christian has long been a matter of significant public debate, and many Christians have begun to look upon the history of the West with a repentance that implies substantive theological reform. Meanwhile, the modern state of Israel has rekindled establishment and empire in Jewish debate, disclosing a whole range of ethical tendencies among Jews. In addition, many Christians have ceased to confess Jesus as the Messiah in any historically recognizable sense, and many Jews of recent times variously understand themselves to live in an age of fulfilled promises. What it means to be "messianic" is once again "up for grabs" among Jews and among Christians.[15] Thus, "the spectrum of differences *within* each of the faith communities is now broader than the distance between their centres; the terrain of their overlap may again become substantial."[16]

Many will no doubt complain at the apparent selectivity of Yoder's historiography. He meets that objection head-on in *JCSR*.[17] He does not stop at the usual cop-out that all historiography is selective and interested. Instead, he presses the question, with what interest should historiography approach the Jewish past of Christianity? His answer, to anticipate what follows, is, with the interest of embracing those excluded.

In facing the unwieldy diversity of the Jewish past, Yoder refuses to succumb to total historical relativism, wherein what really happened doesn't matter because historiographical truthfulness about Jewishness is impossible (i.e., there was supposedly no such thing as Jewishness, nothing real that held diverse Jews together as Jews). He

15. Ibid., 62–63, Yoder also elaborates on the current scenario on 108–12, with particular concern for Jewish-Christian dialogue.
16. Ibid., 62, emphasis his.
17. Ibid., 112–17.

insists that while overwhelmingly complex, ancient Jewish existence was not utterly amorphous but of a relatively discernible shape: "Jewishness was not vague."[18] In other words, it is possible to tell a story of the Jewish community that is wrong, and some generalizations are better than others. This also seems to preclude a voluntarist theological historiography, wherein claims about Jewishness (or Christianness) are not contingent upon historiographical truthfulness because history is supposedly so diverse as to exert no pressure on, say, Christology or ethics; there is, on this supposition, no Jewish or Christian story, only disparate data whose theological construal as any kind of whole is historically arbitrary or willed. Yoder criticizes this kind of ahistorical theology as "enshrining the observer's own identity as a functional absolute."[19] What really happened does matter.

Yoder also notes the usual approach of sifting historical testimony with a priori criteria. This approach tends to confirm the perspective of "any reasonable person," "an ideal observer," or "all reasonable people."[20] It defines the terms of analysis up front, independently of the material to be analyzed, and excludes testimony to what seems unrepeatable or too peculiar. The result is a picture of the past and

18. Ibid., 58. By "vague," Yoder does not mean ambiguous, which he happily admits that Jewishness was. He means totally indeterminate. In other words, there was a real difference between being Jewish and being not Jewish.

19. Ibid., 113. Yoder names James Gustafson as one who succumbs to this approach (in Christology in his case). One variant of this methodological commitment is to say that Jewishness is for Jews to decide. This fails to recognize the historical contingency of Jewishness and Christianness. It ignores that the church was once Jewish and somehow ceased to be so and that this is an important subject of inquiry for Christians and others. It also assumes that Christian identity is safe from Jewish identity, which it isn't, or that Jewish identity has not been shaped by Christian identity, which it has been. It may even harbor imperialist Christian ways of excluding Jewish participation in the determination of Christian existence by consigning Jewishness to Jewish self-definition. This attitude seems to have promoted Christian ignorance of Judaism, which likely helped make Jews killable. Politically peaceful conflict with due humility, rather than segregating competing views (in governance or scholarly method), is an alternative to violent enmity (cf. Yoder's critique of Krister Stendahl in *JCSR*, 156).

20. Ibid., 113.

its subjects that cannot be unsettlingly different from the present as understood by the historian, a hermeneutic that knows no empathy with those it studies. It "cuts out most of the flesh of past reality . . . in the interest of being absolutely sure about the skeleton."[21] This approach finds a more "messianic" tack to history particularly suspect.

> Medieval European imperial Christendom, or Imperial Russian Orthodoxy, or the Enlightenment claims of the French encyclopedists, or the arbitrage today of the news media, or the professional historians, or university academics, have all claimed and can consistently claim that the place where they stand is in some sense more reasonable, more universal, than other places. The missionary messianic community renounces such claims in principle.[22]

But the common obsession with occupying a stable place from which to read the past makes the Jewish story an important historical case. The Jewish story is "a test *par excellence*" of the problem of selectivity, of being true to history.[23] There is no central Jewish institution or territorial limit to govern historical inquiry. Readers of the Jewish past cannot claim to go to or to read from any place that adequately limits their own influence on the account they produce. The historical subject simply sprawls out of control across time and space.

Having noted the problems with conventional approaches to historiographical selectivity, Yoder articulates the following as his alternative way of telling the Jewish story. He does so in general terms, that is, in terms of *any* historical consideration of *any* "other" of the past, but, for the sake of clarity, I will exposit his approach in terms of Jews and Christians. Christian misunderstandings of the Jewish past seem typically to result from reading past subjects in light of the readers' supposedly different identity. The Jews are rendered

21. Ibid., 114.
22. Ibid.
23. Ibid.

intelligible by virtue of being *not* who Christians are, so that the Jews of the past can "appear" or be storied only in terms of Christian self-understanding. The usual critical response is to oppose such Christian hegemony by seeking more neutral or objective terms of analysis, but neither can such terms avoid being the projection of the readers' assumptions.

> So instead of pretending to avoid the danger of seeing the Other in the light of Our own identity, the right way forward must rather be a constructive appropriation of the other's identity. We cannot not be selective; we can ask that the selectivity should contribute to reciprocal recognition, finding in the other what one needs, for the sake of one's own integrity, to esteem.[24]

This does not mean that Yoder is willing to impose what he "esteems" on the Jewish past, to co-opt "the Jews" of the past in order to strengthen his own political program in the present. He claims to find something in the past that was really there and has come in time to make him its own.

> I make then no apology for reading the vast melee of the Jewish experience in such a way that Yochanan [Jochanan ben Zakkai] is more representative than Menachem, Abraham Joshua Heschel than David Ben Gurion, Arnold Wolf than Meir Kahane, Anne Frank than Golda Meir. What goes on here is *not* that I am "co-opting" Jews to enlist them in my cause. It is that I am finding a story, which is really there, coming all the way down from Abraham, that has the grace to adopt me.[25]

But of what precisely are Jochanan ben Zakkai, Heschel, Wolf, and Frank "more representative" than Menachem, Ben Gurion, Kahane, and Meir? They are more representative of what Yoder calls Jewish "virtues," which, according to Yoder, themselves constitute Jewishness. Anticipating the charge that he has simply "discovered"

24. Ibid., 115.
25. Ibid., emphasis his.

what he already esteemed, Yoder lists several criteria by which the fairness of his rendition of Jewishness can be verified: for example, literary coherence, sociohistorical viability, narrative and causative coherence, and especially the criteria of typological connaturality or congruence that are basic to the "empathy" of Yoder's own approach, which identifies diasporic Jewry and peace churches as of basically the same political type.[26]

This comment about representative virtue reveals what is perhaps the crucial feature of Yoder's theological historiography. Historical, material Jewishness (like Christianness) was not amoral. Yoder has told the story not of a Jewish community abstracted from the ethos of its historical constitution—such a community has arguably never existed—but of an already ethically shaped people. Its ethical patterns, over time, determined in which ways it was materially possible to be Jewish, including, for example, under which conditions children were born to Jewish parents or which political tendencies in fact led to assimilation and which managed to resist assimilation over generations. In *JCSR*, Yoder has not offered an account of the Jewishness of every historical person who may have identified him or herself as Jewish nor of every historical movement known as Jewish in one quarter or another. He has offered a historical account of what in fact made the Jewish people, including early Christianity, tick.

Yoder acknowledges that his understanding implies that a historical account will always involve the judgment of the historian and can be countered according to opposing historical judgment. But he claims to proceed with the right kind of judgment (i.e., that which "contributes to reciprocal recognition") *and* to find something in the past that was really there. What made the Jewish people tick is not a nonhistorical or historically inscrutable matter. It is in the evidence.

26. Ibid. Yoder's political types are not merely heuristic. He claims that they fit historical realities.

Yoder seems to imply that Jews who lived like everyone else were not particularly representative *because such living cannot have sustained Jewishness among other real possibilities*. The Jews who were peculiarly Jewish, that is, faithful to the God revealed in Torah, made the Jews as a community who they were over time and therefore those capable of resisting assimilation. Thus, the prophetic and oppressed figures whom Yoder names (above) are "more representative" than their counterparts in violent Jewish establishments. What has historically passed under the name "Jew" or "Christian" must be historically tested to determine whether it was more or less so, even truly or falsely so, and the material difference between Jews and non-Jews was fundamentally ethical, not merely nominal. Moreover, this is not the imposition of present anxieties, for the integrity of Jewishness was also at issue among the historical actors under consideration.

So how does Yoder's (or anyone else's) being wrong or right in his historical account of Judaism affect the ethos of the Christian life? That we would even ask this question is part of Yoder's point, for the Christian tendency has been to trivialize history in the interest of a supposedly firmer basis of faith. But just as how Jesus actually lived determines what it means to be his disciples, so how Israel has actually lived conditions what it means to be the people of God.[27] Though this subjects us to the uncomfortable contingency of history, it is this contingency that God did not refuse but inhabited, in God's people and as God's Son. Much like *The Politics of Jesus*, *JCSR* is perhaps finally a work in Christology, an attempt to take God's revelation in the flesh seriously. Jesus is not taken seriously if his Jewishness is ignored or despised. The flesh of Jesus did not come from nowhere

---

27. This is not to say that Jesus conditions what it means to be his disciples in the same way that the history of Israel conditions what it means to be Israel. Jesus is normative for Christian existence in a way that the Israelite past is not for the people of Israel (e.g., the past of Israel furnishes some negative examples of how to be Israel). But in both cases, how the current generation should live cannot be understood apart from the concrete history to which it looks for guidance.

or exist in isolation.[28] It was embedded in the history of his people, which he claimed to fulfill. In *The Politics of Jesus*, Yoder insists that Jesus' life in the flesh was itself ethically normative rather than a nonethical object of belief from which ethics or politics must then be derived by reasoning from some other ethical premise.[29] Likewise in *JCSR*, the life of the Jews was not the non- or pre-ethical repository of religious truth (or foil thereof) but the unfolding, dramatic political existence that was itself, in the flesh, the witness to the truth. Who Jesus is and how Christians are to live can be discerned only by attending to the ethically charged history of the people that Jesus fulfilled as Christ. That history does not simply tell us where the politics of Jesus came from but what that politics is and what we have to work with in continuing it today. It is important to get that history right because, if we get it wrong, we will misread the people Christians are called to be; we will misread Jesus.

In *JCSR*, Yoder argues that the theological purpose of Christian historical study is therefore to examine the process whereby a holy people has been formed so that its current instantiation might discern how to live faithfully. The continuity of God's revelation across time does not consist fundamentally in theoretical purity but in the political ethos of a holy people (which does not preclude concern for theoretical integrity). Only this sort of incarnate continuity can claim to be God's mouthpiece, that is, to disclose what God is like and to hold promise for the world.[30]

---

28. This is part of why Jesus' mother is so important to the Jewish flesh at the heart of Christian faith, as indicated in the Apostles' Creed. We cannot take Jesus' Jewish flesh seriously without considering his ancestors, most directly the Virgin Mary.
29. *The Politics of Jesus: Vicit agnus noster*, rev. ed. (Grand Rapids, MI: William B. Eerdmans, 1994 [1972]), esp. 1–20.
30. Peter Ochs rightly criticizes Yoder for minimizing, if not disparaging, the place of the land of Israel in the formation of the people of Israel (*JCSR*, 120, 203). As noted above, Yoder does not despise land altogether in the constitution of the people of God. But he seems to have no way of articulating how the land of Israel in particular determines who the people of Israel is, and this is indeed a problem.

Yoder and the Election of Israel

Yoder has clarified to some extent why a Christian account of peoplehood must attend to Israel, but he says next to nothing about God's election of Israel. The biblical testimony to God's election of Israel is perhaps difficult for Yoder to integrate into his account. It threatens to undermine his whole understanding of peoplehood, according to which the people of God is the people faithful to the love of God revealed in Torah and finally Messiah. Yoder understands the people of God to be constituted conditionally and revocably by the human response of obedience to God's call. But God's election constitutes Israel unconditionally and irrevocably. It is not primarily the faithfulness of the people but God's election that makes the people of God who it is. Israel remains Israel even in its unfaithfulness according to Scripture, where its unfaithfulness is a basis of its judgment precisely *as* Israel. God does not protect himself from association with the unfaithful in Israel but invests the integrity of his own name—God's very Self—in the drama of the people of Israel with all of its moral ambiguity. Thus, the people of God cannot police the border of its identity; it can only respond to the identity that God gives it over time. Circumscribing the identity of Israel with subjective political adequacy to God's revelation, as Yoder does, cannot avoid policing the border of the people of God according to criteria of such adequacy, whether historically or ethically (e.g., Jewishness is reduced to Jewish virtue as shown above). My criticism of Yoder here and in the rest of the book therefore focuses on why God's unconditional election of Israel is crucial to a Christian account of peoplehood. Note that this is not primarily a matter of Israel's self-understanding according God's election but a matter of God's election itself.

To say that there was and is a people of God implies God's initiative. It implies that God has chosen to make a people of God's own accord, that is, as God. Yoder is certainly not oblivious to God's initiative and ongoing activity in his theological historiography or Christian ethics. Yoder even associates that initiative directly with peoplehood. He claims that God's initiative was not to reveal theoretical truths or to heal persons one at a time but to form a holy people and to be present in and through that people to heal the world of violence and death. To do so, God issued a covenant call and promised to keep calling until the world's healing is complete. But the resulting people, according to Yoder's description, consists only of those who heeded God's call in obedience, that is, of those who have been Jewish as Yoder has defined Jewishness. Only those Jews came collectively to be a suffering servant, an unlikely savior that has borne all creation's promise in its wandering, peaceful, and costly way of life. Not as the one born of the Virgin Mary, then, but only as the obedient one, according to Yoder, was Jesus the embodiment of God's calling. The resurrection of Jesus revealed *that* one Jew—that one, faithful person—to be the cornerstone of this faithful people, stretching from Abraham to the present.

Yoder is eager to declare that God chose to form a people, but he is reticent to say that God chose the people itself. For if the people is to be God's way of healing the world, it must be politically different from the rest of the world, and to be politically different, according to Yoder, is to live differently, finally to love and not to kill. Thus, if humanity has any meaningful agency at all in God's economy on Yoder's understanding, God can have chosen only the people who have chosen God. It is not God's call but Israel's obedience that makes Israel who it is. This is the sense in which the people of God is *self-constituted* on Yoder's account.

We should not be surprised that Yoder seems uneasy with talk of election. In its traditional valences, the concept of election affords communities and persons a status apparently invulnerable to the way they actually live; it seems to trivialize or preempt history, faithfulness, and patient social process.[31] Election seems to do this by guaranteeing a good future for those chosen as the people of God. This supposed guarantee provides a false sense of security that is ethically devastating: it promotes political insolence and self-worship, which are utterly foreign to the faithful suffering of covenant life, especially that of Jesus. The following is therefore illustrative of Yoder's concern about election:

> The future of the Church is sure in the sense that God is a God who gives life to the dead. Yet the future of *our* church, that of any given community, enjoys no security. Thus when I distil from the radical reformation's historical witness a vision of the believing community, I do not say that such fidelity is assured, nor that it cannot be interrupted.[32]

What constitutes the people of God is fundamentally its unguaranteed fidelity to God. When a community (or person) ceases decisively to be faithful, it must cease to be part of the people. Anything else Yoder might call "Constantinian identity security." The threshold between the people of God and others cannot be basically institutional or sacramental or ethnic or doctrinal or territorial. It must be moral, and it must be both collective and

---

31. This is the case even if people must "confirm" their being elect by the way they live. Such simply inflates human moral judgment (i.e., about what constitutes confirmation) with divine importance and finality. Yoder prefers that we just admit the humanness and fallibility of our moral judgment.

32. *JCSR*, 123, emphasis his. Notice the conflation here of "future" and "fidelity." Cf. Yoder's discussion (with Schwarzchild) of the dialectic of covenant on 84. Perhaps Yoder would allow that the Jews and other peace churches have been who they have been by virtue of God's election as long as this is understood in terms of God's moving them to live faithfully. But he would no doubt worry that such a claim undermines human freedom and responsibility.

personal. It is admittedly somewhat ambiguous and can be identified only through ongoing, scripturally accountable social processes. But the threshold is there, and the integrity and persistence of the holy people depend on it.

While attractive to many modern (and some premodern) sensibilities,[33] Yoder's understanding immediately (and rightly) raises concerns about Christian supersessionism,[34] which has become a muddled concept of late. Given Christianity's complicity in recent atrocities against the Jews (which Yoder invokes often in *JCSR*), many flinch at any Christian claim to decide, through any human process, who counts and who doesn't count as the people of God. Yoder's ethical account may include most Jews, but its decisionist logic does not seem fundamentally different from that which segregated the Jews, and then rendered them replaceable, even disposable, and finally worthy of extermination.[35]

Yet, if we are to say that the people of God is a morally accountable identity and that judgment is not indefinitely postponed (i.e., to a future general resurrection), then we seem committed to observing a moral border to the people of God. Doesn't everyone want to say that there are some people who are only *falsely* the people of God because, say, they are guilty of some atrocious evil? This is precisely what Jewish scholar David Novak concludes in *The Election of Israel:*

---

33. I am thinking particularly here of the modern centering of the human subject, at least of a certain understanding of the human subject, as self-constituting. Nevertheless, Yoder's account of peoplehood is certainly not attractive to all modern sensibilities. He refuses to say what many would like to say, which is that God's action neutralizes sociopolitical differences. Such a claim cannot help but imply that such differences are bad and that God's action has been terribly ineffective, given the proliferation of difference in God's creation. Yoder is rightly concerned to specify which differences are God's work and which are human corruptions of God's work. Nevertheless, he does this always with a view to human subjective responsibility for who a person or community is.

34. These punctuate Peter Ochs's and Michael Cartwright's editorial comments throughout *JCSR*.

35. It is "decisionist" whether the constitution be determined by how persons decide to live, or the decision, through social processes, to regard particular persons or communities as excluded (i.e., as *not* Jewish or Christian), or otherwise to specify criteria of political authenticity.

The Idea of a Chosen People. Novak argues that God's election is not a ground for Jewish privilege, nor can ethnicity finally avail for the identity of the chosen people. It is an invitation to obedience, for Torah must "reign supreme."[36] Election means that some in Israel will always remain faithful, but others relinquish election by extreme unfaithfulness.[37]

> In spite of "even though Israel has sinned, she is still Israel," it has been recognized by normative Jewish tradition that there are cases when Jews can stray so far from the Torah that for all intents and purposes, they—and even more so their children and grandchildren—do indeed forfeit their election and its privileges.[38]

Similarly, Jacob Neusner insists that Israel is a unique social organism that is fundamentally "a moral entity."[39] Accordingly,

> In the law of the Mishnah, Israel does not constitute an ethnic group, a nation or people defined by culture or measured by this-worldly matters of practical consequence. Status as an Israelite, part of "Israel," comes about by reason of the Torah. Israel forms the holy community of those destined for life eternal, and that constitutes not an ethnic group, nation, or people, but a social entity that is *sui generis*.[40]

Neusner cites *m. Sanh.* 10:1, which begins with "All Israelites have a share in the age to come," and proceeds to list several classes

---

36. David Novak, *The Election of Israel: The Idea of a Chosen People* (Cambridge: Cambridge University Press, 1995), 247. Novak criticizes Michael Wyschogrod's understanding (in e.g., *The Body of Faith: Judaism as Corporeal Election* [New York: Seabury, 1983]) for effectively subordinating Torah to the Jewish people, who, according to Wyschogrod, can be defined independently of obedience to Torah.
37. Novak, 246, citing b. Kiddushin 68b on Deut. 7:4. Cf. Yoder's "Church" vs. "church" above. Note that for Novak, in contrast to Yoder, it is not the people who make themselves obedient to Torah but Torah that makes the people obedient. Novak of course maintains, over against Baruch Spinoza and those who follow him, that God indeed chose Israel before Israel chose God.
38. Ibid.
39. The title of ch. 4 of *Making God's Word Work: A Guide to the Mishnah* (London: Continuum International, 2004) is "Corporate Israel As a Moral Entity" (85–99).
40. Ibid., 82.

of "Israelites" and individual "Israelites" who, for indicated moral failures, "have no portion in the world to come" and therefore are not finally part of all Israel.[41] He goes on to read the Mishnah to indicate that gentiles may share in the blessings promised to the righteous, but only as they become part of Israel.[42]

Jewish scholars Novak and Neusner therefore seem to agree with Yoder (and many other Christians), whatever their differences with him, that to be the people of God is to be a community of particular ethical discipline and moral quality. Any account of election must fit Israel's moral constitution, lest the God revealed in and to the people of Israel through Torah be himself morally questionable.

Yoder obviously does not hold to traditional supersessionism, wherein the Christian church is understood to have replaced the Jews as Israel because the Jews refused to become Christian. But the problem with traditional supersessionism for Yoder is not its presumption that the unfaithful cease to belong to Israel and are conditionally excluded. The problem is what it presumes faithfulness and unfaithfulness to be, which in turn has allowed many Christians to imagine a "replacement" and justify violent exclusion of Jews and others (who have been deemed inauthentic members of the people of God). If simply excluding part of the people from membership "nonviolently" because that part has become extremely unfaithful counts as "supersessionism," then Yoder's problem with the traditional Christian understanding is not that it is supersessionist but that its supersessionism is not Jewish.[43]

---

41. Ibid., 70–71. Yet, Neusner says on 133 that "failure to keep the law does not bring about exclusion from Israel." Here he seems to be talking not about the kind of unfaithfulness described in *m. Sanh.* 10:1 but a lesser degree of unfaithfulness. If not, maybe he would say that the exclusions of *m. Sanh.* 10 take place only at the resurrection. One suspects that they are somehow anticipated in present-age Jewish life, however.

42. Ibid., 72–82.

43. Cf. Yoder, *The Original Revolution*, 58 and 180n7. I put "nonviolently" in scare quotes because I will question whether such exclusion should be considered nonviolent.

I should point out that Yoder can apparently conceive of an ethically fitting understanding of election. He entitles the closing section of one of *JCSR*'s crucial chapters "The World-View of the Elect Underdogs."[44] In a 1992 sermon entitled "Salvation Is of the Jews" (John 4:22), Yoder says the following regarding the God of Abraham: "Such a God affirms a given people's tribal identity and posterity as a good thing, but not as over against their enemies and adversaries."[45]

Here is an important sense in which Israel's tribal identity and posterity is "a good thing":

> The notion that God's own people are especially subject to having their sins punished, by virtue of the special privileges of their election, may have become more weighty in the Jewish thought of a later age than it was in the canonical period, but it is already present in the prophets. As soon as that attitude toward one's own sufferings is possible, the injustices suffered by God's people take on a different meaning, and seeking to prevent them becomes impious.[46]

Yoder does not develop this political function of election, which he tellingly locates in Israelite subjectivity as an "attitude," rather than in God's own determination of Israel. In the Tanakh and New Testament, election is the activity of God before it is ever the activity of human beings. Nevertheless, that the election of Israel can be understood to exert this kind of political influence is an important

44. Yoder, *JCSR*, 174.
45. Ibid., 243.
46. Ibid, 191. Cf. John Howard Yoder, *For the Nations: Essays Evangelical and Public* (Grand Rapids, MI: William B. Eerdmans, 1997), 86. Yoder also appeals to the election of the people of God in "Why Ecclesiology is Social Ethics," in *The Royal Priesthood: Essays Ecclesiastical and Ecumenical*, ed. Michael G. Cartwright (Grand Rapids, MI: William B. Eerdmans, 1994), 115. But note how Yoder claims here that the "Abraham-Jesus story" is a story of the rise of a faithful people as opposed to a Constantinian people, whereas, against Yoder, the biblical story of the elect people, of Abraham to Jesus, includes in the covenant community the likes of Saul, Jeroboam, Caiaphas, and Judas. This is a people constituted by God's election rather than its own faithfulness. Thanks to Mark Nation for reminding me of Yoder's discussion of election in this essay.

insight, especially if it can be developed without confining it, as Yoder does, to Israelite subjectivity. How might more careful consideration of the election of Israel challenge and perhaps extend Yoder's theological historiography and thus his account of peoplehood? Can the election of Israel avoid the theological and ethical pitfalls identified by Yoder, Novak, and Neusner? What does it say about the meaning and imperative of Christian nonviolence and the distinctiveness of "the church" within Israel? In an attempt to articulate a theological understanding of peoplehood that can resist the violent tendencies of the modern "peoples" that claim Christians and others today, I will pursue these questions in the remaining chapters of the book. Here I will briefly adumbrate some of the central concerns and arguments of those chapters in conversation with Yoder's account of peoplehood, particularly as it builds on a revisionist understanding of the Jewish-Christian schism.

Adumbration of Arguments to Come

Yoder exemplifies the modern preoccupation with human self-determination and with the human subject (i.e., the human as agent, whether collective or individual). In response to intolerable forms of heteronomy, whether of communities or persons, such preoccupation has sought accounts of political or personal identity capable of self-determination, although the constitution of the identity in question has often been ascribed to God (e.g., by self-evident, divine endowment of inalienable rights that nevertheless have not obtained in the cases of underclasses or enemies). Such accounts provide a sense of personal or collective self. In the (very "creative") political historiography of such accounts, as Partha Chatterjee shows, this quest for peoplehood has often taken the form of the modern nation's search for its historical self. Imagined "bonds of nation-ness. . . justify the identification of the historian with the consciousness of a solidarity that is supposed to act itself out in history."[47] This sounds conspicuously like what Yoder does with the theological historiography of the Jews in *JCSR*.

Modern efforts to claim continuity with a quite different political past have frequently involved a narrative of refinement or progress, which, as Stuart Hall suggests, received its intelligibility and validity through European contact with non-European "savages."[48] Accordingly, modern biblical scholars and others have understood Israel's history as a progression from ancient Near Eastern, polytheistic tribalism to the prophets' "ethical monotheism," which Jesus supposedly perfected and universalized.[49] Yoder, too, conceives of peoplehood in terms of historical progress, even if in *The Jewish-Christian Schism Revisited* he moves the crucial turn in the narrative back from Jesus to Jeremiah (with a view to justifying exilic life as the political calling of the people of God). Indeed, he seems to *reduce* Israel to a political progression, which becomes the condition of the Christian community's ability to "own" its Israelite past.[50] Prior to modern times, Christian thinkers do not seem to have tried to "own" Israel's story by construing Jesus (and the church) as the culmination of a *narrative* of progress.[51] Their supersessionist concepts

47. Partha Chatterjee, *The Nation and Its Fragments: Colonial and Postcolonial Histories* (Princeton: Princeton University Press, 1993), 84.
48. Stuart Hall and Bram Gieben, eds., *Formations of Modernity* (Cambridge: Polity, 1992), 311. With the help of a Christian imagination, this contact with previously unknown, very different communities seems also to have helped provide the conditions for the modern concept of race. See J. Kameron Carter, *Race: A Theological Account* (Oxford: Oxford University Press, 2008); Willie James Jennings, *The Christian Imagination: Theology and the Origins of Race* (New Haven: Yale University Press, 2010). I will take up this matter in ch. 3.
49. Julius Wellhausen was an important figure in the development of this understanding (*Prolegomena to the History of Israel, with a Reprint of the Article "Israel" from the Encyclopedia Britannica* [Atlanta: Scholars, 1994], reprint of the first edition [Edinburgh: A & C Black, 1885]). See also Charles Edward Carter and Carol L. Meyers, eds., *Community, Identity, and Ideology: Social Science Approaches to the Hebrew Bible* (Winona Lake, Indiana: Eisenbrauns, 1996).
50. John Howard Yoder, *The Politics of Jesus*, 87; Yoder, *The Original Revolution*, 101.
51. In *The Star of Redemption*, trans. Barbara E. Galli (Madison, Wisconsin: University of Wisconsin Press, 2005), Franz Rosenzweig criticizes the modern Euro-American tendency in

of "fulfillment" did not depend on a notion of historical progress or evolution. This does not imply that premodern understandings are better or worse than Yoder's, only that we should scrutinize the shift from appropriations of the past that do not depend on a concept of progress to progress-determined ones like Yoder's.

The modern quest for peoplehood, like Yoder's, turned to "Israel" to develop both personal and collective political selves, most notably in the cases of Great Britain, Germany, Holland, and the United States (the provenances of a great deal of modern biblical scholarship), as Anthony Smith demonstrates.[52] "Israel" provided a powerful trope and mythic identity for modern national consolidation—not for reconciliation with the past, however, but for breaking from it into something brand new, a "new Israel" altogether. This is not what Yoder does. He does not ignore or demonize Israel's Jewish past and present in order to render Israel a free-floating, deserted identity awaiting new, nationalist occupation. His Christian identification with the people of Israel aims not at justifying violent revolution or expansion, as it did for the American colonies of Britain or for Britain's imperialist competition with France, but at nonviolent resistance and missionary dispersion. Yoder turns to the Jews to combat modern nationalism and its artificial roots in divine election, not to enable it. Nevertheless, Yoder's Christian appropriation of Jewishness shares something with modern seizures of "Israel," namely, the common weapon of claiming to know or be the true

---

theological discourse to assimilate the past to the present with a concept of progress in order to render the past inoffensive and "ours." The effect is equal and opposite to rendering the past null and void so as to "free" the present (111). By contrast, Rosenzweig insists that the present can never unhinge itself from the past. Cf. Leora Batnitzky, *Idolatry and Representation: The Philosophy of Franz Rosenzweig Reconsidered* (Princeton: Princeton University Press, 2000), 35.

52. Anthony D. Smith, *Chosen Peoples: Sacred Sources of National Identity* (Oxford: Oxford University Press, 2003). Sacvan Bercovitch provides a gripping account of the United States' self-understanding as God's chosen, new Israel in *The Rites of Assent: Transformations in the Symbolic Construction of America* (New York: Routledge, 1993).

embodiment of the reputable identity of Israel over against false pretenders, that is, of claiming a pure theopolitical identity. Influential modern constructions of peoplehood have claimed to be the true, purified, elect "Israel" over against a defunct "Israel" or "Egyptian" slave master. Moreover, as Étienne Balibar indicates, the foil of Jewishness seems to have provided national peoplehood with a way of essentializing itself and consolidating internal fragmentation in relation to enemies.[53] Jewishness was the measure of what a modern people was essentially *not* (i.e., not Jewish) and only therefore of what it was (i.e., true/elect Israel). For Yoder, Jewishness is the measure of what the people of God both was and is (i.e., the true people of God is Jewish). But either way, what is claimed is a total view of the identity of the people of God in relation to the Jews, and those who speak for the people of God claim to command that view. Somehow, then, it must be *decided* by human beings who truly belongs and who doesn't, and those who decide are responsible for enacting the difference. Whether this decision is that of the people who measure up or of those who don't, or of those who claim to command a view of the difference, the result is a finally voluntarist foundation of peoplehood (whatever the claim to embody God's decree, to be obedient to scriptural commands, to be true to history, or to be true to nature).

Yoder tries to make this voluntarist foundation of peoplehood nonviolent in the case of the people of God by locating the human determination of identity not in coercive imposition or high-level usurpation of power but "voluntary" individual choice and "voluntary" social processes of discernment, thereby denying the generational dimension of the people of God (among other things). The people gathered by Jesus "was a society with no second

---

53. Étienne Balibar, "Racism and Nationalism," in *Race, Nation, Class: Ambiguous Identities*, ed. Étienne Balibar and Immanuel Wallerstein, trans. Chris Turner (London: Verso, 1991), 62.

generation members."[54] "Only an adult can enter a covenant."[55] But this conceals the manifold ways in which persons' and communities' decisions are made possible and constrained by their past and present. It ignores the importance of naming God's presence and the complexity of human action and inaction in determining those possibilities and constraints (i.e., the people is more than a cumulative string of decisions; it is bodily).[56] I will argue in subsequent chapters that to have been gathered as the people of God is not for a given person or community as a subject to have laid hold of an identity that once dangled before it. It is for the God of Israel to have laid hold of a given person or community through a holy, impure, preexisting people, and it is to know freedom only as patient response (i.e., as subject to the rule of the God of Israel). This will require an account of election that is alternative to that of modern peoplehood, particularly that informed by a secularized notion of election such as American exceptionalism. In the meantime, one can see how Yoder's account of Christian peoplehood may struggle to resist the violence of modern peoplehood to the extent that it is locked inside the logic that characterizes modern peoplehood, namely, that of pure political identity and voluntarist self-constitution.

Yoder's theological historiography of the people of Israel is typological in the sense that it tells the developing story of one type of people among other political types. On historical and scriptural grounds, he commends that type as normative and exclusive as well as the one with which he has come to identify himself. In Yoder's approach, different types did not and cannot live within the same people, even if they seem to have passed historically as doing so for a time, because the identity of the people inheres in the particular

54. Yoder, *The Original Revolution*, 28n1.
55. Yoder, *JCSR*, 126.
56. Nonhuman actions and conditions (e.g., land, animals, weather) are also important for an account of the formation of the people of God, as we will see in ch. 5.

political type that Yoder "discovers" in the past and finds to be authorized by Scripture. It is only that pure type, the politically faithful one, that finally counts as Israel or Jewishness or church. Otherwise, Yoder surmises, there is no meaningful difference between the people of God and the rest of the world; there is no authentic people, no real promise.

Because Yoder understands Israel to be constituted not by God's open-ended, Self-implicating, irrevocable electing over time but the human response of obedience to God's call, Yoder cannot avoid policing the border of the people of God. The effect on historiography is the formal removal of the unfaithful from Israel and the minimization of historical ambiguity in order to "decide" what Israelite identity was and is. It exerts a homogenizing pressure in order to conceive and utilize representativity (i.e., what represents the "true" people of God) in the ongoing life of the people (this is where historiography and political discipline are one). Like modern historiography that Yoder has criticized, perhaps he too "cuts out most of the flesh of past reality . . . in the interest of being absolutely sure about the [political] skeleton."[57] Yoder cannot help but disown Israel's unfaithful ancestors as not really ancestors. But Christian Scripture teaches the current generation of the people of the God of Israel (including non-Jews) not to disown unfaithful ancestors but to remember them as our own and learn from their example (e.g., 1 Cor. 10:1ff). The people is constituted not by Israelite faithfulness to the exclusion of unfaithfulness. It is constituted by God's faithfully holding Israelite faithfulness and unfaithfulness together with remembrance and forgiveness. This covenant drama is neither a discernible "progress" nor a historically motionless equilibrium. But it is a history. As such it is the work of God that is patient with

57. *JCSR*, 114.

God's people and inspires its faithfulness and thus its hope (Eph. 2:8-10). "Honor your father and your mother, which is the first commandment with a promise" (Eph. 6:2), writes Paul. Children are to honor their Israelite parents not because they are obedient but because they are their parents. However much they disappoint, they remain, like their children, God's effective gift (cf. Mal. 4:6).

As we will see, Yoder does not need to worry about letting the unfaithful count as Israelite (the unfaithful would in fact be unintelligible as such if they did not). God does not need people to protect God's holiness but commands that they observe it. The unfaithful throughout Israel's history may have suffered the death penalty, been killed in war, or been assimilated over generations into surrounding gentile communities before or after exile.[58] But it is God, not the people, who finally and materially weaves certain human strands into Israel's future in the flesh and others out of it. Those who in retrospect were on their way out (e.g., most of the people of the ten tribes of the northern kingdom of Israel) do not need historians or ethicists to preempt God's writing them out of Israel's present or future. Quite the contrary: they must be remembered as ancestors so long as there is the slightest trace of them. Israelite identity is not an honorary status that can be removed from a particular person or community by their own unfaithfulness or by a human court that pronounces them excluded on that basis or some other. Unfaithfulness only makes being Israel a curse inside of a promise, a curse that bodes suffering, sometimes even the extinction of a strand of the people or even of whole tribes, but finally the reformation of the covenant people and blessing for the whole world. Being irrevocably Israel by God's ongoing election, therefore, does not afford false security indefinitely (a false security that reflects a

---

58. They may also seem to have gotten off scot-free while the righteous have suffered, as the psalmist complains.

misunderstanding of the grammar of election, a misuse of the language of it). In truth, being Israel is often much more dangerous and depressing than not being Israel. Consequently, it is not theologically (or historically) insignificant that unfaithful Israelite persons or communities have managed to pass as Israelite or Jewish or Christian in biblical or other human memory. Nor is it insignificant how they have been remembered. More important than the difference between historical faithfulness and unfaithfulness within Israel is that between the part of Israel that has been remembered at all and the gentiles. The former difference is derived from the latter.[59]

Yoder's rather truncated historiography of the Jews is not oblivious to this ebb and flow of the history of Israel in the flesh. He is right that the Jews were somebody and not anybody, and he observes that certain Jewish ways thrived as others deteriorated. But it is not true that only the faithful thrived and only the unfaithful deteriorated. And those who deteriorated should not be disinherited or disowned by subsequent generations. In response to Yoder's worries about the way election underplays the normativity of the law and of Jesus and thus promotes violence, my thesis is that to be chosen by the God of Israel is not to be chosen to thrive at others' expense but to die a life-giving death. Even the unfaithful are swept up into this kind of death.

Similar to its effect on historiography, Yoder's construing the people of God as constituted by obedience introduces into the politics of the people of God a weapon of identity ascription or removal, a human weapon that is supposedly invested with divine authority. It underestimates the extent to which covenant faithfulness bears

---

59. Understanding the history of Israel or the church in this way might ease the apologetic pressure that has informed so much Jewish and Christian historiography. The identity or integrity of the people of God does not depend upon establishing its virtue in the past, despite the contrary assumptions of modern readers who have been schooled to justify the present with fictitiously pure pasts. Instead, present virtue is increased by the honesty of current generations about the inadequacy of their ancestors, as we see in the Tanakh as well as the New Testament.

patiently with covenant unfaithfulness. It attempts to preempt what we will see below as God's material determination of the shape of the people over time, that is, God's election. It does not trust God to reform the sinful ways of a current generation and so ensure the future of the people. Moreover, using identity as a weapon can confuse faithfulness and unfaithfulness and lead those who wield it to find themselves fighting against God. To be sure, political discipline is both indispensable and inescapable, and how to discipline the people is typically the real subject of questions about the identity of the people. But Yoder's weapon of identity pronouncement is not a good kind of discipline because it is inadequately responsive to the often unsettling historical activity of God's election (e.g., God's allowing those we despise, even those whom God despises, to bear our name as well as God's).

As Yoder has so eloquently insisted in other contexts and as we see in Jesus, love is first and foremost patient. Like other prophets before him, Jesus refused to disown the unfaithful among his people. Instead, he embraced Israel's sins as his own, confessing them in John's baptism and later setting his face to go to Jerusalem rather than somewhere else apparently more promising. Dying as he did, instead of starting over with a "faithful" people, was the faithfulness that culminated in resurrection and the forgiveness of Israel's sins, the light that draws gentiles to Zion to grow with Jews into one Israel of covenant peace. Political faithfulness, then, does not exclude the unfaithful but refuses to abandon them as alien. Let us call this solidarity with the sin of the people of the God of Israel the catholicity of Jesus. The catholicity of Jesus responds to and is the culmination of the election of Israel; it is the incarnation of the election of Israel. An understanding of election without this catholicity cannot overcome a hiatus between God's elect people and God's elect one, that is, the Christ.

I conclude by returning to the words with which I began chapter 1: the words of Rabbi Gamaliel in Acts 5. Yoder's reading is perhaps that this Pharisee, "held in honor by all the people," exemplifies the Jewish political ethos. He does not locate God in the province of the Sanhedrin. He does not take belief to define the limits of the people of God. He is concerned with how the authorities of the Sanhedrin are to walk in response to a local, emergent, messianic movement. He is a Pharisee concerned with Israel's obedience to the Torah, not with staying in control. And of course he opposes the violence with which the rest of the Sanhedrin wishes to enforce its will. Thus, he testifies that God's rule calls for patient nonviolence. The life of Israel is not immediately incompatible with Jesus' way; the relation must be allowed to remain ambiguous for the time being. Rabbi Gamaliel thus finds himself an unwitting enabler of the gospel, for which the apostles are honored to suffer, just as Gamaliel himself is apparently ready to suffer shame and loss in the observance of God's sovereignty. Yet, on what we may imagine to be Yoder's reading, Gamaliel is primarily engaged in a social decision-making process rather than responding to God's election or God's movement of history. In another case, in the interest of Israel's faithfulness and God's holiness, Rabbi Gamaliel may have rightly moved against the death penalty but in favor of pronouncing the accused no longer Jewish and treating them accordingly. The identity of the people of God, on Yoder's understanding, is a decision that Gamaliel or a formal social process can make. And so we must press beyond a Yoderian reading.

Rabbi Gamaliel points the Sanhedrin as "men of Israel" to the specific historical cases of two other messianic movements, that of Theudas and that of Judas the Galilean. He notes that those movements were dissolved without lethal repression by Israelite authorities. He claims that God can be trusted to weave unfaithful ways out of Israel over time, often by means of Israel's relation to gentiles, in this case by oppressive, Roman rule. Thus, God's well-attested control of Israel's history bids the authorities of Jerusalem be patient and nonviolent. They enjoy no total view of Israel,[60] no authority to decide who counts as Israel and who doesn't, and no preemptive power to kill. Figures in Israel can at times prophesy that one way leads out of Israel's future while another way leads to it, but God will have to enact that judgment in time. Israel can finally only respond to God's election. Neither the people nor its authorities can dictate it. So the Sanhedrin should wait and see what God does with the Jesus movement. If it does not, Gamaliel the Pharisee warns, if it preempts God's judgment and forsakes God's incomprehensible sovereignty, it may find itself fighting against God. And the Jerusalem establishment agreed.

---

60. Note Michael Cartwright's comment on Bonhoeffer's understanding that Christianity can have "no overview of itself" (*JCSR*, 212). Cf. 2 Samuel 24; 1 Chronicles 21. Cartwright notes that he is drawing on the fine work of David F. Ford, *Self and Salvation: Being Transformed* (Cambridge: Cambridge University Press, 1999), esp. 241–65.

3

"Israel" and the Modern Discourse of Peoplehood

No attempt to describe the people of Israel of yesterday and today can escape the constraints of the politically charged, modern discourse of peoplehood. The discursive patterns in which diverse persons and communities have come to be associated across time and space as this or that "people," as distinct from others, constitute a contingent field in and through which we live and think in the wake of modernity.[1] This discourse influences the sense we make of the Israelite past, the way we read biblical texts about the people of God (or even what we take biblical texts to be about), and the implications any description of the people of Israel will have for the way Christians or a certain "people" should live. Specialists such as historians, biblical

---

1. On "discourse" as key to political formations and a subject of analysis, see Michel Foucault, *The Archaeology of Knowledge*, trans. A. M. Sheridan Smith (New York: Pantheon Books, 1972); Foucault, "Politics and the Study of Discourse," in *The Foucault Effect: Studies in Governmentality*, ed. Graham Burchell, Colin Gordon, and Peter Miller (Chicago: The University of Chicago Press, 1991), 53–72.

exegetes, philosophers, and ethicists may buffer the influence of this discourse—even affect the discourse itself—with the help of their "disciplines," but they cannot avoid it or address it from without. Such disciplines have, after all, done much to generate the discourse in the first place and came to exist as such (i.e., as relatively discrete modes of specialized enquiry) concurrently with the rise of modern peoplehood.[2]

The question of the people of Israel, it turns out, is not incidental to the modern discourse of peoplehood. As I will show in this chapter, certain modern understandings of the biblical people of Israel—and specifically debates about who can still claim truthfully to be that people as chosen by the one God—have to a large extent structured the modern discourse of peoplehood and its key conception of "the people," namely, the nation-state. The purpose here, then, is not to analyze how religious talk of "the people of God" has been influenced by the modern discourse of peoplehood, but how the modern discourse of peoplehood itself has been created and shaped by (often poor) Christian understandings of the people of the God of Israel. Given the pervasiveness of the discourse and the importance of "the chosen people of Israel" in its production, it seems wise to situate the central question of this book—what it means to be the people of God as determined by God's election of Israel—in the context of a summary analysis of this discourse. This will help us to articulate some appropriate resistance to its central tendencies in the sense we

---

2. For an account of the influence of biblical study and theology on the shape of the modern world, see Jonathan Sheehan, *The Enlightenment Bible: Translation, Scholarship, Culture* (Princeton: Princeton University Press, 2005), esp. 120ff. See also Thomas Albert Howard, *Protestant Theology and the Making of the Modern German University* (Oxford: Oxford University Press, 2006), esp. 24–35, 212–266; J. Kameron Carter, *Race: A Theological Account* (Oxford: Oxford University Press, 2008), 39–121; Willie James Jennings, *The Christian Imagination: Theology and the Origins of Race* (New Haven: Yale University Press, 2010), 207–88; Shawn Kelley, *Racializing Jesus: Race, Ideology, and the Formation of Modern Biblical Scholarship* (London: Routledge, 2002).

make of the Israelite past, the way we read influential biblical texts, and how we describe human community and the way it should live. At the very least, it will help us see that what it means to be a people today is not what being a people has always meant or has to mean or should mean.

With the below analysis of the admittedly sprawling modern discourse of peoplehood, I will attempt to show that the relevant challenge facing many Christian communities today is not merely that we do not understand the Christian life as that of a particular political community, as part of what Scripture calls "the holy people." Nor is it simply that we are more concerned to be "the people" of this or that modern nation-state than the people of the God of Israel and thus participate in and even justify theologically the violent ways of our national societies. These are indeed vexing problems, and John Howard Yoder and others have sought to address them by describing the people of God in ways that resist both the dualism of religion and politics and the violence of modern nationalism.[3] The challenge I mean to identify and address is subtler, and it is this: even when Christian descriptions of the people of God aim to resist violent contemporary movements of peoplehood, central tendencies in the modern discourse of peoplehood are uncritically reinforced in the very way that "the people" is described and used.

Specifically, in the Christian descriptions I have in mind (e.g., Yoder's), the identity or being of the people (e.g., "the church") is conceived and performed as effectively *pure* vis-à-vis other communities, especially opposing (e.g., unfaithful, unorthodox, unbelieving, or immoral) communities or persons. A *total* view of the people of God is claimed so that the people of reference can be called to account, its mission undertaken with integrity rather than

3. See ch. 1 above, "The Gospel of a People."

forsaken: "Only those who live as the people of God can claim to be the people of God," the logic goes. With the limits of Christian identity clearly in view, what it means to be Christian is, in effect, reduced to an exclusive, policing description. Thus, a total view of the people enables its claimants to associate certain imperatives (e.g., creedal, ethical) with the identity of the people itself and, by implication, to hold and treat as excluded from the people those not committed to those imperatives. Such persons or communities do not "truly" belong to the people of God and are subtly and not so subtly discouraged from continuing to live the way they do. Similarly, the place of those who are sufficiently committed to those imperatives within the people of God is assured, and they are spurred to remain steadfast. They "truly" belong to the people of God and should endeavor to stay that way. Here we see the use of one important concept of "true" and "false" belonging to the people of God, a sort of technology of identity.

However innocent or indispensable they may seem, such understandings of the people of God constitute what has been a most violent weapon in the shaping of the modern world, particularly the West, as I will demonstrate below. Imaginarily purified of "false" claimants, be they past or present, the people of God has been construed as a conveniently free-floating, deserted identity prepared by God for conquest and possession by the elect, its "natural" inhabitants. It is considered *pure* vis-à-vis its enemies, self-constituted, and endowed by divine authority with a view of its self that is total enough to know who is excluded (e.g., who is killable) and to form and discipline its self accordingly. Its spokespersons conceive "the people," particularly its representatives, as in full possession of—even embodying—the standard of conformity, a standard identified finally as what is "truly" human. For a while this project of peoplehood was rooted enough in the language of the

Bible for the new, national people to be known in some sense as "Israel" (i.e., "the new Israel" or "the true Israel"). It has since moved to the secular messianism of "we the people" and has individualized and biologized the theological voluntarism that has long entitled Christian authorities to decide who the (true) people of God is and are. The entity that is the national people of modernity is accordingly understood as constituted by persons who are who they decide to be and who thus achieve freedom, enact their nature, and realize their humanity.

In this modern political context, Christian attempts like Yoder's to describe the "true" people of God as constituted by its/their subjecivity (e.g., its/their own faithfulness to Torah or Jesus) over against a competing understanding of peoplehood (e.g., a nation-state) remain captive to the modern discourse of peoplehood. They reinforce the very peoplehood they seek to subvert (e.g., they reinforce the violent peoplehood of "We the People of the United States" by obeying its discursive patterns or logic). Because they have not attended to the Christian theological roots of the modern discourse of peoplehood, they are simply not subversive enough.[4]

I should stress, lest it be overlooked, that the concern in Christian appeals such as Yoder's to the unique identity of the people of God is an understandable and important one. It is not merely to exclude for the sake of exclusion or self-assertion, for what can the people of God be if it is not set apart in some sense (i.e., "holy") by what its constituents believe or how they live? How is the Christian community meaningfully different from other communities so that to be Christian is not to be just anything but to be something particular (e.g., to witness to the kingdom of God)? Surely some

---

4. For a brief description of Christendom as the politics of supersessionism, and the national supersessionism of modernity, see Scott Bader-Saye, *Church and Israel after Christendom: The Politics of Election* (Eugene, Oregon: Wipf & Stock Publishers, 1999), 57–69. What follows is an attempt to get at the development of the discursive grammar that Bader-Saye identifies.

who have been baptized in the Triune name, say Hitler, or certain others who claim to be Christian, are not "truly" Christian, are they?! Do not most Christians subscribe to some version of this conviction, however diverse their understandings of what counts as "truly" Christian? If God does in fact elect people as the Bible says, it seems that we are happy for God to elect only those who elect God.

As we saw in Yoder's account in chapters 1 and 2 above, the concern in thus appealing to the identity of the people of God is to insist that it be accountable to the basis and hope of its existence, that is, morally accountable to God as revealed through Torah and finally in Jesus. It is to ensure that faithfulness be understood as constitutive of the identity of the people, that its identity be determinably about becoming who that people is called to be, that its particularity—and correspondingly the particularity of God—be acknowledged and observed. According to Yoder, there can be no politically neutral reserve to the identity of the people of God, no dualistic shielding of its life from the peace-making imperative of God's revelation. Otherwise, being the people of God is allowed to act as a powerful cipher for justifying the violence of what are in fact political ways at cross-purposes with the God revealed in Jesus. This concern rightly implies that the question of who the people of God is amounts to a question of how that people should live and how its integrity and vocation will be promoted. But, it assumes that this question must be addressed from and with a *total* view of the people of God, which is available to, perhaps entrusted to or even embodied in, some human court (e.g., scholarly research, an ecclesiastical authority, a discerning gathering of Christians). It treats the identity of this people as functionally pure vis-à-vis those it polemically excludes as (sufficiently) unfaithful to the standard of conformity. Thus, the being of the people of God is construed as a sort of form to which some persons or communities make a compelling claim as material instantiations while others make an inadequate and therefore false claim.

Notice the following about this modern technology of identity: insofar as the difference between being truly and falsely the people of God is predicated on some human agency whereby persons or groups with some claim to be "in" are treated as "in" or "out," or those claimed by some to be "out" are treated as "in" or "out,"[5] the identity of the people of God—who the people is—is deemed a matter of *human* making, doing, or decision.[6] This is the case whatever the supposed ontic equivalence of this human activity to the activity of God (e.g., God's election).[7] As this concept of the identity or being of the people of God has operated in recent centuries in the West, preoccupied as modernity has been with *self*-determination, communities or persons have often been understood to be Christian (or national) by virtue of some choice or other (voluntary) activity of their own (or of their ancestors), and the church (or nation) is understood to be endowed with the (divine) power to determine

5. This agency is often ascribed finally to those being judged and not to those making judgments. Thus, certain persons or communities "exclude themselves" by unfaithful activity, and authoritative ecclesial figures or processes simply "recognize" what those excluded have already made the case. Alternatively, this agency is ascribed to those making judgments, in which case they become ontically equivalent to God (e.g., by the Spirit), or it is ascribed to God by a troubling theory of double predestination.

6. Cf. the claim by Carl Schmitt: "Every legal order is based on a decision. . . . Like every other order, the legal order rests on a decision and not on a norm" (*Political Theology: Four Chapters on the Concept of Sovereignty*, trans. George Schwab [Chicago: The University of Chicago Press, 1985], 10). In other words, political identity is not simply given or natural. It is made by human hands (cf. χειροποίητος, Eph. 2:11).

7. This decision may seem insignificant to the extent that religious associations do not seem to be the most determinative sort of human association in our time. But it corresponds discursively to the decision of the nation-state whereby communities or persons are deemed foreign or killable, a decision that was once—before "secularization"—the nation-state's claim to divine power over life and death, that is, to inflict death in policing or warfare under divine authority or on a God-given errand. Secularization is of course far from complete, as the religious nature of modern warfare and the sanctity of the national cause readily attest. The question of who belongs to the people and who does not is therefore of immense material importance, regulating not only who is killable but the internal distribution of power "within" the people as it is disciplined by the regnant ideological form of itself. The nature and function of this ideological form will be analyzed below.

its own existence. Here, a commitment to self-determination and autonomy is thought a bulwark against the heteronomous absolutism of the past.

But as we will soon see, this move toward self-determination and self-constitution has hardly thrown off God's election. Instead, it has made God's election equivalent to the self-election of those who decide who or what counts as elect and of those who conform to that decision, what I would call a false incarnation. Without something tantamount to God's election, the political self lacks necessary basis or authority. Yet, without some human conditioning of God's election, God's activity is perceived as arbitrary and human activity as immaterial or uncontrollable, much too problematic to accept or "use" politically. God's unconditional election of a people is thought ethically irresponsible, disempowering, and/or politically oppressive. Accordingly, the modern discourse of peoplehood has in time found ways to keep "God" in the background of peoplehood, shifting the political drama from "the chosen people of Israel" to "the people of God" to "we the people." The former two have been consigned to the stuff of "religion," regardless of how much "religion" influences the political ways of particular communities and persons or crops up in explicitly political claims (e.g., "God bless America"). Meanwhile, the secularized "we the people" has inherited the divine authority characteristic of voluntarist Christian ecclesiology, claiming all the time to be religiously neutral. God's election of a people has thus become at once an empty, irresponsible religious claim and the hidden basis of liberal democratic nationalism. At the same time, we seem to be left with no way of saying that the people of God is God's doing without effectively reducing God's activity to human activity or inflating corruptible human power with the air of divinity.[8]

---

8. This is not to imply that God's activity and human activity are necessarily mutually competitive. But it is to say that they should be understood in a certain (christological) relationship rather

Below we will consider in some detail several tendencies of the modern discourse of peoplehood adumbrated above (e.g., pure identity, a total view of the people, self-constitution) in their originating, Christian idiom in hopes of identifying how their problematic influence is often reinforced in Christian descriptions of what it means to be the people of God. Occasionally, I will illustrate them by referring to aspects of Yoder's account of peoplehood as presented in the previous two chapters. The analysis of these tendencies will lay important groundwork for articulating resistance to the violence of modern peoplehood in the four chapters following this one. As we will see, these tendencies present a formidable challenge because, even in the course of trying to resist the violent political closure of race or territory or class that characterizes the modern discourse of peoplehood, such Christian descriptions typically trade in the very self-assertive "purity" and totalized self-understanding that have empowered modern racialization, territorialization, and economic chauvinism. In fact, while the violent tendencies of the modern discourse of peoplehood now reach far beyond the church (and deceptively appear to be "secular"), they have historically Christian roots and so remain somewhat at home in Christian language. Structuring these tendencies, I will contend, are poor Christian understandings of "Israel" and "the Jews."

Before turning directly to the modern discourse of peoplehood, let me state briefly the alternative understanding of peoplehood that I will propose and defend in subsequent chapters, building on the criticism of this and the previous two chapters. Against Yoder and the technology of identity that has shaped so much of the modern Christian tradition and its secular political derivatives, I submit that the people of God is not self-constituted by the political faithfulness

than as identical. We are dealing here, in political terms, with the theological issue that divided Augustine and Pelagius and later Calvinism and Arminius.

of its members because the people of God is constituted by the uniting power of God's election. As the elect one of the elect people, Jesus' solidarity *with* the unfaithful among his people is the culminating revelation of God's election. In chapter 1, I exposited Yoder's argument that being Christian is about living as a particular people in the world, which, he understands, is living as part of the visibly gathering people of Israel (who are not necessarily "orthodox" in belief). This is a claim that I simply wish to endorse and will try to further substantiate below. It is what we should expect if the Christian life is about serving the God of Israel and following Jesus as the Christ and Son of that God, for there is no Christian God who is not the God of Israel and no Christ the Lord other than the Messiah of the people of Israel. I questioned in chapter 2, however, the basic terms in which Yoder describes the people of Israel, namely, as those who are politically faithful to God, that is, politically "Jewish," both before and after Jesus.[9] I suggested that Gamaliel the Pharisee in Acts 5, and other biblical witnesses, urge Christians against understanding, remembering, or seeking to discipline ourselves or others as the people of God in this way, and that God's election of Israel entails a different, more patient kind of historiography, political discipline, and notion of collective identity. Gamaliel points to a people of God who is holy but not pure, who is always visible but not totally visible to itself as it unfolds in time, and who is constituted by God rather than its collective self or component selves.

The central claim of my argument against modern understandings of peoplehood like Yoder's (but in keeping with his concern to

---

9. I did not question Yoder's designation of Christians as part of Israel. In light of what it has traditionally meant for ("true") Christians to "be" Israel (i.e., to be all of Israel to the exclusion of non-Christian Jews) and the pressing need to discontinue the violent Christian displacement of Jews, many will balk at this designation. The concern seems to be to carve out a Jewish identity that is safe from Christian identity. I don't think this can be done or should be attempted for reasons that will emerge below.

promote a peoplehood of peace) provides the christological basis of Gamaliel's witness, and it is this: contrary to the contention (and correlative political discipline) that persons or communities fail to count as the people of God by virtue of their unfaithful living or that they are constituted as such by virtue of their faithful living, Jesus himself did not disown Israel's unfaithful. Instead, he loved them as his very self. In fact, Jesus' nonviolent solidarity *with* the unfaithful is crucial to his life, death, and resurrection as Israel's Messiah and the one Christians confess as Lord, that is, as God's elect. "He was numbered with transgressors" (Luke 22:37; Isa. 53:12). Jesus is thus the incarnation of God's unconditional and irrevocable election of Israel, that is, the revelation of the very Self of the God of Israel who refuses to leave or forsake the covenant people.

Solidarity with the unfaithful in the people of God, be they Christian or not, is thus an essential dimension of Christian faithfulness and precludes the replacement theopolitics of modern peoplehood that I am about to analyze. This implies that the people of the God of Israel is held together and distinguishable in the world by something deeper than the faithfulness of its member communities and persons (or any other internal basis of purity and corollary criteria of exclusion and internal order), and this uniting power is God's election, an account of which is the subject of chapters 4–7 below. In the second chapter, I summed up the solidarity of Jesus with the unfaithful as "the catholicity of Jesus." I suggested near the end of the chapter that Yoder's failure to do justice to the catholicity of Jesus or the election of Israel that he embodies seems due to an inadequately critical engagement in and with the modern discourse of peoplehood and its characteristic historiography. And so to several key contours of that discourse we now turn. After a summary analysis of the discourse, I will assess its theopolitical import and apply that import critically to the Christian understanding of peoplehood that Yoder represents.

The Modern Discourse of Peoplehood

In "The Nation Form: History and Ideology," Étienne Balibar describes and analyzes what we might call the modern nationalization of peoplehood, and finally the nationalization of the human.[10] That so many Christians and others read "the people of Israel" or "nation" in the Bible to be politically and conceptually equivalent to what counts as a nation in modernity reflects the grip of the modern discourse of peoplehood (to say nothing of neatly identifying "Israel" in the Bible with the modern nation-state of Israel). To be a people in recent centuries is to be a nation, and "the state" is typically understood as a nation-state—the representation, guardian, and mediator of "the people."

But the nation form that has come to monopolize peoplehood and pervaded almost all human societies over more than two centuries of violent conflict is not in fact what "peoples" have always been. Rather, the nation form has shaped what being a people has come to mean through a peculiar, modern, religious history. The result is that we know "the world" or "humanity" today as a system of

10. Étienne Balibar, "The Nation Form," in *Race, Nation, Class: Ambiguous Identities*, ed. Étienne Balibar and Immanuel Wallerstein, trans. Chris Turner (London: Verso, 1991), 88. The analysis below follows the account of Étienne Balibar, who is a political philosopher and critical theorist influenced by Althusser and Foucault. Balibar has written extensively and critically on the philosophy (or nonphilosophy as he says) of Marx, and is considered by some the principal representative of a "neo-Marxist" school of thought in Europe (some would say "post-Marxist"). I have turned to him not only because of his concentration on the question of peoplehood, but because peoplehood for him is best understood as a matter of discourse rather than timeless metaphysical structures. At the same time, he evinces a certain theological sensibility, discerning the centrality of the Jew in the modern political imagination, theological anti-Judaism as the basis of this imagination, and the possibility of theological ways forward. He also offers several constructive trajectories, contending that criticism of modern peoplehood requires an alternative social imaginary. Such a social imaginary is what I attempt to develop theologically in chapters 4–7.

relatively sovereign national states, and we tend to recognize and engage persons and communities primarily as they belong or do not belong to, or are friends or enemies of, such "peoples."[11]

Balibar begins his essay on the nation form with this statement: "The history of nations . . . is always already presented to us in the form of a narrative which attributes to these entities the continuity of a subject."[12] The implied "retrospective illusion" is "that the generations which succeed one another over centuries on a reasonably stable territory, under a reasonably univocal designation, have handed down to each other an invariant substance."[13] The nature of this substance has of course been construed differently, typically as subsisting in an ambiguous interrelation of territory, ethnicity, and/or language. Those who are not properly related to a particular territory (e.g., born there), do not hail from the proper ethnic lineage, and/or do not speak the proper language in the proper way lack the pure and autonomous substance of the national people. Thus, they are formally excluded from it (even if juridically included as citizens) and materially marginalized. In some cases they may be understood to acquire that national substance, but then often dubitably, only in relation to the national people of reference, and only through a process regulated by representatives of those who are already the people and therefore empowered to confer the substance of the people on (some) others.

---

11. Balibar, "The Nation Form," 88–90. For an account of the religious, colonialist influence on the nationalization of land as national territory, see Anthony Smith, *Chosen Peoples: Sacred Sources of National Identity* (Oxford: Oxford University Press, 2003), 131–44, 151–65.

12. Balibar, "The Nation Form," 86.

13. Ibid. According to Balibar, it was Jean-Jacques Rousseau who first explicitly conceived the question, "What makes a people a people?" (94). Cf. Smith, *Chosen Peoples*, 31. Contrast the classical, premodern understanding in which political community is defined not by anything intrinsic to the subjectivity of its human constituents (e.g., their will) but by the law which is common to it. This is thematic, for example, to Marcus Aurelius's *Meditations*, expressed most clearly in book 4.

For Yoder and many others, the substance of the Israelite or Jewish people to whom faithful Christians belong is fundamentally ethical and inheres as such in member communities and persons by virtue of the faithfulness of their political existence. This ethical substance is consequently lacking in communities or persons—whatever their claims to belong to the people of God—whose way of living is unfaithful to the God revealed in Torah and as Jesus. Yoder of course rejects typical modern notions that the substance of the people is territorial, ethnic, or monolingual. In fact, he understands the ethical substance of the people of the God of Israel to be constituted by its nonviolent *defiance* of territorial, ethnic, and linguistic borders in its historical development, self-understanding, and self-discipline. Nevertheless, his Christian account of peoplehood[14] finds in the people of God an *ethically* "invariant substance" and in this sense attributes to this people "the continuity of a subject" or purity of identity across time and space.[15] Thus, Jeremiah, many Second Temple Jews, Jesus, New Testament Christians, "rabbinic" Jews, and radical reformation Christians exhibit the same "Jewishness" in virtue of their particular way of life, their political ethos.[16] Yoder contends that the political identity of the people of God cannot be segregated from the way people live, and so to be the people of God is to live in a certain way, a faithful way, a Jewish way.

The diversity of the Jewish and Christian past, like any other, makes it difficult for Yoder or anyone else to claim for those who are "truly" the people any simple and immediate material correspondence

---

14. In, e.g., *The Jewish-Christian Schism Revisited*, ed. Michael G. Cartwright and Peter Ochs (Grand Rapids, MI: William B. Eerdmans, 2003), hereafter *JCSR*, as exposited in chapters 1 and 2 above.

15. Accordingly, we must ask whether the assertion of an "invariant substance" that claims to defy territorial, ethnic, or linguistic closure in modernity does not in fact perform a territorial, ethnic, or linguistic self-definition, one that is unable to resist or subvert the same violent closure it claims to overcome.

16. Yoder, *JCSR*, e.g., 141, 170.

to an ideal form of peoplehood. To negotiate this difficulty in positing the subjective continuity of the people, the modern discourse of peoplehood has typically turned to a narrative of active development or progress as well as conformity to a single political type (e.g., democracy, free church).[17] These devices can deal with the inadequacy of those in the past whose belonging to the people is indispensable or of those who are unquestionably citizens in the present but do not live up to the ideal form of the people.

In Yoder's case, the narrative is one of ethical development within a singular political type: starting with Jeremiah (though anticipated by Abraham and the pre-kingdom "Mosaic project"), Israel learned to be not the people of this or that ethnic lineage or territory or dynasty but of one particular nonethnic, nonterritorial, nonviolent ethos, that is, of "one particular social-political-ethical option."[18] Within the political type of this ethos or moving determinably "toward" this ethos, diversity does not disqualify claims to membership and the people of God is indeed present. But other types of living—not moving determinably "toward" this ethos—fail to qualify as the life of the people of God. Those following David, Solomon, the Sadducees,

17. Stuart Hall and Bram Gieben, eds., *Formations of Modernity* (Cambridge: Polity Press, 1992), 311. See also Smith, *Chosen Peoples*, 212–13: "One obvious function of . . . myth-memories is to provide a sense of *continuity* between the present and a (preferably glorious) past or pasts. This can be achieved in two ways. The most common is through an evolutionary sequence, which posits the gradual growth of the *ethnie* from rudimentary beginnings to the pinnacle of its cultural expression in one or more ages of heroism and/or creativity, followed by a slow decline or catastrophe, from which the nationalists aim to rescue it and re-establish the community as a political nation. . . . [Golden ages] embody and reveal the 'true essence' of the community," (emphasis his). Cf. John Howard Yoder, *The Original Revolution: Essays on Christian Pacifism* (Scottdale, PA: Herald, 1971), 101.

18. John Howard Yoder, *The Politics of Jesus: vicit Agnus noster*, rev. ed. (Grand Rapids, MI: William B. Eerdmans, 1972, 1994), 11; *JCSR*, 71, 170. One might ask if Yoder's narrative account does not allow for some variance in the substance of the people. It would not properly be analyzed as "substance" if it did. It might so allow if Yoder did not predicate the continuity of the people itself on ethical progress and on fitting a single political type. Because he does this, he implies that all communities and persons who have been advancing along this line of ethical progress and fit this political type (and only these) are of the same substance and therefore count as the people of God.

Constantine, or the Magisterial reformers are "out," that is, they have lost peoplehood and do not belong to the people of God in any meaningful sense. Those following Abraham, Moses, Jeremiah, Jesus, the Christian apostles, Jochanan ben Zakkai, the rabbis, or the radical reformers are "in," that is, they have peoplehood or belong to the people of God. These latter constitute the same subject and embody the same substance, which is in turn basic to Yoder's historiographical hermeneutic as well as his understanding of what "represents" Jewishness.[19] Whatever the differences among formations of this people in the past or present, they are *the same people*. They are all—to use a concept characteristic of the modern discourse of peoplehood—endowed with an original personality.[20] Christians must therefore be guided by this personality—which in Yoder's account is mediated by Scripture and the Spirit as these converge in the church's social process—in order *to be* the people of God, that is, to be a faithfully disciplined community.

It is important to emphasize that "the continuity of a subject," "invariant substance," and "original personality" characteristic of the modern discourse of peoplehood serve a formative and interpellating function, for which historiography is crucial. The purity of its "subject," "substance," and "personality" (e.g., what makes the people

19. See ch. 2 above. Cf. John Howard Yoder, *For the Nations: Essays Evangelical and Public* (Grand Rapids, MI: William B. Eerdmans, 1997), 83.

20. Balibar, "The Nation Form," 88 (note that the printed translation has wrongly rendered "dotées d'une personnalité ethnique originale" as "original ethical personality"; it should be "original ethnic personality"). See Étienne Balibar, "La forme nation: histoire et ideologie," in *Race, nation, classe: les identités ambiguës* (Paris: La Découverte, 1988), 119. Thus, Yoder seems to follow the way that the modern discourse of peoplehood appropriates for a national people "its" pre-national past. As we saw in his theological historiography in *JCSR*, he avoids the nationalist myth of a linear destiny whereby things had to turn out the way they have, with earlier events implying later ones. But he minimizes certain political differences and perhaps the contributions of non-Jewish communities by describing a past that belongs to one determinate people by virtue of internal ethical continuity. Balibar claims that "one determinate people" simply cannot exist. Below I will suggest that it can and does exist, but we cannot predicate its identity on ethical continuity or a similar concept of internal purity.

of Israel or of the United States what or who it is) is not constructed in a vacuum or without political aims. It is constructed and invoked in the service of continually *producing* the people by neutralizing or exploiting certain opposition past and present, displacing or relativizing competing bases of identity, encouraging certain persons and communities to "own" the past and present of "their people," envisioning what the people is destined to become, and promoting various other perceived political goods. Thus, the history of the people is narrated so as to exclude those who are not the people, justify the violent birth and endurance of the people, discourage what is undesirable and therefore "uncharacteristic" of the people, consolidate certain existing persons and communities as the people, and mobilize those persons and communities by supplying them with a destiny on the basis of which to act or not act. Existing persons and socioeconomic structures must give up certain self-understandings and behavioral tendencies in order to embrace alternatives that will establish, maintain, and nourish the people.[21] This is, for example, how some people are recruited for war or economic consumption while others are made killable and exploitable. It is also how some are taught to "value education."

In order to produce the people along the above lines, the formative and interpellating power of the modern discourse of peoplehood has depended on two poles. These poles are thematized and guide the discourse over time, having emerged from the Christian theology that characterized the context of the discourse's early development. They are 1) a *foil*, that is, the ongoing articulation of whoever or

---

21. Balibar, "The Nation Form," 90–95. Cf. Smith, *Chosen Peoples*, 258–60. Ernest Renan, a key figure in the nationalization of peoplehood, confirms Balibar's analysis by exhibiting the main contours of the modern discourse of peoplehood. Note for example the identification of peoplehood with a "spiritual principle," the corresponding importance of historiography, and the self-constituted nature of "the people" in his famous essay "Qu'est-ce qu'une nation?" ("What Is a Nation?," trans. Martin Thom, in *Nation and Narration*, ed. Homi K. Bhabha [London: Routledge, 1990], 8–22, esp. 18–20).

whatever is *not* the people, inhibits peoplehood, and threatens the people; and 2) a *pure* foundation of peoplehood (which implies a mission), that is, the continual projection of the people's sublime origin, true nature, and destiny vis-à-vis the foil and its various contemporary tentacles. A pure foundation makes it possible to imagine "the continuity of a subject," "invariant substance," and "original personality" introduced above, while the foil works to define the purity of the people negatively and so discipline its embodiment. "The continuity of the subject" is rendered as a narrative (i.e., "national history"), wherein the people is not *constituted* by external factors but only internal ones vis-à-vis the foil. The people is thus formed, understood, and celebrated as an independent unit.[22]

According to Balibar, the foil and pure foundation at work in the modern discourse of peoplehood—to anticipate the most pertinent import of what follows—crystallized as "the Jew" and *fictive ethnicity* respectively. Ironically, in some of the most outstanding cases of modern peoplehood (e.g., the United States, Great Britain, Germany, the Netherlands) this anti-Jewish, fictive, pure ethnicity was itself conceived explicitly as the "true people of Israel."[23]

Producing the People

National peoples have of course emerged from previous, competitive political configurations, and have been made in the midst of various dangers and conflicts that have threatened to keep "the people" from coming to be or to tear it apart once relatively established. Balibar mentions "unequal development of town and countryside,

---

22. For example, Israel is rendered discursively as not depending on Egypt for its constitution, and the United States as not depending on Great Britain or people indigenous to "the New World" for its constitution. The people is "independent" and thus "free," a self-made nation.

23. Note the prominence of these outstanding cases of nationalized peoplehood in generating and dominating the modern "fields" of biblical scholarship and theology.

colonization and decolonization, wars and the revolutions which they have sometimes sparked off, the constitution of supranational blocs" and other class hostilities as examples of such threats.[24] As the nation form developed, national peoples were also made in alliance and enmity with one another as well as with supranational, Christian authorities.[25] Amidst resistant sociopolitical structures, then,

> the fundamental problem is . . . to produce the people. More exactly, it is to make the people produce itself continually as national community. Or again, it is to produce the effect of unity by virtue of which the people will appear, in everyone's eyes, "as a people", that is, as the basis and origin of political power.[26]

What must be formed and mobilized, especially for war and economic "development," is

> a community which recognizes itself in advance in the institution of the state, which recognizes that state as "its own" in opposition to other states and, in particular, inscribes its political struggles within the horizon of that state—by, for example, formulating its aspirations for reform and social revolution as projects for the transformation of "its national state."[27]

"The state"—that transgenerational, divinely appointed administrator and guardian of centralized, commercial political order in a contested territory—predates the nation-state by at least a century.[28] But the

---

24. Balibar, "The Nation Form," 92. Cf. Smith, *Chosen Peoples*, 3–5.
25. Balibar, "Racism and Nationalism," in *Race, Nation, Class*, 62.
26. Balibar, "The Nation Form," 93.
27. Ibid. Certain tragedies, too, are inscribed within the horizon of the people's state such that they can become "national" and call for a "national response." The bonds produced by the modern discourse of peoplehood are thus perceptible (and strengthened) when the tragic loss of some among the people is felt acutely by distant others among the same people, who in turn feel little to no loss when a similar tragedy befalls persons who are deemed not to belong to that people.
28. See, e.g., Hendrik Spruyt, *The Sovereign State and Its Competitors* (Princeton, New Jersey: Princeton University Press, 1994). Failing to historicize "the state" and reifying an abstraction of it creates major problems for biblical exegesis and allows it to simply reinscribe a particular modern state into the drama of the Bible and of life as we know it (e.g., the early church's persecution by or subjection to "the state," Romans 13 as "about the state").

development of the nation form identifies one such administrative state with the people (by a concept of political representation and a constellation of formative institutions and practices) and correspondingly expands the state's socioeconomic domain of intervention in the life of the people. Thus, the people is represented in

> a state "intervening" in the very reproduction of the economy and particularly in the formation of individuals, in family structures, the structures of public health and, more generally, in the whole space of "private life." This is a tendency that was present from the very beginnings of the nation form . . . the result of which is entirely to subordinate the existence of [acceptable] individuals of all classes to their status as citizens of the nation-state, to the fact of their being "nationals" that is.[29]

The discursive production of national peoplehood outlined above has drawn upon two key ideological resources that are deeply intertwined: a national narrative and an activist political anthropology. The modern discourse of peoplehood links state "interventions" or "decisions" together in a single story. It begins with an originating, revolutionary intervention or decision, the primary agent (and continuous, pure subject) of which is understood as "the people," who rose up to claim what was already its own,

29. Balibar, "The Nation Form," 92. For the people to be sovereign, their representing themselves in the nation-state (by choosing those who govern and thereby monitoring them) becomes the act of sovereignty par excellence (Étienne Balibar, "Citizen Subject," in *Who Comes after the Subject?*, ed. Eduardo Cadava, Peter Connor, and Jean-Luc Nancy [New York: Routledge, 1991], 47). This sovereignty is rooted in anthropological claims about what human being must be in order to be capable of sovereignty, "a *new* concept of man [i.e., the sovereignty of the human subject as citizen] that contradicts what the term ["subject"] previously connoted [i.e., subjection to divinely chosen human authorities]" (ibid., 44). One central dilemma that results is the question of the authority of law, for the citizens must be both over and under the law, those who are the subjects (i.e., agents) of the law and subject to the law (ibid., 48–49). Another is the representation of the people in the national government that must protect the people, while the people must at once be protected from the national government (ibid., 45). As we will see, the constitution of the nation-state is such that this legal authority and this political representation cannot help but be "White."

as later enshrined in national hymnody and liturgy.[30] By virtue of a national narrative, the nation-state is deemed responsible for its citizens' original and ongoing life and freedom.

In addition to developing a national narrative, the discourse presents human being not merely as political animal but as political *agent*. The people comes into being and into its/their humanity *as* those who act, as those who contradictorily both receive and decide their destiny, as those who *choose* or *elect*. The people is no longer constituted by divine authority through a political hierarchy as political order was in the previous age. It must constitute itself (per divine authority). This involves not simply the modern "turn to the subject" but the construal of human subjectivity as primarily that of citizenship and the interpellation of persons and their complex associations as fundamentally national.[31] It is not enough for the political unit as a whole to be understood as active and history-making in the modern discourse of peoplehood, however. With the nation form, political agency must be understood as diffuse among the constituents of the people, the putative authors of personal and collective self-determination.[32]

To say that the nation form allowed for the rise and diffusion of pure and self-constituted political identity is not to say that the modern discourse of peoplehood has suppressed all differences and existing social structures (e.g., configurations of family,

---

30. "The character of the nation is often most genuinely and movingly expressed in the poetry, songs, and music of the 'homeland', and in the 'authentic' art and architecture of the people; for it is through such media that the 'true' nature of the nation is frequently revealed" (Smith, *Chosen Peoples*, 22).

31. Balibar, "Citizen Subject," 33–37.

32. Cf. Smith, *Chosen Peoples*, 39–40 and Renan, "What Is a Nation?" 18: "Man is everything in the formation of this sacred thing which is called a people." This understanding overlooks the manifold ways in which human communities and persons are in fact determined by what they do not decide or control, a matter to which we shall turn in subsequent chapters, particularly chapter 5.

socioeconomic classes) in favor of an absolutely uniform citizenry. That could hardly have been done. The nation form has taken hold

> not by suppressing all differences, but by relativizing them and subordinating them to itself in such a way that it is the symbolic difference between "ourselves" and "foreigners" which wins out and which is lived as irreducible. In other words, to use the terminology proposed by [Johann Gottlieb] Fichte in his *Reden an die deutsche Nation* of 1808, the "external frontiers" of the state have to become "internal frontiers" or—which amounts to the same thing—external frontiers have to be imagined constantly as a projection and protection of an internal collective personality, which each of us carries within ourselves and enables us to inhabit the space of the state as a place where we have always been—and always will be—"at home."[33]

Note here how the border between the people in question and the rest of the world must be understood as totally perceptible to that people so that the "difference between 'ourselves' and 'foreigners'" can win out and be lived as irreducible, the people embodied as pure. This difference need not dissolve all other differences. It need only "win out."

Note also that this border must become immanent for the internal formation of the people (as structured by the variously rehearsed story of the nation-state's "interventions," the story in which its people find and know themselves). This is how the difference between what or who is conceived as "foreign" or "not us" and who "we" are functions as the guiding principle of purity of both the national body-politic and the subjectivity of its constituent members and groups. It is also how the claims of modern nation-states to be "egalitarian societies" can never overcome the internal and external limits of the national community. The equality they claim to embody "is, first and foremost, an equality in respect of nationality."[34]

---

33. Balibar, "The Nation Form," 94. Cf. Smith's description of the ethno-political construction of Irishness (*Chosen Peoples*, 154).

As mentioned above, the formation of national peoples has involved not simply the modern "turn to the subject" but the construal of human subjectivity as primarily that of citizenship. A reader of modern literature might easily forget that "subject" once meant to be subject *to* this or that (divinely appointed) authority[35] and not agent or the primary bearer of human identity. The subjects of (i.e., those subject to) a king, a dynasty, and finally the sovereign God of Christian revelation as mediated by various, institutionalized human authorities could be understood as "peoples" in the pre-Enlightenment West, even if that was not their most common denomination. But in the struggle to hold sway over stratified societies in the colonialist scramble for survival and dominance, competing powers conceded increased authority in political determination to those of lower social strata, who were quick to own their patrons' denunciations of their marginalization and to demand increased political agency.[36] Thus, the modern discourse

---

34. Balibar, "Racism and Nationalism," 50. The need to relativize all differences for the sake of national equality renders citizenship the basis of functional universality. "Every practice, every condition must be measured by [equality], for an exception destroys it. . . . Civic equality is indissociable from universality but separates it from the *community*" (Balibar, "Citizen Subject," 46, emphasis his).

35. What it still means for Descartes, contrary to current understandings of the "Cartesian subject" (Balibar, "Citizen Subject," 33–37).

36. See Balibar, "Nation Form," 90–92, where Balibar emphasizes that this was a "process without a subject" (90). This process sought a theoretical anchor finally in "developed" human nature as endowed with the power of self-determination and thus citizenship. It was by way of the citizen that universality (i.e., the universality of humanness) came to "the subject." This left nationalist anthropology with the need to naturalize national divisions and to negotiate the aporia of "sovereign equality" (Balibar, "Citizen Subject," 44–46; cf. Smith, *Chosen Peoples*, 34–35). Regarding the case of the United States, note the claim of T. H. Breen: "A newly aggressive English state forced the Americans to leap out of history and to defend colonial and human equality on the basis of timeless natural rights." ("Ideology and Nationalism on the Eve of the American Revolution: Revisions Once More in Need of Revising," *The Journal of American History*, 84, no. 1 [Jun. 1997]: 38). Regarding the formation of European peoples, note Linda Colley's summary statement: "A number of European monarchs start appealing to the people to carry out the Protestant Reformation" (interviewed in Alexander Stille, "Historians Trace an Unholy Alliance: Religion as the Root of Nationalist Feeling, " *NY Times*, May 31, 2003, online edition, http://www.nytimes.com/2003/05/31/arts/historians-trace-an-

of peoplehood facilitated the transfer from human subjection as determined by divinely appointed authority to human subjectivity as self-determined by divine appointment.[37]

In the course of the transition from the subjection of the human to the subjectivity of the human, which was rendered discursively as the course of nature, that is, of "natural man," the self-determination of the Euro-American, nationalized subject came to define what it means to be free and to be human.[38] To realize freedom and humanity has thereby come to be predicated on "actively" belonging to a national people amidst its manifold opposition. This is how the modern discourse of peoplehood has produced the people, rendering the border between "ourselves" and "foreigners" immanent in the formation of "our" persons and diverse social configurations. "The 'new individual,' it would seem, could represent the history of his life only by inscribing it in the narrative of the nation" and acting accordingly.[39] Thus, whatever purity has been understood to lie at the foundation of the people has come to determine the subjectivity (i.e.,

unholy-alliance-religion-as-the-root-of-nationalist-feeling.html). See also Linda Colley, *Britons: Forging the Nation 1707–1837* (New Haven: Yale University Press, 1992), 46–47.

37. Its secularizing tendencies have since produced human subjectivity as self-determination over against any public "religious" claim, i.e., divine authority. But because the threat of "religion" was more a matter of its being foreign and "established" rather than simply religious, the modern discourse of peoplehood developed an intractable dispute between those who associate peoplehood with a certain kind of Christianity, and those who insist that religion not be public except as pluralistic ornamentation. Hence, the dispute in the United States between the "Religious Right" and advocates of "the separation of Church and State," both of whom claim to be contending for the freedom and integrity of the nation.

38. "In the last instance the transcendental subject that effectuates the nonsubstantial unity of the conditions of experience is *the same* as the one that, prescribing its acts to itself in the mode of the categorical imperative, inscribes freedom in nature (it is tempting to say that it *ex*scribes it: Heidegger is an excellent guide on this point), that is, the same as the one identified in a teleological perspective with the humanity of man" (Balibar, "Citizen Subject," 37, emphasis his. See also 44). Cf. Smith, *Chosen Peoples*, 31–37.

39. Partha Chatterjee, *The Nation and Its Fragments: Colonial and Postcolonial Histories* (Princeton: Princeton University Press, 1993), 138. This could also be said of the other social configurations that are subordinated to that of the national people (e.g., the family). Chatterjee goes on to qualify this generalization for women, since nationalist ideology has not been as adept at inscribing femaleness in national narratives.

identity and correlative sense of agency) of its constituent persons and "associations" (e.g., families, schools, corporations, unions, religious communities). One symptom of this is the frequent claim among Christian communities that they owe their "freedom" in general and their "freedom to worship" in particular to the nation-state and its violent power. Another is the proliferation of these associations as "national" (e.g., the American family, the American church, etc.).

The Jewish Foil of the People

But who exactly is this national subject? Who is or are "the people"? I have thus far described the modern discursive production of the people in the relatively abstract terms typical of modern political theory, anthropology, and sociology. But the modern discourse of peoplehood cannot be analyzed adequately without recovering what can only later have been termed the "religious" concreteness of its anthropology and national subject. It is difficult to come to grips with the fact that the production of the people was (and in fact still is) a religiously charged process. "It is usual to see in nationalism a modern, secular ideology that replaces the religious systems found in premodern, traditional societies."[40] But, as Balibar, Anthony Smith, and others have observed, the modern discourse of peoplehood has drawn stories, figures, and concepts from its presecularized context of Christendom and developed them in the service of various competing, nationalist aims.[41] This has gone unnoticed by many modernists because the discourse has often been "antireligious" in the sense of opposing certain "religious" establishments, notions, and practices.[42] But it is not the case that the modern discourse of peoplehood itself—despite a superficial hostility to "religion" in

40. Smith, *Chosen Peoples*, 9.
41. "All significant concepts of the modern theory of the state are secularized theological concepts," (Schmitt, *Political Theology*, 36).

it—has ever ceased to be religious, as we will see in the nature of the personal and collective political self that it has produced.[43]

Under the legacy of Christendom, the "continuity of a subject," "invariant substance," and "original personality" characteristic of the modern discourse of peoplehood drew meaning and power in the face of manifold threats from a foil—the formative and interpellating foil that was the negative background of nationalization. Against this foil, the people could be formed (and form itself) into existence and ongoing vitality vis-à-vis that which it was supposedly not. Existing bonds that undermined the peoplehood of the population could be loosened and reordered in subordination to the emergent national people. With this foil a national story could be told, the masses could become citizens, and a people could be made. It is here that we find the question of the people of Israel in the roots of the modern discourse of peoplehood.

Anti-Semitism[44] functioned on a European scale: each nationalism saw in the Jew (who was himself contradictorily conceived as both irreducibly inassimilable to others and cosmopolitan, as member of an "original" people and as rootless) its own specific enemy and the representative of all other "hereditary enemies": this meant, then, that

42. Smith cites Ernest Gellner, *Thought and Change* (London: Weidenfeld and Nicolson, 1964), and Karl Deutsch, *Nationalism and Social Communication*, 2d ed. (New York: MIT Press, 1966) as primary representatives of this understanding (*Chosen Peoples*, 13).

43. Cf. Smith, *Chosen Peoples*, 17–18, who calls the nation a "sacred communion." Balibar agrees with analyses that make "nationalism and patriotism out to be a religion—if not indeed *the* religion—of modern times" ("The Nation Form," 95, emphasis his). Indeed "national ideology involves ideal signifiers (first and foremost the very *name* of the nation or 'fatherland') on to which may be transferred the sense of the sacred and the affects of love, respect, sacrifice and fear which have cemented religious communities" (ibid., emphasis his). But he also points out that "that transfer only takes place because *another type* of community is involved here. The analogy [between religious and national communities] is itself based on a deeper difference. If it were not, it would be impossible to understand why national identity, more or less completely integrating the forms of religious identity, ends up tending to replace it, and forcing it itself to become 'nationalized'" (ibid., emphasis his). This other type of community Balibar terms "fictive ethnicity," as discussed below.

44. I suspect Balibar is aware of Semitic communities who are not Jewish. Here he follows the convention of identifying Semite and Jew and therefore anti-Semitism and anti-Judaism.

all nationalisms were defined against the *same* foil, the same "stateless other", and this has been a component of the very idea of Europe as the land of "modern" nation-states or, in other words, of civilization.[45]

The Jew thus epitomized opposition to the formation of national peoples and "civilization." Under the emerging and colonizing powers of the modern West, to be a people—to belong to a people—was to be *not* Jewish. In some cases, it would even come to mean the eradication of Jewishness from the emerging and threatened national self. The Shoah, then, far from the devilish aberration we would like it to be, is the progression of a disease in the norm of Euro-American orders of peoplehood.

But we must also recognize the force of the modern colonial context in which Jewishness was conceived as the foil to peoplehood. National peoples were and are understood to constitute a "civilized" community in contradistinction to those societies being colonized, and this difference between the civilized and the uncivilized has been crucial to the formation of modern peoples, indicating the peculiar racism that has informed the nationalism of modern peoplehood.

> The European or Euro-American nations, locked in a bitter struggle to divide up the world into colonial empires, recognized that they formed a community and shared an "equality" through that very competition, a community and an equality to which they gave the name "White". … When historians speak of this universalist project within nationalism, meaning by that an aspiration towards—and a programme of—cultural imperialism (imposing an "English", "German", "French", "American",

---

45. Balibar, "Racism and Nationalism," 62, emphasis his. On the Jew as inassimilable in the United States, see Michael N. Dobkowski, *The Tarnished Dream: The Basis of American Anti-Semitism* (Westport, Conn.: Greenwood Press, 1979), 143–69. Cf. the following two claims by Renan, who, it must not be forgotten, was an influential biblical scholar and historian of Israel and Jesus: 1) "The Semitic race is to be recognized almost entirely by negative characteristics," which he proceeds to enumerate (qtd. Kelley, *Racializing Jesus*, 86); and 2) "Through their various and often opposed powers, nations participate in the common work of civilization; each sounds a note in the great concert of humanity, which, after all is the highest ideal reality that we are capable of attaining" ("What Is a Nation?," 20).

or "Soviet" conception of man and universal culture on the whole of humanity) and yet evade the question of racism, their arguments are at best incomplete, for it is only as "racism"—that is to say, only to the extent that the imperialist nation has been imagined and presented as the specific instrument of a more essential mission and destiny which other peoples cannot but recognize—that imperialism has been able to turn itself from a mere enterprise of conquest into an enterprise of universal domination, the founding of a "civilization."[46]

Here Balibar identifies a reciprocity between racism and nationalism in the modern discourse of peoplehood. Racism supplies nationalism with its universal or "transcendent" mission (e.g., civilization) while at the same time particularizing the universal that nationalism claims to represent.[47]

Now we are in a position to articulate how the Jewish foil to modern peoplehood worked as an "internal" basis or pole of the colonialist construction of race at and from the periphery of the imagined national self (i.e., in relation to populations being conquered in Euro-American colonies). Recall Fichte's claim above that external frontiers "have to be imagined constantly as a projection and protection of an internal collective personality" and thus correlated to internal challenges to the formation of the national people. The reciprocity of racism and nationalism thus

shows itself initially in the way in which the development of nationalism and its official utilization by the state transforms antagonisms and

46. Balibar, "Racism and Nationalism," 62, emphasis his. Whatever the "community" of colonialist powers, they of course acted competitively. "The other White is also the bad White. Each White nation is spiritually 'the whitest'" (43). Cf. the Afrikaner case described by Smith, especially the association of chosenness and Whiteness, 81–85; Colley's remark: "Well into the twentieth century, contact with and dominion over manifestly alien peoples nourished Britons' sense of superior difference" (*Britons*, 368–69). "There was much outrage in the German camp that the French and British had the audacity to deny that Germans were civilized, for was Germany not a white nation, located at the very heart of Europe?" (Marcia Klotz, "The Weimar Republic: A Postcolonial State in a Still-Colonial World," in *Germany's Colonial Pasts*, ed. Eric Ames, Marcia Klotz, and Lora Wildenthal [Lincoln: University of Nebraska Press, 2005], 139).
47. Balibar, "Racism and Nationalism," 54.

persecutions that have quite other origins into racism in the modern sense (and ascribes the verbal markers of ethnicity to them). This runs from the way in which, since the times of the *Reconquista* in Spain, theological anti-Judaism was transposed into genealogical exclusion based on "purity of blood" at the same time as the *raza* was launching itself upon the conquest of the New World, down to the way in which, in modern Europe [and the US], the new "dangerous classes" of the international proletariat tend to be subsumed under the category of "immigration", which becomes the main name given to race within the crisis-torn nations of the post-colonial era. This reciprocal determination shows itself again in the way in which all the "official nationalisms" of the nineteenth and twentieth centuries, aiming to confer the political and cultural unity of a nation on the heterogeneity of a pluri-ethnic state, have used anti-Semitism: as if the domination of a culture and a more or less fictively unified nationality . . . over a hierarchically ordered diversity of "minority" ethnicities and cultures marked down for assimilation should be "compensated" and mirrored by the racializing persecution of an absolutely singular *pseudo-ethnic group* (without their own territory and without a "national" language) which represents the common internal enemy of all cultures and all dominant populations.[48]

The Jew provided nationalism with a foil by which to articulate the colonialist mission that exceeded the existing condition of the emerging national people, a racial signifier that surpassed internal national differences, ordered transnational solidarities, and thus promoted negatively the efficacy of nationalism.[49]

Constructing a Jewish foil to peoplehood entailed the discursive circumscription of the Jew, a political definition of Jewishness that

---

48. Ibid., 52–53, emphasis his. The domestic presence of a massive slave population from the African continent distinguishes somewhat the national peoplehood of the US from those of Europe, making other phenomena in addition to immigration the main names of race in the US. Meanwhile, the Jewish foil of modern, Euro-American peoplehood played out in direct reference to Jesus: "Rejecting Jesus's Jewishness and defining him as Aryan was about not only redefining Christianity, but racializing Europe: reassuring Europeans that they were white. Images of Jesus were crucial to racism in establishing the primary criterion of whiteness: Christ himself" (Susannah Heschel, *The Aryan Jesus: Christian Theologians and the Bible in Nazi Germany* [Princeton: Princeton University Press, 2008], 28).

49. Balibar, "Racism and Nationalism," 62.

would free a national people to become its distinct self and its members to become citizens in pursuit of the national mission. Christian communities had been engaging in the circumscription of Jewishness for a long time, but the colonialist context facilitated the racialization of this circumscription and thus the racialized nature of national peoplehood. Christian powers saw themselves as missionaries of a pure genealogy (attested by their Whiteness) bringing to "underdeveloped" branches of humanity the "civilization" that had superseded the Jews as Israel under Jesus and the apostles. Jewry was thus conceived and further exteriorized as a territorially "internal" race that was key to Christian self-understanding in relation to the "uncivilized races" of the "New World."[50]

Balibar does not name as *Christian* the "equality" and "community" to which Euro-American national powers gave the name "White." But besides relatively lighter skin pigmentation and a monopoly on violent force, Christianity (as the most total designation for their way of life) was of course what those powers shared in contradistinction to the societies they were colonizing, and Christianity was where, and from where, anti-Jewishness lived. The program of those competing, nationalizing powers had not departed substantially from the evangelizing mission of Christopher Columbus, which was undertaken with a view to recovering the Christian possession of Jerusalem.[51] Moreover, the racism that supplied those nationalist

50. Balibar describes this tendency as a way of at once owning *and* exteriorizing by translating an internal exclusion to a group being colonized. This phenomenon continues to characterize the internal relations of Western societies that have received "immigrants" from formerly colonized places and is basic to the modern conceptual construct of ethnicity. It also characterizes the nationalization of formerly colonized places (ibid., 42–45). See also Stuart Hall, "Ethnicity: Identity and Difference," *Radical America* 23 (1989): 17–20. For documentation of the tendency to construe the Jews as the counter-race of national peoplehood in the United States, see Dobkowski, *The Tarnished Dream*, 143–69.

51. See, e.g., *The Four Voyages of Christopher Columbus*, ed. and trans. J. M. Cohen (London: Penguin Books, 1969), 55. Note in this connection how Columbus concludes a letter to the Spanish Crown in 1493. The massive booty, human and nonhuman, that he is accumulating is "for the war and conquest of Jerusalem, *for which purpose this enterprise was undertaken*" (qtd.

programs with their universalist "cause" of "civilization" claimed nothing less than the nature and future of "man" and therefore constituted a kind of anti-Jewish, Christian anthropology. Thus, Jewishness functioned as the negative foundation on which Christian powers found themselves constructing race and nation as the basic, mutually informing sociopolitical structures of the modern world.[52] As such, these structures provided the framework for the formation of modern peoples and emerging "international" relations.

That the Jews should become the foil to political integrity and human nature in the modern discourse of peoplehood is not altogether surprising. One may wonder at the "religious" nature of that foil only by ignoring that national peoplehood was born under Christian political powers, not after but *with* the onset of what has been misleadingly termed "secularization." To be Christian had meant precisely to be *not* Jewish long before modernity, even if that difference had not yet been racialized, nationalized, naturalized, and predicated on human subjectivity as it was under modern, colonialist powers. One could trace how the Jews were typically *the* local foreign

Margarita Zamora, *Reading Columbus* [Berkeley, Calif.: University of California Press, 1993], 19, emphasis mine; cf. 138–39). Jerusalem is understood as belonging to Christendom, which is *verus Israel*, and reclaiming it was the purpose of Columbus's voyage in search of an alternative trade route to the Indies. "The true Israel" was thus the regnant ideology under which European Christians encountered the indigenous people of lands previously unknown to them.

52. Balibar warns against reducing racism to a virtually ahistorical, abstract psychological tendency with various concrete instantiations in racist persons and movements, now against the Jews, now against black people, now against others. "For racism is a social relation, not the mere ravings of racist subjects. The fact remains that the present is bound to the singular imprint of the past. Thus when we come to ask in what sense the fixation of racial hatreds upon immigrants from the Maghreb reproduces certain classic features of anti-Semitism, we should not only point to an analogy between the situation of Jewish minorities in Europe at the turn of the twentieth century and 'Arabo-Islamic' minorities in present-day France, nor simply refer these hatreds to the abstract model of an 'internal racism' in which a society projects its frustrations and anxieties (or rather those of the individuals who make it up) on to a part of itself; *rather we need also to inquire into the unique drift of anti-Semitism out beyond 'Jewish identity', starting out from the repetition of its themes within what is very much a French tradition and from the fresh impulse given to it by Hitler*" (Balibar, "Racism and Nationalism," 41, emphasis mine). This story must also be told with respect to the structural racism in the US against people of African descent or those immigrating from Latin America.

community in medieval Christendom.[53] But we must not overlook that the New Testament itself presents the Christian community—which remains largely Jewish in the New Testament—in tense relation to the Israelite and Jewish past and its own Jewish present (even where that tense relation is characterized as "fulfillment").[54] Amidst profound political crises in the wake of Protestantism and a growing culture of Bible study and exposition in Europe and North America, reading "the Jews" of the Bible (and their contemporary instantiation) as representative of the manifold opposition to civilization and national peoplehood was a ready-to-hand trope. The nature of the Jews and the bonds that "the people" must break in order to fulfill its God-given destiny were conceptualized and constructed in mutual relation.[55] Thus, Jewishness was ethnicized and acquired the form of a counterrace and a counternation, with all the attendant spirituality of modern racism and nationalism.[56] This Christian, violent reading of the Bible is still

53. That is, the visible, material basis of political difference that is also codified in the Christian tradition. Islam, by contrast, was associated with a distinct, encroaching territory and categorized as a corruption of Christianity rather than its hostile ancestor, i.e., as heretical rather than "carnal." On the medieval Christian construction of "the Jew," see Jeremy Cohen, *Living Letters of the Law: Ideas of the Jew in Medieval Christianity* (Berkeley, California: University of California Press, 1999).

54. The presentation of the Christian community in relation to Israel and the Jewish past and present in the New Testament is the subject of chapters 6 and 7.

55. The invention of the printing press and the mass production and consumption of printed material have been identified as key factors in the development of the modern discourse of peoplehood. See Benedict Anderson, *Imagined Communities: Reflections on the Origin and Spread of Nationalism* (London: Verso, 1983); David A. Bell, *The Cult of the Nation in France: Inventing Nationalism, 1680–1800* (Cambridge, Mass.: Harvard University Press, 2003); Linda Colley, *Britons*; Smith, *Chosen Peoples*, 20–21. The availability of printed material appears to have been important for the emergent activist political anthropology of nationalism and helped produce populist understandings of the authority of the Bible, which has been "the book" of the societies being shaped by the modern discourse of peoplehood (Smith, *Chosen Peoples*, 49, 80, 129, 190–91; Sacvan Bercovitch, *The Rites of Assent: Transformations in the Symbolic Construction of America* [New York: Routledge, 1993], 69–70).

56. See Heschel, *The Aryan Jesus*, 21, 47 for the spiritual basis of biology in the telling example of modern German ideology, where race subsists in the soul. Heschel also elucidates the German examples of Christ as "Whiteness," dejudaization as the key to Christian evangelism, and Jews as the common enemy uniting the divided German Christians (28, 76, 140–41). Balibar helps

very much with us and is, as we've already seen, one that Yoder perceived and worked very hard to discredit.[57] And to the extent that this reading of the Bible has informed the modern discourse of peoplehood and its racializing tendencies, nationalism and racism are deeply ingrained in the modern performance (including the academic study) of the Bible.[58]

Balibar's claim that "the Jew" was *the* foil of modern peoplehood and its nationalization of the human by Euro-American powers is a sweeping and astounding one. Let me pause to clarify the limited sense in which I intend to develop it in what follows. I do not understand this claim to constitute an "explanation" of the nation form of peoplehood or of modern nationalism. Such "explanations" will always leave out something important, and I have already mentioned a number of other factors that Balibar and others identify as contributing to the development of the nation form and its pervasion of the modern world. Instead, I understand Balibar's claim to point out a key trope and optic for describing and envisioning national identity in the modern discourse of peoplehood, as well

dispel the mistaken notion that these German phenomena were uniquely German and an aberration in the development of Western democracies. Furthermore, in clarifying the religious quality of modern nationalism, he argues that its ethnicizing nature enables it not only to integrate distinct forms of religious identity but to replace them, that is, to nationalize religion ("The Nation Form," 95).

57. By seeking to trouble Christian understandings of Jewish-Christian difference, Yoder demonstrates his perception that those understandings have played a powerful role in encouraging Christian violence. What remains is the question as to whether "defining" the people of the God of Israel ethically, as Yoder does, adequately resists the violence of those understandings and of the correlative, anti-Jewish reading of the Bible.

58. See the works by Sheehan and Heschel cited above. The biblical Jews could of course simultaneously function as the foil of peoplehood and a romanticized past to be retrieved, i.e., a past of liberation and exemplary peoplehood, given a hiatus between the Old and New Testaments (this was especially the case in German Romanticism). Yet, the exclusive nature of nationalist appropriations of that past rendered contemporary Jews the *betrayal* of that romantic Old Testament past or, at best, those whose resistance to Christianity was the final obstacle to be overcome and Christianized for the consummation of God's purpose for the New Testament Christian nation. See Bercovitch's account of Cotton Mather's attitude toward the Jews for an example (*The Rites of Assent*, 126–27).

as stimulating its assumption and enactment by diverse persons and social structures in the Western world, beginning before secularization. I am thus concerned not primarily with anti-Jewishness as a *cause* of the kind of peoplehood that has been so powerful in the modern world but with the *function* of the Jewish foil in the modern discursive conception and formation of "peoples."[59]

The Pure Foundation of the People

Balibar tersely designates the type of peoplehood instituted by the modern nation-state as "fictive ethnicity."[60] If the Jewish foil is the one, negative pole of modern peoplehood, fictive ethnicity is the other, positive one. With this concept, Balibar aims to outline the pure foundation and implicit ideal of "the people" in the modern discourse of peoplehood.

> No nation possesses an ethnic base naturally, but as social formations are nationalized, the populations included within them, divided up among them or dominated by them are ethnicized—that is, represented in the past or in the future *as if* they formed a natural community, possessing of itself an identity of origins, culture and interests which transcends individuals and social conditions. . . . It is fictive ethnicity which makes it possible for the expression of a pre-existing unity to be seen in the

59. To fully document the historical basis of Balibar's claim lies beyond the scope of this chapter. Beyond the few references I have already provided, I will also note its corroboration by others (such as Karl Barth) as the occasion arises. "There is . . . another modern concept which is important in this connexion, constituting as it does an unmistakeable secular imitation of the election of the community. . . . Elected man . . . according to Fascism . . . is the nation as constituted by race, language and history. . . . [The] totalitarian state . . . becomes the proper bearer of election" (Karl Barth, *Church Dogmatics*, ed. G. W. Bromiley and T. F. Torrance, 4 vols. in 13 parts [Edinburgh: T & T Clark, 1956–77], II/2, 312; hereafter *CD*). The danger of citing the modern fascist case is that it will be perceived as an aberration of the norm of modern nationalism rather than what it is, namely, a particularly full development of the norm. See, e.g., Edward W. Said, *Orientalism* (New York: Vintage Books, 1979); Léon Poliakov, *The History of Anti-Semitism*, vol. 3: *From Voltaire to Wagner*, trans. Miriam Kochan (Philadelphia: University of Pennsylvania Press, 2003 [1975]). Note also the confirmation supplied by Renan above.

60. Cf. Smith's discussion of the ethnic root of modern nationalism (*Chosen Peoples*, 32) and "the myth of ethnic election" (48–49).

state, and continually to measure the state against its "historic mission" in the service of the nation and, as a consequence, to idealize politics.[61]

To describe the material formation of modern peoples, we cannot simply adduce relevant "conquests, population movements and administrative practices of 'territorialization.'"[62] Those who function as a national people have come from various geographical origins, and, even for those born in the nationalized territory, their mutual relation as "of the same people" has been produced under the influence of an ideological form of peoplehood.

> The people is constituted out of various populations subject to a common law. In each case, however, a model of their unity must "anticipate" that constitution: the process of unification (the effectiveness of which can be measured, for example, in the collective mobilization in wartime, that is, in the capacity to confront death collectively) presupposes the constitution of a specific ideological form.[63]

According to Balibar, fictive ethnicity is this ideological form.[64] Thus, fictive ethnicity attempts to name a conception of deep (i.e.,

---

61. Balibar, "The Nation Form," 96, emphasis his. Balibar continues, "By constituting the people as a fictively ethnic unity against the background of a universalist representation which attributes to each individual one, and only one, ethnic identity and which thus divides up the whole of humanity between different ethnic groups corresponding potentially to so many nations, national ideology does much more than justify the strategies employed by the state to control populations. It inscribes their demands in advance in a sense of belonging in the double sense of the term—both what it is that makes one belong to oneself and also what makes one belong to other fellow human beings. Which means that one can be interpellated, as an individual, *in the name of* the collectivity whose name one bears. The naturalization of belonging and the sublimation of the ideal nation are two aspects of the same process" (ibid., emphasis his). Cf. Smith, *Chosen Peoples*, 24, who notes that the ideal nature of the nation means that the goal of nationalism "ever eludes its pursuers."

62. Balibar, "The Nation Form," 94.

63. Ibid., 96. Smith notes how the anticipatory unity of national peoplehood was at times displayed with maps, so that modern geography "created" nations such as Siam (*Chosen Peoples*, 133). On this making of Siam, Smith cites Thongchai Winichakul, "Maps and the Formation of the Geobody of Siam," in *Asian Forms of the Nation*, ed. Stein Tønneson and Hans Antlöv (Richmond, Va.: Curzon, 1996), 84.

64. It was conceived in the postmedieval context of Christendom in crisis, however, so that it is also a theological form, as I will briefly explore below. Cf. Smith, *Chosen Peoples*, 32–33.

effectively irreducible) political difference operative in the modern discourse of peoplehood from well before secularization to the present. It is the pure foundation of the "continuity of a subject," "invariant substance," and "original personality" used in the modern discourse of peoplehood to construct a national story and unify diverse populations, over against others, as the national citizenry, that is, to make a people.[65]

Ethnicity has typically been constructed by appeal to common language and race in complementary relation, making it possible "for the 'people' to be represented as an absolutely autonomous unit. Both [language and race] express the idea that the national character (which might also be called its soul or spirit) is immanent in the people."[66] In other words, appealing to common language and race, whose diverse configuration across the known world appears to be predestined, serves to naturalize the people and minimize its contingency.[67] Such appeals posit a historic "family" to which a plethora of persons and associations belong. A living language appears to have no beginning, and it has a tremendous capacity to assimilate and to adapt, while a racial imaginary supposes that the filiation of persons across generations transmits "a substance both biological and spiritual and thereby inscribes them in a temporal

---

65. A national bond is "based on a belief in ancestral relationship, which, being immune to change and even counter-evidence, is outside time, and which defines and sustains the nation. . . . [It] comes from an overriding belief in shared kinship and common ethnicity, irrespective of the historical evidence. This is an intuitive conviction, it is felt 'in the bones'" (Smith, 22). Smith is here supporting the conclusions of William Connor, *Ethno-Nationalism: The Quest for Understanding* (Princeton: Princeton University Press, 1994), 195–209, and Joshua Fishman, "Social Theory and Ethnography: Neglected Perspectives on Language and Ethnicity in Eastern Europe," in *Ethnic Conflict and Diversity in Eastern Europe*, ed. Peter Sugar (Santa Barbara, California: ABC-Clio, 1980), 69–99, esp. 85.

66. Balibar, "The Nation Form," 96. Cf. Smith, *Chosen Peoples*, 24.

67. "This naturalization is extended to a land as 'a homeland,' as the land of 'our' ancestors, and of our birth, life, work, and death. It was a landscape distinguished from other landscapes through its close associations with a particular people and its culture and history" (Smith, *Chosen Peoples*, 36). Landscape has been crucial to the modern discourse of peoplehood in the United States from very early, as we will see below.

community known as 'kinship.'"[68] Balibar claims that this racial imaginary is at work whenever national ideology claims that persons belong to the same people by constituting "a circle of extended kinship" or "brotherhood" and should therefore behave as such.[69]

Before the development of the modern discourse of peoplehood, "the old empires and the *Ancien Régime* societies were still based on the juxtaposition of linguistically separate populations, on the superimposition of mutually incompatible 'languages' for the dominant and the dominated and for the sacred and profane spheres."[70] But with the concerns of modernity, social differences have been expressed and relativized "as different ways of speaking the national language, which supposes a common code and even a common norm. This latter is . . . inculcated by universal schooling, whose primary function it is to perform precisely this task."[71]

Linguistic association has not been enough to construct ethnicity, however, because "the linguistic construction of identity is by definition *open*."[72] No one "chooses" her "mother tongue." This threatens the activist political anthropology at work in the modern discourse of peoplehood. But more significantly, a language naturalizes new acquisitions too quickly. For example, "second

---

68. Balibar, "The Nation Form," 100. While he explicitly opposes the prevalent undertanding of the racial constitution of peoplehood of his time (indicating its currency) and is criticized by Kant for this resistance, Johann Gottfried Herder remains a crucial figure in the development of fictive ethnicity as constituted by common language and the spirituality of peoplehood. See J. G. Herder, *Herder on Social and Political Culture: A Selection of Texts*, trans. and ed. F. M. Barnard (Cambridge: Cambridge University Press, 1969), 169, 181, 257–58.

69. "The criteria for [racial] differentiation can never be 'neutral' in a real context. They contain within them sociopolitical values which are contested in practice and which have to be imposed, in a roundabout way, by the use of ethnicity or culture" (Balibar, "Racism and Nationalism," 56).

70. Balibar, "The Nation Form," 97.

71. Ibid. Balibar goes on to say, "That the school should also be the site of the inculcation of a nationalist ideology—and also where it is contested—is a secondary phenomenon. ... Let us simply say that schooling is the principal institution which produces ethnicity as linguistic community" (98). Cf. Smith on the nationalizing power of the vernacular, *Chosen Peoples*, 205–12.

72. Balibar, "The Nation Form," 98, emphasis his.

generation immigrants" or other classes to remain marginalized can function in the national language in a manner as spontaneous and "hereditary" as those more "naturally" national.[73] Nationals can also function in other languages as naturally as they do in the national language. A language therefore provides no particular destiny for successive generations and is too hospitable to those identified as distinct from, threatening to, or subservient to, the people. The same language can even serve distinct national peoples. Consequently, while the immense power of a language to bind diverse persons and communities together has typically been important for the national construction of ethnicity, it has not been enough. "For it [i.e., fictive ethnicity] to be tied down to the frontiers of a particular people, it therefore needs an extra degree . . . of particularity, or a principle of closure."[74]

This principle of closure has been provided by the imaginary of race. Race "ethnicizes the social difference which is an expression of irreconcilable antagonisms by lending it the form of a division between the 'genuinely' and the 'falsely' national," (e.g., truly American or anti-American).[75] It imagines the unity of a national people as a historic family that supposedly minimizes divisive "internal" differences by treating as basic the difference between the national self and others. This difference is policed internally as that between "true" nationals and those "falsely" participating in the life of the nation (e.g., dwelling or working among nationals illegally) or otherwise threatening the life of the people. Kinship does not come into existence suddenly but implies a temporal, "biological"

---

73. Ibid., 99.
74. Ibid.
75. Ibid., 100. "At the centre of the nationalist belief-system stands the cult of authenticity, and at the heart of this cult is the quest for the true self" (Smith, *Chosen Peoples*, 37; cf. Smith's remarks on 190 regarding the invention of golden ages "to discover the 'true self' of the people . . . and to draw from it [the golden age] the moral lessons needed to mobilize and unify the people.").

development (of enigmatic origin) whereby a supposedly discrete, extended family has come to be and continues in fulfillment of its intrinsic, natural, or God-given destiny (over against other such "races" whose nature is inferior or whose future is not promised).[76] Its particularity or internal purity is finally secret (since its unity is not infallibly recognizable and is everywhere questionable), typically residing "in the blood" or "in the bones." Yet, it is characteristically associated in modernity with certain (unstable) physical features that are understood to indicate substantive historical and spiritual continuity. Thus, theoretically speaking, the racism at work in the modern discourse of peoplehood "is a philosophy of history or, more accurately, a *historiosophy* which makes history the consequence of a hidden secret revealed to men about their own nature and their own birth. It is a philosophy which makes visible the invisible cause of the fate of societies and peoples."[77]

In order to establish and regulate the difference between true and false nationality, the people is understood to exceed (metaphysically) its current condition and, accordingly, to differentiate among its

76. Kinship is thus not merely a metaphor for describing a unity that is conceived in explicitly multiethnic, ideational terms, as has the national unity of the United States in recent political rhetoric (a people united by "certain ideas," or "the spirit of America"). All ideas and spirits have a history, and the kinship language of peoplehood implies particular genealogical lines of descent from past to present, however imaginary, even where the ideas held to make the people what it is are presented as multiethnic and independent of their history of development. It also remains the case that the most "natural" citizens of national peoples are those born to national parents. Others must be naturalized, a process more difficult for those less White, such as immigrants from Latin America.

77. Balibar, "Racism and Nationalism," 54–55, emphasis his. Accordingly, "genealogy is no longer either a body of theoretical knowledge or an object of oral memory, nor is it recorded *privately*: today *it is the state which draws up and keeps the archive of filiations and alliances*" (Balibar, "The Nation Form," 101, emphasis his). Historiography is thus crucial to racialized constructions of a national past for the sake of political purity or integrity: "Nowhere does the cult of authenticity come into sharper focus than in the selection, and description, of golden ages. For they provide models of the nation's 'true self', uncontaminated by later accretions and unimpaired by corruption and decline. Golden ages represent, for nationalists, the pure and pristine nature of the nation, its essential goodness" (Smith, *Chosen Peoples*, 215). Earlier, Smith has noted that such historiography is always conducted by certain "bearers" of the national identity or ideal (ibid.).

internal constituents, privileging those who are more "natural" to the historic people (i.e., more promising), and marginalizing those who are less so. This excess constitutes the racist principle of closure, supplying what otherwise seems a dangerously and chaotically open form of political community with the particularity, history, and mission of peoplehood. Thus, the racist mission of national peoplehood is evident in the way that emergent nation-states, established in contested territories, have sought to control population movements in an effort to produce the people.[78] It is also evident in "the family policy of the state, which projects into the public sphere the new notion of population and the demographic techniques for measuring it, of the supervision of its health and morals, and of its reproduction,"[79] what Foucault calls "bio-politics" structured by "bio-powers."[80]

The decisive feature of the racial imaginary of fictive ethnicity for our present purposes is that it

constantly induces an excess of "purism" as far as the nation is concerned: for the nation to be itself, it has to be racially or [derivatively] culturally pure. It therefore has to isolate within its bosom, before eliminating or expelling them, the "false", "exogenous", "cross-bred", "cosmopolitan" elements.[81] This is an obsessional imperative which is directly responsible for the racialization of social groups whose collectivizing features will be set up as stigmata of exteriority and impurity, whether these relate to style of life, beliefs or ethnic origins.[82]

78. Balibar, "Racism and Nationalism," 48. Accordingly, nation-states have also territorialized the people by claiming that the people is natural to certain lands or that certain lands belong to the people by divine right or promise.

79. Balibar, "The Nation Form," 101.

80. Michel Foucault, *The History of Sexuality: An Introduction*, trans. Robert Hurley (New York: Vintage Books, 1990), e.g., 140–43.

81. "Cosmopolitan elements" are objectionable because they are by definition unparticular and unpatriotic. Recall that being cosmopolitan has been, in the modern discourse of peoplehood, among the base and inassimilable features of Jewishness.

82. Balibar, "Racism and Nationalism," 60. Cf. Smith, *Chosen Peoples*, 20: "For nationalists the nation, whatever the acts committed in its name, is essentially and ultimately good, as the future will reveal; the conviction of its virtue is a matter not of empirical evidence, but of faith."

The distinction between nationals and foreigners, and correspondingly, the truly national and the falsely national, is predicated on the supposedly intrinsic purity of the people.[83] This historiosophic purity, as Balibar described it above, is "a hidden secret revealed to [some] men about their own nature and their own birth," namely, that they naturally belong to the people while others naturally do not. Accordingly, in the formation of the modern peoples of the West "the racial-cultural identity of 'true nationals' remains invisible"; their imaginary purity, signaled by what Balibar calls "Whiteness," is the nameless (i.e., exnominated) standard by which all else is configured and differentiated and according to which the story of the national people is told. Yet, despite its invisibility, the pure identity of those who truly belong to the people and therefore represent the people

> can be inferred (and is ensured) *a contrario* by the alleged, quasi-hallucinatory visibility of the "false nationals": the Jews, "wogs", immigrants, "Pakis", natives, Blacks. . . . In other words, it remains constantly in doubt and in danger; the fact that the "false" is too visible will never guarantee that the "true" is visible enough.[84]

The anti-Jewish purity of the racial imaginary of fictive ethnicity has given the modern discourse of peoplehood a powerful technology of identity. It is what is taken to make a people what it is and to distinguish one people from another. It renders a particular difference between "us" and enemies as essential and foundational to peoplehood and citizenship.[85] It makes the discourse of peoplehood

83. "The ideals of purity and purification, which are such common motifs of nationalist movements, were soon seen as intrinsic elements of the authentic national self, in contrast to the accretions of the ages and the ensuing corruptions which contact with alien ways so often bred" (Smith, *Chosen Peoples*, 38–39).

84. Balibar, "Racism and Nationalism," 60.

85. For a clear, sympathetic, theoretical formulation of the difference between friend and enemy as the foundation of peoplehood, see Carl Schmitt, *The Concept of the Political*, trans. George

finally about who is killable, who can and must be sacrificed. The people lives insofar as its human enemies are destroyed and the power of "false nationals" is controlled. Claims about who the people really is may have shed the "religious" nature of this purity, but the purity itself has remained in force throughout the modern discourse of peoplehood and remains operative today.[86] It serves to produce a people and set it apart from others, forming, disciplining, and mobilizing its persons and social structures. It allows for the people to be construed and disciplined in terms of "the continuity of a subject," an "invariant substance," and an "original personality," each of which can be rendered narratively and exclusively with the help of a national story.[87] Thus, pure, fictive ethnicity—however multiethnic it claims to be—has been historically and materially at work in the politics of what represents the people, that is, what makes the people who or what it is.

Given the "ethnic" purity of the people in the above sense, as it has developed over time, historiography and other analytic and classificatory modes of discourse about the people (e.g., typology) can scarcely avoid setting themselves up as in some sense the diagnosis

Schwab (Chicago: The University of Chicago Press, 2007). Schmitt aims to develop this understanding by demonstrating that enemies of the people must also be pursued domestically.

86. Carl Schmitt, *Political Theology*, 36. Cf. Smith's account of the religious nature of secular Zionism on 85–94 and his comment on the national handling of the war dead: "The political religion of nationalism draws upon Christian traditions but uses them for national ends, in order to evoke a sense of sacred communion with the 'glorious dead' and their posterity, and to encourage a profound desire to work for self-renewal and national regeneration" (249–50).

87. None of this is to suggest that the political function of kinship metaphors is uniquely modern. What is peculiar to Christian fictive ethnicity in the modern discourse of peoplehood is its relation to the nation form, its anti-Jewish racializing tendency per its relation to societies being colonized (such that it informs anthropology as a science of classifying human diversity), and its diffusion of a certain kind of political subjectivity constitutive of human personhood and peoplehood. The purist nature of modern notions of ethnicity also implies that persons can supposedly belong to one and only one ethnicity, that that identity is unchangeable, and that it inheres in "blood relation." See Smith, *Chosen Peoples*, 45, for a brief description of the Pietist influence on concepts of national uniqueness. For classical concepts of ethnic bonds in relation to Jewish and Christian ones, see Love L. Sechrest, *A Former Jew: Paul and the Dialectics of Race* (London: T & T Clark, 2009).

of the normal and the pathological (e.g., which Jews "represent" Jewishness and which "Jews" don't; which Americans "represent" America and which "Americans" don't; which Christians "represent" the church and which don't). Opposing arguments echo and reinforce one another in the discursive battle for true representation. Such modes of discourse cannot avoid value judgments and policing effects, however purely or innocently descriptive they claim to be.[88]

This often has very little, if anything, to do with the intentions of those participating in the discourse. It is simply in the discursive air breathed and spoken in modernity. Thus, to the extent that they imply a claim to a pure and circumscribable identity, Christian attempts to resist national peoplehood by naming and developing an alternative, pure political community such as "the people of God" trade in the imagined purity that empowers the violence of modern peoplehood. Correspondingly, in the struggle for adequate embodiment of the purity of Christian peoplehood, they often display the same internal divisiveness that characterizes the (national) productions of peoplehood they mean to subvert. Such attempts have not relinquished the claim to political purity that is itself a violent legacy of modern Christian theopolitics, which I will further concretize below.

It is not enough, then, to simply claim that the people of God (or any other people) is nonethnic or (worse) multiethnic (where various putatively pure ethnicities are understood to constitute some kind of supposedly nonethnic unity). Whether the nature of the claim to peoplehood be formally ethical or creedal or ideological, the question remains as to whether it is, in the modern context, in fact an *ethnicized* ethics, creed, or ideology, or whether the transmission of identity is understood and promoted in such a way as to resist

88. Balibar, "Racism and Nationalism," 51. There is, in fact, no such thing as value-neutral description.

the historiosophy of fictive ethnicity. To resist that historiosophy, an understanding of peoplehood will either have to abandon any sense of mission (which it cannot do unless it is happy for the people in question to be dissolved and assimilated by other communities over time), or it must conceive of the people not as pure but as impure. It must abandon attempts to isolate, possess, and wield the technology of what "represents" the people. It can hardly do this if it claims a total view of the people, that is, of the difference between those who are "truly" the people of God and those who are "falsely" so. As I claimed above, such Christian understandings of peoplehood are simply not subversive enough.

We saw the modern discourse of peoplehood at work in Yoder's revisionist historiography of the Jewish-Christian schism, where some Jews represent Jewishness and other "Jews" do not, and the true Jews are self-constituting by virtue of their faithful way of life. Yoder is of course advocating Jewishness, but he does so with the anti-Jewish technology of identity developed in the modern discourse of peoplehood. Many others have done likewise but have not been so pro-Jewish.[89] Yoder is therefore a telling case of modern claims to peoplehood (even if the people he describes and invokes is premodern as well as modern) precisely because he can be in this way unwittingly both pro- and anti-Jewish.

One should not infer from the above analysis that "imaginary" or "fictive" means simply "unreal." What is imaginary or fictive in the modern discourse of peoplehood may be based on falsehoods or lies, but, as Balibar makes clear, it is not for that reason "a pure and simple illusion without historical effects."[90] It is deeply embedded in sociopolitical structures and habits of living. It encourages the

---

89. Take for example the ubiquitous Christian claim that it is "Jewish" to mix politics and religion (e.g., "the Jews" rejected Jesus because they were expecting a "political" kingdom instead of the true, spiritual kingdom of God). This Christian claim to be nonpolitical or above politics is of course itself political.

killing of some and the preservation of others. It profoundly shapes economic relations and distribution. It affects who marries whom and which children are born. It therefore determines to some extent the human beings that come into existence and the manner and time of their death, which persons and communities prosper materially and which don't, and the manifold relations that make up the lives that human communities and persons actually live. In this way the imaginary or fictive, even if it is a lie, is very real.[91] Thus, with the nation form, diverse persons and communities are fictively woven together in "a collective narrative, on the recognition of a common name and on traditions lived as the trace of an immemorial past (even when they have been fabricated and inculcated in the recent past). ... The imaginary which inscribes itself in the real in this way is that of the 'people.'"[92]

Competing "Peoples" of Israel

I have tried to concretize somewhat the foil of modern peoplehood—its negative pole—by identifying it as "Jewish." But I have yet to do the same for its other pole, that is, the people as a fictive ethnicity with pure foundation.[93] In each case of modern peoplehood, "the people" acquired a sacred name and emerged in

90. Balibar, "The Nation Form," 96. See also Smith, *Chosen Peoples*, 49, on the "reality" of "a myth of ethnic election." For Bercovitch's appreciation of the reality of the imaginary and the rhetorical in the case of the production of the American people in the revolutionary and antebellum periods as well as in the 1960s, see *The Rites of Assent*, 11–12, 29–30. He also notes the contribution of his own field of American Studies to this phenomenon. The achievement of its cognitive analysis "of the American 'mind',' 'heart,' and 'character'" has been "to reconstitute history itself as American" (11–12).

91. One thinks of Thomas Hobbes' famous claim: *autoritas, non veritas facit legem*. Given this fact, some readers will no doubt wonder whether peoplehood is a good place to focus the question of how Christians should live. Is peoplehood the right category? For my purposes it is enough to observe that the power that manages to "represent the people" has passed for some time as the primary bearer of the authority to decide between life and death, including the authority to kill, to demand sacrifice. We must also not forget that the language of "people" is, not coincidentally, thematic to Christian Scripture.

92. Balibar, "The Nation Form," 93.

particular historical conditions that, as I have said, owed much to the legacy of Christendom. The imaginary ethnic bonds of peoplehood that I have analyzed following Balibar were thus initially constructed with the grammar of the Christian faith and not with naked or non-Christian political theory. In order to concretize somewhat the fictive ethnicity of modern peoplehood, then, I will here highlight one central theme of Christian theology that has been salient in naming, ethnicizing, and constructing the pure foundation (and subjective continuity) of "the people," namely, the chosen people of Israel. The children or family of Israel names the fictive ethnicity, the particular kinship, that has been foundational to the modern discourse of peoplehood.

What Balibar and Smith have described as the tendency in the modern discourse of peoplehood to naturalize certain configurations of "the people" and minimize their contingency was typically performed in the idiom of *election*, that is, of being the one people chosen by the God of Christian revelation to be itself and to fulfill its mission in, for, and against the world.[94] "The people" of each of the most geopolitically powerful Euro-American nations of modernity thus came into being, in mutual competition, *as* the new, true, and chosen people of Israel.[95]

93. Insofar as the above analysis operates at a significant level of abstraction, it no doubt needs to be nuanced and problematized according to the distinct contexts of national peoplehood, which I will now only scarcely begin to do. That we seek to generalize across diverse contexts of national peoplehood is itself symptomatic of the power of the nation form.

94. Smith notes that "the cult of authenticity" in the modern discourse of peoplehood, which is predicated on the purity I have analyzed above, is derived from "an idea of necessity: the authentic is the irreplaceable and fundamental, that which we cannot do without or think away. It is this necessity that separates 'us' from 'them', our nation from all others, and makes it and its culture unique and irreplaceable. In that sense, the nation becomes the source of collective meaning, and hence 'sacred'" (*Chosen Peoples*, 40). Concretely, this "necessity" was named "chosen by God" or "election."

95. As these nationalizing powers oversaw the formation of nation-states among colonized societies, they bequeathed to them this form of peoplehood, albeit as a patronized "sovereignty" without local "religious" establishment.

Likening the recent deliverance of the Netherlands . . . to the Exodus of the children of Israel from Egypt, many Netherlands predikants, rhetoricians, and artists portrayed a new chosen people fleeing a modern tyranny and fighting the Lord's battles against latter-day Egyptians, Amalekites, and Philistines.[96]

The Protestant worldview which allowed so many Britons to see themselves as a distinct and chosen people persisted long after the battle of Waterloo, and long after the passing of the Catholic Emancipation Act in 1829 as well. For most Victorians, the massive overseas empire which was the fruit of so much successful warfare represented final and conclusive proof of Great Britain's providential destiny. God had entrusted Britons with empire, they believed, so as to further the worldwide spread of the Gospel and as a testimony to their status as the Protestant Israel.[97]

Milton captures the way in which this British chosenness as the true Israel had shifted from the people as subject *to* a hierarchy elected by God, to the people as itself/themselves the subjects or agents *of* elect political identity and action:

---

96. Smith, *Chosen Peoples*, 46. For documentation, he cites Simon Schama, *The Embarrassment of Riches: An Interpretation of Dutch Culture in the Golden Age* (New York: Random House, 1987). Cf. Hartmut Lehmann's conclusion regarding the German case: "The political model followed by the Pietists who were laboring towards a union of Pietism and nationalism was the children of Israel of the Old Testament." See "Pietism and Nationalism: The Relationship between Protestant Revivalism and National Renewal in 19th Century Germany," *Church History* 51 (1982): 51–52; see also 48. Cf. Smith's account of the Israelite ideology of the Afrikaner nationalist movement, *Chosen Peoples*, 77–85; the Russian case in the 1860s as summed up by V. I. Kel'siev: "The people continue to believe that Moscow is the Third Rome and that there will be no fourth. So Russia is the new Israel, a chosen people, a prophetic land, in which shall be fulfilled all the prophecies of the Old and New Testaments, and in which even the Antichrist will appear, as Christ appeared in the previous Holy Land. The representative of Orthodoxy, the Russian Tsar, is the most legitimate emperor on earth, for he occupies the throne of Constantine" (qtd. Geoffrey A. Hosking, *Russia: People and Empire, 1552–1917* [Cambridge, Mass: Harvard University Press, 1997], 73, ctd. Smith, *Chosen Peoples*, 185). For other examples, including that of Italy, see Michael Riff, "Nationalism," in *Dictionary of Modern Political Ideologies*, ed. M. A. Riff (New York: St. Martin's, 1987), 154–65.

97. Colley, *Britons*, 368. Cf. Smith, *Chosen Peoples*, 119. Smith also notes Scotland's claim to Israelite ancestry in its bid for independence from England (125–26). A claim to belong to the people of Israel could thus be competitive with the very same claim made by an oppressive power, just as these same political formations competed to be the Whitest.

> What wants there to such a towardly and pregnant soil, but wise and faithful labourers, to make a knowing people, a nation of prophets, of sages, and of worthies? . . . Moses the great prophet may sit in heaven rejoicing to see that memorable and glorious wish of his fulfilled, when not only our seventy elders, but all the Lord's people are become prophets.[98]

Smith notes that Britain eventually and superficially shed Christianity as basic to its national identity, but "the sacred foundation of a belief in English chosenness (perhaps by 'history' instead of by God) remained intact, and sentiments of English, and later British, election and mission were regularly expressed, albeit increasingly in secular garb."[99] In fact,

> the earliest use of the term "nationalism" in the English language appeared during the mid-nineteenth century, to express the doctrine of the divine election of a nation. . . . The roots of this fundamental conviction go back much further, being deeply entwined in a centuries-long Christian tradition of ethnic election, to which the English and other early modern European nations were heirs.[100]

Thus, while the Romantic rhetoric of the naturalness, greatness, and destiny of "the people" appears non- or even antireligious as well as generic to the modern nation-state, the "idea of destiny and glory, so crucial to the political religion of nationalism and its sacred communion of the people, however secularized and rhetorical, traces itself back to the early medieval religious conviction of divine

98. *The Prose Works of John Milton* (London: Westley and Davis, 1835), 115–16, qtd. Smith, *Chosen Peoples*, 121. As Smith notes, Christopher Hill sums up Milton's claim this way: "So the chosen nation became the chosen people—the common people, not the royal government" (*Milton and the English Revolution* [London: Faber, 1977], 281). This is illustrative of the activist political anthropology of the modern discourse of peoplehood.
99. Smith, *Chosen Peoples*, 48.
100. Ibid. For the development of French claims to Israel's election and its secular vestiges after the French Revolution, see 106–15. Smith also cites David Bell, *The Cult of the Nation in France, 1680–1800* (Cambridge, Mass.: Harvard University Press, 2001), in which see esp. 1–3, 38–40, 43; and Robert Gildea, *The Past in French History* (New Haven: Yale University Press, 1994), in which note particularly the section on the heritage of French grandeur, 112–65.

election of a kingdom and a people with a special mission."[101] Let us also be abundantly clear that, whatever the power of chosenness to resist oppression and stimulate more democratic practices of governance, to be God's chosen was also to be licensed to kill. And a license to kill remains to the present the patrimony of the sovereign states of national peoplehood.

Perhaps the most outstanding case of naming and building a national people as the chosen people of Israel is that of the United States, which is worth lingering over a bit longer than I have the previous cases. The purpose of doing so is to discern more concretely, in an age of intoxicating American power, the tendencies of the modern discourse of peoplehood in prevalent Christian accounts of the people of God and to clarify what it is that must be resisted.

"The two best-sellers of 1776 were Samuel Sherwood's sermon, *The Church's Flight into the Wilderness*, which politicizes the metaphor of sacred history, and Tom Paine's *Common Sense*, which heralds the American republic as New Israel."[102] Sacvan Bercovitch's rich and penetrating account of the development of the United States as the new and true Israel in *The Rites of Assent: Transformations in the Symbolic Construction of America* confirms, illustrates, and elaborates various aspects of the above analysis of the modern discourse of peoplehood and so will be worth quoting at length. In doing so I will attempt to elucidate the discourse's historiosophy, "continuity of a subject," "invariant substance," "original personality," and subjectivity as citizenship.[103]

---

101. Smith, *Chosen Peoples*, 115.
102. Bercovitch, *The Rites of Assent*, 70. This imaginary was not foreign to the American halls of power. "The first proposals for the Seal of the United States, submitted by Franklin and Jefferson, featured Moses leading the chosen people" (162); "Nor is it by accident that so many of the electoral debates through the Jacksonian and antebellum periods turned on which party was the legitimate heir to the title of American Israel" (44). Tom Paine provided "the figural blueprint for American exceptionalism" (162).

Bercovitch's presentation of American subjectivity as citizenship goes a step further than Balibar by describing in detail American "representative selfhood," wherein national persons are understood individually to represent the national people, and personal achievement is understood as national achievement. What makes this mutual representation possible is the supposition of an original personality of America, delivered as an invariant substance from the romantic past to each citizen of the present generation, which is always a generation under threat yet poised to fulfill its glorious future. Following the course from the people of America as God's chosen nation to American exceptionalism and the American Dream as we have come to know them, Bercovitch shows how the foundation of the People of the United States was and is conceived as "pure." Accordingly, the people has been continually summoned to live up to its original and eschatological purity, whose incarnation has passed from being "American Israel" to simply "America."

The production of the People of the United States, on Bercovitch's account, owes an enormous debt to Puritan Christianity. Bercovitch understands that Puritans accounted for only a part of American beginnings. Yet, "the Puritans provided their heirs, in New England first and then the United States, with a useful, flexible, durable, and compelling fantasy of American identity."[104] The symbology of American identity

> has succeeded in uniting nationality and universality, civic and spiritual selfhood, sacred and secular history, the country's past and paradise to be, in a single transcendent ideal. I do not say that the Puritans did

---

103. His analysis of the emergent peoplehood of the United States also points to various differences between the national project of the United States and that of European nation-states. Many of these are due to the "wilderness" context of the United States. European nation-states had to reckon with more immediately present and established forms of political and economic authority and resistance to nationalization. The land of America was "virgin."

104. Bercovitch, *The Rites of Assent*, 7.

all this. But they established a visionary framework within which that symbology could evolve and develop.[105]

This Puritan achievement in the discourse of America went something like this:

[The] Puritans felt free to incorporate Renaissance geo-mythology, as it suited their purposes, into their own vision. . . . They adapted the European images of America (land of gold, second paradise, utopia, primitivism as moral regeneration) to fit the Protestant view of progress. And having thus taken possession of the rhetoric of America, they proceeded one crucial step further. Reorienting their vision from a transatlantic to a transcontinental direction, they situated the Protestant apocalypse . . . in the New World. . . . New Canaan was not a metaphor for them, as it was for other colonists. It was the New World reserved from eternity for God's latter-day elect nation, which He would gather as choice grain from the chaff of Europe/Babylon/Egypt.[106]

The Puritans took possession first by imposing their own image on the land, and then by seeing themselves reflected back in the image they had imposed. The wilderness became their mirror of prophecy. What they saw in it alternated between "wilderness purity" and an Army of Christ advancing into a continental New Canaan. In either case, the identity it yielded pertained not just to a particular geographical region, but, primarily, to a chosen nation in progress—a New Israel whose constituency was as numerous, potentially, as the entire people of God, and potentially as vast as America.[107]

Federalism then allowed the Puritan vision to consolidate a diverse population under one covenantal mission of peoplehood:

---

105. Ibid, 79. "Puritanism came most fully to be absorbed in the national consciousness . . . as image and metaphor, as mythico-historiography, and, paradigmatically, as the dream of an ideal personal-corporate identity which perpetuates itself—in different forms corresponding to the vocabularies of different cultural moments—as an apocalyptic wakefulness destined to overcome the sleep of time, a fusion of Exodus and Garden embodied simultaneously in the ever-new nation and its representative men" (146). See also 32–36, 39, 76, 79, 82, 86–87.

106. Ibid., 75–76.

107. Ibid., 35. For a similar portrait of the American Puritan legacy, especially with respect to the land of America, see Smith, *Chosen Peoples,* 137–41.

> When they adopted the rhetoric of federalism as their "peculiar" social bond, the covenant of national election flowered, and the elect nation of Jeremiah, Isaiah, and John the Divine became incarnate in the first wholly Protestant contribution to modern nationalism, the American Israel.[108]

Under the Puritan legacy, "America" came to name a discrete, if also expanding, people and territory chosen by the God of Israel. The decision to make America was thus undertaken as a decision already made by God. The making of America was a God-given "errand."

> The rhetoric that prepared the colonists for revolution provided their leaders with a vehicle of social control: the pattern has become so familiar as to seem a condition of modern nationalism. . . . Once and for all, the errand took on a special, self-enclosed *American* form. Independence from England completed the separation of the New World from the Old.[109]

As we have seen in Balibar's analysis of the modern discourse of peoplehood and its nationalization of the human, what is imagined as setting "the people" apart must become immanent in the interpellation and formation of its "internal" constituents.[110] In America, this political formation as "errand" seized upon the representative capacity of (certain) selves, who represented—and were themselves represented in—the American ideal. This representativity identifies directly the powerful presence of the racist, nationlist form of "elect Israel." A "common framework of representative selfhood"[111]

---

108. Bercovitch, *The Rites of Assent*, 83.
109. Ibid., 38, emphasis his.
110. Bercovitch focuses interpellation on "individuals," and American "representative selfhood" encourages us to do the same. It is not only "individuals," however, that are interpellated as American but various other associations and structures. Besides Mexican-American, African-American, etc., and White American individuals (the last of which tellingly require no hyphenated modifier), we also have the American family, American business, American history, American education, American government, American church, etc. To the extent that such associations and structures name needed resources for America and Americanization, they are also "constituents" of America.

intertwined individual and national destiny as the outworking of the American people's original and originating personality. Thus, in the mid-eighteenth century,

> the benefits of the errand as pilgrimage—the special sense of oneself as representing God's New Israel—were extended to every patriotic white Protestant American. Of course, this involved a general redefinition of the self.[112]

> Independence became the norm of representative selfhood: independence of mind, independence of means, and these twin blessings, sacred and secular, the mirror of a rising nation—what could better demonstrate the bond of personal and social identity? Elsewhere, to be independent was to challenge society. In the United States, it was to be a model of consensus. Above all, independence gave a distinctive national shape to the idea of progress.[113]

111. Ibid., 33. This framework continues to seek "representatives" of America like "Joe the Plumber" in waging political campaigns for elected office. "Virtually every one of the hundreds of mid-nineteenth-century biographers of 'great Americans' insisted that his subject was not someone unique, but the emblem of American enterprise: a self-reliant man who was therefore, paradoxically, a cultural pattern, the model of a rising nation. The same paradox of representation (self and community entwined, as in a secular incarnation) applied to the countless rags-to-riches stories. However humble their origins, these heroes were not members of the working class, nor were they, after their success, nouveau riche, and certainly they never became upper-class. They were rather, every fatherless son of them, aspiring, self-motivated (even when, like Whitman, they were inspired by Emerson), self-reliant (even when, like Alger's Sam Barker, they depended on employers), self-educated (even when, like Thoreau, they were Harvard graduates), mobile (even if they decided, like Hawthorne's Holgrave, to settle down), and independent. And independence, of course, signified not so much an economic state as a state of mind and being, an entire system of moral, political, and religious values. In short, the American hero could represent no particular set of interests because he represented the general good—which is to say, a cultural myth" (47–48). This was also a racial and racist myth.

112. Ibid., 35. Bercovitch notes elsewhere that males and females represented America differently and unequally, as American women were primarily the mothers and trainers of up and coming Americans (48–49). Thus, women represented America and were represented by America only at a crucial remove, i.e., as those who married American men, had American children, and trained both American men and future trainers of American men. This illustrates the shortcomings of the political concept of representation, which is of course gendered and is briefly discussed below. For a more complete account of the construction of the American self, see Sacvan Bercovitch, *The Puritan Origins of the American Self* (New Haven: Yale University Press, 2011).

113. *The Rites of Assent*, 38. Representative selfhood displays the concern with "voluntary" political formation so typical of the ideology of the United States.

It is easy to forget in our time that this personal and collective "progress" made sense only as "errand" and was understood in Christian terms of sanctification. It was a way of baptizing self-constitution and autonomy, both national and personal, as ordained by God.

> Every sign of an individual's success, moral or material, made New England's destiny visible. . . . Whatever furthered the errand hastened the kingdom. As migration, then, the errand rationalized the expansive and acquisitive aspects of settlement. As pilgrimage, the errand provided for internal control by rooting personal identity in social enterprise. . . . By definition, the errand meant progress. It implied a teleology reaching from Genesis to the Apocalypse. As a community on an errand, New England was a movement from sacred past to sacred future, a shifting point somewhere between migration and millennium.[114]

> The Old World ideal of society was vertical, a model of class harmony. Ideally New England was a "way," a road into the future. Virtually all of its rituals of control—its doctrines of calling and preparation, its covenants of church, state, and grace—were directed toward that ideal. They were rites of voluntarism designed at once to yoke the personal to the political and to spur the venture forward to completion.[115]

Bercovitch sums up the Puritan production of the people that would come to be that of the United States this way: "Both in revival and in war, representative selfhood bound the rights of personal ascent to the rites of social assent."[116]

---

114. Ibid., 33–34.

115. Ibid., 34.

116. Ibid., 36. Perry Miller observes that the revivals of America were not so much preaching nationalism as "enacting it" (*The Life of the Mind in America: From the Revolution to the Civil War* [New York: Harcourt, Brace & World, 1965], 11). "What they [American revivalists] undertook, in effect, was a nationwide cooptation of the conversion experience—a wholesale reversal of spiritual communitas into a rite of socialization" (Bercovitch, *The Rites of Assent*, 54). For the influence of Jonathan Edwards and the Edwardseans on American peoplehood, see ibid., 156–58.

Representative selfhood remains a stock implement in the ongoing social formation of US society. In a widely published recent article by Matt Volz, "World's Oldest Man Dies at 114," whose subject is Walter Breuning, we find these words about one of his last interviews:

But social assent was no easy task even for so apparently homogenous and aspiring a "group" as White, patriotic, landholding Protestant males in America.[117] The fragile process of producing the people had therefore begun and trudged along under the aegis of an ideal unity, an irreducible political purity or inviolability that, through every contestation, was beyond contestation, because the development of America was the errand of God, the people and land of God's choosing.

> The American Way . . . was a web spun out of scriptural myth and liberal ideology that allowed virtually no avenue of escape. Technology and religion, individualism and social progress, spiritual, political, and economic values—all the fragmented aspects of life and thought in this pluralistic society flowed into "America," the symbol of cultural consensus, and then, in a ritual balance of anxiety and reaggregation, flowed outward again to each independent unit of society. To celebrate the future was to criticize the present. To denounce American life was to endorse the national dream. Whether one felt "humble," "fearful," or "hopeful," the sense of crisis that attended those feelings affirmed a single, omnivorous mission.[118]

"Breuning recounted the past century—and what its revelations and advances meant to him—with the wit and plain-spokenness that defined him. His life story is, in a way, a slice of the story of the country itself over more than a century." Recall Chatterjee's observation above: "The 'new individual,' it would seem, could represent the history of his life only by inscribing it in the narrative of the nation" (*The Nation and Its Fragments*,138). Breuning's "life story" is understood not as the story of a town or a church, etc.; it is the story of "the country," the story of America. The modern discourse of peoplehood has inscribed the history of his life in the narrative of the nation and thus presented him and his memory as a representative self of America (see Matt Volz, "World's Oldest Man Dies at 114," *Missoulian*, April 15, 2011, n. pag.).

117. We may also add to Balibar's list of the forces resisting modern peoplehood the "wilderness" conditions of European settlements in the "New World." Domesticating the land of America was crucial to the production of "the people" of America.

118. Bercovitch, *The Rites of Assent*, 56. See Bercovitch's reply to claims that excluded groups or classes could "use" American ideology and patriotism to improve their condition. There is a measure of truth to such claims, but enfranchisement by America has also come at a cost (49–51). The purity of "America" as described above—which is structured by the understanding that it is the elect of the one true God—has encouraged claims to multiethnicity, pluralism, gender-equality, etc. to be absorbed and utilized in an ethnocentric, chauvinist, male-dominated project of peoplehood. While liberating concessions have at times been made under pressure and acceptable conditions of conformity, and the threat of impurity has been

"America" came to define the discursive frame of reference for political formation, for becoming, being, and acting "the people." Thus, dissenters of various stripes

> were conforming to a ritual of consensus that defused all issues in debate by restricting the debate itself, symbolically *and substantively,* to the meaning of America. . . . Nothing more clearly attests to the continuing power of the myth than does the proliferation of "radical" manifestoes in antebellum America. . . . The summons to dissent, because it was grounded in prescribed ritual forms, circumscribed the threat of basic social alternatives. It facilitated process in such a way as to enlist radicalism itself in the cause of institutional stability.[119]

Being on the errand of God's chosen afforded American people-production an imagination and power to co-opt as "American" even the voices that were questioning the project of America itself. They were in fact nourishing the independent "spirit" of America and therefore resisting America *for the sake of* America.[120] In many cases, the most ardent critics of America found themselves claiming to represent America.[121] Chosenness was not simply a symbol but the invariant substance that irresistibly set the people of America apart from the rest of the world and gave it a mission to the whole world. Recall in Balibar's analysis (above) that the nation form relativizes other differences and subordinates them to itself "in such a way that it is the symbolic difference between 'ourselves' and 'foreigners' which wins out and which is lived as irreducible."[122] As long as

---

disassociated from certain excluded groups to some extent, American purity requires that inclusion be effected by means of exclusion.

119. Ibid., 49–50, emphasis his. American historiography has reinforced the myth of American purity by repressing adverse pieces of American history or, especially, by presenting these as "a violation of the nation's promise and original intent" (ibid., 12).

120. Incidentally, this is how someone like Stanley Hauerwas can be named by *Time* magazine—an important outlet of Americanism—"America's best theologian" (2001).

121. Bercovitch mentions several of these figures and movements in *The Rites of Assent*, 50.

122. "The Nation Form," 94.

America itself was treated as inviolable, it could process, temper, and domesticate all manner of resistance.[123]

But this chosenness, this purity, had constantly to labor at identifying, marginalizing, and neutralizing what was foreign vis-à-vis a pure, idealized image of its self. It simply could not represent everyone and also be the one chosen people amidst the manifold competition for its inheritance. It could represent only the elect.

> One major characteristic of the [antebellum] period was its astonishing variety of official or self-appointed committees to keep America pure: "progressivists" for eradicating the Indians; "American Christians" for deporting the Catholics; "benevolent societies" for returning the blacks to Africa; "Young Americans" for banning European culture.[124]

"Omnivorous mission" is therefore an apt designation of the errand of American peoplehood. For while the errand of God's elect nation was of cosmic dimensions, it could incorporate resistant movements, associations, and persons only by consuming and digesting them, assimilating them to its mythically pure self. In many cases, to be thus processed by the people of America was not only to be domesticated but to be excised or eradicated. This has made American peoplehood a fiercely violent enterprise even as it has brought some relief to many of those despised or not enfranchised by previous political orders. America was limitless, for who could limit the God who had chosen the people of America and yet claimed the whole world as his own? Yet, God called America to be a particular people, a people of certain (e.g., ideological) limits that must therefore be the modes of America's limitlessness.

123. For an account of the American political discipline that invokes a romantic biblical past to reform a present on the brink of failure so as to realize an eschatological hope, see Sacvan Bercovitch, *The American Jeremiad* (Madison: University of Wisconsin Press, 1978).
124. Bercovitch, *The Rites of Assent*, 49–50, emphasis his.

This self-proclaimed latter-day Israel was unlike any other community, sacred or secular. It was not limited by genealogy, as was Israel of old. Nor was it circumscribed by territory, tradition, and custom, as was modern England or Germany. Nor was it a wandering congregation of Christians seeking a haven in the world's wilderness, as were the Plymouth Pilgrims or the Pennsylvania Quakers. And yet the Puritans insisted on incorporating all of these aspects, tribal, territorial, personal, and spiritual. Their key to incorporation, I have suggested, was the Protestant concept of national election.[125]

The limits of American particularity constituted a principle of closure that channeled its omnivorous mission. The only ways open to those "inside" or "outside" America were either subordination and conformity to America's calling, or crumbling under the American wheel of progress. National election was therefore the limit of the people of America that channeled its limitlessness. This open-ended, tribal, territorial, personal, and spiritual vision defined the particularity or substance of America. It was a political particularity that was inhospitable to "the Indians," Blacks, Jews, and others. In some cases, such "foreign" elements could be adopted into the tribe, but only on condition that they display a sufficient measure of conformity and subordination to its natural members and therefore representatives, that is, that they become sufficiently White, Protestant, and capitalist, that they subscribe and witness to the purity and inviolability of America. Even so, their belonging would not be altogether natural or immediate. It would be mediated by the Americanness of reference, those representative persons, associations, and structures who have been designated as "American" *simpliciter* (who require no modifier to signal impurity, as "African-American," "Mexican-American," etc., do), whose features remain nameless because they constitute the hallowed standard for the differentiation of the rest (i.e., exnomination). For America "to be tied down to the

125. Ibid., 82.

frontiers of a particular people, it therefore needs an extra degree …
of particularity, or a principle of closure."[126] As Balibar contends, this
principle of closure is supplied by the imaginary of race, the anti-
Jewish, Christian purity that has generated and brought the chosen
people from a romantic and immemorial past into a threatened
present in anticipation of a triumphant future.

The limit of national election that rendered the people of America
a fictive ethnicity was an American Protestant development of the
Christian historiosophy of race. However apparently sudden in
appearance, the omnivorous mission of American peoplehood issued
from the past. American historiosophy illuminated the long-hidden
chosenness of the People of the United States to lead and represent
humankind. It made "history the consequence of a hidden secret
revealed to [representative Americans] about their own nature and
their own birth" and made "visible the invisible cause of the fate of
societies and peoples."[127] The fate of societies and peoples was to be
ordered in relation to God's election of the People of the United
States. In this way, the racist historiosophy of Protestant Christian
immigrants to the "New World" from Europe, what Bercovitch
calls "mythico-historiography,"[128] developed a nationalizing trend
typical of European Protestantism, a trend of election that has fed on
competition with other national peoples.

Not unlike the feat of some early non-Jewish Christian
communities vis-à-vis non-Christian Jews, communities of
Protestants, individually and collectively, redefined "the chosen
people" as those who worshiped the God of Israel *rightly*, that is, the
way Protestants did and not the way the Roman Catholic Church
did. There was first the big, "false" Church and the little, "true"

---

126. Balibar, "The Nation Form," 99.
127. Balibar, "Racism and Nationalism," 55.
128. Bercovitch, *The Rites of Assent*, 146.

church.[129] Then there was the big, "false," Protestant church and the little, "true," protestant people, divisiveness reaching specious completion at elect nationality. Empowered by the newness, geographic remove, "virginity," and enchantment of America vis-à-vis European Protestant powers, the Puritans in the "New World" presented America as the city on the hill, and the United States became God's chosen bearer of history. The Puritans "used their self-declared newness to create a vision of America that reconceived history at large (including that of the Old World) as hinging on *their* failure or success."[130]

But I must emphasize that the historiosophic continuity of the subject of the people of America, from its enigmatic prehistory through its incarnation as nationalization, was not merely that of political ideas or certain Christian convictions. The invariant substance of America that crystallized with the formation of the People of the United States was supposedly the stuff of a concrete, culturally particular body of pilgrims descended from a common past and transmitted from one generation to the next "naturally" and providentially by birth. Their chosenness was understood as immediate and genealogical.[131] These White Protestants became God's chosen family as Americans by nature. Others, those not inscribed in Protestant historiography as the people of promise, could therefore be American only by adoption and unending struggle. Regarding "the dream of national election,"

---

129. Recall Linda Colley's remark above: "The *Protestant* worldview which allowed so many Britons to see themselves as a distinct and chosen people persisted long after the battle of Waterloo, and long after the passing of the Catholic Emancipation Act in 1829 as well" (*Britons*, 368, emphasis mine).

130. Bercovitch, *The Rites of Assent*, 86, emphasis his. See Bercovitch's description of Federalist leaders' presentation of the American enterprise as "the redemption of mankind" (42–43). America was charged "by the design of Heaven" with "the cause of mankind" (44).

131. Consider, accordingly, the legacy of Puritan notions of immediate relationship with God: "No Protestant sect insisted more adamantly than they did on the unmediated relation between man and God" (ibid., 77).

As nonseparating congregationalists they [American Puritans] had effectually de-historicized their venture. Their effort at intellectual synthesis ("visible saints," "church-state") deprived them of their concrete connections with the past—all their English antiquities, except those inscribed in Protestant historiography—just as the past they invented for America deprived the continent's native inhabitants of *their* past, all their indigenous antiquities except those inscribed in the Christian-progressive view of history.[132]

Through the rituals of continuing revolution, the middle-class leaders of the republic recast the Declaration to read, "all propertied, white, Anglo-Saxon Protestant males are created equal." Through those rituals they confined the meaning of revolution to American progress, American progress to God's chosen, and God's chosen to people of their own kind. It is no accident that under Jefferson's administration, the Revolution issued in an increasing violation—for blacks and Indians—of life, liberty, and the pursuit of happiness. Nor is it by accident that so many of the electoral debates through the Jacksonian and antebellum periods turned on which party was the legitimate heir to the title of American Israel, and which candidate the true son of the Revolutionary fathers and Puritan forefathers. Nor is it by accident, finally, that while France and Latin America degenerated into factional pandemoniums, the United States generated a conformist spirit that foreign observers termed a "tyranny of the majority."[133]

The historiosophy of American peoplehood began as a feat of biblical exegesis in the Protestant tradition. But with "America" as its hermeneutical key, it has since followed its lines behind and beyond the Bible to keep pace with the mission of America. Ironically, Christian authorities, afraid of losing control of the United States, have continually furnished the tropes that have allowed the passage of the People of the United States from "American Israel" to just "America."

132. Ibid., 83, emphasis his.
133. Ibid., 44.

The Puritan millennialists saw their errand into the wilderness as part of the final stage of history. In doing so, they distorted traditional forms of exegesis, but they were careful to justify themselves by recourse to scripture. They always rooted their interpretations (however strained) in biblical texts, and they appealed to (even as they departed from) a common tradition of Reformed hermeneutics. Their Yankee heirs felt relatively free of such constraints. During the Enlightenment, the meaning of Protestant identity became increasingly vague; typology took on the hazy significance of image and symbol; what passed for the divine plan lost its strict grounding in scripture; providence itself was shaken loose from its religious framework to become part of the belief in human progress. The eighteenth-century clergy took advantage of this movement to shift the focus of figural authority, from Bible history to the American experience. In effect, they substituted a regional for a biblical past, consecrated the American present as a movement from promise to fulfillment, and translated fulfillment, from its meaning within the closed system of sacred history, into a metaphor for limitless secular improvement.[134]

The Theopolitical Import of the Modern Discourse of Peoplehood

Yoder describes the development of modern political order in relation to the church as successive iterations of Constantinianism, each one the mortal enemy of the previous one.[135] Constantinianism is that tendency of Christian churches to identify themselves "with the power structures of their respective societies instead of seeing

134. Ibid., 147. Bercovitch quotes (66–67) a telling *New York Times* report in April of 1980 on the inception of a new "Citizen's Party"—telling because of how well it illustrates the myth of America and because it shows how conservative the most left-wing American movements are: "Some 275 delegates represented 30 states at the founding of what they call a "second party" rather than a third, on the frequently stated contention that the Republicans and Democrats and their prospective candidates were one indistinguishable mass. . . . Delegates included old radicals of the Socialist era, young environmentalists, ardent feminists and labor union activists; almost everyone was a "ist" of some kind . . . . Speaker after speaker emphasized how different the Citizens Party convention would be from those of the major parties. . . . .Keynoting the convention . . . Studs Terkel, the Chicago writer, predicted that the new party would "reclaim the American dream from the predators who've stolen it—that's what this meeting is all about." (Warren Weaver, Jr., "Citizens Party Born in Unorthodox Way," *The New York Times*, April 13, 1980, 15.)"

135. In a section entitled "Constantinianism Old and New," in *The Original Revolution*, 150–54.

their duty as that of calling these powers to modesty and resisting their recurrent rebellion."[136] The medieval Constantinian identification of the Holy Roman Church with the Holy Roman Empire gave way to Protestant, separated churches who were identified with specific nation-states (neo-Constantinianism). Next came the severance of formal bonds between church and national government, accompanied by their continued association in the minds and practices of most citizens (as in the United States) or the retention of formal bonds without popular support (as in Scandinavia)—in either case "the secularization of the Constantinian dream" (neo-neo-Constantinianism).[137] Since then, says Yoder, "peoples" have come to be led by non- or antireligious philosophy with Christian support, as it is thought that "the process of secularization can best succeed when favored and fostered by the church"[138]—the neo-neo-neo-Constantinianism of the church's alliance with postreligious secularism so long as it remains popular. In the latest iteration, we find the church's tendency to look to the future in hopes of identifying itself with the most promising political cause of the time—since we are assured that history is guided by such a political cause—so that the church will not be discredited or further disenfranchised when the present order collapses—neo-neo-neo-neo-Constantinianism.[139]

As insightful and amusing as this account of reiterative Constantinianism is, it leaves out a crucial dimension whose discursive performance I have analyzed above. At each stage of the Constantinianism Yoder criticizes, (part of) the church has invoked God's authority to claim for itself, and only itself, a powerful mythic identity of God's chosen with a view to consolidation as a new,

136. Ibid., 150.
137. Ibid., 151.
138. Ibid., 153.
139. Ibid., 153–54.

discrete, and independent political unity. Beginning with neo-Constantinianism, churches did this as competitive "peoples." The hope of forgiveness and reconciliation was abandoned, "the people of God" of the past superseded by the "new" and "true" people of God, who in turn is as old and legitimate as biblical antiquity or nature, founded by God's election before the foundation of the world.[140] The identity of "the people of God" (i.e., "Israel") is thus conveniently emptied of its rival inhabitants, who have ceased to qualify as the "true" people of God, the elect. Purified of its enemies, the "new" and "true" Israel has achieved its independence, the fulfillment of its self. It has decreed, on the authority of Scripture, that the now "false" people of God, the "old" Israel, has been replaced.

All of this has of course taken place by the power of God's grace and election, as Christians are justified by faith alone and can claim nothing before God that has not been given them. Nevertheless, what God has supposedly given this new Israel is a knowledge of its self that is total enough to determine who it is not, that is, to determine who is disownable or killable, and who are to serve it as slaves. It therefore forms and disciplines itself in conformity with its inner purity, which is not only its possession but the spirit of its political body.

For much of the Christian past this supersessionist project of peoplehood was rooted enough in the language of the Bible for the new people to be called "Israel," whatever that was worth. But with the Protestant multiplication of Israels and the embattled intelligibililty of the oneness of Israel's God, the project has moved to the secular messianism of simply "we the people." The Christian story and its ecclesiastical authorities ceased to be compelling, as

140. Here the hope of forgiveness and reconciliation would not mean what it is often taken to mean, that is, the anticipation that things will be better in the future when "they" realize that they're wrong. Instead, that hope would be the ongoing practice of refusing to disown those "we" are calling upon to repent and assuming our complicity in their crimes (i.e., their impact).

modern peoplehood reached for conceptual authorities that appeared less theologically particular and more "humanly" accessible. But with the continued supersessionism of the modern discourse of peoplehood came the theological voluntarism that long entitled Christian authorities to decree who the "true" people of God is instead of living in response to God's election (which I will clarify in chapters 4-7). In the modern crisis of theopolitical authority, that theological voluntarism has been individualized and biologized with the rise of both the modern subject and the agent of "nature." The national people is thus understood as constituted by persons who are who they decide to be, and in this way achieve their freedom, enact their nature, and realize their humanity, all at the atrocious price of mass enslavement, mass exploitation, and mass killing.[141]

Modern Christian supersessionism is therefore not simply an isolated theological tendency that has contributed to atrocities against Jewish communities. It is a violent theopolitical imaginary that has empowered the racialization and nationalization of the political configuration, social habits, and predominant sense of self of the modern world. It is not enough, then, to refuse the Constantinian temptation of identifying the church with the power structures of a society. This is especially not enough if Christians are at the same time presiding over the people of God as itself a disembodied, pure form whose putative material instantiations in the flesh can be judged "true" or "false," whether on the basis of Scripture or some other authority. That kind of technology of identity remains Constantinian

---

141. Cf. Barth's observation: "If it is the case that this [individualist] orientation of the Church's doctrine of predestination certainly did not arise apart from the earlier way of secular individualism, it is equally certain that as orientated in this way the doctrine is not merely one of those factors which have paved the way for Pietism and Rationalism within the Church itself, but is also one of the presuppositions without which the further development of secular individualism would have been inconceivable (the development from J. J. Rousseau and the younger Schleiermacher through Max Stirner and Kierkegaard to Ibsen and Nietzsche)" (CD, II/2, 308).

in the purview it claims for itself and the vicious cycle of revolution it remains within. It also plays into the hands of modern racist and nationalist political formations, even if it explicitly aims to resist them.

To resist the supersessionist violence of modern peoplehood, Christians must stop claiming against one another or against others that the people of God is only that people who gets the God of Israel right, for this God has not chosen only those who choose this God.[142] Accordingly, it is important not to disown or domesticate a prerevolutionary past or its troubling present articulations, not to imagine that the people of God is purely itself or totally visible to itself vis-à-vis its enemies or "false" claimants to its identity, not to define the people of God past or present by any supposed "representatives," and not to disappear the "external" contributions to its personal and collective constitution or subjectivity. In short, the people of God must heed the witness of Gamaliel the Pharisee (chapters 1 and 2 above) by refusing to impose a principle of closure on its identity. It must forgive instead of forgetting, and love its enemies as itself. It must, as the psalmist insists again and again, wait upon the God of Israel as the author of the people.[143]

I have yet to provide much of a theological or biblical basis for resistance to the modern discourse of peoplehood. Nor have I attended to the question of where the above criticism of Christian contributions to modern peoplehood leaves the particularity of the Christian community. If we cannot limit the people of God to those

---

142. Notice that the basis of this claim is not that "we could be wrong about ourselves or others." Nor is it that we're supposed to embrace those who are wrong while presuming that "we" are right. The point here is neither the need for more "humility" that is self-doubt nor patronizing acceptance of those we have historically despised. It is rather that the God of Israel has not put his people in charge of who they are, thereby precluding our ability to circumscribe our identity. This inability is itself ethically significant as we will see in the remainder of the book.

143. The sense in which the God of Israel is the author of the people of God will be clarified in the remaining chapters.

who get God right, then what makes the people of the God of Israel who it is and how can it be that the Christian gospel is true? On what basis can it be said that this is the way to be the people of God and not that? How is the people of God to be disciplined so as to be faithful and good? The purpose of this chapter has been to raise these questions and signal some inadequate answers to them rather than develop any answers of my own. It has been to demythologize the nation form of peoplehood, to expose its Christian basis and themes, and to point up some problematic ways of reading the Bible before we turn to a more constructive theological account of the people of God in the remaining chapters. There I will eschew notions of the purity of the people of God vis-à-vis the rest of the world without denying the difference between the two. I will treat with suspicion claims that the people of God is constituted ethnically (or nonethnically) without overlooking the fact that the children born to the people of God are gifts of God. I will try not to perform the typical Christian reduction of Jewishness to a single something by which to define the people of God, whether to embrace the Jews as a pure foundation of the people of God or to supersede them as the foil in supposed fulfillment of God's purpose. This will involve an account of the people of the God of Israel that is not constituted by its own faithfulness as ontically equivalent to God's election, but by God's faithful election as it is embodied in its (impure) covenant response. And finally, I will be careful in making any Christian claims about peoplehood in relation to generic concepts of "humanity" or "nature."

As the above analysis of the modern discourse of peoplehood has indicated at various points, it has been a discourse in anthropology, a struggle to understand what it means to be human as political community and what one community in one place means for everyone else. The ahistorical, anthropological generalization at work in the discourse has encouraged its Christian voices to try to comprehend "humanity" in debates internal to the Judeo-Christian tradition. Thus, in some way, certain Jews or certain Christians, good or bad, are thought to *represent* this group or that, or to *represent* all humanity or some feature characteristic of all humanity. External frontiers are imagined as projections of internal struggle, as we rush to define a perceived danger, often before we have even met it. This is not only a phenomenon of Christian theological discourse but also occurs under the auspices of Western humanism insofar as it trades in anthropological universals. A theoretical humanism that makes humanity as a species the origin and end of ethics is perfectly capable of naturalizing and reinforcing both the nationalist and racist tendencies of the modern discourse peoplehood.[144]

But the question of what it means to be human should not and will not go away, especially as societies are forced to recognize their economic dependence on others. That is why Balibar sees resistance to the violence of the modern discourse of peoplehood as inevitably "pitting one idea of man against another" and "setting an internationalist politics of citizenship against a nationalist one."[145]

But Christians know of no revelation of universal "man," much less of an idea of "man." Christian anthropology, if we can call it that, must work from the messy details of a particular history which claims to hold promise for all. It is a history mediated by but not contained in the Bible, where the people of God is never a pure, autonomous unit but itself only as an impure community in relation to other communities, often unfaithfully so. It can seek to discipline itself and engage others not in the full knowledge of itself much less of others, but only in hope and by the light of God's heteronomous revelation. In studying this history for ethical guidance in the present, Christian

144. Balibar, "Racism and Nationalism," 63.
145. Ibid., 64.

concern with the people of God must fix its gaze upon one person whom it confesses as Israel's Messiah: the one who, in time, brings the forgiveness of Israel's sins, calling his fellow Jews to covenant *shalom* and drawing gentiles to forsake the gods who keep them at war with one another and with Israel; the one who knew Israel's sins only as his own, who joined his people in the baptism of repentance at the Jordan, who set his face to go nowhere but Jerusalem, even when that road of solidarity led to the cross. He who knew no sin became sin that we might become the justice of God in him (2 Cor. 5:21). In Jesus we see the wisdom to which Gamaliel the Pharisee bears witness, the life that shows why the people of God cannot impose any closure on its own identity, for "he himself is our peace" (Eph. 2:14).

In order to offer a Christian description of the people of the God of Israel, we will consider, in the next chapter, Karl Barth's christological account of the election of the people of Israel. In his account, the people of God is not the pure, Christian replacement of an impure, Jewish attempt at instantiating the form of Israel but the one, Jew-gentile covenant people determined by the God of Israel to be one in both unfaithfulness and faithfulness. Jesus is not the chosen, the Christ, at any remove from the impurity of sin, but precisely in his solidarity with sinners. He is the elect one only as the rejected one. Thus, I will not purport to engage the modern discourse of peoplehood from without, nor propose a supposedly new and better understanding of "the human."[146] Nor will I pretend that an engagement in and with that discourse in terms of Jesus Christ can avoid implying something about the Jewish past or present, as a guilty Christian imagination is wont to pretend. For that is simply to be in denial about the Jewishness of Jesus and the inevitable impact of Christian claims to serve the God of Israel under Jesus as Lord; it is to

---

146. Balibar, too, thinks that the violence of modern peoplehood can be resisted with theology (ibid., 63).

hide behind a false shield of fictitious independence. Being Christian always has implications for those being Jewish and vice versa, and Christian arguments about these matters should be vulnerable to Jewish contestation rather than aloof in a futile effort to protect Jews from Christians. Instead of these false starts, then, with Barth's help I will engage the modern discourse of peoplehood in its own themes of Israel and Christology and meet the modern political challenge of Christian supersessionism head-on, hopefully without reiterating it.

4

The Politics of the Election of Israel

Help from Karl Barth

The only God who exists is the God of Israel. The only people of God is God's elect people Israel. That God elects this people means that "the people" is not self-made but made by God. Its constituents do not decide who they are. "Israel" is not an identity that can be expropriated or appropriated by human beings. It is not predicated on human adequacy to any standard. Those who claim to be the people of God cannot justify their claim by adducing anything that they do or have done (e.g., believing, being good or faithful). They bear no intrinsic integrity, whether that integrity be conceived as moral or ethnic or something else. The people of Israel is the people uniquely formed, and thus compromised by(!), the electing presence of God, that is, uniquely united to and thus participant in the one true God. This participation by election is the meaning of covenant. Therefore, God's election upsets any claim by "the people" to intrinsic integrity, purity, independence, or sovereignty. God's election is the power of God that makes this covenant people, and the apocalypse of this compromising election is the elect one, Israel's Messiah Jesus.

The aim of this chapter is, with the help of Karl Barth, to substantiate and develop the above understanding of the elect people of God in response to the supersessionist, self-made peoplehood of modernity, whose theologically derived racism and nationalism have been the source of such diabolical violence. I begin with Karl Barth because, with his emphasis on God's election as attested in Scripture, he takes us a long way toward an adequate response to modern peoplehood. But then, in the next chapter, we must move beyond Barth.

In a letter dated Sept. 1, 1933, Barth addressed the following words to Frau Dalmann:

Die Judenfrage ist sicherlich, theologisch betrachtet, der Exponent des ganzen Geschehens unserer Zeit.[1]

The Jewish Question is surely, as seen theologically, the exponent of the entire event of our time.

He goes on in the same letter, as reported by Eberhard Busch, to write

Gerade in der Judenfrage könnte ich nicht den kleinsten Schritt mittun mit dem Nationalsozialismus. Wenn irgendwo, so meine ich, müßte man hier das Halt hören und die Grenze sehen, über die hinaus man eigentlich nur unter ›Verrat‹ am Evangelium . . . weitergehen kann.

It is precisely on the Jewish Question that I could not join in taking the slightest step with National Socialism. I believe that if anywhere it is here that one must hear the halt and see the limit, past which one can go only as a *betrayal* of the gospel.[2]

---

1. Qtd. Eberhard Busch, *Unter dem Bogen des einen Bundes: Karl Barth und die Juden 1933–1945* (Neukirchen-Vluyn: Neukirchener, 1996), 49, translation mine.

The "entire event of our time" is not merely the end of Weimar Germany and the rise of National Socialism. Writing in the shadow of "The Great War," Barth is well aware that the tumult in Germany is part of a much wider colonialist scramble for global dominance.[3] Given what we have seen in the previous chapter, Barth's identification of the Jewish Question as *the* issue of that event is most perceptive. Not only does it touch the violent pulse of the modern West; it goes, as he says, to the heart of the gospel. Barth's theological response to the Jewish Question will therefore provide my starting point for an exposition of his Christian account of the people of God.

Instead of pretending to circumvent the modern discourse of peoplehood, this and the remaining chapters will knowingly engage in it by describing who the people of the God of Israel is according to the gospel story, which is an Israelite story. To do this I must try to say both how God's election of the people of Israel determines what it means to be Christian and explicate the interrelation of the election of Israel and the elect one, Jesus Messiah. As we have seen in the previous chapter, the question of the election of Israel lies deep in the grammar of the modern discourse of peoplehood. If this question is not taken up or addressed adequately, the violent tendencies of modern supersessionism will be reinscribed in descriptions of the Christian community as the people of God, to say nothing of non-Christian descriptions of "we the people." We turn, then, to Barth's Christian account of peoplehood in response to the Jewish Question.

In considering Barth's account, I wish to highlight a difficulty right on the surface of his presentation of the people of God according to

2. Ibid. Cf. "He who is a radical enemy of the Jews, were he in every other regard an angel of light, shows himself, as such, to be a radical enemy of Jesus Christ" (Karl Barth, *The Church and the Political Problem of Our Day* [New York: Charles Scribner's Sons, 1939], 51).

3. For a brief but illuminating account of the colonialism and racism at work in the political context to which Barth is speaking, see Marcia Klotz, "The Weimar Republic: A Postcolonial State in a Still-Colonial World," in *Germany's Colonial Pasts*, ed. Eric Ames, Marcia Klotz, and Lora Wildenthal (Lincoln: University of Nebraska Press, 2005), 135–47.

God's election. In his fine book, *Church and Israel after Christendom: The Politics of Election*, Scott Bader-Saye rightly criticizes Barth for succumbing to a metaphysical subordination of the collective to the individual on the matter of election.[4] As Bader-Saye acknowledges, Barth is concerned to subvert a discourse of peoplehood that predetermines individuality to conform to an overwhelming collective nourished by a degenerate, nationalist appropriation of Israel's election.[5] Barth opposes this destructive tendency by making God's election of the community the *mediation* of God's healing election of the individual, to whom election is ultimately directed. While Barth formally denies any rivalry between the collective and the individual,[6] apparently he cannot avoid the conclusion that the particularity of individuals is finally more determinative than the particularity of the community.[7] This understanding, Barth argues, enables the community to avoid the arrogance of modern movements

4. Scott Bader-Saye, *Church and Israel after Christendom: The Politics of Election* (Eugene, OR: Wipf & Stock, 1999), 73–77. Nevertheless, as Barth argues in the *Römerbrief*, the election of the individual does not mean for him what it had previously meant for Reformed theology, namely, the psychological unity of this or that individual as elected or rejected, or the quantity of the elect and the damned. To speak of election in such terms is to speak "mythologically" (*The Epistle to the Romans*, trans. Edwyn C. Hoskyns [Oxford: Oxford University Press, 1933], 347). See Katherine Sonderegger, *That Christ Was Born a Jew: Karl Barth's "Doctrine of Israel"* (University Park, Pennsylvania: The Pennsylvania State University Press, 1992), 29.

5. E.g., *Church Dogmatics*, ed. G. W. Bromiley and T. F. Torrance, 4 vols. in 13 parts (Edinburgh: T & T Clark, 1956–77), II/2, 312, 366.

6. E.g., ibid., 313, 718.

7. E.g., ibid., 314, 727. Thus, Barth seems to cave to a dualism of the individual and the collective. Barth justifies his claim that the election of the community mediates (unidirectionally) the election of the individual by appealing to the individuality of God and Christ, but this simply begs the question. It is not as self-evident as Barth assumes that Christ is more an individual than a community, nor that the one God is more individual than plural in God's oneness. We must learn what both individuality and community are from the Triune God in the full revelation of that God in the Son by the Spirit, rather than assume that either God or Christ corresponds directly to a certain concept of individuality (as Barth himself instructs in *CD*, IV/1, 205). We are better off sticking with Barth's formal contention that human individuality and community are not competitive. God's election in Christ reaches humanity precisely as a community fulfilled in the particularity of its member persons and as persons fulfilled in their community. Such is the "oneness in Christ" of the New Testament, where the oneness of persons is not more determinative than the oneness of their community (e.g., Gal. 3:26–29).

of peoplehood in the West and to be patient in its service to individual persons as determined by God in Christ.[8]

But Bader-Saye is right that we do not need to resort, as Barth does, to this metaphysical hierachy in order to resist a violent collective. Instead, we should insist that the identity of the elect community and that of its member persons are mutually determined, made *for* each other so to speak, with neither more final than the other in their relation to God: the community becomes what it is through the growth of its member persons in their interrelationships, and persons grow in their particularity in and through the life of the community.[9] Nevertheless, while I agree with Bader-Saye's critique and so will not follow Barth's subordination of the election of the community to the election of the individual, I wish to clarify and strengthen the crucial resistance offered to the modern discourse of peoplehood by Barth's account of the elect people of the God of Israel, focusing on his most systematic presentation of that account in *CD* II/2.[10]

We will concentrate on two key features of Barth's presentation of election and then, in the next chapter, address one of its significant and far-reaching liabilities. The key features are 1) God's election of the people rather than a predicate of human subjectivity as primary in the description of who the people is (i.e., the people is not that community that does this or that but that community chosen by God); and 2) insisting that election is unequivocally both good news

---

8. That is, the community must never regard itself as more than "the environment" of the election of Christ and individual persons in him (*CD*, II/2, 196).

9. Yet, we should not overlook that persons are welcomed into the community that preexists them rather than vice versa, and the community continues through and beyond the death of its members, uniting persons across death.

10. I owe some of the impetus to turn to Barth on this matter to Jacob Taubes's critique of Carl Schmitt in *The Political Theology of Paul*, trans. Dana Hollander (Stanford: Stanford University Press, 2004), as well as to J. Kameron Carter, from whom I have learned much, especially in his lectures at Duke University on Christology.

and judgment for the people of God because it transforms its political object. These two features will clarify Barth's response to the *Judenfrage*.

The significant liability of Barth's account lies in the excessively formal character of his description of the elect community. Abstracted from the complexity of its history, Barth's description cannot adequately name the temporal content of God's election, that is, the electing presence of God that holds the people of Israel together across time and space and informs its ethics of forgiveness. In other words, Barth's description cannot adequately describe (or tell) the history of Israel in the flesh. Instead, he resorts to a concept of representation: the people of God is that people represented in Christ. The concept of representation shifts the ground of Barth's description from the winding path of Israel through time among the gentile nations as attested by Scripture to a realm of "christological" forms.

As we will see, by operating within this realm of representation (i.e., where the elect community is represented in the elect one), Barth's formal Christology cannot help but eclipse the material history of the elect community, including the material history of the elect one. As the everywhere-contingent history of Israel attested in the Bible, the election of Israel in fact defies the forms of Barth's Christology. But that those forms are considered Christology, which Barth rightly identifies as theopolitically primary, preemptively determines the shape of the people in time and therefore undermines the Christian ethics of peoplehood. Thus, Barth's account encourages a neat and problematic *twoness* of "Israel and the church," a vestige of traditional Christian supersessionism that has, as we've seen in the previous chapter, been constitutive of the modern discourse of peoplehood. As Yoder has argued (see chapters 1 and 2 above), the history of the elect community defies this twoness. Its historical complexity counsels against subgrouping the people of the God of

Israel into clean, ethically charged blocs (e.g., Israel and the church), even if in the same breath their unity is declared primary and inviolable.[11] Moreover, the proper political defiance of the division of the elect community is what the catholicity of Jesus, the full revelation of God's election in the flesh, is all about. Accordingly, I will argue in the remaining chapters that the election of Israel is the living history of Israel in the flesh, which continues in the present. Jesus is not the representative of the (opposing) forms of the elect community but the cornerstone of its complex history. As such he is the forgiveness of sins, the reconciler of Israel with God and the gentile nations (Matt. 1:21; 26:28; Rom. 11:27).

The Primacy of Election:
Questioning the Divisibility and Self-Constitution of the People

I begin by reiterating briefly the political challenge that Barth inherits, so that I might better articulate the dramatic implications of his claims about the primacy of God's election for the nature of peoplehood. Zygmunt Bauman writes that with the arrival of modernity

> order *was to be made*; there was to be *no other order*. Hence the urge, the desperation: there would be as much order in the world as we manage to put into it. The practice stemming from a conviction that order can be only man-made, that it is bound to remain an artificial imposition on the unruly natural state of things and humans, that for this reason it will forever remain vulnerable and in need of constant supervision and policing, is the main (and, indeed, unique) distinguishing mark of modernity.[12]

---

11. Particularly problematic is the corresponding identification of the Jew with the bloc that bears witness to God's judgment, rejection, or "No," even if this identification is supposedly synecdochical, as Barth says it is (*CD*, II/2, 199), for ways of responding to God's election current in *both* Jewish and Christian communities.
12. *Intimations of Postmodernity* (London: Routledge, 1991), xv, emphasis his.

Modern peoples have been produced in this violent desperation. A well-deserved shadow of suspicion had fallen over European Christian institutions claiming divine, monarchical right to rule over the masses. The resulting crisis of authority that is characteristic of modernity made it difficult to understand speaking or thinking "God" in the West as anything other than speaking or thinking "man." It was painfully obvious that established Christian powers had often been speaking only for themselves when they had supposedly been speaking for God. A new and improved (Protestant) basis of political authority was therefore sought and located "in the people," *in der Volk*. The West translated the divine right of kings to the divine right of peoples and then to the natural right of peoples.[13] But, as Bauman says, orders of peoplehood did not come to exist all by themselves. They had to be made. Their political ontology was voluntarist. They had to choose and make their selves. And yet, this assertion is somewhat misleading, for peoples could not make themselves from scratch and could hardly be promoted as "artificial." They could be made only with reference to their metaphysical unity, which is what rendered them representable and compelling in the process of their production. They indeed claimed to be self-constituted, but their collective selves were also somehow metaphysically *given* (e.g., "elected" by God or "natural") and thus treated as intrinsically pure vis-à-vis their parent regimes, rival peoples, or societies to be colonized.[14]

13. See Étienne Balibar, "Citizen Subject," in *Who Comes after the Subject?*, ed. Eduardo Cadava, Peter Connor, and Jean-Luc Nancy (New York: Routledge, 1991), 33–57. For an excellent discussion of the political and anthopological aporias of the transition from the divine right of kings to the divine right of peoples to the natural right of peoples, see 47.

14. For Carl Schmitt's attempt to address the crisis of political authority of modernity, see *Political Theology: Four Chapters on the Concept of Sovereignty*, trans. George Schwab (Chicago: The University of Chicago Press, 2005 [1985]). According to Schmitt, this political purity or independence is derived within humanity from the primordial friend-enemy distinction, the enemy being that of "the people" as determined by the sovereign authority of the same

As we have seen in the previous chapter, the metaphysical unity informing the modern production of the most powerful peoples of the West and their colonies was imagined with an anti-Jewish, nationalist appropriation of the divine election of Israel. Jewishness became the foil of "the given" of modern peoplehood. To be a people was thus to have overcome the inadequacies of Jewishness by God's grace, as Euro-American projects of peoplehood competed with one another to be the new and true Israel (i.e., the "Whitest" people), and resistance movements in their colonies mimicked them in opposition to colonial rule.[15] The Christian supersessionism at work in Christendom leading up to modernity therefore provided a key language and optic for the imagination of modern peoplehood and the production of its peoples, and it is *with* a development of Christian supersessionism that such modern political order was to be *made*.[16]

Barth answers this far-reaching, Western philosophy of peoplehood with a resounding theological "No!" "The people" of which Christians can and must speak is the people of God rather than a self-made, God-less people, and this God is none other than the God of Israel, that is, the God of all Israel and not merely some new Israel of our own making.[17] The order of peoplehood is not made by

"people." See also his *The Concept of the Political: Expanded Edition*, trans. George Schwab (Chicago: The University of Chicago Press, 2007 [1996]).

15. For an account of this mimicry, see Partha Chatterjee, *The Nation and Its Fragments: Colonial and Postcolonial Histories* (Princeton: Princeton University Press, 1993).

16. "There is, however, another modern concept which is important in this connexion, constituting as it does an unmistakeable secular imitation of the election of the community. . . . Elected man . . . according to Fascism . . . is the nation as constituted by race, language and history. . . . [The] totalitarian state . . . becomes the proper bearer of election" (Barth, *CD*, II/2, 312). Also, see Schmitt's totalitarian claim that political order is based fundamentally on a human decision (*Political Theology*, 53–66). He argues this against the more "organic"—if also human-made—process-driven view of political liberalism and attempts to expose the inadequacy of such a process to account for political order.

17. "Apart from Israel, no people as such is God's people." (*CD*, II/2, 196). See also *CD*, II/2, 410–11 for a summary statement. Now that the peoplehood of the modern nation-state has monopolized our imagination, this will sound to many like an unqualified endorsement of the

human beings but by God, and God's making of the people of Israel is the activity of election. To say that Israel is not made by human beings but by God is to say that Israel is not an idea or a disembodied spirit or form that may be invoked to name and produce a "new" people (i.e., by violent revolution or by cleansing sources of "ethnic impurity"). It is not a free-floating, deserted identity prepared by God for conquest and possession by some newly "elect" community, its supposedly "natural" inhabitants. Israel is a people that, against the voluntarism of modernity, is already there in the flesh, for God has sustained its existence to the present according to the loving promise of God's election.

The elect people is therefore not ontically equivalent to the life or existence or history of any modern people, because Israel preexists and exceeds any such people; most significantly for Barth, Israel preexists and exceeds such peoples in the form of the Jews. The people that is of God, then, opposes its own peoplehood if it disowns any of its Israelite past, present, or future, if it "makes" itself as an anti-Jewish replacement of Israel, that is, as a new Israel. Doing so is arrogantly to deny the faithfulness of the electing God that grounds and sustains the very existence of the people of God and so promises its future. In fact, it is to attempt to replace that electing God. There is no such thing as a new Israel that replaces the old Israel or otherwise leaves it behind. Moreover, the promised future of the people of God, revealed in Israel's crucified and risen Messiah, is not that of the chosen people at the expense of others, be they parent regimes, rival peoples, or indigenous societies slated for colonization. It is, according to Barth, mercy and peace for all human beings as well as the rest of creation, for such is the work of God's election of Israel in Christ, the elect one.

modern state of Israel. But as Yoder argues (chapters 1 and 2 above), the modern state of Israel is itself an iteration of the supersessionist modern project of national peoplehood.

Barth thus exposes the still absolutist violence of both modern national election and the natural rights of humanity. Such attempts at making political order either deny God's election or falsely claim it as an exclusive possession rather than responding to it in obedience by remaining committed to all the Israelite existence in the flesh that God has already made and continues to make. Barth's alternative to the ontological voluntarism of Western political philosophy is, however, not a retreat to the problematic, "revealed" authority of Christendom, but a christological articulation of the election of Israel. The election of Israel means that modern "peoples," particularly Christians within them, cannot and must not attempt to choose or make themselves into existence on the back of the Jews or as independent units relative to one another or other political communities. They cannot impose closure upon who they are by claiming their own beginning or a pure constitution of their own. To be Christian participants in the people of the God of Israel, Barth insists, is always to be in the middle, in solidarity with the Jews and joined in the peaceful unity of Christ to all human beings. The church must insist that there is no "national interest" other than this.

We may understand the primacy of election according to Barth particularly in terms of 1) the *oneness* of Israel and the church and 2) the *secondary* character of human subjectivity in the constitution of the people of God.

1. The Oneness of Israel and the Church

Barth opts for the term "community" (*Gemeinde*) in describing the elect people of God "because it covers the reality both of Israel and of the Church," implying their oneness.[18] The church has contributed to the violent tendencies of the modern discourse of peoplehood by

18. Ibid., 196.

falsely claiming the independence of some Christian people of God vis-à-vis the Jews (or all non-Christian Jews), by imagining itself as a "new people" that is constituted by replacing and disowning the "old people." And what Christians have done to the Jews, they have done to one another. Thus, the Christian supersessionist imagination has made possible the division of the Christian community into competing peoples, each of them supposedly new and independent relative to a previous political configuration or to other peoples. It has enabled the racist operation whereby Euro-American nationalist movements, many of them still Christian in their initial phases, have rendered their constituencies the "natural" bearers of a falsely pure collective identity, the "natural" inhabitants of a particular (expanding) territory, and those accordingly justified in destroying their enemies.

But for God to have elected a people precludes God's replacing or disowning all or part of that people. The people is one as God is one. The people is therefore responsible for negotiating its growth, defeats, and differences with patience and forgiveness rather than violence and supersession. That is simply what election means politically. The people of God, which Barth understands to be a political community,[19]

> is as Israel and as the Church indissolubly one. . . . It is as the Church indeed that it is Israel and as Israel indeed that it is the Church.[20]

> Only where the calling that rests on election had not occurred is it possible to play off the special form of the Church within the one community against this unity with the people of the Jews, to forget and deny the unity of Israel and the Church.[21]

19. E.g., ibid., 731.
20. Ibid., 198.
21. Ibid., 201. See also 213.

Consequently, the church, or any "people" attempting to usurp the election of the people of God, cannot disinherit the Jews of the promises given to Israel and thus arrogate exclusively to itself the unity and identity of the people of the God of Israel. Whatever promises, unity, and identity the church claims for itself it shares with the Jews, and denying this fact can lead only to the violence borne of trying to sustain a lie.[22]

The fundamental basis of Barth's assertion of the oneness of Israel and the church as the people elected by God is that Jesus, who is the elect one in whom the people of God is elected, was a Jew.[23] Jesus is the one who makes the church who and what it is, and Jesus was a Jew. The church can no more replace or disown the Jews in being the people of God than it can replace or disown Jesus.[24]

22. "The Church lives by the covenants made between God and Israel" (ibid., 203). "The Church can understand its own origin and its own goal only as it understands its unity with Israel" (ibid., 284).
23. As is well known, the Son of God is, according to Barth, the proper object (and subject) of God's election: God's choosing God's self in God's Son who becomes flesh in Jesus, who in turn is God's choosing humanity. The beloved Son is thus the basis and purpose of the entire will and work of God *ad extra* (i.e., creation). The Son himself is thus object and subject of election proper, rendering people elect only in him. The election of the community that is the environment of the electing revelation of this Son (i.e., the community of Israel and the church) is therefore the "other election"—the election whereby all people are united to the Son (see e.g., ibid., 195–97).

  While I am sympathetic with Barth's account of the christological basis of election, I worry about his characterization of all God's activity *ad extra* as "election" because of the resulting inadequate distinction between that activity and the election of God's people in particular. God's election of Messiah and the people in him seems to me, according to Scripture, not an "other election" but election proper, and God's other activity *ad extra* should be characterized as related but different. This has implications for the dispute between Bruce McCormack and George Hunsinger on whether the differentiation of Trinitarian persons is predicated on God's election, although I cannot pursue those here. See George Hunsinger, "Election and the Trinity: Twenty-Five Theses on the Theology of Karl Barth," *Modern Theology* 24, no. 2 (April 2008): 179–98; Bruce McCormack, "Grace and Being: The Role of God's Gracious Election in Karl Barth's Theological Ontology," in *The Cambridge Companion to Karl Barth*, ed. John Webster (Cambridge: Cambridge University Press, 2000), 92–110.
24. This raises the question of how the Jewishness of Jesus is the Jewishness of "the Jews," a question that points up the limits of Barth's formal approach. I will take this question up in the next chapter.

But it is from Israel that this man has come and been snatched. Not from Greece, not from Rome, not from Germany, but from Israel! This is simply a fact. It is independent either of Israel's unbelief or the faith of the Church. It cannot be destroyed by Israel's unbelief and therefore it is not to be denied in the faith of the Church but openly confessed: "Salvation is of the Jews" (John 4:22).[25]

Christian voices in modern projects of peoplehood such as Germany may wish to claim Jesus as their own or identify him romantically with their own supposedly Greco-Roman "roots" rather than with the Jewish past, but they cannot because Jesus is and remains irrevocably of the Jews.[26] They may wish to separate Jesus from the Jews by appealing to Jewish unbelief or their own non-Jewish Christian virtue, but the identity of Jesus, and therefore the identity of those who participate in the benefits of his life, is not attributable to the quality of Jewish or Christian living. That Jesus is Jewish is who Jesus is as God's elect. If it is not, if Jesus can be severed from the Jews through the replacement or redefinition of the people of God, then what promise is there to God's election? If the elect one can leave the elect people behind, the object of the church's own faith is empty, and the church itself is without hope. "Whoever has Jesus Christ in faith cannot wish not to have the Jews. He must have them along with Jesus Christ as His ancestors and kinsmen. Otherwise he cannot have even the Jew Jesus."[27] The implication is that modern peoples

25. *CD*, II/2, 204. Romanticizing the Greek or Roman past of Christian or post-Christian European society or "Western Civilization," so that its Jewish past is overshadowed, became a motif of the modern discourse of peoplehood (and a trend in biblical scholarship). See Nell Irvin Painter, *The History of White People* (New York: W. W. Norton & Company, 2010), e.g., 101. See also Susannah Heschel, *The Aryan Jesus: Christian Theologians and the Bible in Nazi Germany* (Princeton: Princeton University Press, 2008), 34, 63, 138.

26. This is not to imply that as a Jew Jesus was not also Greco-Roman in a number of senses. See the now-classic work of Martin Hengel that exposed the myth of a purely Jewish society in first-century Galilee and Judea: *Judaism and Hellenism: Studies in Their Encounter in Palestine During the Early Hellenistic Period*, trans. John Bowden (Philadelphia: Fortress Press, 1981 [1974]). We must hold together with historical vulnerability the two propositions that there is no such thing as pure Jewishness and that there has been a real difference between Jews and others (more on this in the next chapter).

that derive their secular identity from Christian supersessionism have arrogated to themselves a false integrity or purity, for they have not escaped the "impurity" of their own Jewish roots and the branches—now alienated by them—that extend from those roots into the present, however much such peoples have come to despise them.

At several points in his presentation in *CD* II/2, Barth notes the political currency of his claim that the church and Israel are one in the Jew Jesus and the urgent imperative that it entails. It is the imperative of Christian peoplehood in solidarity with, rather than hostility toward, the Jews. Perhaps most immediately this involves Christians not standing idly by while their Jewish neighbors are persecuted or rounded up for destruction, but taking active responsibility for their well-being as that of their very self.

> How can he [Paul], or the union of Jew and apostle to the Gentiles admittedly consummated in him, have for his people any more than the significance of an exception which can only prove the rule that God has rejected this people? Questions of this kind had perhaps already been asked in Gentile Christian circles in relation to the Jews. Later, and right up to the present time, this has certainly been the case. The question which Paul faces is the question asked by Christian anti-semitism, whether the crucifixion of Jesus Christ does not settle the fact that the Jews are now to be regarded and treated only as the people accursed by God.[28]

> It is not, then, only the zeal of Paul, but that of the whole New Testament, which bursts into flame at this point. It is palpable, however, that this is a zeal which includes rather than excludes, which seeks rather than rejects, which loves rather than hates. It is the zeal for the house of the Lord grounded in Israel. An antisemitism which mistakes and disputes Israel's election from outside can have nothing to do with this zeal (to which indeed this mistaking and disputing is essentially foreign).[29]

27. *CD*, II/2, 289.
28. Ibid., 269.

What this striking second νῦν [of Rom. 11:31] makes quite impossible for Christian anti-semitism (he that has ears to hear, let him hear) is the relegation of the Jewish question [*Judenfrage*] into the realm of eschatology. That Israel's hope is really the *hope* of Israel and the Church, and is therefore *future*, makes no difference to the fact that in relation to Israel the responsibility of the Church, which itself lives by God's mercy, is already a wholly present reality.[30]

As these quotations indicate, the Jewishness of Jesus is not, for Barth, simply the timeless assertion of a transcendental and mythical Jewish substance. It is the testimony of the biblical story. It is the character of Jesus within the drama of God's covenant history with Israel. It is this Jesus in this story that precludes any fundamental division between the Jews and the church. In his account of the primacy of election as revealed in the oneness of the Jews and the church, Barth therefore draws on a wide range of biblical texts. I will deal with the Gospel of Matthew and Romans 9–11 more carefully in chapters 6 and 7, respectively, and not engage any of Barth's exegesis in detail here, but I should note illustratively a couple moments in the biblical story of Israel that Barth highlights. This will clarify what the primacy of election is, according to Barth, and how it entails the oneness of the Jews and the church in Christ the Jew.

The Christian attempt to supersede the Jews is not, Barth observes, without Israelite precedent.[31] From power centers in Bethel and Dan after the death of King Solomon, Jeroboam seceded from the united kingdom of Israel and tried to disinherit the Israelite order of Judah

---

29. Ibid., 204–5. Cf. 234: "A Church that becomes antisemitic or even only a-semitic sooner or later suffers the loss of its faith by losing the object of it."

30. Ibid., 305, emphasis his. Cf. Barth's critique of the classic and current argument for Christian antisemitism on 290. Barth also responds directly to the tendency in German churches to deny the possibility of Jews' becoming Christian and therefore to exclude them from the ecclesial community. The oneness of Jews and Christians means that Jews, far from being merely tolerated in the ecclesial community, ought to be particularly welcomed as a "special honour" (ibid., 213; see also 267).

31. Ibid., 393–409.

by heading a "new" Israel of the ten northern tribes. The tragedy of this division of the one people of the one God into two—Israel and Judah, a tragedy nevertheless unable to assail the indivisiblity of God and therefore the people of God—is pictured in 1 Kings 13. There "a man of God" of Judah prophesies against Jeroboam in Bethel but is finally duped into sharing an idolatrous table with "an old prophet in Bethel," resulting in the former's being killed by a lion per the word of the Lord. Yet, the story concludes this way:

> The prophet [of Bethel] took up the body of the man of God [of Judah], laid it on the donkey, and brought it back to the city, to mourn and to bury him. He laid the body in his own grave; and they mourned over him, saying, "Alas, my brother!" After he had buried him, he said to his sons, "When I die, bury me in the grave in which the man of God is buried; lay my bones beside his bones. For the saying that he proclaimed by the word of the Lord against the altar in Bethel, and against all the houses of the high places that are in the cities of Samaria, shall surely come to pass. (1 Kgs. 13:29-32)[32]

Jeroboam cannot constitute a "new" Israel. Not because he is not good enough, but because Israel is already stubbornly there as twelve tribes in the flesh according to God's election and can therefore not be superseded by a northern kingdom of ten tribes.[33] What is more,

---

32. Cf. ibid., 409 and 2 Kgs. 23:15-18. All biblical quotations in this chapter are from the NRSV unless otherwise noted.

33. It is crucial to notice, as Barth does (CD, II/2, 400), that Jeroboam does not seek to constitute a new Israel in the name of some god other than the God of Israel. Just as Aaron had at the foot of Sinai, Jeroboam invites his kingdom of Israel to worship the God of Israel in a form other than the one already revealed by that God: "Then Jeroboam said to himself, 'Now the kingdom may well revert to the house of David. If this people continues to go up to offer sacrifices in the house of the Lord at Jerusalem, the heart of this people will turn again to their master, King Rehoboam of Judah; they will kill me and return to King Rehoboam of Judah.' So the king took counsel, and made two calves of gold. He said to the people, 'You have gone up to Jerusalem long enough. Here are your gods, O Israel, who brought you up out of the land of Egypt.' He set one in Bethel, and the other he put in Dan. And this thing became a sin, for the people went to worship before the one at Bethel and before the other as far as Dan" (1 Kgs. 12:26-30; cf. Exod. 32:4). The most destructive kind of idolatry is not that which calls out to the names of gods other than the God of Israel, but that which calls out to the God of Israel so as to supersede and forget the way in which that God is already served by the people as it already exists. In these

Jeroboam and the northern tribes remain Israel by God's election even in their violent opposition to that election. But because of that unfaithful opposition, their election means judgment for them. The oneness that God's election affords to Israel in the flesh cannot finally be undone, only temporarliy denied and futilely opposed.[34]

> For what is the real subject of the whole ensuing history [i.e., of the people of Israel divided into two rival kingdoms]? For one thing, it is obviously the unity of the will of God for the whole people whom He led out of Egypt, through the wilderness and into the land of Canaan. To this extent it is also the unity of the people itself, of the relatedness of its whole history, of all its tribes and kings and prophets. . . . But the will of God . . . does not cease to be one and the same for all Israel; His faithfulness is unshaken. His promise continues open. If the separation and opposition in Israel's course and destiny are necessary, they can exist only in such a way that they point beyond themselves. They must still witness to the unity of God's will, and therefore also to the unity of Israel; to the truth which is now eschatological, but which is all the more true for that very reason.[35]

Barth's exegesis of 1 Kings 13 emphasizes the way that the prophetic witness to Israel's rebellion (i.e., the prophet of Bethel) remains, like the errant kingdom for whom he seems to speak, a participant in and servant of God's election—part of the one elect people Israel.

> The point now seems to have been reached when all Israel must sink into the abyss of its common guilt; an abyss into which the grace of Judah also falls, and with it every hope for the whole. But it is in this very situation that the miracle happens to Israel itself and its lying prophet. The evil and ungrateful man, addressed by the Word of God, becomes himself its bearer and messenger. This is not, of course, because he has any merit or worth. It is apart from and even against his own intention.

---

two instances of betrayal, like many others, the concern was political survival and therefore not faith.

34. *CD*, II/2, 400.

35. Ibid., 403.

It is simply because God is always God, because He has not cast away His people, His whole people Israel.[36]

Thus, the way that rebellion within Israel cannot undo or fail to serve finally the oneness of Israel evinces the primacy of God's election for who the people is.

> But the very fact that this [opposition to what the prophet of Bethel formerly served] is possible and actual, even in the form of a contradiction which is all that it can have, is not just a sign but a concrete part of the reality of the grace of Israel's God, which has not destroyed him [the false prophet that now speaks the truth] but now claims and uses him, which is not simply lost and forfeited by the whole realm of Bethel and Samaria, for all the tremendous sins of that realm and the menacing approach of the year 722 (and the day of Josiah). The God of David [i.e., of Judah] has neither forgotten nor abandoned the lost sheep of the house of Israel. There is no occasion for the men of Jerusalem to disdain [the northern kingdom of] Israel; and for Israel itself there is no reason for despair. There is an election and calling of the ungodly also. Is there any other?[37]

There is therefore no such thing as two Israels, or the right Israel and the wrong Israel, or the good Israel and the bad Israel, or the true Israel and the false Israel, or the new Israel and the old Israel. The church is to learn from this chapter and the rest of the story of Israel that it must not dualize Israel so as to identify itself as the right, good, true, or new Israel and the Jews as its superseded counterpart. Because of God's election, the church enjoys no such dualistic integrity or purity. There are indeed right ways and wrong ways of Israelite living. But any internal distinction—and internal distinction is indeed important, as we will soon see—is for the sake of the solidarity of the one Israel. Israel in the south (Judah) "has no right to an existence

---

36. Ibid., 407.
37. Ibid., 402. Cf. 405: "On the contrary, the story now moves on to its sequel, that the very tempter and destroyer must now take up the flag which the other had let fall."

which is tranquil and settled in itself. It cannot possibly rejoice or boast in its election to the derogation" of Israel in the north.[38]

> Nor can it come to terms with it and accept it without at once addressing itself afresh to this Israel. There is, therefore, no possibility of self-sufficiently leaving this false Israel to its error and destruction. On the contrary, it is under obligation to Israel.[39]

> The disruption did not mean that the north was released and expelled from the sphere of the Word of God, and therefore from the scope of His grace. The disruption was hardly completed before salvation began to appear more than ever in the place where grace had been repudiated—and from that place where it had been received as grace, from the Jews. And the right to existence of these Jews was their message, the Word of God given them for themselves—yet not for themselves alone, but for all Israel. It is only by going to the north with this Word that the man of the south can confirm and justify his own election. Thus the cause of Jeroboam and his prophet was vindicated even before it was expressed and executed in its folly. Long before and in a very different way God Himself had provided a common table for His whole people. Nothing could come, therefore, from that arbitrary table fellowship [initiated by the false prophet of Bethel] . . . . It is not from a secure elevation, but from the depths of the same distress, sustained by the unmerited grace of God alone [i.e., election], that Judah addresses and necessarily must address Israel by the mouth of its prophets, and must speak to it the one Word, i.e., the Word of God, which is its own support.[40]

> And if the cry of mourning uttered in Bethel over the man from Judah: "Alas, my brother!", could only be a cry of mourning, yet it did express an objective truth. . . . This one was his brother.[41]

---

38. Ibid., 404.
39. Ibid.
40. Ibid.
41. Ibid., 406. In the run-up to and aftermath of the Shoah and in an effort to expose the antihistorical illusions of modern anti-Judaism, Marcel Simon was among the first to expose the historical errors of the standard Christian account of the Jewish-Christian schism. He pointed to relatively late evidence of brotherhood analogous to that between Israel and Judah, namely, that between divided non-Christian Jews and non-Jewish Christians, not incidentally in places of burial. In fact, in many places the later division does not seem to have been characterized by the hostility of the earlier one. See *Verus Israel: A Study of the Relations between Christians*

The election of Israel means that there can be no possibility of the "faithful" disowning the "unfaithful," as Yoder's account cannot help but do (chapter 2 above). Some may claim to do so, but such claims are empty, as will be borne out in time. The oneness of the people that derives from God's election implies that the faithful in Israel share in the guilt of the unfaithful in Israel.[42] In fact, far from disowning errant Israelite communities, faithfulness to the God who elects Israel means living in solidarity with those in Israel who are straying. Faithfulness "assumes the responsibility and initiative" with respect to the unfaithful in Israel.[43]

We must not overlook, however, that the oneness of Israel, which is analytic of the primacy of God's election for who Israel is, does not preclude internal difference. In fact, the difference between God and Israel, the difference that is the covenant relation, implies not only the differentiation of Israel from the gentile nations who serve other gods, but also differentiation within the people of Israel. That God has elected Israel and will therefore move Israel to the fulfilment of the promise of election not only allows but requires internal distinction. Why? Because Israel is not a formless, motionless mass but a dynamic political community being formed by God's electing revelation in and to it, the formation from which Israel's covenant faithfulness is derived and to which it is a participatory response. Yet, the internal distinctions within the people of Israel—which are subject to, and themselves become, the ongoing, living revelation of God—serve the whole people, and finally the whole creation of the one God, rather than one part of it at the expense of others. One

and Jews in the Roman Empire, 135–425, trans. H. McKeating (New York: Oxford University Press, 1986), e.g., 78, 124. "The apparently clear distinction between Judaism and Christianity turns out on closer examination to be rather more vague than appeared at first sight" (95). The original French edition was published in 1948.

42. Barth, *CD*, II/2, 404–5, 407.
43. Ibid., 405.

such internal distinction is that of authority or rule (e.g., parents, prophets, priests, kings), whereby Israel is ordered over time—in relation to particular persons, places, and institutions (e.g., the house of David)—according to the rule of God that will finally avail for the covenant blessing of all Israel according to God's unconditional covenant promises. This rule of God is ultimately God's making an Israelite society of peace, which involves its peaceful unity with the gentiles of the world under the kingdom of Israel's God. The oneness of all humanity in and through Israel's Messiah is thus the goal of God's election of Israel.[44] The distinctions that God's election of Israel effects within Israel are therefore predicated on the oneness of Israel and are thus the promise and hope of all Israel.[45]

On Barth's reading, the life of Israel after the patriarchs "was directed towards one individual figure," namely, King David, who was the key forbear of Messiah.[46] David is thus an important witness to the internally distinguishing activity of God's election of Israel. Just as Israel was not Isaac's first son but his second, so David was not Israel's first king but its second. There is nothing "natural" or automatic about the ascendancy of David and Judah over Saul and Benjamin. God's election cannot be reduced to the intuitive primacy

44. Here I am anticipating what is to come. My concern is that the reader not be settled with an understanding of election that imposes closure on its political object, whether people or king, such that the telos of election is merely the differentiation of that object from others. The telos of election is not merely the differentiation of Israel from the gentiles but the oneness of Israel and the gentiles (i.e., the fullness of Israel and the gentiles' joining Israel) under the peace of the one true God, just as the telos of the election of the king of Israel is not merely the differentiation of that king from rivals or the rest of the people but the oneness of Israel (i.e., in which all share the kingdom as in, e.g., the "democratization" characteristic of Isa. 40–55 or the kingly anointing that is extended to all the people in Joel 2).

45. The internal distinctions of election are correlative, if also subordinate, to the distinction between Israel and the gentile nations. They constitute the order of election that restrains the idolatry and injustice of Israel, which would otherwise lead toward the dissolution of Israel as a people before God. Though Barth does not make this claim in this way as far as I know, the correlation between the internal distinctions of election and the distinction between Israel and the gentiles is important to note at this juncture.

46. Barth, CD, II/2, 55–56.

of the first over the second or any "natural" or automatic process. Moreover, for David to be chosen by God was for him not to preempt God's removal of Saul, who was himself irrevocably God's anointed, but to wait upon the electing movement of God to give David the throne.[47] This is, again, what election means politically. The people of Israel is not a "natural," automatic, or human-made order. It is an order patient with God's election.

> It is necessary that he [David] should first go through that long period of concealment. It is necessary that he himself should not lift a finger to shorten that period; that he should prefer to let himself be driven to the southern heathen; that he should prefer to serve the Philistines (1 Sam. 21:11f; 27:1f; 28:1f; 29:1f), rather than to tread the path of rebellion against Saul's government; that he should prefer to expose himself to constant perils of death rather than shed Saul's blood. It is necessary that he should show absolute reverence for Saul as the Lord's anointed, not only throughout his whole life, but even after his death. All this is necessary because he is the elect of God as distinct from the elect of man or from any self-election; because he cannot seek its confirmation through men, but can only in fact find and receive it—at the moment of its divine confirmation. Further, it is necessary that he should be persecuted unto death by Saul as the (divinely instituted) bearer of the kingship by Israel's grace, and be continually saved only as by a miracle from the fate planned for him. "There is but a step between me and death" (1 Sam. 20:3). "The king of Israel is come out to seek a flea, as when one doth hunt a partridge in the mountains" (1 Sam. 26:20). This is as necessary as the condemnation of Jesus at the hands of Pilate, who himself did not act without power given him from above. For only as one harried unto death and delivered from such distress by God does David seal with his being the decree of God that he shall become the prince of a people which is itself continually harried but also continually delivered.[48]

---

47. Ibid., 289.

48. Ibid., 373–74. The limit on violence implied by election is borne out in the way Barth continues: "And it is further necessary that not only in respect of Saul, but in general, David should not be bloodguilty, as is visible in his remarkable last instructions (1 Kgs. 2). In his own person he is again to manifest the divinely elected king in the fact that it is really left to God to avenge him fittingly upon his enemies. The fact that for this reason David orders the

That God's election effects distinctions within the elect community (that one or some are elect within the elect) does not imply that the elect within are elect to the absolute exclusion of the other(s). God's election of one or some remains for the sake of all the elect. God has elected not only David but also Saul, just as God elected not only Judah but also Israel, and so no voice can claim, in the name of the Son of David or any derivative, secular messianism, to be the "new" elect over against the elect of the past. Christians cannot disown any boughs or limbs of that past that have branched into the present, however disdained or feared they may be.[49] They cannot preempt the decision of God, no matter the danger. "The Lord forbid that I should raise my hand against the Lord's anointed" (1 Sam. 26:11). God's election, which is primary in the constitution of the people, both shapes Israel as a unique whole and differentiates within Israel for the sake of the whole of Israel's promised future. The distinguishing activity of God's election is thus the basis and development of Israel's oneness. Impatience with this activity and the destruction that such impatience invites is key to the history of the northern kingdom of Israel. "The peculiar sinful element in the sins of Jeroboam and of the northern Israelites as a whole is . . . [that] they compromise the house of David, and his people, and the temple in Jerusalem and therefore the promise and hope of Israel."[50]

The internally distinguishing movement of God's election through Israel's history is revealed in its fullness in the elect one Jesus, the Son of David. As Israel's Messiah, he does not despise or disown

---

eventual removal of his most loyal, but bloody assistant Joab, and that this Joab is buried in the wilderness (1 Kgs. 2:34), is of a piece with this. In short, it is necessary that the being of David should exhibit a series of features which, as far as any palpable likeness is concerned, make him absolutely and consistently dissimilar to the typical figure of the oriental melek of the period." See also 408 on the unity of David and Saul in their witness to the one true king.

49. Cf. David's treatment of his supporters Rechab and Baanah (2 Samuel 4) as well as Mephibosheth (2 Samuel 9).

50. Barth, CD, II/2, 401. See also 326.

Israel's corruption but receives it as his very own, in the flesh, so that, crucified and raised from the dead, he represents the oneness of God's election of Israel. Much as the prophet of Bethel was united to the man of God of Judah in a common grave, in death and judgment (1 Kgs. 13:26-32),[51] Jesus was united with all Israel in dying on a cross, the life of this oneness culminating in his resurrection. There is therefore no messianic political existence beyond the covenant community of Israel, much less a people *made* by overcoming the inadequacies of Jewishness. That the people of the God of Israel is elect means that those who are already the people of Israel are fundamentally irreplaceable and indivisible, whatever their internal differences. Such differences can be ordered finally and only to the oneness of the people.

> We cannot aspire to get beyond the existence of the Israel, and hidden in it the Church of Jesus Christ, which then and there [at the hearing of the command] moved towards and derived from the fulfilment of the covenant of grace. The people of God in *all* its members and in the whole life of its members can only be this people—Abraham and Peter.[52]

Christians have tried to "get beyond" the existence of Israel in more ways than one. For example, hand in hand with modern, Euro-American political revolution and order (ch. 3 above) have gone the historiography and biblical scholarship whereby some description of ancient Near Eastern religion renders the "they" of the Israelite past fundamentally different from "us." More often, the moral distinction is less veiled, as when we openly declare that we have reached some moral superiority vis-à-vis Israel of long ago when it had yet to graduate from religio-political tribalism to the ethical monotheism of the prophets and Jesus.[53] One way or another, those carried along by the narrative of the West have wanted "the people" to be a predicate

---

51. Ibid., 406.
52. Ibid., 706, emphasis his. Cf. the unity of Judas and Peter in Christ on 282, 475.

of human subjectivity (e.g., what "we" have achieved and how "they" failed), that is, we have predicated the identity of the people of God on what some have done and others have not done, particularly on what some have believed and others have not believed. We have then hallowed and grounded that subjectivity with claims to divine election or, its God-less equivalent, nature. In effect, we have claimed to constitute our political self, to be the makers of the people that we are, having distinguished ourselves from those who are not. Against this tendency Barth insists that the people of God is not a predicate of human subjectivity; it is not a human-made order. In addition to the oneness of Israel and the church, the second way in which we may understand the primacy of election according to Barth, then, is the *secondary* character of human subjectivity in the constitution of the people of the God of Israel. To be sure, the subjectivity of Israel is not immaterial to who it is, for God's election works on and in its subjectivity. But we may speak of the constitution of Israel in terms of its subjectivity, Barth insists, only as its/their *response to* and fulfillment of God's primary, electing activity.

---

53. The Jews that have branched from then to the present easily find themselves on the negative side of this distinction, representing what good Christians have left behind in order to be ourselves. Or, in other cases, Jews find themselves trading in the Christian dualization of Israel in order to repudiate their share in Israel's darkness and secure a share in its Christian light (e.g., proving their "spirituality"). This is analogous to the way people "of color" in modernity have found themselves having to trade in Whiteness, to become as White as possible, to secure a share in the benefits of a society dominated by the representatives of Whiteness. As we saw in chapter 3 above, this analogical relation is not incidental or merely formal, but material and historically derivative. The historiography whereby Israel is taken to have passed into "ethical monotheism" from something obviously inferior owes a great deal to Abraham Geiger and to the history of religions school, as shaped by Julius Wellhausen and popularized by figures such as Ernst Troeltsch.

2. The Secondary Nature of Human Subjectivity
in the Constitution of the People of God

I realize that this claim offends the most sacred of modern sensibilities, as we desperately want to have decided who we are and be in control of our future. So many of our popular films deliver the lesson that we are who we choose to be. We have designated such self-determination "freedom," and we bristle at any suggestion that the shape of our existence is not up to us. To be a people has come to mean to choose our own existence. One variation of this offense at God's determination of who we are, evident in Yoder's account of peoplehood in chapters 1 and 2 above, is the complaint that the ongoing membership of the unfaithful in the people of God renders the people itself false and inconsequential, its ethics immaterial to who it is. Such a "people" cannot be the people of God, it is thought, for it cannot witness to the holy and loving God who is; supposedly only a righteous and loving people can do that.[54] But as Barth insists time and again, according to Scripture our existence is thankfully not up to us, and that is because the loving God who created the world has refused to leave us to our own devices. God has determined the existence of the people of God—in Christ—to become one of loving God and one another, and this free determination by God is called election, which cannot be undone along the way by human failure to love as God has loved us. Thus, the election of Israel cannot be undone by Israel's failure.

Not surprisingly then, perhaps the clearest indication that the people of God is not a predicate of its own subjectivity is the inability

---

54. Offense at the scandal of the election of Israel, in fact, cannot be limited to the modern West. Premodern churches, too, insisted on various measures of exclusion of the Jews, if not their outright destruction, lest the activity of the church (e.g., its doctrine, institutions, achievements) be deemed inconsequential to God's revelation, that is, to the truth. See, e.g., Justin Martyr, *Dialogue with Trypho*; Jeremy Cohen, *Living Letters of the Law: Ideas of the Jew in Medieval Christianity* (Berkeley: University of California Press, 1999).

of its rebellion or corruption to undo who the people is. Israel remains itself in its deepest sin, because Israel is who it is by God's election rather than anything Israelites do or don't do; Israel cannot be disinherited even by its own unfaithfulness or injustice.[55] In fact, as Barth has said above, the possibility and actuality of rebellion and contradiction among the people of God "is not just a sign but a concrete part of the reality of the grace of Israel's God," who refuses to forget or abandon the rebellious but claims and uses them for the sake of the blessing of all Israel and, with it, the rest of the world.[56] The subjective division and opposition in Israel's historical course and destiny thus witness to the primacy of election for who Israel is

> with a force which was impossible for the undivided kingdom, monarchy and prophecy. For the human division speaks much more loudly than any human solidarity could ever do of God Himself as the real basis of Israel, and not its own kings and prophets. Just because of the division there are now authentic relations in the history of Israel. Just because these men—the peoples, kings and prophets—on both sides of this relation show themselves to be so incomplete and so helpless on their own account, they become completely authentic occasions for authentic revelations of God, and as such reveal the authentic meaning of the existence of Israel.[57]

There is no election that is not the election of the ungodly,[58] and it is precisely the failures of Israel's history that give crucial testimony to God's election of Israel. In those failures, Israel is revealed to be not the people who is subjectively right in relation to God but the one

---

55. Cf. Barth's remark above that Jesus' being Israelite "is independent either of Israel's unbelief or the faith of the Church. It cannot be destroyed by Israel's unbelief and therefore it is not to be denied in the faith of the Church but openly confessed" (*CD*, II/2, 204).

56. Ibid., 402. Cf. 1 Tim. 1:12-17.

57. *CD*, II/2, 403. One might be tempted by this claim to say, as Paul anticipates in Rom. 3:8, "Let us do evil so that good may come." But God's faithfulness never justifies our unfaithfulness. It only testifies to its futility and thus promotes faithfulness. Below, I will question Barth's claim that human division witnesses "more loudly" than human solidarity to God's election.

58. The christological basis of this assertion will be clarified below under "The Judgment of the Elect."

people whom God has chosen and is thus making right. Moreover, it is only the God who holds a subjectively mixed people together across time and space that enables some of them to be good and promises that the whole people will be saved from its injustice. Even in its disobedience, then, Israel remains not only Israel but, as such, the servant of God.

> It is also God's aim that Israel should become obedient to its election . . . in order that in this way the differentiation within the community should confirm its unity. But God does not wait till Israel is obedient before employing it in His service. This is settled and completed in and with its election as such, so that Israel cannot in any way evade it, whether it is obedient or disobedient. God does not make the purpose He has with Israel dependent on Israel's attitude to it.[59]

In the course of his argument for the primacy of God's election over human subjectivity in the constitution of the people of God, and how this impinges upon its political formation and ethics, Barth takes aim at several watchwords of the modern discourse of peoplehood: words such as "self-determination" and *tabula rasa*, words that claim that the people and its derivative persons are self-made. On the contrary, Barth insists, "His [i.e., God's] decision precedes every creaturely decision. Over against all creaturely self-determination it is pre-determination—*prae-destinatio*."[60]

---

59. Barth, *CD*, II/2, 207. See also ibid., 573: "It is clear, therefore, that what Israel does and fails to do under God's claim is one thing, but the fact that it is always the people claimed by God, that God does not cease to declare His will to it, is another. And this other holds whatever has to be thought and said about this people's answer to what God says. Its disobedience may be exposed and it may be convicted of its unfaithfulness, but it still has the Law. . . . It is never released from the obligation which this imposes. It is allowed no escape from this obligation. It may set little or no store at all by the fact that it is characterised in this way. Yet it always has the honour done it by the fact that it stands under this obligation. It bears it always, and therefore against all its deserts, in and in spite of its utter unworthiness, it also bears the grace which is the secret of this claim." Cf. 235–37, 261.
60. Ibid., 19. Cf. 31.

We are never *tabula rasa*, and we cannot and must not try to make ourselves such. Integral to the humility in which we must ask what we are according to the divine command is the sober recognition that we always come from the school of the divine command and that we have not been in vain to that school.[61]

What must be made explicit in this context, although Barth himself does not do so, is that the predetermination of the people of God involves the whole of the people of God who have lived and continue to live in the flesh, among them the Jews. Predetermination is not the work of a docetic God. The determining presence of the whole people, that is, of God's election in the flesh, belies any claim to constitute a *tabula rasa*. Whatever the force of members' subjectivity in their existence as the people of God, it is not original or originating but the fruit of a relation to God and to the rest of the people whom God has already elected into being (e.g., their parents, whom they are commanded to honor, among the many others that shape them). A Christian community of a particular time or place is therefore unable to constitute itself a unique and independent people (or themselves as unique and independent persons); such a community can live only as part of the people whom God has already constituted by election and will continue to constitute by that same election.[62]

61. Ibid., 644–45.
62. Carl Schmitt recognized the contrived nature of modern peoples' claims to natural or otherwise legal constitutions. But this leads him to a political theory that usurps God's election of Israel in the form of an originating, human decision that can emanate only *ex nihilo*: "That constitutive, specific element of a decision is, from the perspective of the content of the underlying norm [e.g., the basis of legality], new and alien. Looked at normatively, the decision emanates from nothingness. The legal force of a decision is different from the result of substantiation. Ascription is not achieved with the aid of a norm; it happens the other way around. A point of ascription first determines what a norm is and what normative rightness is" (*Political Theology*, 32). The fundamental political question that a norm or concept of legality is unable address, according to Schmitt, is that of who. Who bears the authority to interpret/apply the norm or the law? From whom does it come in the first place? This is *the* aporia of modern peoplehood, since it has despised God's election of Israel in the flesh. Schmitt, however, does not realize this, and so he develops a disastrous "christological" theory of the human Führer, whose ascribed sovereign power of decision is the ground of political and legal order, the determinant of friend and enemy, and the possibility of democracy. This theory has found application in the

Turning to the scriptural basis of Barth's claim that the people of God is not a predicate of human subjectivity but of God's election, we need only point out some illustrative features of the biblical moments already cited in support of the oneness of the elect people.[63] First, the witness of the false prophet of Bethel:

> One thing at least is made perfectly clear in the figure of this prophet [the prophet of Bethel]: that the one true God of Israel, even if He is completely misunderstood and even if He is revered in a way which is quite false and illegitimate, has not ceased to be its God; that His Law and also His promise continue to stand even in relation to Israel. He, God, is the substance of the covenant of grace between Himself and His people. Therefore this substance is indestructible, however much it may be attacked by seducers and seduced, by Israel and then by Judah itself.[64]

The lying prophet of Bethel became the bearer and messenger of the Word of God "apart from and against his own intention . . . simply because God is always God, because He has not cast away His people, His whole people Israel."[65] Even in its most overt rebellion all Israel remains, however unwittingly, the elect servant of God. Likewise, David's becoming God's chosen ruler of Israel cannot be predicated on anything that David did. David's egregious sins show that his overshadowing Saul was "certainly not because he was hewn from another kind of wood."[66] It was because he was God's elect. Even

---

growing emergency powers of the executive of the United States, which no longer require constitutional basis (see Giorgio Agamben, *The State of Exception*, trans. Kevin Attell [Chicago: The University of Chicago Press, 2005]).

63. The biblical and christological basis of election is of course crucial. Without it, election has often been understood as a divine determination of human existence as such (i.e., as an act of mere sovereignty), apart from the particular way in which the Bible and Jesus reveal that determination to us, apart from the particular history in which we find ourselves. "Once we are freed from this presupposition [of election as the determination of human existence as such], there is no further point in attempting in some way or other to derive the divine election of grace from the existence of heathen and Christians, or of good Christians and bad. There is no further point in attempting to understand and fashion the doctrine of election as an answer to questions raised by the facts of experience" (Barth, *CD*, II/2, 44).

64. Ibid., 402.

65. Ibid., 407.

Judas, the betrayer of the elect one in whom the people of God is elect, does not cease to figure among the elect because of his betrayal. Quite the contrary: there "can be no doubt that—in a way which is basic—he [Judas] co-operated positively, against his will and deserts, in the task of the apostolate and the Church as it is grounded on the election of Jesus Christ."[67] As the Jew that Judas was, he was an apostle of Jesus, a disciple of Christ, a Christian. We may and should say that the course of his existence was not complete in his betrayal of the Messiah and his suicide. But we must also say that by God's election, as the betrayer he is a constitutive part of the people of God, not an aberration of some timeless, nonchristological standard by force of his own subjectivity (i.e., his sins).

The "standard" of Christ himself is for Barth the fundamental basis of the claim that the people of God is not a predicate of human subjectivity. Jesus did not do or not do something whereby he made himself God's elect. His own doing and not doing was a response to the election of God that constituted him the political being that he was and is. "It is not that He [Jesus] does not also elect as man, i.e., elect God in faith. But this election can only follow His prior election, and that means that it follows the divine electing which is the basic and proper determination of His existence."[68] It is not as Jesus chooses the good or who to be but "as He is elected by the grace of God that the good is done."[69] And this good that is done in Jesus is not a supersession of Israel, much less an overcoming of Jewishness or even a repudiation of Israel's sinners. This good is his solidarity with

---

66. Ibid., 382. See also 383.
67. Ibid., 503. Here it is clear that God's election does not operate on some plane separate from human subjectivity. God's election claims human subjectivity, such that what the people think they've done or wanted to do is not the same as what they have in fact done according to God's election. Retrospection is crucial to the ability to discern the difference. See also 477, 480, 488, 504.
68. Ibid., 103.
69. Ibid., 517.

the people of Israel even to the depths of its subjective corruption, to the depths of Israel's opposition to its calling by election, which thus claims Israel in its opposition.[70] Such is the obedience of Jesus' death and the representation of God's election of Israel in the flesh.

The people is therefore not a predicate of its subjectivity but, by God's election, the predicate of the Subject who is God in Messiah.[71] The people is not defined by its deciding rightly according to the way Jesus decided rightly, nor by enacting its freedom and independence from political oppressors or "foreign" elements. The people is held together by God's election in Christ even in its/their deciding wrongly.[72] Israelite oppressors of Israel must indeed be opposed but not disowned or forgotten. The church is thus one with others who have heard the call of the God of Israel, however alien they may seem or hostile they may be.

That the existence of the people of God is not predicated on its subjectivity but on God's election also means that it must engage those outside the people of Israel in the trust that the integrity of the people of God is not a matter of preserving itself or of imposing closure upon its identity. Its integrity is a matter of God's election, which does not impose such closure but opens into the hospitable fullness of Christ, God's love for the whole world made flesh.

When Barth does describe the people of God with reference to its subjectivity, he characteristically does so in terms of its response to and fulfillment of the electing activity of the God of Israel. Israel is the people that *hears* the word of God rather than only the people that obeys that word. Whatever the people does, good or bad, it

---

70. Ibid., 425–26; 475.
71. Ibid., 539–40.
72. This is why the people of God cannot be reduced to a mythological community of those who obediently follow Jesus—not because following Jesus is not entirely possible, but because Jesus embraced as his own those who did not follow him. And this act of Jesus is not something that Jesus rightly decided to do at some point but who Jesus is from beginning to end as God's elect, in whom the elect people is represented.

can do only in response to God's election, and can never thereby become or cease to be the people of God.[73] Those who respond rightly to hearing the word of God remain united to those who don't.[74] The people does not create or sever its relation to God, and thus itself, by the way that it responds.[75] The people can respond only because that relation, and thus itself, has already been created by God.[76] Its subjectivity can take place only within its determination by God's election. It is therefore not in possession of any standard of conformity to its identity. Rather, as Gamaliel bears faithful witness in Acts 5 (see chapters 1 and 2 above), the people continues to meet the electing power of the living God from outside itself, somewhat hidden from its view, as the power of Christ was hidden in the weakness of the cross.[77]

That the people of the God of Israel is a predicate of God's election rather than its own subjectivity is good news. Because God's election is prior to and stronger than the subjectivity of the people of God, the people cannot undo or forget itself (or be undone or forgotten by

73. Ibid., 235–40. See also 199, 735.
74. The Christian life is therefore a life of confessing sin and solidarity with those who respond to God's election unfaithfully (ibid., 213, 769). Accordingly, it makes no sense to wonder whether one figures among the elect of the God of Israel, as if that depended on some quality of human consciousness or moral achievement, for to ask about that God's election is already to have been seized by it, to have heard the word of God, to find oneself called and among the elect (ibid., 186). In other words, to be able to name sin as transgression is already to be on the way to forgiveness.
75. Ibid., 632. Here Barth speaks particularly to the relation created by the command of God. The people of God does not create that relation by obeying it. The people of God already finds itself in that relation when it has heard it. The command is itself electing.
76. That the people is creation rather than creator—and particularly that it is a sinful part of creation—means that it cannot decide who it is. That eternal decision is the election of God (ibid., 754, 756). Any human attempt to make such a decision is precisely what Barth calls sin.
77. Ibid., 637. See in this connection Bonhoeffer's claim that Jesus is and acts "in the incognito of history, in the flesh. . . . The nearer the revelation, the thicker must be the disguise; the more penetrating the question of Christ becomes, the more impenetrable must be the incognito" (Dietrich Bonhoeffer, *Christ the Center*, trans. Edwin H. Robertson [San Francisco: Harper Collins, 1960, 1978], 38, 110). The electing power of God in the weakness of Christ is revealed only by the light of the resurrection and exaltation of Christ, which never cease to be the resurrection and exaltation of the crucified (111). See also Dietrich Bonhoeffer, *The Cost of Discipleship*, trans. R. H. Fuller (New York: Touchstone, 1995), 183–88.

other peoples). Because of God's election, the people of Israel is the people of promise; in the flesh the people is the political condition of the possibility of forgiveness as well as the locus of that forgiveness when it comes.[78] This is what is ignored when the people of God is predicated on its subjectivity (e.g., on its faithfulness). When we say that the election of God holds only where it is confirmed in human faithfulness, that it is ontically equivalent to a community of the faithful, we say in effect that God's election is no stronger than our faith, that God's forgiveness has no corollary in the way the people of God forgive one another. That is to deny God's election, and it brings with it the violence of human attempts at *making* the people with our own politics, at hardening the borders of the people of the past and replacing them. This is simply the refusal to forgive as God has forgiven us.

God, however, is faithful even when Israel is unfaithful. Election is God's making Israel by creating and owning the people of Israel in the flesh, making Israel the bearer of God's name, so that for God to forsake Israel in its unfaithfulness would be for God to deny God's self.[79] Instead of denying God's self, God continually meets the people in the abyss of its disobedience with the hope of repentance and forgiveness.

> Where else but in the depths of this abyss has He [Jesus] established His kingdom? Sinking into this abyss man will continually encounter Him and in Him will continually find and have One who does not desire his loss in this abyss and who, in spite of all the power of his impotence, will not tolerate or accept it.[80]

---

78. As we will see in ch. 6, the forgiveness of sins is not a timeless status or a feeling, but a material reality, the healing of the body of God's people, finally the resurrection of the dead.

79. Josh. 7:8-9; Dan. 9:15-19. Israel is the history of the name that God has made for God's self (Neh. 9:10; Ps. 79:10; Jer. 32:20). Cf. 2 Tim. 2:13: "If we are faithless, he [Messiah] remains faithful, for he cannot deny himself."

80. Barth, *CD*, II/2, 623.

Contrary to the presupposition of modern peoplehood, hearing the word of God as God's elect does not stand the hearers in a place of neutrality, whence the faithful could constitute themselves the "true" people of God over against those who respond unfaithfully. To have been seized by God's election in time is already to have been seized irrevocably by God's faithfulness and to have been made to stand as God's people. One may wish to distinguish oneself from another in the people of God by pointing to one's own faithful response to the "opportunity" of God's word and to the other's failure to respond faithfully. "But more is to be gained from noting the opportunity offered than how badly [the other] let it slip."[81] In refusing to forsake God's people, God refuses to let us finally forsake one another. Because the people of God is held together across time and space by God's election, because its checkered past has not been replaced and forgotten despite violent attempts to supersede it, the people's ongoing existence itself witnesses to the presence of the eternal God in its midst and to a future of blessing. It does this both for itself and for others who will participate in its forgiveness. In this way it is the people of promise.

To those who infer from the above that Barth has deprived humanity of its dignity, that the primacy of election renders human subjectivity immaterial to who the people of God is, Barth replies that human subjectivity is not disregarded but embraced and enabled within the purview of God's election. What is more, self-determination without God's election is not dignity but a denial of the (political) self, who is created and determined by God. Self-determination of the people and its persons is not the freedom in which the people constitutes itself, but the freedom for which God constitutes the people (assuming for a moment with Barth that self-determination is a concept worth redeeming).[82] While this freedom

81. Ibid., 618.

involves the limited possibility of unfaithfulness as occasioned by God's election, "the purpose and meaning of the eternal divine election of grace consists in the fact that the one who is elected from all eternity can and does elect God in return."[83] Election is indeed finally a determination to obedience, and the demand of God's election is such that finally "it can be fulfilled willingly or not at all."[84] Here we see that election cannot be understood as a dead decision of God that forever remains outside human subjectivity. Instead, election is the living presence of God that is both prior to and *in* human subjectivity, completed in the death and resurrection of the Messiah of Israel, the electing God and elected human being who elects God in response. The elect people of God finds its subjectivity, its obedience, its freedom, in him.[85]

But what we have seen of Barth's account may leave some with the mistaken impression that the living election of the people of God is a mild, always-inviting movement of God in time. And perhaps the principal complaint brought against the doctrinal primacy of election in the constitution of the people of God—indeed Yoder's complaint—is that it is not accountable to the loving God who is. How can a morally compromised people bear witness to the holy

---

82. Cf. Augustine, *Lib.* 1:15, 2:13.
83. Barth, *CD*, II/2, 178. See also 322, 413, 417–18.
84. Ibid., 569.
85. Barth develops this understanding with respect to the election of the individual, but it need not be limited to the individual. "The perfection of God's giving of Himself to man in the person of Jesus Christ consists in the fact that far from merely playing with man, far from merely moving or using him, far from merely dealing with him as an object, this self-giving sets man up as a subject, awakens him to genuine individuality and autonomy, frees him, makes him a king, so that in his rule the kingly rule of God Himself attains form and revelation. ... The Lion of Judah which has gained the victory—man in a state of utter and most abject responsibility over against God, who even in this responsibility, even in the acknowledgment of the absolute pre-eminence of God Himself, is and becomes an individual, and autonomous, and in the sphere of creation a sovereign being, and as such the image of God" (ibid., 179). As this rather Kantian moment shows, for Barth there is no fundamental conflict between the heteronomy of the human that is theonomy on the one hand and human autonomy on the other. Human autonomy is the culmination of the theonomy of election in covenant.

God? How can God's election avoid promoting a cool, imperious security? To such questions Barth answers that God's election, in the christological history in which the people of God finds itself, means judgment. God does not turn a blind eye to Israel's injustice. Election is not cheap grace. "There is no grace without the lordship and claim of grace."[86] The people of God "has to pay dearly for being God's chosen people."[87]

The Judgment of the Elect

That election is "good news" has been the assumption of the modern discourse of peoplehood—good news for the elect, that is. It has been bad news for those not elect, however. Having passed them over, or having selected them for exclusion, election has been understood as God's judgment for them, God's rejection of them. In fact, the judgment of those not elect (or elected for destruction) has often been itself the good news of election, as the life of the elect is supposedly built upon the destruction or subordination of those not elect, upon the elimination or subjugation of the enemy. Not to figure among "the people" has thus involved not only exclusion from the benefits of fictive modern peoplehood but often colonization and enslavement for the sake of the people that is considered elect. This remains, for example, the messianic or exceptionalist identity of the People of the United States, for the sake of which some simply must be exploited and destroyed.[88] As the elect, the people itself supposedly constitutes a good that justifies the destruction of those who seem to stand in

---

86. Ibid., 12.
87. Ibid., 261. It is in the historical course of this people that God's name is vindicated, that injustice is opposed and finally overcome by the justice of God. And because God has attached God's own name to the whole of Israel by God's own election, this vindication is finally the healing of all Israel. And because Israel cannot be healed apart from peace with the gentile nations, this vindication is finally the healing of the world.
88. See, e.g., Donald E. Pease, *The New American Exceptionalism*, Critical American Studies (Minneapolis: University of Minnesota Press, 2009).

the way of its predestined prosperity or are deemed the utilities of its success. Judgment is thus reserved for those who are excluded from the elect, while election is understood as precisely what spares the elect from God's judgment.[89] God's putative rejection of the Jews lies at the heart of this modern exceptionalism.

Barth opposes this tendency by arguing that the elect people is only itself as the judged people. The election of the people of God is indeed good news for the elect, but this is precisely because God does not leave that people alone in its corruption. Rather, the God of Israel judges the people and thus transforms it according to God's merciful purpose, which avails for both the elect people of Israel and the gentile nations. Because of the judgment of the elect, election finally means the peaceful oneness of the two, the peace of oneness for all (Eph. 2:11-22).

God has not elected an obedient people. God has taught Israel not to romanticize itself but to remember itself as "a stubborn people" (e.g., Deut. 9:6).[90] The living election of God therefore means judgment for Israel. This is, as mentioned above, what election meant for Jeroboam and the northern kingdom of Israel in their rebellion against the house of David. It is also what election meant for David and the southern kingdom in their own sins against the God of Israel. Judgment is crucial to the way that election orders Israel, excluding certain "possible" developments from Israel's future (e.g., a royal dynasty of Saul's or Jeroboam's descendants, the dissolution

---

89. Thus, on this traditional view operative in the modern discourse of peoplehood (i.e., that election means to be spared judgment), any judgment that is recognized as determining the elect people internally can be only a different judgment from that which determines those not elect, one that effects and confirms the distinction of the elect from those who are not elect. This dichotomization of the one God's judgment is precisely what Barth is criticizing.

90. Rather than predicating our identity on our moral superiority to Israel of old, the church would do well to follow the lead of the Tanakh (and the New Testament) and be more impressed by the failures of our history than our successes. This is the promising way of a repentant people rather than a triumphalist political memory whose lies about the past wreak havoc in the present. See, e.g., 1 Cor. 10:1-22.

of Judah into the northern kingdom or neighboring gentile peoples) while bringing about other developments (e.g., the absence of heirs to the throne in the line of Jeroboam, the royal dynasty of David's descendants, the life and promise of Judah).

But the gracious judgment of election does not limit and resist Israel's unfaithfulness at the final expense of Israel or of the gentile nations, Barth contends.[91] God's election, which identifies God's name with the whole of one people in the flesh and is revealed in its fullness in the cross and resurrection of the elect one, does not give up on Israel, whatever its unfaithfulness. It continues until the promise of Israel's election is realized, its covenant blessings fulfilled.[92] Because God cannot deny God's self, God's election of Israel persists *in* judgment through the unfaithfulness of the people, in whom God has invested God's self by name. This unrelenting resistance by God to unfaithfulness in Israel is good news, keeping the promise of forgiveness alive and forming Israel to serve God's purpose of blessing for the whole world. Yet, it makes the covenant history of Israel turbulent, as God refuses to leave beloved Israel alone. The people of God endures the refining fires of judgment, as God opposes Israel's idolatry and injustice. In its hottest moments in the Bible, the

91. Barth, *CD*, II/2, 13.

92. "[God's] anger is but for a moment; his favor is for a lifetime" (Ps. 30:5) so that judgment is not an opposing principle but a subordinate moment of life-giving election (ibid., 224). Yet, God's anger did endure some. While the judgment of the elect did not destroy the people, death still reigned. The judgment of election in Israel's turbulent history thus retains a certain ambiguity before the resurrection of Messiah, insofar as Israel can cling only to a promise not yet totally fulfilled (ibid., 387–88). But with the resurrection of Jesus, the good news of the judgment of the elect is finally disclosed. Not only does election entail judgment; the judgment of the elect is the grace that leads to resurrection. In the resurrection of Israel's Messiah the promise at work in the judgment of the elect is fulfilled. It is the dawning of the day of reconciliation promised in the covenant (e.g., Deuteronomy 30). Here we should note, though Barth does not, that the covenant blessings of this promise include peaceful unity with the gentile nations. Barth brings gentiles into the blessings of the covenant by the way they are represented in Christ "as man." But the blessing of peace with gentiles is not a represented but a historical reality of the covenant in the Tanakh, not a matter of timeless correspondence to christological "man" but fulfillment of Israelite prophecy in time (e.g., Isaiah 2).

judgment of the elect means war against Israel and the exile of many generations;[93] finally, it means the crucifixion of Israel's Messiah at the hands of disciples and friends, of other fellow Jews, and of Israel's gentile enemies.

Unlike the supersessionist election of modern peoplehood, the election of Israel is not a recipe for Israel's acting with impunity. God's election is the very basis for Israel's responsibility; it means the most terrible judgment when Israel responds to the justice of God's covenant commands with injustice. Because election means judgment *for Israel*, it does not authorize the violent assertion of the people of God against enemies in the name of God's judgment of others. Election does not translate to an imperative of political survival or dominance. On the contrary, politically, election means that Israel is to trust God with its survival and prosperity, at the mercy of God's commands (e.g., Isaiah's call upon Ahaz to trust God's provision for Judah and the house of David in Isa. 7). Nor does election entail disowning the judged in an effort to constitute a people "free" of judgment. The life and freedom of the people of God does not consist in inflicting, spurning, or escaping God's judgment. The people is created, sustained, and ordered *in* God's judgment of it, in God's opposition to Israel's unfaithfulness. The people is therefore called to the faithful endurance and remembrance of judgment, the life of oneness with the judged. This is the life in which the judgment of the elect culminates in forgiveness, in which election is good news even in judgment. It is finally the life of Messiah, in whom the people lives. He came to "save his people from their sins" (Matt. 1:21).[94]

---

93. This is also what it meant for non-Israelite peoples in the Bible. The difference is that without some remnant of worship of the one God in such non-Israelite peoples, they had no way of remembering who they were across generations, no way of finding final forgiveness, no way of surviving as peoples. A future of remembrance and forgiveness lay only in the worship of the one God who refuses the fragmentation of idolatry, the God of Israel.

94. Barth, *CD*, II/2, 361, 741. The electing God "avenges sin not by regarding but by forgiving it" (ibid., 35).

That election means judgment primarily for the elect is among the most crucial revisions that Barth makes to the Christian theological tradition. Traditionally, election has been precisely what spares the elect the divine judgment that is directed to others, who are in turn consigned to destruction, whether as passed over by election or elected for destruction (i.e., the reprobate). In this way, God's revelation, including God's self-revelation in Christ, was understood as the mechanism that simply *applies* the eternal divine decree of election lying hidden behind revelation, dividing humanity eternally. The eternal decree of election itself, that is, the word of God's very self, is supposedly not revealed.[95]

On the basis of an arbitrary division assigned to the hidden eternal decree, the church could conceive of itself as the "new" elect people of Israel that had replaced the "old," ambiguously "elect" people of Israel, that is, the people of salvation that had replaced the people of judgment. As we saw in the previous chapter, this move allowed the modern discourse of peoplehood to conceive of "the people" itself as pure vis-à-vis those it had replaced, and therefore pure vis-à-vis those it was not. Whether those associated with a parent or rival regime or with the societies the elect were authorized to colonize and destroy, the enemies of the elect could be consigned to the fires of judgment so that the elect could enjoy the exclusive benefits of election. To be the elect people was not only to be spared these excluding fires but often to unleash them on the enemy, who had been rendered killable by a doctrine of election that storied them, and not the elect, as the judged. Of course, an elect people of this nature was constantly in need of proving itself by distinguishing itself from the judged, whom God had chosen for destruction, whom God had not chosen at all, or who had not chosen God. And so election ironically promoted

95. Ibid., 65.

the elect people's attempt to make itself according to a metaphysical representation of itself as the new and exclusive Israel.[96]

But this whole imaginary of the division between the elect and the judged is to understand election as a principle of differentiation more determinative than the election of which we learn in the Bible, namely, the election of the Messiah and the people of God in him. Barth insists that the fullness of God's revelation in the Messiah and the story of Israel that the Bible relates are incompatible with such a hidden principle of differentiation.[97] There can be no hidden decree that is not fully revealed in Jesus the Son of God. What we are shown in Christ and what we are plainly told in the biblical story of Israel is that judgment falls within the purview of God's election of the people rather than falling primarily to a human realm excluded by God's election (cf. 1 Pet. 4:17).[98] Any realm of election *ad extra* that is devoid of God's judgment is mythical, for to be the elect is to be none other than the damned.[99]

Barth hardly needs to adduce a biblical basis for the judgment of the elect people Israel. While full of promise and blessing, the biblical history of Israel is also manifestly a history of judgment. One might think that the story changes in the New Testament, and that suddenly the elect people is that community spared the judgment that had afflicted Israel. Well, the story may advance or fill out in the New Testament, but it does not change. The people of God in the New Testament remains the people of Israel, and, as we've seen in the discussion of the oneness of the elect people above, the Christian

---

96. Ibid., 113. And here in "the perseverance of the saints" we find the Protestant roots of modern capitalism. See Max Weber's classic treatment of this in *The Protestant Ethic and the Spirit of Capitalism* (London: Routledge, 2001).
97. Barth, *CD*, II/2, 64–65, 110, 325–26, 423.
98. Barth recognizes that what distinguishes his revision from the Christian tradition that preceded him is not some better theological schema. "The decisive point is the reading of the Bible itself" (ibid., 148).
99. Thanks to Stanley Hauerwas for suggesting that the matter be put this way.

community enjoys the benefits of election only insofar as it shares in the judgment that is the lot of the elect. To be elect is to be judged. The people of God does not suddenly become morally unambiguous in the New Testament, obviously superior to the corrupt people of Israel of the preceding generations (or opponent communities). It includes both Judas, the betrayer of Jesus, and Peter, the foundational rock of Jesus' church who plays the Satan and then denies him three times in his greatest hour of need. And while it is true that Israelite communities or persons who overtly and even violently oppose Jesus' Messiahship endure judgment according to the New Testament, they do not thereby exclude themselves from the elect people. They have no power to do that. "According to the election, they are beloved because of the ancestors" (Rom. 11:28, my translation). They have found themselves irrevocably within the people of the God of Israel in time, and thus remain sisters and brothers of the church of Jesus.[100] Thus, Barth resists the destructive tendencies of the modern discourse of peoplehood by depriving it of an election that divorces the elect from the judged. According to the Bible, any such theopolitical identity is a violent and unsustainable fiction.

The primary basis for Barth's claim that election is both good news and judgment for the elect people of God, as borne witness by the biblical moments and figures already cited, is the crucified and risen Messiah of Israel, the elect one. The fullness of God's judgment can be sought nowhere but in the fullness of God's self-revelation, for in him is the fullness of God (Col. 1:19; 2:9). Jesus himself is the Word of God, both the Word of God's judgment and the Word of

---

100. "The New Testament account of Judas does not say that among the genuine apostles there was one who was an apostle only in appearance, or that among the presumed and supposed elect there was one who was actually rejected. What it does say is that it was one of the genuine apostles, one of the genuinely elect, who was at the same time rejected as the betrayer of Jesus" (Barth, *CD*, II/2, 459). Judas shows us that the rejected "cannot have the authority, dignity or power of an objective opponent of Jesus," but only an identity relative to the saving action of Jesus, which thus embraces the rejected (ibid., 504).

God's deliverance. In Jesus, the political indivisibility of judgment and election, as well as the relation between the two, is revealed. The judgment of Jesus' death is therefore not a departure from his election but the climax of his life as the elect one.

> He is elected man not only in His passion and in spite of His passion, but for His Passion.[101]

> That the elected man Jesus had to suffer and die means no more and no less than that in becoming man God makes Himself responsible for man who became His enemy, and that He takes upon Himself all the consequences of man's action—his rejection and his death. This is what is involved in the self-giving of God. This is the radicalness of His grace. . . . The wrath of God, the judgment and the penalty, fall, then, upon Him. And this means upon His own Son, upon Himself. . . . Why not upon the disobedient? Why this interposition of the just for the unjust by which in some incomprehensible manner the eternal Judge becomes Himself the judged? Because His justice is a merciful and for this reason a perfect justice. Because the sin of the disobedient is also their need, and even while it affronts Him it also moves Him to pity.[102]

> The truth is rather that as God fulfils this judgment in Jesus Christ, He treats this One who is judged as His Elect and eternally Beloved. The very condemnation and reprobation here executed on man are the decree and the work of the love in which He has, from all eternity and here and now in time, loved man and drawn him to Himself. Even this judgment is the form of God's eternal predestination and the effectual working out of it in time.[103]

In Christ, the elect people can be no people other than the judged people. Any attempt to identify its enemies as the judged is only to identify its enemies with Christ and therefore with itself. In the oneness of the elect one, there is no hiatus between judgment and election but rather the fulness of judgment and thus the fulness of

---

101. Ibid., 117. Here Barth cites the work of Gottlob Schrenk.
102. Ibid., 123–24.
103. Ibid., 739. See also 778. Barth of course entitles an entire section "The Judge Judged in Our Place" in *CD*, IV/1, 211ff.

election. These do not cancel one another out, but are together the life of Israel's Messiah, which culminates in the resurrection of the body. It is therefore in this judgment of the elect one, and the elect people in him, that the grace and mercy of God's election are finally revealed, however turbulent the history of the people along the way.[104]

We may clarify Barth's claim that the judgment of God reaches its fullness in and as the judgment of the elect by asking how deep the solidarity of Messiah with the judged goes, how far the catholicity of Jesus reaches. Barth's answer is that the rejected—the human life excluded by God's election in so much of the Christian tradition—is none other than Christ himself. As the elect one, he is the rejected of God.

> The death of Jesus unites what was divided, the elected and the rejected.[105]

> He is the Rejected, as and because He is the Elect. In view of His election, there is no other rejected but Himself.[106]

---

104. Precisely because Jesus is a person in Israel rather than a timeless principle, the people of God is not judged in the same way its Messiah is judged, as if the people were simply another instance of Christ. The people is judged *in* Christ. For Barth, because Jesus is God made flesh, the judgment that would otherwise destroy sinful humanity is taken into God's self, leaving for Jesus as human, and all those in him, the eternal life of resurrection, that is, the Spirit of God (Barth, *CD*, II/2, 162). The elect people is the circle in which human persons are in Christ and thus elect, the elect people mediating in this way the election of its persons. There is, nevertheless, a problem in Barth's account here (besides the counterfactual of "otherwise"). He wants to retain double predestination by saying that in Christ, God elected God for judgment and humanity for salvation, but Jesus' deity and humanity cannot be divided in this way. Whatever Jesus endures, he endures as both God and human. Against Barth, I submit that Jesus' being God for humanity does not preclude humanity's participation in his reprobation. But it is just that—humanity's historical *participation* in his reprobation, not humanity's enduring reprobation just as he does, not its repetition of the judgment of Messiah. Here we see an instance of the difficulties that attend Barth's placing the people in the formal domain of representation in Christ. In this case it runs aground on the Christology of Chalcedon, on the oneness of the *hypostasis* that precludes the twoness of Barth's double predestination.

105. Ibid., 229. "For this, in our flesh, according to His human nature, as the Son of David, He must be the Rejected. . . . But in Him, who was very God and very man, in perfect unity, the glory and the shame and abandonment were reality, one reality" (ibid., 365). See also 351.

God, by the decree He made in the beginning of all His works and ways, has taken upon Himself the rejection merited by the man isolated in relation to Him; that on the basis of this decree of His the only truly rejected man is His own Son; that God's rejection has taken its course and been fulfilled and reached its goal, with all that that involves, against this One, so that it can no longer fall on other men or be their concern.[107]

But, again, it is strictly and narrowly only in the portrait of the one Jesus Christ that we may perceive who and what a rejected man is. It is He who—just because of His election—is cast out from the presence of God by His righteous law and judgment, and delivered to eternal death. In the genuine fulfilment of genuine election it is His life which is truly the life of the man who must suffer the destructive hostility of God. The peculiarity of the position which He occupies among all others is that He took it upon Himself to be this man. God has made Him who is uniquely His Son and Friend "to be sin" [2 Cor. 5:21]. It is He who is the rejected individual.[108]

The judgment, rejection, and wrath of God, then, cannot be understood as rivals to God's love in Christ and therefore the lot only of God's enemies, as the modern discourse of peoplehood would have it. However counterintuitive, judgment, rejection, and wrath can be understood, in Christ, only as expressions of God's love. The rejected

is as such surrounded by the election and kingdom of Jesus Christ, and as such confronted by the superiority of the love of God. This love may

---

106. Ibid., 353. Barth goes on to say that because Christ is the elect only as he is the rejected, the rejected of the world cannot help but bear witness to Christ and so be embraced by God's election in him.

107. Ibid., 319. "Why is it that in the very desire to glorify this grace they [those of older predestinarian teaching] were so intent on opening up the gulf of this absolute contrast between the "elect" and the "rejected" ungodly? The only reason we can see is that they were not seriously prepared with childlike consistency to understand the grace of God as 'the grace of our Lord Jesus Christ.' It is for this reason that we are compelled at this point to arrive at a different conclusion" (ibid., 329).

108. Ibid., 352. "Since no one outside or alongside Him is elected as the bearer of divine rejection—no one outside or alongside Him is rejected. Where else can we seek and find the rejection which others have merited except in the rejection which has come on Him and which He has borne for them? This rejection cannot, then, fall on others or be their concern" (ibid., 421). See also 450–51, 495.

burn and consume him as a rejected man, as is fitting, but even so it is still to him the almighty, holy and compassionate love of God. And this very love does not permit but debars him from any independent life of his own alongside or apart from the life of the elect.[109]

Barth claims that the subjectivity of human communities and persons cannot undo their determination in Christ, and so those who reject the revelation of the God of Israel cannot be understood thereby to remove themselves from the embrace of God's election.[110] God rejects their rejection in Christ the rejected one. Thus, even the force of election that divides Israel—the force that makes internal distinctions within Israel (e.g., Israel and Judah, Saul and David)—can only serve finally to embrace the rejected and thus to embrace all Israel.[111] Furthermore, it is precisely the tension of election within Israel that draws the rejected gentile nations into the embrace of God's election of Israel, the election that is in its Messiah, who is Lord of all.[112]

> He is both the Elect of God and the Rejected of God, rejected because He is elect and elect in His rejection. But if this is so according to the exegesis of the New Testament, then we must understand the election stories of the Old Testament, if at all, as a prophecy of Christ even in their striking duality . . . not only in the type of the Israelite nation but also in the very different type of the excluded and yet not utterly excluded heathen nations.[113]

Election does not afford the people a basis for the exclusion of its enemies (i.e., of the Jews and whomever these are taken to represent). The politics of election, as revealed in Christ, can only be a politics of solidarity with the enemy. It can only be a politics of sharing in the

---

109. Ibid., 450–51.
110. Ibid., 356.
111. Ibid., 366, 378, 392, 406, 425–26.
112. Ibid., 275, 347. Cf. Matt. 10:17–18; 27:54; Rom. 11:11–36.
113. Ibid., 366. "And at this first and decisive place [i.e., Judas] . . . the Church stands and acts in identity with the Israel which rejected its Messiah, together with the heathen world which allied itself with this Israel, and made itself a partner in its guilt" (ibid., 460). See also 475.

judgment of the unjust, of taking responsibility for them, of seeing itself in them.[114] "What other kind of reality can the elect predicate of the rejected in the form of his neighbour than the peculiar reality of this 'beingwith'?"[115] Anything else will be the people's opposition to its own election in Christ, which can meet only with judgment, albeit the judgment of the elect.[116] This solidarity does not preclude discipline but is the very substance of the discipline of the people. Any measures that are taken to address injustice within the people or the threat of enemies will insist on the solidarity of the people with those judged in the endurance of those measures.[117] Any other course has disregarded the judgment of the elect and the corresponding hope of judgment. "With Jesus Christ the rejected can only *have been* rejected. He cannot be rejected any more,"[118] for it is none other than the Rejected who was raised from the dead.

> And at a first glance we may say that Jesus Christ did not suffer this [the judgment that befalls the disobedient], since it was in obedience that He humbled Himself unto death. But what follows from this obvious incongruity between His action and His suffering? It is certainly not that He suffered something different from the torment and death, the fate, which the rejected have earned and prepared for themselves. It is rather that He suffered this torment and death, this fate, which by His obedience He had not earned or prepared for Himself, for them, in the place of these rejected. . . . "For us"—who when we believe and confess it must consider ourselves to be in solidarity with those rejected Jews and Gentiles.[119]

---

114. Ibid., 450–53.

115. Ibid., 452–53. Per ch. 3 above, the refusal of this "beingwith" is the germ of what has since become the color line.

116. Because this is the judgment of Christ, it is not a judgment without hope. Even in the judgment of the elect in Christ, the people participates in Christ's death and may live in the sure hope of the resurrection that is the fruit of that judgment when it has run its course.

117. It is very difficult to claim to be engaged in this solidarity when those measures involve killing.

118. Barth, *CD*, II/2, 453, emphasis mine. For the constructive role of the unjust within the people according to election, see 456–58. Human beings under judgment and therefore among the elect cannot be denied or forgotten if the gospel of the grace of election is to be rightly lived and proclaimed.

For if in faith we can confess this for ourselves, we can do so seriously only as we recognise that we no less than they have deserved to be handed over to bondage by the wrath of God. We can confess it seriously only when we are in solidarity with them. . . . The recollection of what God has done for the world—He delivered His own Son for us—is not weakened, but strengthened, the more clearly we see what rejection means for others—or, better still, for ourselves—and what judgment it involves to be a man rejected by God.[120]

The catholicity of Jesus reaches not only to the obedient in Israel but to all Israel. And in reaching to all Israel, the catholicity of Jesus reaches to the whole world, as gentiles are moved to embrace the God of Israel as their own in the name of that God's Son, crucified as and for the rejected, and then raised. The election of Israel in its Messiah is thus ordered to God's making one people of peace of the whole world. It is God's very judgment of the elect under the power of Israel's promise—finally the death of Israel's Messiah—that makes this people.[121] In the judgment of the elect, we see that election is not a recipe for self-assertion and impunity. God's election bids

---

119. Ibid., 495.
120. Ibid., 497.
121. See my concern above about Barth's characterization of the election of the people in the Messiah as "another election" relative to the election that is all God's activity *ad extra* in Christ. Barth's account of the election of the people does not resolve all eschatological questions, of course. It does exclude an eschatology of disembodied, individual souls going to either heaven or hell forever, an eschatology totally foreign to the Bible, as the promised future is bodily in the whole creation healed of sin and death (ibid., 424). "But whereas the Church's doctrine of predestination ends and halts with this definition as in a cul-de-sac, and whereas its last word is to the effect that the elect finally 'go to heaven' as distinct from the rejected, the biblical view—in a deeper understanding of what is meant by the clothing of men with God's eternal glory—opens at this point another door. For as those who expect and finally receive eternal life, as the heirs in faith of eternal glory, the elect are accepted for this employment and placed in this service. They are made witnesses" (ibid., 423). Because Christ the elect one is the Word of God, the one who is with God and is God, the rejection that derives from election is the rejection of God's self such that there can be no rejection that is not thoroughly and finally the love of grace (ibid., 100–1). Instead of resolving all eschatological questions in defiance of God's revelation in time, Barth's account deprives us of any argument whereby we might anticipate the final exclusion of our enemies by destroying them. Because of Christ, we must hold out hope for the participation of all in the eternal life of resurrection, and we must love accordingly. Because of Christ, we *can* love accordingly, that is, as God has loved us.

God's people come and die. This is a death in the service of God's catholic and covenant love, a death that the elect people cannot finally avoid.[122]

The question of the elect people of God had long been understood in the Christian tradition as the most basic question about both God and humanity, about the who and how of being human according to the God of Christian revelation.[123] And so it remained for the modern discourse of peoplehood, whatever the secularizing tendencies and poverty of its answer. The *Judenfrage* that that discourse developed in time tests the truth and hope of the gospel by questioning the power of God *as* the God of Israel. It compels us to ask who the God of Jesus the Jew is, and what it means to be human as determined by that God and not some other of our own making. It prevents us from continuing to enquire into election in the abstract, at a supersessionist remove from Israel and Jesus in the flesh. It requires us to ask what it means to be the people of the God of Israel as disclosed in the Messiah and by what hope that people lives. Because the God of Israel is the creator, this is to ask by what hope the entire creation lives. Such are the stakes of the Jewish Question.

Barth sees that the gospel is betrayed by the claim that God has disowned or demoted the Jews. Faithful proclamation of the gospel must therefore refuse simply to nourish the modern discourse of peoplehood. Nor can it remain aloof, as it already finds itself in the fray. It must confront the violence of modern peoplehood with the

---

122. "When Christ calls a man, he bids him come and die" (Bonhoeffer, *Cost of Discipleship*, 89).

123. "The question was not merely an incidental question, as the older theologians knew only too well. It was the question of the beginning of all things. It was the question of the knowledge of God's absolutely decisive disposing which takes place in the eternity before time was, and which legislates for salvation or damnation, for life or death, both in time and in the eternity when time shall have ceased to be. It was the question of the knowledge of the specific order of the kingdom or rule of God, with all that that means for the existence, the preservation, the history and the destiny of creation and man. The question was in fact the actual and burning question: What is to become of us at the hand of God?" (Barth, *CD*, II/2, 151–52).

peace of the elect people of God as revealed in Israel's Messiah, the elect one. Barth does this by refusing to offer yet another Christian description of the people of God whose promise is predicated on the subjective rightness of its own constituency, whether in what they believe or the way they live. The peace of the people of God as revealed in Israel's Messiah is predicated on God who loves humanity rather than on humanity, on God's election of Israel in Christ rather than on Israel's obedience. Barth exposes the election of modern peoplehood as not God's election but self-election. Contrary to modern assumptions, there simply is no self-constituted people or person. Claims to self-constitution can only deny the material contingency of the collective or individual self in question, and the violence of such modern claims has been manifest. It is God's election rather than a human society that constitutes the political solidarity in and through which peace unfolds in the midst of violence.

To expose the self-election of modern peoplehood is for Barth to name its christological heresy, its docetic denial of the Jewish flesh of the God who has created the world. By remembering God's irrevocable election of Israel, Barth refuses the Jewish foil of modern peoplehood. Jewish flesh cannot be shorn away from the people of God so as to retain a "pure" or "spiritual" constituency that is supposedly of the people's own making. The mythically pure political identity of reference for modern peoples is simply false. They are neither natural nor elect peoples. "We the people" cannot be accepted in these supersessionist terms, which are corruptions of the Bible's teaching on election. The elect people is not based on an original personality of its own but descends from a wandering Aramean, adopted by God, not a natural child. It consists of no invariant substance across time but has always been in constant variation in response to the Word of God, contingent at every point on the faithful and sustaining presence of God in the midst of its own unfaithfulness and lack of self-sustaining identity. Without the possession of its identity as a timeless essence, Israel knows who it is only by looking back upon its history as the faithfulness of God, a history whose future must therefore remain open and somewhat dark, as must the people's knowledge of itself. Supersessionist, modern orders of peoplehood have imposed closure on the identity of "we the people" and claimed false independence for themselves in defiance of the history of the people of God per its biblical witness. Such "peoples" can be nothing more than contingent political orders of only relative integrity, dependent in manifold ways upon what they say they are not, and determined not by themselves but by the rule and presence of the God of Israel in Christ. This determination, unlike the election of the people of God, is their passing away and only in this way their service to God. Modern peoplehoood must therefore be resisted in and by the church wherever it promotes a human existence that is not humanity in Christ. That is to say, its violence must be resisted with the Christian love that witnesses to God's election, as the church embodies God's alternative to the modern desperation of human-made order, as it participates in the people made by God through the cruciform discipline of forgiveness.

I have focused on the way the election of Israel according to Barth confronts modern claims to peoplehood. But given the way in which the modern discourse of peoplehood has constructed selves that somehow "represent" the people (chapter 3 above), we might also say that the election of Israel refuses the false integrity or independence of such representative selves, whether they be individual persons or "intermediate associations" such as churches. We imagine our selves in possession of some mythological integrity whereby we can do without one another, disown one another, forget one another, even destroy one another. But the election of Israel in its Messiah insists that we are neither independent nor in possession of any such integrity but are made by the God of Israel out of one another and for one another.

The History of the Election of Israel in the Flesh

God's Story of Hope

Having articulated some key resources of Karl Barth's account of God's election for resisting the violent tendencies of the modern discourse of peoplehood, I now turn to address its principal liability. This liability stems from the formal register of his Christology as it bears on his account of election, rendering it inadequately responsive to the messy history of God's electing activity and thus losing sight of that history. Barth's account can hold in view only a mythological struggle between two christological forms (i.e., natures) of the people—Israel and the church. Instead of pointing to how the people has been determined historically by God's election in Christ, which should be able not only to confirm but increase our knowledge of Christ, Barth's account tends to eclipse the history of God's electing the people with the formal categories of his Christology. One might think that a more historical account of God's election can only push the account away from a christological foundation that is so crucial according to Barth. But I submit that Christology itself can and must be more historical, particularly with respect to the history of Israel. In this chapter, I intend to show that a more historically implicated and responsive account of God's election in Christ 1) subverts the problematic tendencies that Barth's account perpetuates and 2) offers resources that Barth's account lacks for being Christian in societies permeated by the modern discourse of peoplehood.

Losing Sight of the History of God's Electing Activity: A Critique of Barth

Barth understands God's election of the people as God's moving it from its Israelite form to its church form. The "history" of God's election is the tension between these two formal poles. Against Barth, I will argue that God's election is the historical formation of the one elect people in the flesh in relation to the gentile nations according to God's christological promise. The key difference of election is not a formal one between Israel and the church but the material one between Israel and the gentiles.[1] This is not a timeless difference, but an unfolding one that gives the people of God the shape that it historically has acquired to the present. Of this people made by God in and through time, Christ is not so much the representative as the promise and cornerstone. In a formal realm of representation the people is rather neatly divisible into two (or any other number), such that a representative Christ divides the people in a way that supposedly corresponds to the twoness of Christ himself (e.g., God and human, election and rejection). But, as we will see, the biblically

---

1. This allows Barth's helpful insights about the christological relation between God and the human to flow into the relation between Israel and the gentiles. As an unfolding material difference, it is not predicated on a timeless distinction that breeds only hostility in time, but on a nearing future of reconciliation in Christ, present through the Spirit of his resurrection.

attested history of the people of God in the flesh defies such twoness, so that imposing such twoness on that history is not to see how God has determined the people materially in Christ, but to underdetermine the description of the people with its supposed representation in Christ.

Let me begin by illustrating the problematic formal register in which Barth describes the elect people of the God of Israel:

> For the sake of His mercy, and therefore for the sake of Jesus Christ and through His agency, God wills to bring into being His community in its form both as Israel and the Church—this one people with its twofold testimony and message which in both respects means the proclamation of the one Lord Jesus Christ: on the one side His death, on the other His resurrection; on the one side the rejection of man which God has taken upon Himself in Christ, on the other the election in which God has turned to man in Him. The history of this one and twofold people as the circumference of the man Jesus of Nazareth, the history of its preparation and guidance to be the witness of the one Saviour, and therefore the witness of God's mercy to the whole world, the Bearer of which both derives from this people and is the origin from which this people springs—this history is the history of God's covenant of grace to which the interest of the whole Bible in both its parts is indissolubly directed.[2]

Admittedly everything has a different form in the two cases. This difference is in the relation of election to the rejection which inevitably accompanies it. And it is in the twofold determination of Christ Himself that this difference has its basis. It consists in the fact that the Israelite form of the elected community reveals its essence in its Old Testament determination, as determined from the side of elected man as such, whilst its Church form, on the other hand, reveals the same essence of the elected community in its New Testament determination, as determined by the electing God as such. This ineffaceable differentiation of its essence is made plain by the fact that the people of the Jews (delivering up Jesus Christ to the Gentiles to be put to death) resists its

---

2. *Church Dogmatics*, ed. G. W. Bromiley and T. F. Torrance, 4 vols. in 13 parts (Edinburgh: T & T Clark, 1956–77), II/2, 677–78.

divine election, whereas the gathering of Jews and Gentiles (believing in the same Jesus Christ) is called on the ground of its election. The decisive factor in the former case is human turning away from the electing God, and in the latter case the turning of the electing God towards man. These are the two forms of the elected community, the two poles between which its history moves (in a unilateral direction, from here to there), but in such a way that the bow of the one covenant arches over the whole.[3]

The formal duality on display in these two programmatic quotations is systemic to Barth's presentation of the election of the people of God in CD II/2.[4] In both "The Election of the Community" (§34) and "The Election of the Individual" (§35), Barth follows the twofold form of God's election. Barth treats "The Election of the Community" according to the following divisions: "1. Israel and the Church"; "2. The Judgment and Mercy of God"; "3. The Promise of God Heard and Believed"; and "4. The Passing and Coming of Man". "The Election of the Individual" follows similar divisions: "1. Jesus Christ, the Promise and Its Recipient"; "2. The Elect and the Rejected"; "3. The Determination of the Elect"; and "4. The Determination of the Rejected." While the Israel and church forms are united in Christ because represented in him, Israel corresponds to the form of judgment, (merely) hearing the promise, humanity passing away, and rejection, whereas the church corresponds to the form of mercy, believing the promise, the coming of humanity, and election. While the people as both Israel and the church falls within the purview of God's irrevocable election, Israel is elected as witness to humanity's rebellion against God as graciously limited by God,

---

3. Ibid., 199. The direction is unilateral because "the Church" is the perfect form while "Israel" is the imperfect form of the elect people (198–99, 213, 266). Thus Israel must "enter" the church (e.g., 208, 298).

4. See Katherine Sonderegger, *That Christ Was Born a Jew: Karl Barth's "Doctrine of Israel"* (University Park, Pennsylvania: The Pennsylvania State University Press, 1992), 81ff. It appears to soften in later volumes of the *CD* but not to undergo any fundamental change (e.g., IV/1, 33).

whereas the church is elected as witness to God's deliverance of humanity. Prior to Jesus, wherever Israel appears to receive mercy and to believe the promise—where it is just, faithful, and not rebellious—it is the preexistent church "hidden" in Israel, a material exception to the form of Israel and anticipatory instantiation of the church form. Israel proper can witness only to the light of Christ by its subjective darkness.[5] In fact, Barth goes so far as to depict Israel's history as a steady decline, the circle of the preexistent church within Israel gradually shrinking to the dimensions of a single man, Jesus of Nazareth.

> The circle of the elect grows continually smaller, or at least continually less visible, in the course of Israel's history, until it is ultimately reduced to the person of one man, Jesus of Nazareth. Strictly speaking, the preexistent life of the Church in Israel consists only in the light which, without changing its character, is provisionally cast on the history of Israel by this one man, who is Israel's future and goal, making visible within this history certain individual, fragmentary, contradictory and transitory prefigurations of the form of the community which will be revealed in and with the appearance, death and resurrection of Jesus Christ. The pre-existent life of the Church in Israel consists in the fact that again and again in its history there is revealed a contradiction against the sin of man, an illumination and clarification of the divine judgment, an obedience and faith which are disclosed and validated in their reality, not indeed by the course and character of this history in itself and as such, but by its future and goal in the person of Jesus of Nazareth and the existence of His Church.[6]

---

5. Barth, *CD*, II/2, 211–12, 227, 266. According to Barth, the church existed only in individuals in Israel; Israel as community could witness only to the judgment and rejection of election (268, 506). Elijah, for example, was an existence of the church in Israel (269). "The remnant" was the church in Israel (273). The presence of these exceptions supposedly attests the unity of the Israel and church forms of the people.

6. Ibid., 212–13. The Church in Israel was a "steadily diminishing remnant" (227). The claim of a shrinking circle of the elect is of course without basis in Israel's biblical history. Barth's fall narrative serves a formal claim of "christological" fulfillment that is defied by Israel's biblical materiality, which cannot be forced to fit it. We must look to something other than a narrative of steady decline or progress for the historical and christological logic of fulfillment.

> By the very means of this judgment—the shame and distress of which He [God] will bear Himself—He will save him [man]. The history of Israel leading up to this goal can be nothing but an increasingly close succession of intimations of this judgment. . . . For the sake of its election and its hope, Israel—otherwise it would not be Israel—must always have in it as well these "vessels of wrath fitted to destruction." Indeed it must finally become a single "vessel of wrath."[7]

This assessment is not the result of any study of Israel at particular times, or of any comparison of Israel in an earlier time to Israel in a later time, or of the exegesis of any particular biblical text. Yet, it is manifestly a claim about the way Israel "as a whole" lived. Given the form of Israel according to God's election, it is simply what the "history" of Israel *must* have been, according to Barth, whatever the material exceptions. The material existence of Israel is therefore historically visible only as the ever-declining form of Israel or as the exceptional, preexisting form of the church. This dualistic, formal construal persists with respect to the church. Where the church fails to live up to the calling of Messiah, it ceases to be itself, at best embodying only the form of Israel.[8]

A key implication of Barth's formal construal is that the people of God was not, as traditional supersessionism would have it, Israel before Jesus and the church after Jesus (i.e., the new Israel). Rather, Israel and the church are ineffaceably distinct forms of the one people of God in Christ, present throughout its history (the tension between them *is* its "history"), which nevertheless somehow "moves" inexorably from Israel to the church. Thus, despite the fact that the people of God exists only in one of its two forms at a time, it is the one people rather than the two forms of its existence in Christ that is

---

7. Ibid., 226. To be sure, for Barth this vessel of wrath is not disowned but taken up in Christ's death and resurrection, as he goes on to say on 227: "Paul has clearly in view that at the goal of Israel's history God will not say No to man but that veiled under the No He will say Yes; that He will not leave Jesus in the grave after being put to death but will raise Him from the dead."

8. Ibid., 204, 293, 481.

always the object of election and rejection. Its forms name the distinct determinations of its existence by God's election, not its existence as the object of God's election.

> We cannot, therefore, call the Jews the "rejected" and the Church the "elected" community. The object of election is neither Israel for itself nor the Church for itself, but both together in their unity. (In speaking of elected Israel or of the elected Church, we must be clear that we are speaking "synecdochically.") What is elected in Jesus Christ (His "body") is the community which has the twofold form of Israel and the Church.[9]

Here Barth names with "synecdoche" the formal duality whereby "Israel" represents the whole of God's people in its rejection of God and God's (electing) rejection of the people while "Church" represents the whole of God's people in its election by God and the people's election of God. With "synecdoche" he attempts to safeguard the fundamental unity of the people of God (i.e., "the community") as determined by God's election.

But this synecdoche cannot keep Barth from retaining the familiar, supersessionist Christian distinction of the "true" Israel and the "false" Israel, terms unknown to the Bible. And Jews who do not join the church—"the synagogue"—correspond to the "false" Israel while

---

9. Ibid., 199. The claim that these two forms are ineffaceable is under tremendous pressure when Barth makes remarks like the following: "And at this first and decisive place . . . the Church stands and acts *in identity with* the Israel which rejected its Messiah, together with the heathen world which allied itself with this Israel, and made itself a partner in its guilt" (ibid., 460, emphasis mine). Here the limits of the formal domain of Barth's account are in view, as it cannot hold together the twoness of Israel and the church on the one hand, and the oneness of the elect people in the flesh on the other. Consider the way that Judas, the apostolate, Israel, the world, and the night are all grouped together as one negative form in the following quotation: "The basic flaw was revealed in Judas, but it was that of the apostolate as a whole. At this decisive point the apostolate was also Israel, and Israel was the murderer of the night. The elect were also rejected and as such elected" (475). Or consider the way that the church is "complete in itself" but somehow also "provisional" so long as Jews remain outside the church, as they represent the "incompleteness of the Church" (281–82). That Barth is forced to make such contradictory and thinning assertions indicates that he has misplaced the duality of God's revelation, having drawn an unwarranted inference about Israel and the church from Christ's death and resurrection (or his human and divine natures).

the church corresponds to the "true" Israel.[10] Barth's formal, "christological" division of the people of God compels him to say this. Thus, the formal domain in which Barth describes the elect people can lead him to make perplexing claims that seem to contradict the unconditional oneness of the people of God as determined by election, and to perpetuate the traditional supersessionist pattern that has, as we've seen in chapter 3, provided for the theopolitical contruction of race and its violent channel of modern nationalism. For example, what is left to Israel by its rejection as represented in Judas is, according to Barth, "a holiness and a mission which are no longer Israel's, but necessarily become those of *an entirely different people*."[11] "His people have ceased here [in the sin of Jeroboam] to be His people."[12] Moreover, God's "unconditional" election somehow becomes forfeitable, humanity empowered to do what Barth has elsewhere insisted it has not the power to do: "If the community tries to be more than His [Jesus'] environment, to do something more than mediate, it has forgotten and forfeited its election."[13] Here Barth finds himself channeling the subjective self-constitution that is so basic to the modern discourse of peoplehood.

The revelation of God constitutes a profound crisis for all of creation, according to Barth, and it is perhaps here that we must

---

10. "Gentile Christians not only belong now to Israel but are, in fact, the true Israel" (ibid., 288. See also 274, 404, 693). But also see 406, where Barth's exegesis rightly resists the true-false duality). On the rejection that the synagogue embodies, see 204–5, 217, 227, 281–82, 287, 291, 294–95. Because the church is for Barth the term for Israel's perfection, the church cannot itself be divided the way that Israel was between hearing and believing (i.e., between Israel and the church hidden in Israel). Only those who both hear and believe, only the faithful, belong to the church (ibid., 428). This is an ever disappearing and reappearing church.

11. Ibid., 469, emphasis mine. Per Barth's own claims elsewhere, this is tantamount to saying that the body of the risen Christ was an entirely different body from the one that died on the cross. This is replacement instead of healing, gnostic salvation rather than resurrection.

12. Ibid., 398.

13. Ibid., 196. See also 425. The forfeiture of election, as claimed here by Barth as well as David Novak (*The Election of Israel: The Idea of a Chosen People* (Cambridge: Cambridge University Press, 1995), is a contradiction in terms. Election is irrevocable and thus unforfeitable. Unforfeitability is simply analytic of election.

look to understand the formal twoness and polarization of the elect people of God as Israel and the church in Barth's account. The crisis of revelation arises not only from the difference between God and creation, but from the impossible possibility of sin, of the finally futile human resistance to God's love. It is a crisis that leaves nothing about creation intact, no nature on which revelation may build, no being to which God may be revealed as analogous. The revelation of God can only divide (i.e., judge) on its way to uniting a corrupted creation. This division must be borne witness, Barth insists, or any claim to the unity and efficacy of revelation will be empty. Sinful humanity cannot avert but must endure this dividing crisis, by which it is determined by the God who has elected it in love. Thus, the way through this crisis cannot come by nature or being. Nor is it the deliverance of any general history. According to Barth, the way through the crisis of revelation is the particular God-human event of faith, which is God's gift in Christ, itself part of revelation.

This crisis of revelation seems to inform the duality of God's election in Barth's account. The church can never claim to be itself without faithfully recognizing itself in the form of Israel, as there is no resurrection without the cross. But then Israel must represent what only the crisis of revelation can touch, what lies beyond any hope of nature or being or general history. It is the form of the people as it hurtles itself into the abyss of sin. Israel remains for Barth the people of God particularly as it kills Christ.[14] Only from (and because of!) this abyss is "the breadth and length and height and depth" of God's electing love revealed. Thus, Barth infers the formal duality of election in the forms of Israel and the church from the cross and resurrection of Christ, who is man and God, such that Israel represents the negative limit to which election reaches.

14. Barth, *CD*, II/2, 57–58, 198–99, 224, 505.

To be sure, this duality holds only within the oneness of Christ, that is, the oneness of God's election and therefore the oneness of God's people, as I have emphasized in the exposition of Barth's account of election in the previous chapter. The failure of Israel is not about what God absolutely excludes but the extent of the inclusion of God's excluding election. In it the deepest corruption of the world is represented and addressed, as Israel is witness to "the misery of man."[15] Yet, because of the way Barth relates Israel to the crisis of revelation, the duality is such that it predetermines anything that happens in time. It is, as any truly formal distinction must remain, ineffaceable. As such, as epic dialectic, it guards against the lifelessness of general principles and provides for the dramatic "life" of God's electing activity.

But we must question whether this duality can in fact be inferred from the cross and resurrection of Christ as man and God and whether it does justice to the history of Israel. The test must be, as Barth says, the reading of the Bible itself. In the scope of this book, I can make only some illustrative exegetical claims. Many of these turn on the way the New Testament is read in relation to the Tanakh, which I shall take up in the final two chapters. We will consider two key New Testament witnesses in more detail there, the Gospel according to Matthew and Rom. 9–11. Here I wish to deal (only broadly) with the history of Israel in the Tanakh in relation to the election of the people of God, the biblical history that the New Testament inherits and within which it speaks. With the biblical commentary that is to follow, I will attempt to show that the formal duality of Barth's account of election is inadequate to the biblical witness and offer an alternative understanding of the drama of the election of Israel, a historical drama *in* the flesh rather than

---

15. Ibid., 212.

in the formal realm of representation. But before I do, let me restate my concern with Barth in relation to the violent tendencies of the modern discourse of peoplehood so as to clarify what I am finally trying to address as we turn more directly to the text of the Bible. My aim is not merely to criticize Barth or to offer an alternative dogmatic proposal. It is to use Barth constructively to articulate in the present time a Christian account of what it means to be the people of the God of Israel.

While the Jews are not an absolute foil to the people of God in Barth's account of election, he presents them as entirely negative in their subjectivity. This serves to maximize the grace of God's election in judging and thereby embracing the people in its Israel form so as to raise it from the dead in its church form, the perfection of Israel. But it sets off a race to the bottom of Jewish inadequacy.[16] Meanwhile Barth presents the church as entirely positive in its/their subjectivity so as to convey the effective mercy of God's election.

16. In other words, the worse the Jews the greater Israel's God. For example, it is properly "the guilt of Israel . . . [that] can confirm its election" (ibid., 258), as it is likewise "just because of the division [between north and south] there are now authentic relations in the history of Israel. Just because these men—the peoples, kings and prophets—on both sides of this relation show themselves to be so incomplete and so helpless on their own account, they become completely authentic occasions for authentic revelations of God, and as such reveal the authentic meaning of the existence of Israel" (ibid., 403). The problem here is the "because" driven by Barth's formal scheme. It is not because of Israel's failure that it is "authentically" elect. The impotence of Israel's failure is simply one of many witnesses to Israel's election, albeit an important one. The relation between God's election and Israel's faithfulness is not a zero-sum game, just as there is no such game to the God-human relation according to Barth.

Barth would do better here to follow his own criticism of the idea "that the grace of God will be magnified if man is represented as a blotted . . . page" (CD, III/2, 278). He may be right in saying, "Does not even Jewish obduracy and melancholy, even Jewish caprice and phantasy, even the Jewish cemetery at Prague—because all this is bound up with the sterile hearing but yet with the hearing of God's Word—still contain objectively and effectively more genuine Gospel than all the unbelieving wisdom of the Goyim put together, and a good part of what is supposed to be believing Christian theory and practice into the bargain? If this witness passes unobserved it is so much the worse for the world and for the Church, but no disproof of the fact that witness—witness of Jesus Christ—is actually being given." But it is as much Jewish righteousness as Jewish unrighteousness that bears the gospel in time and witnesses to the Messiah, and all Jewish righteousness cannot be claimed as Christian even if Christians rightly want to learn it.

As "the new Israel" the church is described as the perfect form of the elect people, formally pure with unquestionable moral adequacy to God, even if, as such, it is formally united in Christ to corrupt, failing Israel.[17] This duality caves to the Jewish foil, false purity, and self-constitution of modern peoplehood, as well as the manifold problems that accompany these. It undermines the solidarity of the people of God with its failing members and therefore its mercifulness toward those who threaten it from without. By formalizing Jewish-Christian difference, it ignores the historical contingency whereby the way of the people of God parted into the ways of Christianity and Judaism. It assures Christians that we are on the right side of the duality within the people of God and that non-Christian Jews (i.e., our supposedly failing members) must become like us to be perfected by election. This last implication has the distinct disadvantage of ignoring that non-Jewish Christians may learn substantively (and not merely negatively) from non-Christian Jews (i.e., "the synagogue"), that many non-Christian Jewish communities may have lived a life more faithful to the God revealed in Jesus (e.g., by observing the law of the covenant) than many confessing Christian communities. It may be that "post-Christian, non-Christian" Jews have more embodied Barth's church form and the church his Israel form!

The duality of an imperfect form and a perfect form of the people of God also invites the people to prove who they formally are, rather than acknowledge who God has materially made them to be in time.[18] It chronically trivializes or postpones confession of sin and corresponding repentance. It wrongly empowers those who

17. I am aware that in other contexts, Barth is quick to recognize the many shortcomings of the church without implying its ceasing to be the church. But in the formal domain of his account of election here, the church must have overcome the shortcomings of Israel—which includes the embrace of Israel in those shortcomings—in order to be the church.

18. See ch. 3 above on the modern "cult of authenticity." The inadequacy of the forms to the people's actual existence comes into view when Barth admits that the elect and the rejected "can exchange their functions" (Barth, *CD*, II/2, 354).

claim to determine the subjective adequacy of competing claims to be the people of God and who thereby define the people. This insidious empowerment is precisely what election renders futile and pretentious according to Scripture, since, as I will demonstrate below, it is God who materially defines the people. The formal domain of Barth's account of the elect people compels him to "find" subjective "confirmation" of what he otherwise describes as the independent and objective activity of God's election.[19] But that confirmation is not in fact to be found in the subjective moral inadequacy or adequacy of those who figure among the people. It is to be found in the course of that people in the flesh in relation to the gentile nations in time.

Recovering Sight of the History of God's Electing Activity

As Barth rightly claims, election is before time *so as to be in time* such that "it can only be history. . . . [It] is something which can only be told, not a system which can be considered and described."[20] But here he is describing the election of Jesus. It is hard for him to "tell" the election of the people of God since it takes place in the realm of representation—representation in Christ—always just

---

19. E.g., "On man's side this election becomes actual in man's own electing of God, by which he is made free to do the will of God, and achieves and possesses individuality and autonomy before God" (ibid., 180). "This, then, is how the elect and others differ from one another: the former by witnessing in their lives to the truth, the latter by lying against the same truth" (ibid., 346). "There will always be those who hear the proclamation of their election, always those who believe it, whom God has chosen in Jesus Christ and therefore determined for this faith and hearing. Those who are really this people by the grace of God will always recognise and confess Jesus Christ, emerging, therefore, as His people, as the communion of saints, recognising and confessing Him" (ibid., 418–19). See also 179, 314, 322, 345, 413, and 569.

The need for subjective confirmation of an identity of the people of God claimed on other grounds (e.g., God's election) also promotes apologetic historiography and exegesis, where the people of the past, including those of the Bible, must be presented in a moral light corresponding to the claims being made about their identity. This happens to Barth when he finds himself minimizing King Saul's sins (369), as it does to Augustine in relation to the Genesis account of Abraham (*Civ.* 16:19), for Augustine wrongly assumes that people must qualify subjectively to belong to the city of God rather than the city of men.

20. *CD*, II/2, 188.

"before" time rather than *in* time. Thus, the election of the people "happens and happens again *before* every moment of time."[21] The election of the people, then, its "history," can be "told" by Barth only as a series of highly occasional and yet repetitive clashes of the Israel and church forms of the people, as the people meets the electing presence of God and is continually divided into two blocs that correspond to its two christological forms. But the Tanakh never divides Israel into such blocs or forms (not even in the division of the kingdom of Israel), and it is only Barth's and other readings of the New Testament that imagine such a division into the Tanakh (so as to distinguish the church from Israel and account for the epic significance of Jesus as Messiah and God).[22] The continuous being of the people itself remains mythological. It remains the presupposed, invisible, representable substance that simply endures the continual crisis of election. How, then, can we describe what Barth rightly expresses as the "indestructible continuity in the being of Israel,"[23] that is, its election, without resorting to an excessively formal presentation like Barth's? How can we describe the election of the people of God *as* its history? How can we *tell* God's election of the people?

"Ethnic" Israel?

The recent answer to the question of the continuous being of Israel by election—an accretion of the modern discourse of peoplehood—has been "ethnicity." It is precisely this discourse that has ethnicized peoplehood and thus the imagination with which

---

21. Ibid., 191, emphasis mine.
22. That formal divisions within Israel like Barth's depend on the New Testament is probably one reason why Jewish exegesis has not seen them in the Tanakh. Nevertheless, a formal division like Barth's is latent in any reading of the Tanakh that claims that inadequate obedience to Torah forfeits election.
23. Barth, *CD*, III/2, 297.

we attempt to name the election of the people of God and read the Bible. This ethnicizing tendency therefore must be addressed before I undertake to tell God's election of the people. The biological determinism of recent decades has only strengthened the supposedly ethnic nature of Israel's history, and therefore the ethnic nature of Israel and of God's election. Ethnicity is assumed or presented as the material foundation of Israel, whether the description of Israel being given is concerned with God or not, whether it is concerned with God's election or not. This is already a symptom of the problem with ethnicity, particularly in theology and biblical exegesis, for we should not be able to make sense of Israel without God. But ethnicity has offered an apparently stable foundation that God no longer can.[24] So in theology and biblical exegesis we resort to identifying the electing activity of God as well as the continuity of Israel with Israelite ethnicity, with Israel "by birth." But this supposedly automatic reality, as we will see, is really no activity at all.

God's election, it is typically assumed, must by definition remain safe from historical contingency, "above" it somehow. After all, how could it be God's election if it were historically contingent? Ethnicity is supposedly the one fact of the people of Israel that is identifiable with election, the one constant of Israel's history, the invariable and pure substance that has been passed from parents to children across time from a mythologically purified and common ancestor (i.e., Abraham). The identity of the people is thus transmitted primarily "by birth." I hesitate to name representatives of this understanding of the history or election of Israel because it is simply ubiquitous.[25]

24. It also provides apparent stability to the otherwise chaotic modes of modern social science. Without ethnicity, we ask, how can we be describing Israel rather than some other community? There seems to be no other human ground for its particularity. Never mind that describing Israel as ethnic makes it simply one instance of a generic category, i.e., of ethnicity.

25. I will engage New Testament exegetes that assume and mobilize this understanding in the next chapter. Joel S. Kaminsky has offered some much-needed nuancing of election with a more careful survey of the biblical witness in *Yet I Loved Jacob: Reclaiming the Biblical Concept*

Within the imaginary of ethnicity, Israelite and Jewish identity are indistinct. Long before the kingdom of Judah or its exile (when it seems that a certain community indeed came to be known as "the Jews"), Israel is imagined as ethnically "Jewish," so that one often hears talk of "the Jewish people" of the exodus (referring not only to the tribe of Judah but to the whole people of Israel). Somehow the people born of Abraham of the Chaldeans, the wandering Aramean, became purely and totally "Jewish" at some point. Such "Jews" are assumed to have been Israelite, too, but the supposedly ethnic constitution of Israel renders trivial any distinction between what is Israelite and what is Jewish. Whatever the wildly varying differences in Israel of old, among the Jews since, or between Israel of old and the Jews since, the elect people is supposedly held together by the unbreakable bond of ethnicity.[26]

Jewish or Israelite ethnicity has come to be an important building block or placeholder of recent theology and biblical exegesis. It is held by many (with whom I am otherwise in deep sympathy) to guard positively against supersessionist attacks on the adequacy of Judaism, as Jewish ethnicity cannot be expropriated by Christians (or anyone else) and is supposedly always taken for granted by certain or all New Testament writers. It also guards against the tendency of Christian theology to treat the life of the people of God as disembodied.[27] At the same time, among Christians less concerned

---

of Election (Nashville: Abingdon, 2007). While he continues the pattern of reifying ethnicity, he notices the following: Israel's election is not neatly ethnocentric or reducible to its ethnicity; people not born into Israel can in fact become Israelite; the racism that is ascribed to Israel is the construction of modernity rather than a biblical concept; and the election of Israel will not yield to a dichotomy of particularism and universalism (see pp. 113, 126–30, 140–57). My account is different from Kaminsky's in its refusal to accommodate the modern notion of ethnicity, its concern with election as the activity of the God of Israel rather than as Israel's self-understanding, and its aim to describe the continuity of Israel over time.

26. As we will see in the final chapter on Romans 9–11, this does not account for the difference between Esau and Jacob (or Ishmael and Isaac). Israel is somehow deemed uniquely Abraham's "ethnic descendants" while arbitrarily excluding many of Abraham's "ethnic" descendants.

about Christian supersessionism, it can serve negatively to specify the limitations of Israel (whether objective or subjective) that were overcome in Jesus, as enacted by Paul in the gentile mission. Here the idea is that the one people of the God of Israel was an ethnicity before Jesus—that is, strictly endogamous or ethnically exclusive—and has been multiethnic in and after Jesus, à la the Pauline church. Thus, the foil to the eschatological movement of God in shaping the people of God according to the New Testament is supposedly "biology" or "ethnicity" (objective).[28] The characteristic feature of

27. E.g., R. Kendall Soulen, *The God of Israel and Christian Theology* (Minneapolis: Fortress Press, 1996), 29, 122–23; Scott Bader-Saye, *Church and Israel after Christendom: The Politics of Election* (Eugene, OR: Wipf & Stock, 1999), 30–37. See also 159n13: "I therefore use the terms 'Israel' and 'the Jews' interchangeably throughout the book as a way of reminding us that there is no ideal 'Israel' that floats above or could be detached from the actual *people* of Israel, the Jews, past and present" (emphasis his). I suggest that this timeless, albeit actual, Jewishness/Israeliteness is not the only or best alternative to what Bader-Saye rightly criticizes as an ideal "Israel."

Both Soulen and Bader-Saye are dependent on Michael Wyschogrod in their accounts, particularly his *The Body of Faith: God in the People of Israel* (Northvale, New Jersey: Jason Aronson, Inc., 1996 [1983]), e.g., 176. Each opts for the language of "flesh" or "carnality" or "natural descent" rather than ethnicity, and Soulen has told me in private conversation that he is against defining Israel ethnically. But each is following Wyschogrod in defining Israel "by birth" or "physical descent." While I am sympathetic with Wyschogrod's insistence on the unconditional nature of God's election "in the flesh" and its transmission "through the body," I don't think that he recognizes the (storiable) contingency of "in the flesh" itself or "through the body" itself, and therefore God's unconditional election in and through such storiable contingency. This contingency is extremely important. It remains open to adopting people from without. It is capable of losing from within. It is what David Novak is wrestling with in his insistence that election not prevent Torah from being "supreme," leading him to render election forfeitable (*The Election of Israel*, 247). And it is what I am trying to articulate in the remainder of this chapter.

Also note the wisdom of the Mishnah on this matter, per Jacob Neusner's helpful observation in *Making God's Word Work: A Guide to the Mishnah* (New York: Continuum International, 2004): "In the law of the Mishnah, Israel does not constitute an ethnic group . . . but a social entity that is *sui generis*" (82). See also his explication of *m. Bik.* 1:4 on p. 97 and his comment in Jacob Neusner, Bruce Chilton, William Graham, *Three Faiths, One God: The Formative Faith and Practice of Judaism* (Boston: Brill, 2002): "Israel is not ethnic at all . . . Israel forms not an ethnic category but a supernatural one" (145).

28. Hermann Strathmann, "Laós in the New Testament" in *Theological Dictionary of the New Testament: Abridged in One Volume*, ed. Geoffrey W. Bromiley (Grand Rapids, MI: Eerdmans, 1985), 502. N. T. Wright, *The New Testament and the People of God* (Minneapolis, MN: Fortress Press, 1992), 224, 365–67, 456, 468. This deep tendency is evident on the surface in remarks like the following: "Election for Paul is corporate. It was in ethnic Israel and is now 'in Christ'" (Ben Witherington, *1 and 2 Thessalonians: A Socio-Rhetorical Commentary* [Grand Rapids, MI:

Paul's opponents, even Jesus' opponents, is imagined as Jewish ethnocentrism (subjective).[29] Accordingly, any rules of endogamy in the Tanakh are understood to be concerned with the ethnic purity of Israel (which was supposedly already a reality and in danger of being lost). Such a concern can be deemed positive or negative or both by Christian writers, depending on whether the ethnic constitution of the people of God plays a positive or negative or temporary role in a salvation-historical account of the people of God or in a soteriological system.

Particularly among those opposing traditional Christian supersessionism, any account of the people of God must regard ethnic Israel as foundational and inviolable. Ethnic or carnal Israel, that is, "the Jews," is Israel proper.[30] Non-Jewish Christian participation in the people of the God of Israel can be based only on its relation to elect, ethnic Israel, at the very least by way of Christians' relation to Jesus, who is presented as ethnically and therefore authentically Jewish and Israelite. "Flesh" is often the biblical word that is taken to stand for ethnicity in this context: "the flesh" is ethnic relation, and Jesus' "Jewish flesh" was his Jewish ethnicity.[31] Jesus' Jewish flesh in this sense preserves difference and particularity at the heart of

William B. Eerdmans, 2006], 65); "In that Day, Jesus says, ethnic boundaries will no longer matter" (Scot McKnight, *The Jesus Creed: Loving God, Loving Others* [Brewster, MA: Paraclete, 2004], 39).

29. Wright, *The New Testament and the People of God*, 123, 365, 456. "Ethnocentrism" is how Frank Thielman identifies Paul's opponents in *Theology of the New Testament: A Canonical and Synthetic Approach* (Grand Rapids, MI: Zondervan, 2005), 273. Ethnocentrism as the key to Paul's opponents is conspicuously absent from premodern exegesis (although there are signs of its emergence in Luther's commentary on Romans (on ch. 9 in particular).

30. See the previous three notes and also Douglas Harink, *Paul among the Postliberals: Pauline Theology beyond Christendom and Modernity* (Grand Rapids, MI: Brazos, 2003), 183. Perhaps it is good that the Jewish community is Israel proper in our imagination. But that is not because of Jewish ethnicity; it is because of the way that the history of the people of God has elevated that community over other communities of the people, just as that history has done with Judah, David, and Jesus. That has to do with God's faithfulness to that community as well as its faithfulness to God. It is the result of this history that calling the Jews "Israel" sounds fitting while calling the Christian church "Israel" sounds hokey and is intuitively construed as in some sense metaphorical.

the Christian faith, warding off Christian claims to intrinsic purity and universality and to Jesus as their possession. Should Jews and Christians be deemed to belong to the same, one people of God, then, it must be as fundamentally separate constituents of the people since, within that one people, timeless Jewish ethnicity can only continue as distinct.[32] Here "Israel" in the New Testament means the Jews, and non-Jewish Christians are only Israel once removed. It is unclear how Jesus has anything to do with the Jews' being Israel, that is, with their being the people *of God* that they are, despite the tremendous christological claims of the New Testament that Barth rightly emphasizes (i.e., that the elect people is elect in the elect one).

Thus, it is Jewish or Israelite ethnicity that is imagined as the "indestructible continuity in the being of Israel." A particular ethnicity is the timeless substance of Israel that is safe from historical contingency (or sustained *despite* rather than in and through historical contingency), making the Jews of today an ethnically pure community and one with all Jews or Israelites of the past. As such, the living Jewish community is the primary, if not only, authentic presence of the Israelite generations of the past, and Jewish ethnicity is the (positive or negative) basis of Christian claims to participate in the people of God. Correspondingly, multiethnicity, particularly among those who conceive the ethnic nature of Israel as a limitation to be overcome, becomes the primary virtue of the church. Christian salvation is "breaking free" from the bonds of ethnicity. In both its positive and negative iterations, ethnicity as described above has come to play a key grammatical role in Christian theology, even

---

31. E.g., James D. G. Dunn, *The Theology of Paul the Apostle* (Grand Rapids, MI: William B. Eerdmans, 1998), 69, 348.

32. See, e.g., Bader-Saye's reading of the "new covenant" according to Paul: "a living covenant that embraces *two peoples* in a relationship of tense reciprocity" (*Church and Israel after Christendom*, 100).

among those who are trying to resist the racialized categories of modernity.

But such Israelite or Jewish ethnicity is a myth. While invoking it has functioned in some ways to promote the embodied nature of the life of the people of God and resist the disinheritance of the Jewish community, it is primarily an ideological force that makes false claims about the material existence of Israel past and present.[33] Moreover, it is no more alive than what Barth rightly criticizes: a hidden divine decree that supposedly separated the elect from the reprobate before time and for eternity independently of Christ and that is merely being applied in history. It is an attempt to reduce the existence of Israel to a dead law (whereas the covenant law of Israel is alive with God's Word by God's Spirit). When identified with the ethnicity of Israel, the election of Israel cannot be "told" as the living work of the living God.[34]

But for reasons we have seen in Barth's account of the election of Christ, the election of Israel must be "told" rather than reduced to a dead principle. Accordingly, Amy Jill Levine rightly criticizes the attempt by Christians and others to identify Jewishness as an ethnicity, for among other things, it "reduces religious practice to an accident of birth, and it ignores the role of the proselyte to Judaism."[35] Ethnicity, or ethnic endogamy and procreation, is not the "indestructible continuity in the being of Israel." Nor is it what distinguishes Israel from the gentile nations. The people of Israel

---

33. For a careful and compelling vindication of ethnicity as a way of naming impure identity under threat, one that helps a community to remember its fugitive past, traditions, etc., see Stuart Hall, "Ethnicity: Identity and Difference," *Radical America* 23.4 (1989), 9–20.

34. It can perhaps be set down as a registry of the children the people of God have managed to produce down through the ages. But then, since such children are in fact far too many to be named and many have been forgotten, how would the children named in such a registry be chosen for remembrance?

35. "'To All the Gentiles': A Jewish Perspective on the Great Commission," *Review and Expositor*, 103 (Winter, 2006): 141. This is particularly unfortunate since Christians no doubt have so much to learn from the practices of being Jewish.

hails from a wandering Aramean of Ur named Abram, has been adopting gentiles under a variety of terms into the people ever since (no doubt both on and off the record), and has been formed up to the present by various practices in addition to that of conceiving and giving birth to children. What distinguishes gentiles from Israel in the Tanakh (and the New Testament), so that their adoption must be regulated, is not their alien ethnicity but their practical service to false gods. The problem with gentiles—what makes them such—is not the timelessly construed accidents of their birth over against the accidents of Israelite birth, but that their idolatrous ways threaten the Israelite way of life that is the worship of the God of Abraham, Isaac, and Jacob. This is the biblical concern with intermarriage.

> Do not intermarry with them [the seven gentile nations of Canaan], giving your daughters to their sons or taking their daughters for your sons, for that would turn away your children from following me, to serve other gods. Then the anger of the LORD would be kindled against you, and he would destroy you quickly. (Deut. 7:3-4)[36]

Intermarriage is the occasion of relational bonds and alliances that affect the sociopolitical and economic patterns of Israel, especially with the passage of time and the generation of children through those intermarriages. Such bonds and alliances can compromise Israel's faithfulness to the law of its covenant with its God. But they do not always do so, and Israel is not presented in the Tanakh as ethnically pure, such that gentiles never become part of Israel. The genealogies of Israel (to say nothing of the foundational stories of key figures like Moses, who married a non-Israelite, Midianite woman and later a Cushite woman) characteristically include women and men born to non-Israelite communities—gentile people who, through a variety of circumstances, found themselves woven into the material life of

---

36. Cf. Gen. 24:1-4. All biblical quotations in this chapter are from the NRSV unless otherwise noted.

Israel and went on to leave behind Israelite descendants. The concern of the genealogies is not ethnic continuity, but the ability to name the winding path by which the life of Israel has sojourned from the past to the present. Prominent in that concern are the implications of that path for land holdings in the promised land, which in turn has sustained Israel's life by God's grace and remains its hope (as is especially clear in the book of Ruth).[37]

Intermarriage is thus ambiguous in the Tanakh because, depending on the gentiles in question and the circumstances, it can be good or bad for Israel. It can be the way that some or all of Israel are drawn away from the God of Israel toward an idolatrous way of life, to a politics that serves false gods (as in the case of early generations' intermarrying with Moabite or Canaanite communities or with Solomon's marriages). Or it can be the way that some or all of Israel is sustained or strengthened in faithfulness to the covenant, in a politics that serves the God of Israel and betokens the promised future of Israel (as in the case of Moses' marriage with Zipporah the Midianite or Boaz's marriage with Ruth the Moabite). Thus, not all gentiles are the same, and none are essentially bad or non-Israelite; the conditions for intermarriage and adoption vary from gentile to gentile and time to time. There would be no such variation if the concern were with timeless ethnic differentiation, and the reason for that variation is a difference in actual historical relations with Israel. For example, Deuteronomy 23 tells us that Moab's and Ammon's betrayals of their Israelite family postpones the participation of their descendants in Israel, whereas Edomites and Egyptians may be fully admitted to Israel after a shorter presence within Israelite society.[38]

---

37. Also a concern (particularly in Ezra and Nehemiah) is the political integrity of the priesthood, which likewise sustains Israel's life in the land and informs its hope (cf. 1 Kgs. 12:31).

38. The faithfulness of Israel rather than the purity of its ethnicity remains the concern of Ezra and Nehemiah with respect to Israelite intermarriage with the gentiles living in the promised land (e.g., the abominations and pollutions of Ezra 9:1, 11; the separation of the Jews to obey the

From its beginning, then, when Israel's God adopted Abram, Israel has been adopting people from without, making Israelites out of gentiles and continuing its generations not only by procreating marriage between people born in the community but also by procreating marriage between Israelites and gentiles or people who were once gentile and have become Israelite.[39] We therefore find provisions in the Tanakh for the Israelization of gentiles, particularly in relation to the rites whereby Israel's history—its peoplehood—is remembered.

law of YHWH in Neh. 10:28-31, and the prohibition of intermarriage for fear of a repetition of King Solomon's sin in Neh. 13:23-27). Gentile wives and children, particularly at this vulnerable stage in Israel's life, threaten to lead Israel away from faithfulness to its God; they indicate the wrong kind of political economic ambition. Likewise, the integrity of the history and practice of the priesthood rather than its ethnic purity is at stake in Ezra 2:59-63 and Neh. 7:61-65. Moreover, the lack of genealogical pedigree and corresponding lack of trustworthiness can be overcome by Urim and Thummim per Ezra 2:63 and Neh. 7:65. The "belonging to Israel" by shared covenant life of certain people has become ambiguous because of the loss of regulating institutions in the land and the brokenness of Israel through invasion and exile, and Ezra and Nehemiah are trying to pick up the pieces. Without remembering the God of Abraham, Isaac, and Jacob as their own, which is jeopardized by the future of existing marital associations with surrounding gentile communities, Israel cannot exist indefinitely. It can forget itself into oblivion over generations, into total assimilation by surrounding gentile communities as ordered by their gods.

On the decisive factor of time for the determination of the limits of the people of Israel, see Neusner, *Making God's Word Work*, 97. He discusses *m. Bik.* 1–4 on Deut. 26:3 (where Israelites name their decisive ancestor as "a wandering Aramean"), which provides for the complete Israelization of the children of "gentile" proselytes but a subtle liturgical distinction whereby the Israelization of the proselyte himself remains incomplete. The proselyte may nevertheless produce fully Israelized children and does not thereby "contaminate" an otherwise pure Israelite ethnicity. Thus, the gentile who has not been born and formed in Israel, but who nevertheless enters Israel, witnesses to the liminal and living transition between the gentile nations and the people of Israel. Here one can see how the being of Israel *takes time*. Nevertheless, this is always a time of hope, and so the one who was gentile and is now proselytized has in fact become a member of the promised family of Israel. See Neusner's summary comment on the rabbinic understanding of gentiles' becoming Israelite in the Tanakh: "Thus, in the law of Judaism, gentile family ties bear no implications for either consanguinity or inheritance. If a gentile becomes an Israelite, his or her prior family ties are null. He or she is viewed as a newborn child. The father and mother of every convert are Abraham our father and Sarah our mother" (*Making God's Word Work*, 89). Accordingly, Neusner insists that Israel is not an ethnic but "a moral entity" (the title of ch. 4 is "Corporate Israel As a Moral Entity").

39. On the ancient history of Israelite adoption of gentiles, see Louis H. Feldman, *Jew and Gentile in the Ancient World: Attitudes and Interactions from Alexander to Justinian* (Princeton: Princeton University Press, 1993).

The Lord said to Moses and Aaron: This is the ordinance for the passover: no foreigner shall eat of it, but any slave who has been purchased may eat of it after he has been circumcised; no bound or hired servant may eat of it. It shall be eaten in one house; you shall not take any of the animal outside the house, and you shall not break any of its bones. The whole congregation of Israel shall celebrate it. If an alien who resides with you wants to celebrate the passover to the Lord, all his males shall be circumcised; then he may draw near to celebrate it; he shall be regarded as a native of the land [ἔσται ὥσπερ καὶ ὁ αὐτόχθων τῆς γῆς or וְהָיָה כְּאֶזְרַח הָאָרֶץ]. But no uncircumcised person shall eat of it; there shall be one law for the native and for the alien who resides among you. (Exod. 12:43-49)[40]

Here in Exodus 12, we see with particular clarity that Israel is not defined by ethnicity. Its border (i.e., the border of its flesh) is regulated (but not originated) by covenant practice over time, particularly by the practice of circumcision. Those who come to Israel from other peoples must abandon false gods and adopt and learn Israel's covenant way of life in joining the people of Israel. Thus, Abraham's family of promise was not to be limited by the ability of its existing members to conceive children, but regulated by the covenant practice of circumcision. This is the rule of how the promise would continue to live in and as the people.

40. See John I. Durham, *Exodus*, Word Biblical Commentary 3 (Waco: Word, 1987), 173, who indicates that the proscription of v. 43 is not absolute but the general rule subject to the subsequent exceptions so that only members of the covenant community, including foreigners Israelized by circumcision, may participate. Despite the explicit injunction of this passage—that upon circumcision, the foreigner shall be regarded as autochthonous—Shaye Cohen insists that the person in question remains a resident alien (*Beginnings of Jewishness: Boundaries, Varieties, Uncertainties* [Berkeley and Los Angeles: University of California Press, 1999], 120–21). One suspects that Cohen has presupposed an Israelite ethnocentrism and ethnic purity that is in fact absent. The concern of such texts, again, is not ethnicity but the threat of idolatry, particularly as conveyed by those who do not live enduringly among the covenant community. Idolatry does not course in the foreigner's blood but in his memory, continued alliances, practices, habits, imagination, etc. The cutting away of that corruption begins with his circumcision, which is his and his household's commitment to live according to the covenant among the covenant community. Circumcision in and by the Israelite community—rather than circumcision in general—must be the point of reference for his and his family's future participation in the people (and land) of Israel. Not all the circumcised are Israel, but all the men of Israel are to be circumcised.

God said to Abraham, "As for you, you shall keep my covenant, you and your offspring after you throughout their generations. This is my covenant, which you shall keep, between me and you and your offspring after you: Every male among you shall be circumcised. You shall circumcise the flesh of your foreskins, and it shall be a sign of the covenant between me and you. Throughout your generations every male among you shall be circumcised when he is eight days old, including the slave born in your house and the one bought with your money from any foreigner who is not of your offspring. Both the slave born in your house and the one bought with your money must be circumcised. So shall my covenant be in your flesh an everlasting covenant." (Gen. 17:9-13)

Abraham's promised family is a visibly gathering people. Those who are to be circumcised are not only those men born into the people but all men who find themselves remaining "among you," that is, among the people of promise. It is by the faithfulness to perform this rite in remembrance of the covenant between Abraham and the God of Israel that men, and the families associated with them, retain a share in the people of Israel (which again, for many generations was particularly a matter of land). Thus, the passage continues, "Any uncircumcised male who is not circumcised in the flesh of his foreskin shall be cut off from his people; he has broken my covenant" (Gen. 17:14).

Given the practical regulation rather than the ethnic definition of Israel, what, then, of God's election? Are we forced here at Gen. 17:14 to recognize that God's election of the people of Israel is ontically equivalent to those whose men have undergone circumcision and who observe other central rites of the people, so that the history of Israel can be no more than the history of those who faithfully practice these rites? So that the people of Israel is not only shaped but originated by its covenant practices? Does this not mean that the people of God is indeed constituted by its own (subjective) faithfulness, however thin that faithfulness becomes when reduced to such rites? Are we not given here in Genesis 17 a representative criterion, whereby the "true" people of God can be distinguished from some "false" people of God, namely, those who do not faithfully perform covenant practices like circumcision and are therefore not the people of God? Does "cut off" mean immediately disowned, a declarative act whereby some are "removed" from Israel or their participation in Israel is decided as "inauthentic"? Here we meet the crux of my attempt to name and describe the "indestructible continuity in the being of Israel"—that is, Israel's election—if I am to tell a history rather than return to the chaotic sea of representation where Christian descriptions of the elect people of God have so often lived. In describing the historical activity of election, I will deal first with the more epic contingency of the people of Israel in the phenomena of being "cut off" and adopting gentiles, and second with the contingency of Israel's history at its most minute. From both perspectives, I will seek to expose the historical contingency of election that the concept of ethnicity attempts to hide, and articulate how God's electing activity can and must be "told."

The Ebb and Flow of Being Cut Off and Adopting Outsiders: The Election of Israel through Intimacy with Gentiles

To be "cut off from" the people of Israel is not to be immediately disowned, to be declared inauthentic. It takes time. How does it happen? The figure in question in Genesis 17 above, like others threatened with being "cut off from" Israel in the Tanakh, is not a mythologically discrete individual. It is the life into which a branch of Israel has grown, which, like other branches, seems to be growing into Israel's future. It is a name. The name of this figure is often already that of a collective, that is, a family or clan within Israel whose name is expected to continue through descendants, both by procreation and adoption (as in Exod. 12:48). But the branch of a "cut-off" Israelite person or family does not grow finally into the material future of Israel. Over time it weaves away from the living sprawl of Israel's history to the point that it atrophies and falls away. In cases such as Achan, the traceable future of the branch in Israel is cut off quickly by burning with fire.[41] A similar, rapid cutting off can occur through war. But should the cut-off branch produce "descendants" in any nameable or traceable sense (e.g., procreated, ideological, economic), they are eventually assimilated by gentile communities, who serve gods other than the God of Israel. This is to go into the wilderness and not return. The nameability or traceability of their descent from Israel—their belonging to Israel—thus decreases with time, finally reaching disintegration when they have been totally assimilated by idolatrous, gentile societies. The presence of their Israelite past becomes unnameable and untraceable, both to them and to the people of Israel that remains. The name and family of the figure who fails to keep the covenant of Genesis 17 shall in this way be "cut off from his people," cut off from Israel, the one people sustained by the promise of God's election.[42] That those who disregard the covenant of circumcision will be cut off from their people is the rule of Israel's life and history.

This fate of disintegration or extinction is what confronts the tribe of Benjamin at the end of the book of Judges, after it has been ravaged in an Israelite civil war. The rest of Israel has killed practically

---

41. Josh. 7:24–26: "Then Joshua and all Israel with him took Achan son of Zerah, with the silver, the mantle, and the bar of gold, with his sons and daughters, with his oxen, donkeys, and sheep, and his tent and all that he had; and they brought them up to the Valley of Achor. Joshua said, 'Why did you bring trouble on us? The LORD is bringing trouble on you today.' And all Israel stoned him to death; they burned them with fire, cast stones on them, and raised over him a great heap of stones that remains to this day. Then the LORD turned from his burning anger. Therefore that place to this day is called the Valley of Achor."

42. The wilderness generation is an important witness to this historical force of God's judgment, which, as God's election, was limited to the destruction of one generation rather than effecting Israel's extinction. "Although all the people who came out [of Egypt] had been circumcised, yet all the people born on the journey through the wilderness after they had come out from Egypt had not been circumcised" (Josh. 5:5).

all Benjamin's men and then destroyed Benjamin's settlements, burning any remaining towns to the ground (Judges 20). The rest of Israel has also sworn not to intermarry with any remnant of Benjamin (Judg. 21:1), thereby cutting off Benjamin from Israel's future.

But the prospect of the disintegration of the tribe of Benjamin over time proves more than the rest of Israel can bear: "But the Israelites had compassion for Benjamin their kin, and said, 'One tribe is cut off from Israel this day'" (Judg. 21:6). The elders of the assembly (τῆς συναγωγῆς) of Israel ask what is to be done for the tiny remnant of Benjamin, so that Benjamin may remain in Israel's future (Judg. 21:16). "There must be heirs for the survivors of Benjamin, in order that a tribe may not be blotted out from Israel" (Judg. 21:17). A future for Benjamin is finally sought in the abduction of Canaanite women of Shiloh for Benjaminite wives. This, the closing scene of the declension narrative of Judges, is hardly promising; it forebodes more of the idolatry and lawlessness that has made Judges the depressing chapter in Israel's history that it is. And so the book of Judges concludes with the refrain of the book: "In those days there was no king in Israel; all the people did what was right in their own eyes."

Being "cut off" or "blotted out" from the people of Israel is perhaps best understood when seen as the fate confronting Israel as a whole across the entirety of the Deuteronomistic History. It is what apparently befalls most of the ten tribes of the northern kingdom, who prove unable to endure exile as a particular Israelite community under the power of Assyria. The beginning of the northern kingdom as distinct within Israel was idolatrous, even though its secession was in the name of the God of Israel (1 Kings 12-13). Any remaining sense or memory of being the people of the God of Abraham, Isaac, and Jacob appears to have mostly deteriorated through its continual affairs with surrounding gentile peoples and their gods and the rampant law-lessness among its tribes. The kings of the northern kingdom ignored the prophets faithful to the God of Israel and welcomed prophetic advisers who were easier to listen to. By the time Assyria invaded and relocated many of the northern kingdom's inhabitants—which was the common practice of Israel's imperial neighbors in their effort to subdue peoples obstructing their aims—the remnants of the northern kingdom found themselves without the resources to resist total assimilation. They had already been at home with the idolatrous, gentile ways in which they found themselves for some time before exile. In a short time in exile, then, they forgot the songs and stories of Israel. They often married members of their host societies, and, even when they didn't, their grandchildren did not understand the language of their grandparents. The rhythm of Israel's salvation through the liturgical year ceased to shape their life.[43]

Who knows how much of Israel's covenant and story the northern kingdom had remembered before exile? What we have in the Deuteronomistic History may be no more than what Judah remembered for them. In any case, in exile they adopted the ways of their host peoples, whose ways, languages, and gods became their own in time. Whatever may have been the genetic "continuity" with previous generations, in exile these descendants of Israel began to live by political and economic patterns that were not those of Israel's covenant, away from the land that had made Israel's covenant harder to forget. Thus, they ceased to know the God of Israel as their own. After generations (perhaps three or four, e.g., Exod. 20:5), to them Israel became a "they." In time they could not even remember when Israel had been a "we," nor could the living Judahites remember them

43. Hezekiah attempted to forestall this destruction according to 2 Chronicles 30. He appears to have succeeded so that a remnant of the northern kingdom was rejoined to the kingdom of Judah and thus ceased to be the remnant of a rival Israelite kingdom.

as once "our brother." One exception to this story of assimilation may be a community known as "the Samaritans." Otherwise, the northern kingdom appears to have left no remnant that was not restored to unity with the surviving remnant of Judah or assimilated by gentile peoples. This history of being cut off by war and assimilation was not a matter of Israelites failing to bear children and so conserve and pass down some timeless, pure, ethnic substance.[44] It was a matter of abandoning the law of the covenant for a gentile way of life over time. It was a matter of forgetting their God.[45]

Meanwhile, the southern kingdom faced the same threat of extinction to which its northern brother succumbed. The history of Judah, too, was fraught with idolatrous alliances and injustice. The Davidic kings often spurned the words of prophets faithful to the God of Abraham, Isaac, and Jacob. Like the northern kings, they attracted prophetic words that seemed more conducive to their security and prosperity, although some heeded the words of prophets who spoke the truth. And so Judah, too, endured the ravages of war, first with Assyria and then with Babylon, culminating in the scorching heat of exile, a death sentence for a people. Such was in fact the death sanctioned by the covenant.[46] The temple that commemorated and mediated the presence of Israel's God in Jerusalem was destroyed, and many of Judah's inhabitants, especially its institutionalized bearers of memory, were relocated throughout Babylonian lands. The people

---

44. I.e., producing children that were 0.5 Israelite, then 0.25 Israelite, then 0.125 Israelite, etc., or similar.

45. E.g., Jer. 23:27: "They [false prophets] plan to make my people forget my name by their dreams that they tell one another, just as their ancestors forgot my name for Baal."

46. The death of Deut. 30:15. See, e.g., Lev. 26:14–39; Deut. 28:15–68. Here we see that the curses of the covenant culminate in exile, but provide various warnings along the way, e.g., sickness of crop plants, animals and people; invasions by plant, animal, and human enemies; infertility of land, animals, and people; pennilessness; waterlessness; lawlessness; hopelessness. In short, the fabric of Israelite society by every possible measure would show signs of disintegration, calling upon Israel to repent.

was slated for absorption and thus extinction like other conquered peoples.

But Judah did not go the way of the northern kingdom.[47] Its people did learn the languages of their host peoples and adopt some of their ways, and many of them were no doubt totally assimilated by surrounding gentile peoples and their gods, much as their Israelite siblings of the north were. But by the grace of their God, some of Judah continued remembering the God of Abraham, Isaac, and Jacob as their own in exile; a remnant of Judah continued singing the story of Israel in languages new to them, struggling to be faithful to the covenant in conditions unimaginable to former generations. Despite knowing the temple and land of Israel only as a memory and a hope, despite the languishing of the line of David, they persisted in the politics of the covenant people of Israel, guided by prophets like Jeremiah. They found themselves unable to forget their God or their history, and thus God sustained in their flesh the promise of Israel's future.

Because the Israelite remnant of Judah was not allowed to succumb to the fate of the rival Israelite kingdom of the north, the history of Judah became the only living history of the people of Israel (perhaps along with that of the Samaritans[48]). And the life they lived bore witness to the one true God amidst fractious gentile societies in such a way that many gentiles found themselves drawn to the light of the God of Israel and joined Israel as proselytes.[49] In fact, the Israelite

---

47. E.g., Deut. 32:26-27: "I thought to scatter them and blot out the memory of them from humankind; but I feared provocation by the enemy, for their adversaries might misunderstand and say, 'Our hand is triumphant; it was not the LORD who did all this.'" Cf. Hosea 1.

48. For Samaritans as not gentile, in some sense Israelite, not adequately Jewish, etc., see, e.g., *m. Ter.* 4:14; *m. Peah* 4:1; cf. 2 Kgs. 17:24-33. Notice in these texts the persistent concern with Samaritan *practice* and Jewish *practice* in relation to Samaritans. Many Samaritans seem to have understood themselves as Israelite (*The Samaritans*, ed. Alan D. Crown [Tübingen: Mohr Siebeck, 1989], 196, 198). Of Tannaitic rabbis, Menachem Mor says, "The Sages during this period have a very positive attitude toward the Samaritans and considered them as part of Israel" (ibid., 22).

remnant of Judah eventually thrived in and through exile. Thus, while exile appeared to threaten all Israel with extinction, the promise of Israel was kept alive in a remnant of Judah that became "the Jews." This history was not merely a matter of Jews' conceiving children with other Jews, though that, along with the continued adoption of gentiles, was certainly involved; it was a matter of God's manifold provision for the future of Israel so that the Jewish remnant was unable to forget its God, the God of Israel. Israel's God promised never to forsake Israel; Israel would never cease to be a people in the world. And as the prophets foretold, Israel would one day know peaceful unity with the gentile nations of the world, a testament to which was the ongoing adoption of gentiles into Israel, even in exile. One day, all the nations of the world would be drawn to join the people of Israel in serving the God of Israel as the one true God and as their own God (e.g., Isa. 2:1-4). It could be no other way, for, however apparently weakened by the fires of judgment, the life of Israel could not be separated from God's life. And as the people of the God of creation, its life was inscribed into the very life of creation.

> Thus says the LORD, who gives the sun for light by day and the fixed order of the moon and the stars for light by night, who stirs up the sea so that its waves roar—the LORD of hosts is his name: If this fixed order were ever to cease from my presence, says the LORD, then also the offspring of Israel would cease to be a nation before me forever. Thus says the LORD: If the heavens above can be measured, and the foundations of the earth below can be explored, then I will reject all the offspring of Israel because of all they have done, says the LORD. (Jer. 31:35-37)

49. See ch. 1 above. For example, several centuries into Israel's dispersion, Seneca bemoans in *De Superstitione* the influence of the Jews: "Sceleratissimae gentis consuetudo conualuit, ut per omnes iam terras recepta sit; uicti uictoribus leges dederunt." "The customs of that most accursed people have gained such strength that they have now been received in all lands; the conquered have given laws to the conquerors" (qtd. Augustine, *Civ.* 6:11).

The sense in which the offspring of Israel would otherwise "cease to be a nation before me forever" is not that Israel would become "false," continuing to exist but not faithfully. It is that Israel would become extinct in the flesh, disintegrated as a people like so many other peoples of the past (e.g., Hittites, Canaanites, Jebusites, Assyrians, Babylonians, Medes). That is what God will prevent, according to Jeremiah, because Israel is a people by God's election, and God's election is the power that gives Israel the shape that it acquires in relation to the gentile nations around it. The ability of the remnant of Israel to endure the death of exile without being utterly destroyed by it attested that the life of Israel is stronger than death. It is the life of an indestructible promise, and so in exile its existence pointed to its promised future, after death had done its worst.

> When all these things have happened to you, the blessings and the curses that I have set before you, if you call them to mind among all the nations where the LORD your God has driven you, and return to the LORD your God, and you and your children obey him with all your heart and with all your soul, just as I am commanding you today, then the LORD your God will restore your fortunes and have compassion on you, gathering you again from all the peoples among whom the LORD your God has scattered you. Even if you are exiled to the ends of the world, from there the LORD your God will gather you, and from there he will bring you back. The LORD your God will bring you into the land that your ancestors possessed, and you will possess it; he will make you more prosperous and numerous than your ancestors. (Deut. 30:1-5)

Israel lived through death with this hope. But this hope was not predicated on Israel's subjective power to remember its God, but on the electing power of its God to remain unforgettable. The Israelite life that would outlast and defeat death was not Israel's own apart from its God but the life of that God *in* Israel, even *in* and *through* Israel's death. The God of Israel had brought the people into existence and would continue to form the people until the full unfolding of its eternal life in time. The above passage continues:

> Moreover, the LORD your God will circumcise your heart and the heart of your descendants, so that you will love the LORD your God with all your heart and with all your soul, in order that you may live. The LORD your God will put all these curses on your enemies and on the adversaries who took advantage of you. Then you shall again obey the LORD, observing all his commandments that I am commanding you today, and the LORD your God will make you abundantly prosperous in all your undertakings, in the fruit of your body, in the fruit of your livestock, and in the fruit of your soil. For the LORD will again take delight in prospering you, just as he delighted in prospering your ancestors, when you obey the LORD your God by observing his commandments and decrees that are written in this book of the law, because you turn to the LORD your God with all your heart and with all your soul. (Deut. 30:6-10)[50]

The Jeremiah passage about the indestructibility of Israel quoted just above was preceded by these words:

> The days are surely coming, says the LORD, when I will make a new covenant with the house of Israel and the house of Judah. It will not be like the covenant that I made with their ancestors when I took them by the hand to bring them out of the land of Egypt—a covenant that they broke, though I was their husband, says the LORD. But this is the covenant that I will make with the house of Israel after those days, says the LORD: I will put my law within them, and I will write it on their hearts; and I will be their God, and they shall be my people. No longer shall they teach one another, or say to each other, "Know the LORD," for they shall all know me, from the least of them to the greatest, says the LORD; for I will forgive their iniquity, and remember their sin no more. (Jer. 31:31-34)

---

50. Cf. "A new heart I will give you, and a new spirit I will put within you; and I will remove from your body the heart of stone and give you a heart of flesh. I will put my spirit within you, and make you follow my statutes and be careful to observe my ordinances. Then you shall live in the land that I gave to your ancestors; and you shall be my people, and I will be your God" (Ezek. 36:26-28).

264

Jeremiah prophesies to a people who are forgetting their God.[51] In generations past, Israel was loosely knit by the worship of the God of Abraham, Isaac, and Jacob, riddled as it was with the presence of rival gods (e.g., Baal), the imaged lure of competing political orders. Now Israel seems to be unraveling altogether, as those who remember the God of Israel have to urge other Israelite survivors in exile, "Know the LORD."[52] Such Israelites find themselves on withering branches of Israel, as their future is being woven over generations into the gentile peoples among whom they live. The overwhelming heat of exile makes the time of the people of Israel seem short; extinction approaches from the horizon.

But Israel's time is not short, promises the LORD through Jeremiah. Israel cannot cease to be a people before its God any more than the sun, moon, and stars can cease to order the heavens and the earth. The days are coming when whoever is left of Israel—not only its priests and great teachers—will know the LORD as their God. The LORD will be the God of reference among the people in that time, as the gentiles and their gods will somehow have ceased to threaten Israel's present and future. This will not be a feat of Israel. Israel's promise does not lie in its faithfulness to the covenant already revealed. The covenant life of Israel's promised future will be the work of the "I" of God's self. God will make the new covenant that will fulfill the everlasting covenant promise of Israel. God will forgive Israel's sins. God will forget Israel's sins so that Israel cannot forget its God.[53]

The Judahite remnant of Israel that God sustained was not morally unambiguous. It did not consist only of the righteous. It was not

---

51. Cf. Deut. 28:45, 62-68; 32:15-18; Hosea 2:13; 4:1-19; 13:6; Isa. 17:4-11; 64:7; Jer. 2:32; 3:21-22; 50:6; 1 Macc. 1:11-15, 41-50; 2 Macc. 2:1-3.

52. The meaning of such passages is obscured if LORD is not read as a proper noun, i.e., the name of Israel's God.

53. Such claims should not be read as speculations about God's inner psychology or a forensic realm, but as commentary on a historical outworking of God's electing presence in Israel, and therefore of the material conditions of Israel's existence.

the true Israel while another, unrighteous Israel was false or not genuinely Israel. Even after being burned down to a Judahite stump of its former glory, so many of its families cut off from their people, the tree of Israel consisted of good and bad Israelites, each Israelite both good and bad, although some were certainly better than others. Nevertheless, what characterized this remnant as a whole was that when they sinned, they kept confessing their sin to the God of Abraham, Isaac, and Jacob, who remained with them by name so as to be remembered by them. God refused to let them turn to false gods and forget the God of Israel as their God, and this was their faith. There remained in and as this remnant of the people the order of Israel's promised covenant relation with its God, and so, unlike those cut off or blotted out from Israel altogether, they continued to call out to the God of Israel. By virtue of God's faithful and electing presence in Israel, they continued to remember the God of Israel, and so they continued to *be* Israel. While many were cut off from Israel over time, dissolved in the gentile sea around them, some were sustained as Israel, growing through the manifold organs of Israel's life and even adopting gentiles from the sea around them. Such has been the ebb and flow of the election of Israel through intimacy with gentiles.

The ebb and flow of Israel's being by election does not obtain only at its border, in the intimacy of its ongoing exchange with gentile peoples there, however. As we saw with Barth in the previous chapter, election is also a matter of distinctions within Israel. The same election of God that forms Israel's being in relation to gentile peoples over time is forming Israel internally, determining its order or shape in the flesh. I have already mentioned Achan as an example of a family/name cut off from Israel, leaving Israel's internal order altered by its departure, and leaving the presence of an admonitory memory. What the ebb and flow of election means internally for

Israel is even clearer in cases like Korah (Numbers 16) and Eli, where it concerns the shape and power of the priesthood. Eli's sons "had no regard for YHWH" (1 Sam. 2:12) and thus corrupted the priesthood. The sentence upon Eli is this:

> See, a time is coming when I will cut off your strength and the strength of your ancestor's family, so that no one in your family will live to old age. Then in distress you will look with greedy eye on all the prosperity that shall be bestowed upon Israel; and no one in your family shall ever live to old age. The only one of you whom I shall not cut off from my altar shall be spared to weep out his eyes and grieve his heart; all the members of your household shall die by the sword. The fate of your two sons, Hophni and Phinehas, shall be the sign to you—both of them shall die on the same day. I will raise up for myself a faithful priest, who shall do according to what is in my heart and in my mind. I will build him a sure house, and he shall go in and out before my anointed one forever. Everyone who is left in your family shall come to implore him for a piece of silver or a loaf of bread, and shall say, "Please put me in one of the priest's places, that I may eat a morsel of bread." (1 Sam. 2:31-36)

The priestly presence of Eli in Israel's future, embattled for generations to come, would finally wither to the point of disintegration.[54] A similar fate befalls the kings of the northern kingdom beginning with Jeroboam. Each one fails to begin a dynastic rule, the male descendants of each one destroyed before any can succeed his father. The same fate threatens the house of David, which itself rose to rule by the ebb and flow that removed Saul's family from power. But the house of David is spared and against all odds continues from son of David to son of David into the Babylonian exile. The way one son of David after the next succeeded his father, however minimal this political stability, is God's election in faithful fulfillment of the promise to David about his and Israel's

---

54. See 1 Sam. 4:12-18; 14:1-3ff; 1 Sam. 21–22; 1 Kgs. 2:27 for this tale of shame and destruction, which finally drifts into oblivion, leaving behind a steady whisper of warning for subsequent generations.

future (e.g., 2 Samuel 7).[55] Thus, election determines not only the shape of Israel as a whole but the particular internal order of that whole.[56]

The epic history of Israel evoked thus far *tells* the election of Israel according to the Tanakh, instead of defining it as a timeless law of ethnicity or in a christological realm of formal representation. Having clarified the sense of being "cut off from" the people of Israel, I can venture a summary description of "the indestructible continuity in the being of Israel." It is the unfolding presence of God in Israel by name, whereby Israel remembers its God as its own, as opposed to forgetting its God by being assimilated by gentile peoples, who in turn remember other gods as their own. God's election is thus what continuously creates and forms Israel as distinguishable from the gentile nations. Like other parts of creation, Israel is flesh subject to decay and corruption, which leads to the disintegration of peoples, save for the electing activity of God that sustains and shapes Israel's life through the death of one generation after the next and all manner of calamity. It is the absence of this electing activity of God (but not the absence of this God) in gentile peoples whereby the same decay can lead—and often has led—to extinction, that is, to a time when no living community remembers such peoples as their ancestors and therefore themselves (e.g., Hittites, Canaanites, Jebusites, Assyrians, Babylonians, Medes).

To tell God's election of Israel according to Scripture in this epic mode, then, is to tell how certain branches and certain ways of living

---

55. While there is much more to the continuity of the Davidic line than "biology," here we see that continuity from parents to children, in this case father to son, is indeed part of how God is present and electing within Israel's history.

56. Sometimes this involves a ruling by God through an Israelite authority in favor of a withering family in Israel, as in the case of God's ruling through Moses for the daughters of Zelophehad (Num. 27:1-11). The narrative of Numbers conspicuously returns to the future of this name in its closing chapter (Num. 36:1-12). In the transmortem life of Zelophehad we see how the God of Israel sustains and shapes the numbers of the people.

in Israel endured while others did not, and this is also to tell how those enduring branches came to live in the particular shape that they did and do. As named by the curses and blessings of the covenant, the God of Israel has made certain branches and ways of living difficult to sustain in Israel. Meanwhile, God has maintained and invigorated other branches and ways of living. Some Israelite communities were cut off, their future in Israel utterly destroyed through the sudden burning of war or more gradually being woven out of Israel and into gentile peoples by assimilation over generations. These branches were burned away from Israel's flesh, whether before exile or in exile, their "biological" or "genetic" descendants eventually losing all memory of their Israelite past and thus any living share in the flesh of Israel. The remnant of Israel had lost the ability to name or trace the relation of those cut off to their common, Israelite past in service to the God of Abraham, Isaac, and Jacob.

For those cut off, a process that can be anticipated but not guaranteed by excommunication (which is what the term "cut off" seems to denote in some places), there eventually remained no basis (e.g., no memory, no occasion, no will) on which any living part of Israel could claim them as Israelite, much less a basis on which they could so claim themselves. They were "handed over" to the idolatry and injustice in which their ancestors and they had been living, eventually blotted out within Israel (some tribes were dissolved within other tribes) or gobbled up by gentile societies as ordered by their gods. Some of the Israelites who found themselves on branches being cut off (e.g., Jeroboam) left legacies of shame, a name of derision in Israel; others left no legacy at all, their memory eradicated as time wore on.[57] Meanwhile, some were not cut off but persisted as the saved remnant so that they continued to participate in the

---

57. They may also have appeared to get off scot-free while the righteous suffered, as the psalmist complains.

ongoing and living remembrance of their Israelite past and thus to be Israel in the present. Still others were adopted into Israel from among the gentiles, and so received the Israelite past and future as their own and became part of the flesh of Israel in the present, remembered as such in Israel's future.

This material shaping of the people of Israel over time and in the flesh, as I've just described it, *is* the electing activity of the God of Israel. That activity is not a decree hidden before time and merely applied in time. It is not the continuity of Israelite genes. Nor is it, as Barth presents it, the activity of God that must remain before every moment of time so as not to lose its freedom by becoming a dead law in time. It is indeed before time but, as such, it is working its way *as* Israel in and through time. It is the history of Israel, the particular shape that, according to the Tanakh, God has given to the flesh of the people of Israel in dangerously intimate, mutual relation to surrounding gentile peoples and continual, internal churning. This is the ongoing drama of election through the covenant.[58] As determined by God's election, Israel is thus the people that remembers the God of Abraham, Isaac, and Jacob as its own as opposed to 1) those who have forgotten that God as their own among gentile peoples and 2) those gentile peoples who as such have not known the God of Israel as their own for time beyond remembrance.[59]

---

58. The implication here is that the promised family of Abraham is a visibly gathering people, its only invisibility the presence of its past and future in the present generation and the rest of their impression on the earth. It is not the people that are invisibly genetic descendants of Abraham or invisibly righteous in relation to God.

59. Although we remember no other people that has known the God of Israel as its own, we do remember other persons who have known that God as their own (e.g., Melchizedek in Genesis 14; see also Gen. 4:26; 24:50). It is also clearly the case that non-Israelite peoples revered the God of Israel, even if they did not know that God as uniquely their own and denied that that God was the only God (e.g., 1 Samuel 5; people in the realm of King Achish of Gath, 1 Sam. 29:6). The way Israel remembers the beginning of creation implies that not knowing the God of Israel as their own is not original to gentile communities, but a departure from distant

The epic history of election is indeed a drama, the tense drama of God's electing Israel into its particular being through the blessings and curses of the covenant, of Israel's wrestling with God. As Barth has rightly claimed, there is a profound disequilibrium to the blessings and curses, to the "Yes" and "No" of God that shaped Israel, for the people persisted. God's "Yes" and "No" did not cancel one another out and add up to Israel's extinction—it is not a zero-sum relation. The intimate, ongoing encounter between Israel and the gentiles—the ebb and flow of Israel's election through the covenant drama—meant a continuity for Israel that it did not mean for its hostile gentile neighbors, for whom it meant a decaying discontinuity, as gentile powers superseded their gentile predecessors one after the other.[60] The curses that Israel endured warned the remnant of Israel against certain ways of living, and so were a subordinate moment in God's blessing Israel with life and sustained the promise of its eternal life by pruning. The curses of the covenant are not rivals to the blessings, but God's "No" to Israel's refusal of God's blessings, and this "No" is itself a blessing that keeps Israel from extinction, guiding Israel back to covenant obedience and drawing the gaze of gentile nations to Israel and its God (e.g., Deut. 28:37; Jer. 24:9; Isa. 49), pointing the way to Israel's faithfulness and future.

The dramatic contingency of the covenant materially gives shape to the people over time, but Israel lives by the underlying, unconditional promise of God's election. Whatever fires Israel endures over time, they cannot burn Israel away altogether. They can only sculpt Israel's body, and the judgment that Israel undergoes in

ancestors who did in fact know the one true God as their own (i.e., Adam and Eve, Enosh in the time of whom "people began to invoke the name of the LORD," Gen. 4:26).

60. E.g., Bar. 3:16-23.

time contributes to its blessing, its life.[61] The epic of the election of Israel is a history of hope.

Exile in the Ebb and Flow of the Election of the People: A Short Engagement with Carl Schmitt

Let us pause here to consider a point of clarification on the politics of election in light of Israel's exile, the culmination of the curse of the covenant. Although I have begun to move beyond Barth in this chapter by attending to the history of Israel in the flesh, my argument here resembles Barth's various claims that God's election is revealed particularly in Israel's breakdown. But whereas for Barth this breakdown is distinctly a matter of Israel's subjective moral failure, I understand Israel's subjectivity to be morally ambiguous in this breakdown. The disintegrating power and culmination of Israel's breakdown in the flesh is, in the language of the covenant, death (e.g., Deut. 30:19), and this means curses on the land, Israel's bodies, its animals, and finally gentile invasion and the exile of the covenant people. It is not only or primarily a matter of Israel's unfaithfulness. Death is its condition, whether the people bear it in faithfulness or unfaithfulness. God's provision for Israel's ongoing remembrance of its God in and through the death of exile has profound implications. Exile is the apocalypse that the people is itself, and persists, only by the gracious faithfulness of its God. Death is not a suspension

---

61. Here we see the relation between the unconditional nature of election in the flesh and the contingency of the covenant drama in that same Israelite flesh. Israel's exile brings into bold relief that the way Israel lives affects the shape of Israel, while that shape is always the work of the God of Israel. Israel has brought the death of exile on itself, *and* it is God who not only brings death upon Israel but brings Israel through death. God gives Israel life unconditionally—and that means in and through death—but the life that God gives Israel, the suffering life that moves through death, is also what Israel's sin has done to Israel. What remains through death is at once what Israel's sin has done to Israel and the life that God has given Israel. Thus, Israel's sin never has the final word, but Israel is always accountable through God's election. This unfolding relation in the flesh between the unconditional election of God and the contingency of corruptible Israel reaches its fulfillment in the cross and resurrection of Jesus Messiah.

of Israel's life but the dramatic revelation of the life that has been unfolding in it from the beginning, disclosed in and through Israel's death. Exile uniquely revealed the electing power of God that constitutes Israel throughout its history, the miracle that is the life of Israel all along, not only in its most precarious moments but also in its most apparently normal and natural moments. Anticipated by the wilderness generation, exiled Israel confronted life in material conditions that seemed only to threaten its very existence as a people—the time and space of the curse: the hopelessness of a recent and most devastating military defeat, no land of its own for economy and security, no fixed center of worship and memory, no established structure of governance—in short, the sentence of death for a people. It had only the hope of God's promise. What, or rather who, can be said to constitute the people in this condition of approaching extinction?

This question is, not incidentally, parallel to Carl Schmitt's modern question about "the *pouvoir constituant* of the people"[62] in what he calls "the state of exception." This modern question arose, he observes, when the presence of God as traditionally and theologically conceived was no longer accepted as providing for political order. "The state of exception" in Schmitt's *Political Theology* is his theoretical attempt to retain "transcendence."[63] Schmitt recognizes that the political order of any "people" is contingent, such that without knowledge of its basis and an institution corresponding to that basis, it is subject to disintegrating instability (continual revolution, i.e., supersession). "The state of exception" thus names the condition of the people in the suspension of its apparently normal political order, and therefore the exceptional condition from which

---

62. Carl Schmitt, *Political Theology: Four Chapters on the Concept of Sovereignty*, trans. George Schwab (Chicago: University of Chicago Press, 2006), 51.
63. Ibid., 50.

its political order must historically and logically be constituted. It is in this condition that the transcendent, sovereign power that in fact constitutes the people is revealed, for "sovereign is he who decides on the exception."[64]

"The state of exception" is a borderline concept and so must remain abstract, a piece of negative theology, as it were. It cannot describe an already known state of emergency, for political order cannot name its own limit. The law of a political order cannot define the limit of the law but is itself defined by that limit. Sovereignty, then, is precisely that power that determines the order or life of a people in the state of exception, that is, when the law of a people is suspended in the face of the threat of its undoing. In fact, sovereign power is that which decides both when the exception obtains and how to address it. It is itself the power that, as the basis of the law, suspends the law for the sake of the political order, that is, for the sake of "the people." The most the law of the people can do, then, according to Schmitt, is to name ahead of time who is to decide on the exception, and then it must entrust itself absolutely to the one so named should the exception arise.

The sovereign power must be a who—a person. Schmitt holds that no people can trace its existence to an order or law that precedes it and that a people is by definition not all people. In other words, a people was and is constituted by an act of differentiating will,[65] itself predicated on the primordial difference between friend and enemy (i.e., the difference between one people and others that is decided and effected by that act of will).[66] What constitutes the people is thus a decision, and only a personal power can make a decision. Only

---

64. Ibid., 5.
65. Thus, peoplehood is voluntarist; claims to another foundation are romantic and false, argues Schmitt.
66. Schmitt, *The Concept of the Political: Expanded Edition*, trans. George Schwab (Chicago: University of Chicago Press, 2007 [1996]), 26.

a personal power can have called a people into existence and then determine the order of the people when there is no law to guide it or when the law is unable to guide it. Only a personal power is "free" from the limit of the law (i.e., transcends it). Only a personal power can determine the difference between friend and enemy so as to save and sustain the people (i.e., save the friends from their enemies). Denying the personal nature of this sovereign power—claiming that such power can be legally contained or operated technically as in modern liberal democratic process, for example—is simply to ignore the personal or subjective dimension of the power that is always coursing through the entire political order. It is to deny the basis of the political order itself, the peoplehood of the people.

But Jacob Taubes pointed out to Schmitt, a Christian Nazi, that he had overlooked (or misunderstood) the sovereign and determining power of God's election of Israel (appealing to Rom. 11:28).[67] Schmitt was seeking a "christological" instantiation of that power with the institution of the *Reichspräsident* (the Weimar antecedent of the Führer of National Socialism). He was trying to find and secure the being of the people ahead of time, abstracted from the flesh, in a political office. But in so doing, in trying to name God's election as a human executive's decision, in trying to present Germany's president as the divine messiah in whom the people's divine life was secure, Schmitt offers some helpful insight. He offers a concept for understanding the sovereign power that was indeed revealed in Israel's exile, the apocalyptic and personal nature of God's electing rule.

Exile was something of the state of exception for Israel, when the people was threatened with its undoing in the face of gentile enemies. The law that guided Israel seemed incomplete, if not inadequate,

---

67. Jacob Taubes, *The Political Theology of Paul*, trans. Dana Hollander (Stanford: Stanford University Press, 2004), 112.

even if the law named, sanctioned, and thus encoded exile itself. If Israel was like other peoples, it could indeed disintegrate in such conditions as many other peoples already had and have since. Who, then, determined the shape of Israel's ongoing existence in and through the death of exile? The Sovereign who has always made Israel the people it has been: the God of Israel.[68] This is not to say that the God of Israel suddenly came to life in Israel's exile, but that in exile the life of God that was always electing Israel into being was starkly revealed, the life of Israel radically disclosed in and through Israel's death. This is God's personal, deciding life in Israel, in the flesh.

The covenant law as legal code could not and did not define this life but was defined by this life. Israel did not constitute itself by obeying the legal code of the covenant and by being blessed accordingly, but was constituted by God so as to be able to obey the covenant and endure the consequences when it didn't (consequences which are themselves part of the covenant). It was constituted by God's election, as attested by the history of the covenant law (the law of the covenant is both history and code). The rule of the law as legal code could shape the people in the flesh, as it named and empowered the future of blessing for the obedient and the curse of withering and being burned away for the disobedient. But it could not originate, constitute, or define the flesh of the people. The rule of blessings and curses derives from the promise of election and is not co-ordinate with it. Thus, failing to perform circumcision, offer sacrifices, practice kashruth, and observe the Sabbath could mean being cut off from the people, but being cut off was not reducible to these failures, nor could such failures mean the cutting off of the people itself. Keeping the hope of Israel's promise alive, God signaled

---

68. This sovereignty of the God of Israel, not only over Israel but over the whole world, is an important theme of the exilic book of Daniel.

both Israel's vulnerability and its indestructibility in the wilderness when circumcision was suspended and a generation was destroyed, when God provided for Israel's security, economy (e.g., food), and memory, when God led and followed Israel in judgment and hope. God further disclosed Israel's vulnerability and indestructibility in exile. The practices of covenant obedience themselves were shaken to their foundation and forced to undergo radical reinterpretation.[69] The people persisted in exile by God's electing activity, by the grace that provided for Israel's remembrance of its God.

Citing Kirkegaard, Schmitt claims, rightly in my view, that the exception "confirms not only the rule but also its existence, which derives only from the exception."[70] The exception of exile confirms not only the rule of the blessings and curses of the covenant but also the very existence of that rule. In other words, the exception of exile confirms not only the rule according to which Israel is shaped by God in the flesh over time, but also the very life of election from which the rule of the covenant issues to form Israel the way that it does. Thus, God's election is not limited by Israel's obedience. If we must speak of the limit of God's election, it is the self-determination of God as this is revealed in the shape that Israel acquires in the flesh over time, especially as it moves through the death of exile. Through the death of Israel by which God reveals and determines God's self, God forms the people of Israel, not out of scratch but out of Israel's death.[71] God's

---

69. While we should not and cannot claim that the whole remnant of Israel continued to practice circumcision, we should note that circumcision, along with kashruth and Sabbath observance, proved relatively practicable in exile relative to other covenant practices, perhaps even growing in importance in such conditions. These became the marks of the Jewish community, according to non-Jewish historians such as Tacitus and poets such as Juvenal. They would become, as we see in the New Testament, the battleground for Israel's response to the final apocalypse of its God's rule in the Messiah.

70. Schmitt, *Political Theology*, 15.

71. That the death of Israel is the self-determination of the God of Israel is borne witness by texts that publish the effect of Israel's exile on its God's name (e.g., Isa. 52:3-6; Ezek. 36:20-38) as well as by God's departure from the temple (Ezekiel 10).

electing activity courses in, through, and as the whole of the history of Israel, in its faith and in its faithlessness, encouraging its faith and discouraging its faithlessness, moving Israel to love God as God loves Israel.

The history of Israel's election through exile helps us to guard against the temptation of describing Israel's election in terms of the remnant's obedience to the covenant law. We might want to say that Israel remembered its God because some Israelites continued to perform circumcision, observe the Sabbath and other festivals, and eat kashruth, or that they obeyed some other crucial subset of the covenant commands. We might want to say that God's election is God's promise that at least some of Israel will not forsake the law of the covenant or that God's election is ontically equivalent to a modicum of Israelite faithfulness (which could then harden into a boundary to be policed, however apparently generous). But the Tanakh won't let us do that. That is not the basis of Israel's hope in exile, for the covenant has been forsaken. The faithfulness of some is therefore not what Israel remembers as its hope. Israel can only hope in the mercy of God's election; God's faithfulness is the only covenant faithfulness that it can remember as the basis of its hope and its life.

> All Israel has transgressed your law and turned aside, refusing to obey your voice. So the curse and the oath written in the law of Moses, the servant of God, have been poured out upon us, because we have sinned against you. He has confirmed his words, which he spoke against us and against our rulers, by bringing upon us a calamity so great that what has been done against Jerusalem has never before been done under the whole heaven. Just as it is written in the law of Moses, all this calamity has come upon us. We did not entreat the favor of the LORD our God, turning from our iniquities and reflecting on his fidelity. So the LORD kept watch over this calamity until he brought it upon us. Indeed, the LORD our God is right in all that he has done; for we have disobeyed his voice. And now, O Lord our God, who brought your people out of the land of Egypt with a mighty hand and made your name renowned

even to this day—we have sinned, we have done wickedly. O Lord, in view of all your righteous acts, let your anger and wrath, we pray, turn away from your city Jerusalem, your holy mountain; because of our sins and the iniquities of our ancestors, Jerusalem and your people have become a disgrace among all our neighbors. Now therefore, O our God, listen to the prayer of your servant and to his supplication, and for your own sake, Lord, let your face shine upon your desolated sanctuary. Incline your ear, O my God, and hear. Open your eyes and look at our desolation and the city that bears your name. We do not present our supplication before you on the ground of our righteousness, but on the ground of your great mercies. O Lord, hear; O Lord, forgive; O Lord, listen and act and do not delay! For your own sake, O my God, because your city and your people bear your name! (Dan. 9:11-19)[72]

The only basis of Israel's appeal is that it bears God's name, that it is remembered as the people of its God. Its only hope is its God, and this hope keeps it from forgetting. The law's sentence of exile and gentile enmity has shut up all Israel in disobedience, so that Israel's life through and beyond the death of exile is presented exclusively as the unconditional and merciful work of its God. No decision or practice of Israel's own constitutes the basis of its life and promise. This does not mean that no one observed any of the covenant law in exile, nor that God's mercy renders Israelite obedience immaterial. It means that Israel's condemned condition was not attenuated by such observance and that practices of obedience were a witness to Israel's hope rather than the basis of it. It also means that Israel's life is the fruit of its disobedience as well as its obedience. The disobedient who have been cut off leave an altered shape of Israel behind, along with a legacy of shame that has subsequently deterred the remnant from the same path of destruction.

Exile left Israel with a story that warns subsequent generations against certain ways of living: idolatrous, faithless, and violent ways that lead to terrible suffering for the people. And yet, exile also left

---

72. Cf. Psalm 44, esp. v. 26; Ps. 115:1-2; Jer. 14:7-9, 19-22; Bar. 2:19—3:8; Ezek. 36:22-38.

Israel with nothing of itself on which to predicate its life, confront its enemies, discipline its membership, or otherwise attempt to ensure its future. The existence of the people, and therefore its identity, cannot be a matter of its own decision or agency. No faithfulness of its own, no ideas of its own, no perceived virtue of its own, can function truthfully as the basis for deciding who is in and who is out, for regulating its life, or for engaging threats to its existence. In other words, here in God's electing activity in the depths of Israel's suffering we see with particular clarity what it means to be "we the people" of God. It means that the existence, and therefore the identity, of the people is given by God, such that the people is empowered to meet the deepest challenges to its life both with powerful measures of resistance and without violence. The people is freed from the presumption that its life depends on its own striving or policing, and so it can be a community of both discipline and unconditional love. In fact, this discipline and this love are not competitive. The unconditional love of God that refuses to settle for anything other than a community of corresponding, nonviolent love lies at the heart of the politics of election. It is the discipline of peoplehood.

The Outline of the Epic Drama of Election in Israel's Covenant Practice

Returning to Genesis 17, we can now see that the promissory covenant of circumcision outlines the epic drama of unconditional election *in and through* the contingency of the covenant. It also implies that Israel is neither a people sustained by mere procreation, nor one whose power or promise lies in its numbers. The many stories of barrenness in its foundational generations, and God's command to sacrifice Isaac, remind Israel that its life and future do not come from itself, from its own striving or any "law of nature" (and this has implications for what nature is). The birth of every child to Israel, like the birth of other children, is a miracle. Israel has never been "an ethnicity," whatever its participants may believe along the way. Its actual, ongoing life is the work of God's election, as shaped over time through circumcision and other practices of the covenant life. In these practices, God continually cuts away the idolatry and injustice of Israel's past and warns it against the idolatry and injustice in its present, which lead to forgetting the God of Israel and thus to oblivion among, and then as, the gentiles. Merely bringing children into the world guarantees nothing about Israel's future, for Israelite children can be born into an Israelite society riddled with idolatry and injustice, a life already in the throes of assimilation by surrounding gentile peoples. Genetic descendants of Israel can be destroyed in war or similar judgments and, over generations, cease to be Israel by being absorbed into gentile peoples, all traces of their relation to Israel disintegrated and forgotten.[73]

For children born to Israel to continue Israel's promise in the flesh, they must be born into a time in which God has provided for Israel's remembrance of its God and forestalled absorption into gentile societies. Circumcision by Abraham's promised family witnesses to that provision and sustenance. The neglect of the practice of circumcision in Israel's history is a bad sign, according to the Tanakh.[74] Thus, what conceiving and bearing children means

---

73. If Kiera Feldman's description is any indication, this is something that the enterprise Birthright Israel has forgotten. Getting young Jewish people together in Israel for all expenses paid, ten-day trips of Zionist narrative and intra-Jewish sex does not promise much for Israel's future, in or out of the land. See Kiera Feldman, "The Romance of Birthright Israel," *The Nation*, July 4–11, 2011, 22–26. Israel in defiance of Torah did not enjoy covenant blessings (including land) in the past, and only Israel as shaped by Torah can hope for the blessings of the land in the present and future.

74. The danger of forgoing circumcision and of intermarriage, i.e., the way they invite idolatry, is given poignant consideration (at a crucial juncture in the narrative) in Exod. 4:24–26, when the LORD (or an angel of the LORD) met Moses in the night "to kill him." Moses was delivered by Zipporah the Midianite when she circumcised their son and touched Moses' "feet" (i.e., genitals) with the foreskin. This striking passage tells us that Moses could not deliver God's firstborn son

for Israel is contingent on the time in which children are born, particularly the conditions of the people's life in that time as provided by God and the derivative vitality of covenant practice among the people. That particular time is more determinative of the shape of Israel's life in that time than the way particular Israelite communities then choose to live in that time (e.g., consider the difference between being born under Solomon or born in Babylon, between being born in a temple-based Israelite society and an Israelite society that knows only a destroyed temple). By God's election, certain times in Israel's history bear certain possibilities for Israel's life that other times simply do not. Thus, by God's election the people is not determined by the way it lives in time, but by the time in which it lives, its time always preceding how it lives in it, but its way of living always affecting the time that it leaves behind for subsequent generations. Consequently, the time of God's election determines, among other things, what it means to obey the commands of the covenant (e.g., the meaning of sacrifice after the temple is destroyed).

But as we have seen in Israel's exile, practices of covenant faithfulness are not the basis of the Israelite remnant's life. It remains primarily the work of God's faithfulness, from which Israel's faithfulness follows. While many who fail to perform certain practices are cut off from their people, and the people is thus shaped by losing the branches that forget their God and adopt other gods, the rest of Israel's ongoing life in the flesh is sustained by God. It is sustained by God even when that remnant of Israel abandons the practices enjoined by the covenant. While the sentence of being

from Egypt for worship or announce the death of Egypt's firstborn without delivering his own son up for worship. Zipporah thus kept blood from coming upon her and Moses' family (much as Israel would do with the blood of the Passover lamb). Moses' seed needed to be consecrated. Here we see that circumcision should not be considered covenant obedience in the abstract. Its power to promote Israel's life depends on the complex of practices that attend the concrete circumcision of a male child or adult (e.g., sacrifice, storytelling, the presence of witnesses). This is why circumcision among other peoples is not what circumcision is in Israel.

cut off from the people is a determinative rule of Israel's life, it is itself a rule determined by God's election and not in itself absolute. God often relents from cutting off unfaithful branches. God always sustains the life of some—those who, unfaithful though they may be, remember that God as their own in the midst of their people's unfaithfulness. But God does not do this because that remnant has obeyed the covenant. God does this for God's own sake (i.e., God's name), which God has bound to Israel by irrevocable promises to Israel's ancestors. As the people of God, Israel stands and falls by God's election. When the life of the people becomes bankrupt and God unleashes the culmination of the covenant curses by exiling Israel, subjecting it as a whole to the electing judgment that cuts off, God spares and forms a remnant in which the future of all Israel continues. The practices of the covenant are thus secondary to God's election in the determination of the shape of Israel, so that we can say that covenant practices shape Israel only insofar as God is *in* Israel as it engages in those practices.

That the election of Israel cannot be reduced to a dead law of ethnicity, but is God's activity in dynamic relation with Israel's secondary, covenant practices such as circumcision, does not render procreation inconsequential for Israel's ongoing life. Quite the contrary: circumcision in particular is intimately related to procreation. It is not incidental that the cutting of circumcision affects the organ of procreation of those who carry the generational names of Israel, the men who bear the named seed of Israel across generations and thus the names according to which the promised land is distributed. Thus, circumcision names Israel's covenant response to and participation in God's gift of continued life, as Israel must live a life of cutting away idolatry and injustice, a life of remembering its God. Procreation is therefore not immaterial to the indestructible continuity in the being of Israel. Bearing children and raising them in the covenant way of life has been an important part of Israel's continuity; children born to Israelite parents have been a gift of God—not a guarantee but part of Israel's being and a testament to its promised future. As the Tanakh testifies again and again, God does not make Israel God's own only after the birth of children but *in* the conception and birth of children to Israel. And it is the relatively stable covenant community of parents bringing up their children together across generations that is able to resist assimilation to gentile society and adopt gentiles into the Israelite way of life (i.e., the covenant). This relative stability, though it is only relative, is the context in which the covenant practices that regulate and shape Israel are maintained. It is what exile threatens with the worst kind of disruption. But the contingency of birth itself and the fact of Israel's adoption of gentiles (even "off the record") preclude "by birth" from being a timeless law of Israel's life. Instead, these call for covenant practices like circumcision whereby the life of Israel has been shaped, recognized, and regulated. That is why the birth of children, far from being "enough" to constitute members of the covenant community as such, is to be followed by practices like circumcision, which image and form the covenant way in which Israel's life continues.

The Contingency of the History of Election in the Minutiae of Israel's Life

To say that birth to Israelite parents is contingent is to go further than saying that procreation guarantees nothing about Israel's future. It is to say that procreation itself requires certain material conditions for its actuality. In addition to the contingency of whether and how children born to Israel are brought up as the people of Israel's God, the life of Israel continues in the peculiar histories, conditions, and circumstances whereby particular women and particular men come together and are able to conceive and have children. Thus, the birth of children depends, for example, upon the land that nourishes the people who have children, the health of their bodies, the political order in which their lives take the shape that they do, the many practices that shape the life of the people, and such trivial matters as weather, traffic patterns, and the subconscious rhythms of daily life. All of these affect who has sexual relations with whom and whether, when, and whom they conceive. This is how particular Israelite people have come together to have particular Israelite children.

Such histories, conditions, and circumstances, down to all the minutiae of Israel's life in relation to its gentile neighbors, are not immaterial to God's election of Israel in the flesh. God's election is *in* such minutiae. Nothing about Israel's ongoing life is automatic. We are always talking about particular people when we say that the people of Israel continued through time, and so if we say that Israel continued in part "by birth," we have to be able to ask, "Which births?" "Which parents?" "At which moments?" "Under what conditions?" and so on. We have to be able to ask such questions even if we can't provide adequate answers to them. Otherwise, "by birth" becomes a lifeless principle, a dead law of ethnicity that hides from historical scrutiny and the community's thankfulness the innumerable, particular, and contingent conditions and circumstances that have availed for the birth of particular children to particular Israelite parents. Conceiving and bearing children is thus one practice among many in and through which the life or being of Israel continues, and these many other practices in turn contribute to the conditions in which Israelites conceive and bear the children that they do.

I have pointed here only to the contingency of Israelite births. Similar gestures should be made in relation to the way children born to Israelite parents are formed as Israelite in community and the way particular gentiles are adopted in particular ways into the people of

Israel. Mythologizing the being of Israel into an ethnicity imagines a false purity and stability into Israel's identity. It attempts to eliminate the manifold contingency of the births of the particular children that have in fact been born to Israel and then raised as Israelite. It ignores the gracious conditions, circumstances, and practices that shape the birth and formation of those lives. And of course it denies the Israelization of gentiles. Imposing closure on Israel's identity in this way inevitably serves a violent regime of power, one that cannot wait upon the God of Israel to determine the shape of the people by God's election in time.

In my account of the epic history of God's electing activity (i.e., the ebb and flow), I have described the "indestructible continuity in the being of Israel" as the activity of God whereby Israel remembers its God as its own as opposed to being dissolved in gentile peoples. But the way that Israel continues in and through the innumerable and not altogether traceable contingencies I have indicated makes even that description seem inadequate. Such summary descriptions will always leave something important out, or remain at a level of abstraction that seems to express little of the actual life of the people. In telling the history of God's election of Israel, the most apparently trivial and abhorrent matters may be adduced as contributing to the actual shape of Israel's life: a talking donkey, that someone was left-handed, the sexual whim of the men of a village, a wedding gift of foreskins, the baldness of a prophet, a famine that drives Israelites into a gentile land, a rape in which an Israelite child is conceived, the lure of some red soup, and pretending to be hairy. There is no end to this list. No contingent factors such as these in Israel's history can be dismissed as irrelevant to who Israel has been in the flesh, and who it therefore is and will be in the flesh, for they have all left their determining mark on the flesh of Israel. Their complexity and incalculability is precisely what overwhelms any claim that the people has been constituted by its obedience, by its own decision(s), by biology, or by any other lifeless law of being.

Yet, these contingencies do not constitute a frenzied crowd, as if every contingency were alone and their sum amounted to nothing. Not all contingencies are the same, and the contingencies of Israel add up to its particular existence. Israel is a particular rather than a general or amorphous history; its contingencies are storiable and call forth a particular story rather than any story. There is thus a meaningful difference (and relation) between Israel and other peoples of the world, between the history of Israel and other histories. To say that Israel is the people elected by the one true God is to say that God has elected Israel in, through, and as the incalculable historical contingencies that have been its existence. God has been *in* those contingencies down to the minutiae, which have not been equal and formless but have constituted an order, a particularity, a people in the flesh.

The formative, electing activity of Israel's God, that is, the people itself as made by God, can therefore be remembered, named, and observed only in relation to a particular past. This particular past is indicated by certain places, figures, institutions, and words that, among the many contingencies of Israel's existence, have apparently done more to form Israel in the flesh than others and so have shaped the living order that is the unfolding life or being of the people. In other words, they have left a lasting impression on the people. Thus, the electing activity of God in Israel is remembered in relation to particular places such as Canaan, Egypt, and Babylon; figures such as Moses, David, and Elijah; and institutions such as the temple, the priesthood, and the Sabbath; all of which is to say that the electing activity of God in Israel is remembered in relation to the living words of the Bible, the selective history of Israel that is its memory and constitutes the written record and command of its existence. The Bible, then, is *the* written witness to God's electing activity.

The God of Abraham, Isaac, and Jacob can be called upon only by the name that the history of election has given that God. It is a history that took hold in the flesh in a wandering Aramean named Abram and has continued in an ongoing gathering of his promised family. Like a restless herd of sheep, it followed its God to Canaan, then to Egypt, then back to Canaan, and then was dispersed across what we know today as the Middle East and the lands surrounding the Mediterranean Sea. The shape of this gathering of people was constantly changing and unfolding in relation to surrounding peoples, adopting non-Israelite people and communities from without, losing some of its own to gentile communities over generations. Those who endured judgment and went on to continue remembering the God of Israel as their own—the elect—thus retained the living condition for knowing one another as parts of one people across abysmal differences. In so doing, they made a powerful impression on the peoples among whom they lived in exile, particularly as their history passed through and was ordered by Jesus of Nazareth.[75] The Jewishness of this man is not a predicate of the purity of his genes—not his ethnicity. Nor is it his faithful politics. It is his particular constitution by the stream of contingencies that made the Jews who they were and thus made Jesus who he was

75. The remembrance of the God of Israel is not a matter of the consciousness of a certain number of Israelite communities or individuals (who would thereby be departicularized by a general criterion of consciousness). Even if some in Israel have all but forgotten Israel's God and past as their own (e.g., some in the northern kingdom of Israel), other Israelite communities who do remember Israel's God and past as their own can remember for them. (This is what older members of the community do for the small children of the community as well as wayward members of the community.) They can do this only insofar as enough of their common past remains traceable and nameable, such that, for example, Judah could remember when it had been united with the rival kingdom of the north as a single kingdom under Kings Saul, David, and Solomon. In this case, the relation eventually deteriorated into oblivion, as Judah was, in time, unable to remember any living communities as the remnant of the northern kingdom (again, perhaps with the exception of the Samaritans).

and is, that is, by the drama of God's election in and through the covenant. This is most important for understanding the claims of the New Testament about Jesus and what has become of the world in and through him.[76]

This history of the people that has remembered the God of Israel as its own is what enables us to mean the particular knowable God rather than any god when Christians say "God." That is why the difference between the people that has remembered the God of Israel as its own by God's election and those who don't is not banal or insignificant. This is the case, however little such remembrance seems to mean in an age convinced that the true God must not be soiled by the contingencies of a history, however little our perceptions can make of that difference in our lust to know good from evil for ourselves and to know the good guys from the bad guys, however unable we are to justify ourselves and our destruction of others. Any claim about the revelation of the God of Israel or what it means to be faithful or unfaithful to God is derivative of the difference between the people that has remembered that God as its own and gentile societies who serve other gods. Attempts to "free" God from this history, to make God a god that is not the God of Israel—the God of Abraham and Sarah, Moses, Ruth, and David, are on a path to forgetting this God and worshipping this God only as a god. As the history of the northern kingdom and Israel's gentile enemies teaches us, such a god in time becomes any god, its people any people, as it drifts away from all remembrance.

---

76. It is also important for intractable problems in the Christian tradition, like the maleness of Jesus. It indicates that Jesus is not absolutely not female but constituted as a male by a great number of female persons, most directly the Virgin Mary. Thus, the maleness of men must be understood according to the particular contingency by which they exist as men, a contingency constituted by many women. The relation of male and female is not best considered in a formal realm of representation that is Christ but in the history that is cornerstoned by Israel's Messiah.

When election is told as I have attempted to do above, one can quickly see the trouble with the supersessionist idea that certain people who claim to serve the God of Israel can somehow be declared *not* to belong to the people, perhaps because of something they believe or don't believe, or because they've been really bad. According to the Tanakh, if they didn't in fact belong to the people, they wouldn't remember the God of Israel as their own, however poorly they do so. Branches of Israel are not finally cut off by any temporary human figure or court. No one but God has that kind of total view of the people, because it is determined by God's election and only revealed over time as outlined above.

This understanding of election renders supersessionism ontologically nonsensical and impossible, an affront to God's self-revelation in the flesh, for no person or community who calls out to the God of Israel as its own can be declared not-Israel on any grounds. If they weren't Israel by God's choosing, they wouldn't bother to call upon that God as their own, and there would be no basis for dispute with them in the name of that God. The one tree of Israel, with its sprawl of interweaving branches, winds across time toward the day when the promise of the people, the messianic life of the people that has been the sap of the tree all along—the Spirit of God—will fill the whole people in the fulness of time. The activity of God that forms Israel across time in this way, sustaining certain branches, hotly pursuing others to the point that they wither and fall off, grafting still others in, is God's unconditional election of Israel in and through the conditions that are Israel's life. The life that seizes Abram as its own, adopts his flesh as its own, lives in him and his children of promise, sustains and shapes his people of promise across generations by continuing in them the remembrance of and service to the God of Abraham, Isaac, and Jacob—the life that is *in* the giving of children to Israelite parents and the adopting of children born to gentiles, that is *in* these children, *in* their collective and personal formation—*this* life in the flesh is the "indestructible continuity in the being of Israel." It is the living, moving being of the people of God as delivered by God in both its pruning and its continuing growth.[77]

Without understanding God's election as the history of Israel as witnessed by the Bible, we cannot reconcile the unconditional promise of election with the conditional curses and blessings of the covenant. We're left torn between the faithfulness of God and the accountability of Israel. Surely God's election accomplishes Israel's faithfulness, we think (but when?). The Christian tradition has typically tried to address this conundrum with timeless criteria that distinguish between the true people of God and the false people of God, with the invisible and the visible church or some such. The true people of God are supposedly those who show that they are elect by being faithful and finally blessed. The false people of God are supposedly those who show that they are not elect by being unfaithful and finally cursed. The only alternative to this sort of true-false dichotomy seems to be that really bad people forfeit their election. But such an alternative makes election incoherent and finally empty. And neither "forfeitable election" nor the true-false dichotomization of the people of God can help but affront God's faithfulness. The Tanakh knows nothing of a pure elect people nor a forfeitable election. Instead, election means judgment for the elect people in time when there is unfaithfulness in the people, and this in turn shapes the remnant who thereby continues toward the fulfillment of the promise. Any attempt at exclusive, ontic equivalence between God's unconditional election of Israel and Israel in terms of its righteousness at some point in the middle of its history

---

77. See note above for Wyschogrod's correct insistence on the unconditional election of Israel in the flesh but also my qualification of his claim based on the contingency of the flesh of Israel itself.

is predicated on a supersession of some of Israel in the flesh. It is impatient with God's election. It also produces a Christology that tends toward docetism, a Jesus who was not in the likeness of sinful flesh (contrary to Rom. 8:3) but remained at some remove from the flesh so as to safeguard his preeminence and purity. The modern political fallout has been staggering and will no doubt continue to be so for some time.

The history of God's election of Israel according to the Tanakh refuses to let the people of God disown any of its members in the flesh, whatever their claim to do so, even when such members become violent enemies. This is not because they have been represented in Christ, who formally embraces the rejected (though this is true), but because they are there in the flesh and have thus been embraced by the election of God that is never without messianic promise. Instead of attempts to disinherit them because they live wrongly in relation to the God of Israel and their neighbors, they are to be engaged in the thankfulness that they still remember the God of Israel as their own. Some may be held to be leading Israel astray, that is, leading it towards idolatry and injustice, to forgetting the God of Israel. But to know what they are in fact doing will take time and will depend on the way that they die and are remembered (as Gamaliel the Pharisee teaches us in Acts 5). They can do nothing to forfeit their election, and they are to be loved as Israel among the rest of the community, so long as there is the slightest trace of the remembrance of the God of Abraham, Isaac, and Jacob, the slightest occasion for encountering them under the name of that God. The point is not to decide who is in and who is out but to love those whom God has determined to bring together. This internal struggle to bear with one another is how Israel learns to be like its God and to love those who have as yet not been swept up by God's election of Israel (i.e., the gentiles). It is how it learns from its history of election the politics of hope.

But understanding the being of Israel in this way will leave many frustrated. It is fine when Israel is a small, minority people in an ancient sea of gentiles who serve other gods. But it suddenly seems problematic when so many of the earth's inhabitants have come to know the God of Abraham, Isaac, and Jacob as their God. It apparently includes too many and seems to underestimate the divisions among such people, to render its peoplehood all but empty. We want to be able to dismiss as "false" some or many of the people who remember the God of Israel as their own.

But this problem is not the Bible's; it is our violent way of naming the elect people. We balk at a description that embraces as Israel so many and such diverse people, because we underestimate the diversity of ancient Israel and the significance of the fact that so many have come to call upon the God of Israel as their own, however inadequately they do so. We have caved to the fractious ways in which gentile societies make themselves and their gods. These are ways that crave independence, autonomy, and the ability to decide who we and others are. But they are not the forgiving way of God's election.

The forgiving way of God's election of Israel is revealed in its fullness in the catholicity of Jesus, when he willingly becomes for Israel what and who is cut off from Israel and then is raised from the dead. As such, he is not the representative of Israel nor its first stone, but the cornerstone and promise of the people in time: the stone by which God holds the whole people together, the stone that destroys Israel's enemies by making those enemies worshipers of the one true God, and the stone on which God grows Israel into a people of resurrection life. It is thus the death of this Israelite king—the fullness of covenant love—that is the culmination of God's electing activity, leading the people to resurrection after he rested in death for all on the Sabbath of Holy Saturday. To be Christian is not to be adequate to that election. It is to have been seized by it, adopted by the God of Israel into the Israelite community that confesses by name and as Lord the elect cornerstone of God's elect people. It is, as we will now see from Matthew and then Romans, to call upon the one who is the forgiveness of Israel's sins and teaches us the politics of sharing in that forgiveness in conformity with our baptism into his death and resurrection.

6

The Election of Israel
according to the First Gospel

Abstracted from the flesh of Israel, the identity of the people of God becomes a weightless concept, easy to lift from people, carry for a while, wield as a weapon, and leave behind for others to fight over. With the recent atomization of all identity claims, concepts of the identity of the people of God have grown particularly light. Identity is now something people can simply choose for themselves. Or it is their sexual orientation or socioeconomic status or profession or political party. All the while it remains their religion or nationality or ethnicity or culture. It is no surprise, then, that readers of the New Testament detect "competing identities" all over the place. "Israel" has come to be conceived and read as a weapon in this chaotic competition, supposedly available for rival communities or persons to deny to one another and claim for themselves as "the true Israel."

But if this were the case, then we would have in the New Testament a radical departure from the Scriptures of Israel that it claims everywhere to be following (i.e., the Tanakh or Old Testament). As we've seen in chapters 4 and 5, "Israel" is no such identity in those Scriptures. It is a people in the flesh, shaped over generations by the electing power of the God of Israel. It is not itself a concept and certainly not a weightless one. It is the name of that people. It cannot be lifted from those who have been seized by it in time. It is not predicated on any timeless purity of that people, a purity in and out of which communities or persons are supposedly constantly passing by virtue of their adequacy to God, now gaining, now losing their "identity." It is not a self-constituted identity. Nor does it emanate from nothingness. It is given by the God of Israel and is the people of Israel in the flesh.

The heaviness of Israelite identity in the flesh per the witness of the Tanakh means that no scriptural text can contain, define, or circumscribe the identity of the people of God, nor can writers or reception communities determine who they themselves are as in some sense "Israel." Their identity is not up to them. It is happening to them. Scriptural texts can only respond to the Israel that already has been and is in the flesh. They can only point to or gesture toward Israel. They can make sound claims about who Israel *is* only in terms of how the people is moving and where it is going, and this can be discerned only in light of how it has been shaped by and through the past.[1] Their witness is always restrospective. Thus, the identity of Israel is extremely heavy, weighted with time, so that it cannot be lifted from the people of God in the flesh and assumed by some supposedly new people. Israel is the name of that one people that has wrestled in the flesh with its God in relation to the gentile nations that have surrounded it and are present in various ways within it. Any newness to the people will be a renewal of the people. No political

---

1. In the course of the people's formation, scriptural words then become words according to which the people is formed.

newness can disinherit or despise any of Israel in the flesh, or it is simply the empty "newness" of forgetting.

If the New Testament has not departed from this Tanakhic understanding of Israel, then we should not find any timeless definition of the people of God in it. We should not find words of secession from Israel or replacement of Israel, for that is ontologically impossible and conceptually incoherent. Israel is simply not the sort of entity that can be replaced, or from which some of its members can secede. I suppose we may find words that constitute such a claim in the New Testament, but if that were the case, according to the Tanakh the claim is baseless. Such a polemical claim itself would attest that the claimants have found themselves a part of the larger people in the flesh in which such claims to be Israel over against other Israelites, however empty, are possible. They have found themselves invoking the God of Israel as their own, and this implies their oneness with all Israel in the flesh, even if they or others may find their current branch burning away over coming generations, in the sense discussed in chapter 5 above. They have found themselves a part of the historic people that remembers the God of Israel as its own. They find themselves *in* that history and as such elected by God.

I have chosen to consider the election of Israel according to the Gospel of Matthew for two reasons. First, it opens the New Testament, setting the tone canonically for what follows. Second, it is frequently read as particularly supersessionist and thus counter the argument I have been making for the irrevocable election of Israel according to the Tanakh. Readers discern in the First Gospel an embrace of the gentiles and a rejection of Israel: a story in which 1) "all the nations" supersede the rebellious "lost sheep of the house of Israel" and 2) judgment is assigned to Israel and salvation to the church. My exegetical thesis is that 1) the scope of Jesus' mission extends from "only the lost sheep of the house of Israel" to "all the nations" as a result of the forgiveness of Israel's sins, which inaugurates the eschatological covenant blessings *of* and *for* Israel; and 2) the only saved people in the First Gospel is the judged people. According to the First Gospel, Jesus is no stranger to the dramatic history of election as outlined in the previous chapter. He does not disown his people—any of them. Instead, as Messiah he is God's election in the flesh, the elect one: the one who holds the people together in its faithfulness and unfaithfulness, and delivers it through death from the threat of its dissolution to its future of promise, that is, finally to resurrection. His name means "he will save his people from their sins" (Matt. 1:21). As the Son of David, he is the chosen ruler come "to shepherd my people Israel" (Matt. 2:6, which splices together Mic. 5:2 and 2 Sam. 5:2; cf. 1 Chron. 11:2).

Could the First Gospel be a story of a "Messiah" who saves and shepherds only those in Israel that respond to him "rightly," disowning the rest? What salvation or shepherding would that be? Would the only security of those saved and shepherded then be their own adequate response to the revelation of God, however that response might be deemed the work of God rather than their own? And what kind of politics would sustain such a self-constituted human community? Does that sort of insecurity fit the life that Jesus calls his disciples to live in the First Gospel? If God's salvation and human faithfulness are ontically equivalent, then God's election is empty and peoplehood is a matter of human policing. In any case, who responds to Jesus rightly in Matthew? By the time the story is over, all have abandoned and rejected him. His messianic way is diversely but universally refused: by disciples, by family, by established Israelite authorities in the land, by gentile rulers, and by the crowd. The only exception may be the few women who dared to mourn him once dead. They had stood with him until the end, though "from a distance" (Matt. 27:55).

298

Nevertheless, Matthew is read by many as the Gospel of a "new people," one that has left the old people behind, while claiming the old people's promises for itself (perhaps because supposedly excluded by the old people). At best, the new people includes only those Israelites in the flesh who have joined the new people by "believing in Jesus." The people of the God of Israel has mysteriously "started over" with Jesus.[2] This is the impression left by widely disseminated, introductory material on the First Gospel, and no doubt the framework within which the text of Matthew is commonly read and taught.[3] Such readings are deeply entrenched in the modern discourse of peoplehood. Ulrich Luz is somewhat more cautious than others,[4] although he, too, reads Matthew under the presumption that the "Matthean community" is a discrete entity empowered to decide who it is relative to other Israelite communities.[5] "That it was now becoming increasingly clear to them ['the Matthean community']

---

2. See, e.g., Graham Stanton, *A Gospel for a New People: Studies in Matthew* (Louisville, KY: Westminster John Knox Press, 1992): "The evangelist and the original recipients of his gospel saw themselves as a 'new people', minority Christian communities over against both Judaism and the Gentile world at large" (378).

3. See, e.g., Stephen C. Barton, "The Gospel according to Matthew," in *The Cambridge Companion to the Gospels*, ed. Stephen C. Barton (Cambridge: Cambridge University Press, 2006), who begins his chapter with the subheading "A New Gospel for a New People." Barton wisely resists a claim of total discontinuity between the old and the new; yet he has little to offer in terms of the substance of the continuity: "The fundamental continuity has to do with God" (121). In other words, the God of Israel is the same God of Jesus. This is good so far as it goes, but, as we have seen, the revelation and knowability of God depend on the oneness of the people of God, that is, Israel in the flesh. God is not revealed in the continuity of ideas or doctrines or even a story in abstraction from the flesh of Israel. God is revealed in the continuity of Israel's flesh, from which Israel's story, ideas, and doctrines derive. This is finally a christological claim, for in Jesus the intimacy of God with the flesh of Israel is not "achieved" for the first time but *fulfilled* (πληρόω). See also, Graham Stanton, *The Gospels and Jesus*, 2nd ed. (Oxford: Oxford University Press, 2002). "Matt. 21:43 with its double emphasis on God's rejection of Israel and his acceptance of gentiles as part of his 'people' is one of the most important verses in the whole gospel" (65).

4. "They [the Matthean church] belonged to Israel. It is noteworthy that a firm 'inside-outside way of thinking' about Israel and corresponding self-designations of the community are still absent from the Gospel of Matthew. It does not yet speak . . . stereotypically of 'the' Jews as a negative other. It does not call the church 'people of God' (cf. 21:43), 'remnant,' or 'true Israel' as opposed to a false Israel" (Ulrich Luz, *Matthew 1–7: A Commentary*, trans. James E. Crouch [Minneapolis: Fortress Press, 2007], 55).

that they were faced with the alternative of defining themselves as Jews *or* Christians was a profound crisis for them and was for the evangelist the main reason he told the story anew for them."[6] Thus, Matthew is a story of Jesus in "conflict with Israel."[7] The community in question is here to be conceived vis-à-vis "Jews." As such it is effectively a pure, self-constituted (or at least self-constituting) community with a personality of its own. We have in this modern exegetical tradition, even in its more cautious adherents, all the main contours of the modern discourse of peoplehood.

Luz's reading has the virtue of trying to hold the Jewish-Christian schism in suspense, rather than making it a foundational fact of the First Gospel. But by making the schism *the* question of the First Gospel, he has assumed its traditional terms for understanding the dramatic tension of the narrative. This cannot help but reinforce those terms, instead of allowing for the possibility that the story questions or resists them, and it easily yields to the discursive pressures of the modern discourse of peoplehood. Accordingly, such exegesis assumes a particular understanding of the schism that did in fact eventuate, namely, that Jews and Christians constitute, in some sense, two separate communities. Yet, without minimizing the differences between those known as Jews and those known as Christians today (and there are some who are both), the Bible invites us to speak of Jews and Christians as belonging to the one people of the God of Israel in the flesh. Only as such can they negotiate their differences peaceably, and only as Israelite sisters and brothers of Jews can the

---

5. Scott Bader-Saye is less cautious at this point: "The context of Matthew's Gospel as a whole pushes toward an allegorical reading in which the vineyard (the kingdom of God) is the fruit of God's election, the displaced people are the Jews, and the new 'people' are the church" (*Church and Israel after Christendom: The Politics of Election* [Eugene, OR: Wipf & Stock, 1999], 53).

6. Luz, *Matthew 1–7*, 55, emphasis his. Notice Luz's assumption that the Matthean community can "define themselves."

7. Ibid., 11.

church repent of the violent politics of the modern discourse of peoplehood.

Luz follows the now-customary hermeneutic in biblical studies of reading the dramatic tension of ancient texts as a mirror of the local drama of their authors and early readers.[8] This two-level-drama approach has tremendous liabilities. It arises from a helpful historicist sensibility that wishes to do justice to the particular origin of the text in time, and to take the occasional nature of the text seriously. Such considerations have often been neglected in "theological" or other "synchronic" readings, and this neglect has cost them to the extent that they have attempted to "free" the text from its skin in the past. But reading a text like Matthew according to a drama that is neatly two-leveled in this way invites us to "explain" the text instead of exegeting it, that is, to "explain" the text as an epiphenomenon of a speculatively reconstructed, discrete social reality (e.g., "the Matthean community"). This is not the only or best way to be historically responsible, and it struggles to exegete the text as a witness to Jesus in the flesh, which is what the text itself claims to be.

On this two-level-drama construal, the words of the text of Matthew (and any other text) are trapped, as it were, within the confines of the subjective reality of its writer and early readers. This totalized subjective reality is taken to circumscribe the substance of the text and is separated from the explicit subject matter of the text (in this case Jesus) by an infinite qualitative distinction. Any reality that in fact determines or exceeds the subjective reality that has "produced" the text is all but denied since meaning is supposedly enclosed in the "experiences" of the writer and early readers. Thus, a totalized human subject (i.e., "the Matthean community") is allowed

---

8. This hermeneutic is spawned and excellently articulated in J. Louis Martyn's *History and Theology in the Fourth Gospel* (Louisville, Kentucky: Westminster John Knox Press, 2003 [1968, 1979]).

to occupy center stage, right where the modern discourse of peoplehood has placed it; it is effectively the maker of meaning, of itself, and of everything else; it is the phenomenon to which all else, including its testimony to Jesus, can be only epiphenomenal. This hermeneutic suffers from the same liabilities as other causal systems of closure. Phenomena are supposedly comprehended by identifying their causes, the "whole" of which can never exceed the sum of the causative parts and is imagined as calculable. There is fundamentally no story to be read with this hermeneutic, only analysis of human projections.

But words are not in fact enclosed in the drama of any single human being or her community. They are shared across time and space in ways that exceed a person and her local community. The drama of the writer(s) and the community in which the writing was conducted is not the cause(s) of which the words of the First Gospel are the effects. It is not a phenomenon that the Gospel words "explain." Whatever we may imagine about the early readers of Matthew, the words of the First Gospel are testimony to the one who has given the Matthean community of yesterday and today (i.e., the church) the reality it is in the first place (a reality that has only recently come to invite "explanation"), a political reality that is contingent, impure, unfinished, and thus not totalizeable. They are not words that an ancient person or community created *ex nihilo* in response to contemporary concerns, but words inherited and held in common with others across time and space, words about Jesus (i.e., not just their experience of Jesus) that have been continuously molded through time.[9] As we have learned from the Tanakh in chapter 5, because of God's election the people of God does not

---

9. Despite the negative effects of Luz's two-level-drama framework on his commentary, it has many strengths, one of which is his attention in exegesis to the church's worship (e.g., his comments on the Lord's Prayer).

determine its words or its life, but is itself determined by the time in which it finds itself living by God's election. Ancient communities were involved in the shape of the First Gospel, but their involvement is itself a participation in the one whom Matthew is about, for he has not only made that involvement possible but made it what it is.

What is decisive, then, is not the force of the words of the First Gospel as determined by an isolated and speculatively reconstructed local drama of long ago, but the coming of the time in which the words of Matthew were not only possible but actual and current, as they remain to the present. The First Gospel can therefore say something that is really about Jesus—not one Jesus among others, or Jesus as distorted by Matthew or his community, but the one Jesus as present, remembered, and made known in and through the community that produced the First Gospel and has transmitted it and read it ever since.[10] Jesus cannot be separated from the remembrance of Jesus. He is not an object alien to the reality of "the Matthean community," whatever it was, but the one who lives in the response of the church to his life in the flesh and his resurrection, even as he remains the one to whom that response is directed. That community in the flesh has become part of his life. The community and Jesus are not two but one.[11] A two-level-drama approach to the First Gospel cannot help but enclose Jesus in the fictitious "identities" of self-constituted peoplehood.

Besides this philosophical-theological problem, another liability of the two-level-drama hermeneutic needs to be named, for it generates

10. Another virtue of Luz's commentary is its attention to the way Matthew has been read in the tradition of the church, which furnishes us with the (fallible) imagination with which we read it. This enables us to read more critically. The way that the words of Matthew were and have been determined by time, whose fullness is Messiah, makes the words open to many, though not any, readings, as they witness to a future that is likewise open. Thus, they are determinate words of hope.

11. Which is not to say that there is no distinction between them, only that the distinction between them is their interrelation, i.e., Jesus and the church are one in the way Jesus is distinct from the church, and Jesus and the church are distinct in the way they are interrelated.

an unwarranted supersessionist drift in readings of Matthew. The second level of the drama is conceived rather arbitrarily. The force of the words is assumed to reflect a certain conflict in the life of "the Matthean community," in this case, a conflict between that community and some configuration of Jews. The presence of such conflicts can hardly be gainsaid. But the way those conflicts have shaped Matthew's story and the terms in which those conflicts should be described are far from obvious, and they are theopolitically fraught. Moreover, such matters may themselves be concerns of the First Gospel, so that we should pause before imposing upon the exegesis of the text terms to be determined by reading the text. When Graham Stanton says provocatively that "Matthew's gospel is Jewish, anti-Jewish, and pro-Gentile," we have a good example of terms that tell us little about Matthew's Gospel and much about the chaotic, beclouding ways in which the second level of the drama is conceived.[12] Perhaps the First Gospel makes claims about what it means to be Jewish and what it means to be gentile, and how these two have come to relate in time. If so, on terms like Stanton's we will not have ears to hear, for the story can only be for or against the totalized entities we have already imagined. Instead of suspending such terms as much as possible, readers assume that the force of Matthew's words reflects a conflict between "Judaism" and "the church."

But why should we name the ancient conflict and array the parties to it in this way? And if Matthew is primarily an epiphenomenon of a church in the throes of what we know only retrospectively as the Jewish-Christian schism, is it so obvious how the story has been shaped by such a conflict? Must certain characters "represent" the enemy Jews and others the church? Luz, for example, suggests

12. Stanton, *The Gospels and Jesus*, 58.

that we read Matthew through the supposition that "the Matthean community, whose mission in the land of Israel has come to an end, no longer belongs to the Jewish synagogue."[13] Is it not equally likely that a prominent Jewish figure in Matthew's local church opposes Matthew's teaching? Or that Matthew is the child of an overbearing Jewish father and a non-Jewish Christian mother? Or that there is a really mean and powerful Jew operating in the local Roman aristocracy? The point is simply that when we try to identify the Matthean community's "situation" as the "cause" of which the First Gospel is an "explanation," we are at sea. We simply cannot assume that "the Matthean community" is so discrete, that it knows clearly who "we" are and who "they" are. Nor can we assume that the conflicts in which it finds itself (i.e., the second-level drama) are not much more complex than the one imagined as the totalized church against the totalized Jews, as "natural" and determinative as this conflict seems to us. The hermeneutical fallacy here is the same one that assumes that a world war has done more to shape a temporal segment of human existence than the invention of the clock. Sometimes the most apparently mundane and insignificant developments prove to be much more determinative of the way things are (and the way the past is storied in writing) than the "big developments" that dominate our imagination and so are assigned the lion's share of causation.

Nevertheless, when it comes to the First Gospel, *the* scenario that dominates our imagination, as shaped by the modern discourse of peoplehood, is that some time after the life of Jesus whom it is about, the community that knows the God of Israel as its own bifurcated into what have since been conceived as two communities: the Jews and the church. And so we are tempted to make this "big

---

13. Luz, *Matthew 1–7*, 54.

development" the decisive background of our readings, decoding the words as struggling in some way with that development, whether it is past, imminent, or future to the composition of the text. Many words in Matthew of course lend themselves to playing the church off against Israel, as the Christian tradition amply attests. But that does not mean that such readings are the most faithful to the text either synchronically or diachronically. Foregrounding the Jewish-Christian schism for exegesis succumbs to the historical and exegetical determinism that Yoder has eloquently criticized (chapter 2 above), where readers "look in earlier texts for explanations of the later polarizations."[14] Moreover, "explaining" the text in this way, as the epiphenomenon of a community in the throes of the Jewish-Christian schism (i.e., the second-level drama), relies heavily on a dubious philosophy of representation (and thus plays into the politics of representation that have been described in earlier chapters). Somehow Jesus' diverse opponents in Matthew are taken to represent "Israel" or "Judaism," and Jesus himself has ceased to be "Israelite" or "Jewish." Instead, Jesus and his disciples represent what is "Christian." Such contrived terms of the drama are already a distortion. Consider a few examples in Ulrich Luz's fine commentary:

1. The disputes of Matt. 12:1—16:20 are supposedly "disputes with Israel."[15]
2. The Matthean community "is a Jewish Christian church that has experienced the painful failure of its own mission *to Israel* and

14. John Howard Yoder, *The Jewish-Christian Schism Revisited*, ed. Michael G. Cartwright and Peter Ochs (Grand Rapids, MI: William B. Eerdmans, 2003), 46. See, e.g., Luz, *Matthew 1–7*, 50: "The Gospel of Matthew tells how it happened that in the end the greatest portion of Israel rejects Jesus." Or Stanton, *A Gospel*, 378: "Matthew's gospel legitimates the recent painful separation of Matthean communities from Judaism by providing divine sanction for the parting of the ways."
15. Luz, *Matthew 1–7*, 9.

its separation from *majority Israel* and that now must reorient itself."[16]

3. The "their" of Matthew refers to Israel and supposedly implies an "our" that is Christian: "Matthew speaks of Christian scribes (13:52; 23:34). When talking about Israel he [Matthew] speaks of 'their synagogues' (four times) and 'their scribes' (7:29) but not of 'their Pharisees.' We may surmise that this happens because there were 'our' scribes and synagogues separate from 'their' scribes and synagogues."[17] But why surmise this?

4. "The community keeps the entire law, but it does so—to state it pointedly—not so much because it belongs to Israel but because Jesus commands it (5:17-18)."[18] But what in the text of Matthew would ever encourage us to play "belonging to Israel" off against Jesus the shepherd of Israel?

5. "The [Matthean] community experienced the destruction of Jerusalem in the Jewish War as God's judgment *on Israel* (22:2-7; 23:37-39)."[19] But so did everyone else![20] Moreover, as we will see below, judgment upon Israel in Matthew is judgment upon Jesus Messiah, and thus any judgment upon Israel in Matthew is for the sake of Israel.

6. "The church . . . failed in its mission *to Israel*."[21]

---

16. Ibid., 11, my emphasis.

17. Ibid., 44.

18. Ibid., 48.

19. Ibid., 50, my emphasis.

20. See, e.g., Jacob Neusner, *In the Aftermath of Catastrophe: Founding Judaism 70–640* (Quebec: McGill-Queen's University Press, 2009), 188. That the destruction of the temple was God's judgment upon Jewish sectarianism is the implication of the entire coalition associated with Yavneh, per the description of Shaye J. D. Cohen in "The Significance of Yavneh: Pharisees, Rabbis, and the End of Jewish Sectarianism," *Hebrew Union College Annual* 55 (1984): 27–53. It is also the summary judgment of Josephus in *The Jewish War* (e.g., 5:13:6). Luz goes on to write of a "new orientation," and by "new" he seems to mean an orientation that leaves "the old" in the flesh behind (*Matthew 1–7*, 50).

21. Luz, *Matthew 1–7*, 50, my emphasis. See also "The Gospel of Matthew [bears] the imprint of the schism with Israel" on the same page.

Somehow, totalized, mutually distinct, social entities known as "Israel" and "the church" have found their way into the First Gospel, variously "represented" in the conflict of its narrative.

In response to the well-established exegetical tendency outlined above, I will consider two features of the First Gospel: 1) the movement from "the lost sheep of the house of Israel" (10:6; 15:24) to "all the nations" (28:19) and 2) the work of judgment. These features will clarify the witness of the First Gospel to the election of Israel, as revealed in the catholicity of Jesus. We will see that Yoder is right that the church of the Messiah is the continuation of God's presence in and for Israel, and here Luz is wrong to read Matthew as a movement beyond or away from Israel. We will also see that, against Yoder and Luz, Barth is right that judgment against Israel in Jesus is judgment for the sake of all Israel.[22]

22. I will reserve my exegetical critique of Barth for the reading of Romans 9–11 in the next chapter. Where the text of Matthew resists Barth's claims is that it defies any formal division of the people of God into rebellious Israel and the obedient church. Those who are obedient are no more the church than they are Israel, and the church that Jesus gathers over the course of the story proves no more faithful to Jesus than those who do not follow Jesus and even those who openly oppose him. In fact, it is precisely in the moment that the church of Jesus is revealed that its foundational rock plays the Satan (Matt. 16:13-28). This does not mean that there is nothing to following Jesus or the particularity of the church, only that following Jesus means solidarity with whatever part of Israel rejects him.

Also against Barth, the First Gospel presents Jesus not as the representative of anyone or anything, but the cornerstone of Israel that holds the whole people together and delivers it to the promise of resurrection. It presents the elect community as one people within whom the church is not one form but an eschatological gathering in the flesh, an embodied witness to the forgiveness of Israel's sins and thus its peace (the peace that ends Israel-gentile enmity and draws the gentile nations to Israel's table of eschatological blessing). Denying the Messiah in Matthew is not only a matter of unbelief but of disobeying his commands, which Christians can do, and often have done, much more than "non-Christian" Jews do or have done (while many Jews have obeyed his commands). As Barth argues on other grounds, even blaspheming the Messiah who is Son of Man does not keep an Israelite community from enjoying the forgiveness of sins that is the Spirit of the kingdom of the God of Israel in Matthew (12:31-32). All Israel is determined not by how it responds to the revelation of the Christ in time but by the time of Christ's revelation, to which it cannot help but respond.

From the Lost Sheep of the House of Israel to All the Nations

In Matt. 10:5-6, Jesus restricts the mission of the newly appointed "twelve apostles" (Matt. 10:2) to "the lost sheep of the house of Israel."[23] This restriction is brought into bolder relief in Matt. 15:21-28, where Jesus reiterates to his disciples that he has been "sent to no one but (εἰ μὴ εἰς) the lost sheep of the house of Israel" (v. 24). Yet, the First Gospel seems to thematize gentile participation in the story, and, at the end, the scope of Jesus' mission extends to "all the nations" (28:19). This is where Luz detects a rupture in Matthew's Gospel:

> On this point—and only on this point—the Gospel of Matthew contains a rupture: the mission commandment of the earthly Jesus (28:19-20; 10:5-6). The entire course of the Jesus story accounts for this radical break: Matthew portrays the conflict of Jesus, Israel's Messiah, with the leaders of the people. It culminates in the passion narrative, where the people side with the leaders who are leading them astray (27:24-25). Thus the Gospel of Matthew tells how it happened that in the end the greatest portion[24] of Israel rejects Jesus (cf. 28:11-15). The risen Lord responds to this rejection by commanding the disciples to make disciples of "all nations" (28:16-20). This rupture in the story of Jesus also took place in the story of the church, which failed in its mission to Israel, experienced the divine judgment of the destruction of Jerusalem, and now in Syria is called by the evangelist to a new task.[25]

In Matthew, we find the striking coincidence of what many have termed the most conservatively "Jewish" portrayal of Jesus (e.g., Matt. 5:17-20), some of the most scathing denunciations of Jewish authorities (e.g., Matt. 23:1-39), and a persistently happy portrayal of

---

23. All biblical quotations in this chapter are my translations. Emphasis in such quotations is of course mine as well.

24. On what basis should we proportion the people of Israel according to Matthew? See ch. 7, "The Election of Israel according to the First Letter: Romans 9–11," on conceiving Jewish opponents of the church as a "majority" of Israel.

25. Luz, *Matthew 1–7*, 50.

(some) gentiles (e.g., Matt. 8:11-12). Readers like Luz attribute this to the above rupture, finding in these seemingly competing "strands" a dissonance within the tradition or social drama underlying Matthew's Gospel.[26] But these "strands" are not so competing or dissonant.

Jesus' mission extends from "only the lost sheep of the house of Israel" to "all the nations" not because God has rejected Israel, but because God has forgiven Israel's sins, and this forgiveness inaugurates the eschatological covenant blessings *of* and *for* Israel.[27] Crucial to this claim is that the people of Israel is at no point set aside, relativized, or replaced, as if Israel were a formal entity with replaceable material content. On the contrary, Israel's promised blessings reach gentiles only *in and through* the people of Israel in the flesh, none of which is left behind or superseded. It is the covenant drama of the election of Israel—curse and blessing, cross and resurrection—that draws gentiles into Israel's own life, finally to peace. The possibility of this sort of gentile participation (i.e., not just any gentile participation) in Israel's covenantal life therefore depends upon a change in the rule of Israel. The modern discourse of peoplehood and the historiography of the Jewish-Christian schism on which it rests encourage us to read the story of Matthew as immediately *defining* the people of God. But from beginning to end, the First Gospel does not claim to define the people of Israel, but

---

26. E.g., Matthew "preserves this outdated tradition in order to show how the mission of the church began and how it developed" (Eung Chun Park, *The Mission Discourse in Matthew's Interpretation*, 2, Reihe 81, Wissenschaftliche Untersuchungen Zum Neuen Testament [Tübingen: J. C. B. Mohr (Paul Siebeck), 1995], 8). David C. Sim finds two parallel missions in Matthew, one to Israel and one to the gentiles. 28:18-20 supposedly acknowledges the legitimacy of the latter while the mission of the Matthean community is only to Israel. See *The Gospel of Matthew and Christian Judaism: The History and Social Setting of the Matthean Community*, Studies in the New Testament and Its World (Edinburgh: T & T Clark, 1998), e.g., 245–46. See also Amy-Jill Levine, *The Social and Ethnic Dimensions of Matthean Salvation History*, Studies in the Bible and Early Christianity, vol. 14 (Lewiston, NY: Mellen House, 1988), 38–52.

27. Cf., e.g., Deut. 30:1-6; Isa. 6:5-7; 22:14; 27:1-13; 33:1-24; Jer. 31:30-40; 33:1-9; Ezek. 16:59-63; 36:33-38; Dan. 9:19-27.

to tell of the messianic struggle for *the rule of Israel*, which mediates the life of the people.[28] This is in part why it is focused on the promised land of Israel, where only a part of the people of Israel is living. That the promised Son of David has come to rule Israel of course has dramatic implications for the people of Israel scattered abroad, but, as the Tanakh has led us to expect, these implications will be worked out in time, in the flesh. They are not a matter of immediate redefinition of the people in some formal domain safe from the slow movement of the flesh.[29] Jesus is heavy with the flesh of all Israel. He shepherds Israel through the death of judgment to eschatological life, thereby embodying the forgiveness of sins. According to Matthew, that forgiveness is what John the Baptist prepared Israel for at the Jordan and what Jesus accomplished in his life, death, and resurrection.

Mission in the Land of Israel: Matt. 10:5-6

The restriction of Jesus' mission to "the lost sheep of the house of Israel" should be read in light of the crucial shift in Jesus' public profile that the narrative has detailed in the run-up to the Mission Discourse (Matthew 10). The shift? Right before the Mission Discourse, Jesus has been decisively rejected by trusted Jewish authorities in the land and his popularity described as unruly. In response to this shift, the force of the restriction in 10:5-6 is that Jesus has come *for* the people of Israel, where the harvest is plentiful and the workers are few (9:36-38). From the time of Jesus' coming

---

28. It begins with a royal geneaological history of Jesus and concludes with Jesus as the promised ruler not only over Israel, but over all creation, as the Israelite ruler of Dan. 7, the promised Son of David and Son of Man who is God with us (Matt. 1:23; Isa. 7:14; cf. Psalm 2).

29. As the modern discourse of peoplehood moved us from notions of human subjection as determined by divinely appointed authority to human subjectivity as self-determined by divine appointment, we could no longer see that the people of God in Matthew is not determined by themselves but by the ruler chosen by the God of Israel (i.e., mediator of election). This determination is not reducible to the people's subjective relation to the ruler.

from Galilee to John at the Jordan, Jesus has maintained a relatively low profile vis-à-vis Israel's authorities, his parents having quietly reintroduced him into the land of Israel after the death of Herod the Great (2:20-23). Immediately before the Mission Discourse, however, Jesus has found himself on a course of public divergence from trusted Jewish authorities in the land. He has presented himself as "the Son of Man" with "authority to forgive sins" (9:6), colliding with some of the scribes, clashing for the first time with Pharisees in Capernaum (9:9-13). Jesus has even distinguished his moment and vocation from those of John the Baptist (9:14-18). Meanwhile, Jesus' popular renown has steadily increased since his baptism (e.g., 4:24-25), swelling in response to his healing of a ruler's daughter (9:26).

But now his popularity is becoming a problem: when people acclaim Jesus "Son of David" (9:27) for the first time in the story,[30] Jesus warns them not to spread the word about him. "But they went away and proclaimed him widely in that whole land" (9:31). The final passage before the Mission Discourse then highlights this apparently decisive combination of an explosive following and the hostility of reputable Israelite authorities in the land: the crowds respond to an exorcism with amazement: "Never has anything like this appeared in Israel" (v. 33),[31] while some Pharisees, in immediate juxtaposition to v. 33, respond to the same exorcism with definitive contempt, "By the ruler of demons he casts out demons" (v. 34).

---

30. The opening genealogy freights the name of David with maximum weight for the revelation of Jesus that is the rest of the Gospel. In addition to David's prominence per Matt. 1:1, 6, and 17, the writer has apparently counted David twice, signaled by naming David twice in 1:17. The genealogy is thus organized numerically with the value of David's Hebrew name. See Barclay M. Newman, Jr., "Matthew 1:1-18: Some Comments and a Suggested Restructuring," *Bible Translator* 27 (1976): 209–12, 210. Note also the angel's way of addressing Joseph in Matt. 1:20: "Joseph, son of David."

31. The crowds are said to specify "in Israel" as the scope of what is without precedent about Jesus, "Israel" having appeared only (and similarly) in 8:10 since Jesus' return to the land in 2:21. This suggests that the Israel-wide implications of Jesus' life are now in the foreground of the narrative.

The setting of Matt. 10:5-6, then, is on the one hand that of eager crowds among whom Jesus has been preaching and healing, and on the other what portends rejection by Israel's current shepherds in the land and a change in the regime of Israel. The writer has already described Jesus, per Mic. 5:2 and 2 Sam. 5:2, as the "ruler who is to shepherd my people Israel" (Matt. 2:6). Now in this setting, we are told that when Jesus "saw the crowds, he had compassion on them, because they were mistreated and helpless, like sheep without a shepherd" (9:36).[32] What gives way directly to the Mission Discourse is what Jesus says in relation to *these* Israelite crowds in the land: "The harvest is plentiful, but the workers are few" (9:37). Jesus has a plentiful harvest to reap *in Israel*.[33]

Jesus' disciples have remained innocuous since their entry into the story at 4:18-22 (5:1; 8:21-23; 9:10-11, 19, 37).[34] But in 10:1, they

32. The language of "lost sheep without a shepherd" seems to invoke Ezekiel's prophecy "against the shepherds of Israel," who "did not strengthen the weak . . . or heal the sick . . . or bandage the mistreated . . . or return those led astray . . . or seek the ruined, and you have subdued the strong with toil. And my sheep were dispersed because of being without shepherds. . . . My sheep were dispersed to every mountain and every high hill and dispersed throughout the face of all the earth, and there was no one to seek them out or turn them back. . . . For this, O shepherds, thus says the Lord himself, 'I am against the shepherds, and I will seek out my sheep out of their hands, and I will turn them away from leading my sheep. The shepherds will no longer feed themselves, and I will rescue my sheep from their mouths, and they will no longer be food for them. . . . I will feed my sheep, and I will give them rest, and they shall know that I am the Lord. . . . I will seek out the sheep that has been lost, and I will turn back the one who is being led astray, and I will bandage the one that has been broken, and I will strengthen the one who has fainted. I will guard against the strong and feed them with judgment.' As for you my sheep, thus says the Lord himself, 'Behold I will judge between sheep and sheep, rams and goats. . . . I will judge between the strong sheep and the weak sheep. . . . Then I will set over them one shepherd, and my servant David will shepherd them, and he will be their shepherd. And I the Lord will be God to them and David in their midst as ruler. I the Lord have spoken" (34:4, 5a, 6, 9-11, 15-17, 23-24 LXX). The various themes of this passage will crop up throughout what follows. Note especially the shepherd's concern to seek out one stray while leaving ninety-nine behind (Matt. 18:12), and the Son of Man's separating the sheep from the goats when the nations—with Israel's lost sheep mixed in—are gathered before him (Matt. 25:32-33). Of all Matthew's material about "lost sheep," only Matt. 9:36 has a synoptic parallel (Mark 6:34). The motif of "lost sheep" is clearly more prevalent in Matthew than Mark or Luke.

33. The language of "harvest" and "laborers" should call to mind the parables still to come in Matthew, not the least of which is that of the vineyard taken from the tradition of Isaiah 5. Like the argument of the narrative here, those parables oppose Jesus not to the people of Israel but to Jewish authorities of his day in the land (see below).

come to life. Jesus "summons his twelve disciples" to give them some of the authority he himself has been exercising, now as "the twelve apostles" (10:2) whom the writer names, indicating that the time to begin gathering the lost sheep of the house of Israel under the rule of the Son of David has come. Israel is lost under its current shepherds, and it is time for God's eschatological government of Israel, the kingdom of God that John and Jesus have been proclaiming. It is fitting, therefore, that Jesus instructs his apostles not to follow any road leading to gentile territory or enter any city of the Samaritans but to go rather to the lost sheep of the house of Israel (10:5-6).

While this limited scope directs the kingdom mission to communities of the house of Israel in the land, it must not be missed that it excludes Jews that live among the gentiles or in Samaritan cities. Few readers seem to notice this and, looking for the totality of Israel to be "represented" in the text, overlook that only some of the people of Israel are in view here, namely, the remnant of Judah that is settled in the promised land. The directions, "do not go down a road of the gentiles or enter a Samaritan city but go rather to the lost sheep of the house of Israel" (εἰς ὁδὸν ἐθνῶν μὴ ἀπέλθητε καὶ εἰς πόλιν Σαμαριτῶν μὴ εἰσέλθητε πορεύεσθε δὲ μᾶλλον πρὸς ...), keep the apostles from leaving the promised land and are primarily *geographic* rather than ethnic or religious in scope (which are both hopelessly overgeneralized categories).[35] To say that the restriction is ethnic or

34. Note that the "disciple" of 8:21 is described as ἕτερος, apparently with respect to the "scribe" of 8:19. Thus, the writer registers that Jesus counted at least some of Israel's scribal authorities in the land as supporters (cf. 13:52) and marks an upcoming shift after which every entrance of "scribes" into the story will be as those hostile to Jesus (although they will be mentioned as simply Israel's teachers, without coming on stage at 17:10).

35. Other εἰς-plus-accusative prepositions in Matthew in which the object of the preposition is a place or other topographical term are also primarily geographic. Luz misses the geographic force of the commission (*Matthew 1–7*, 73–74). Davies and Allison seem to miss it as well, although they speak ambiguously of "the borders of Israel" and "Jewish territory" (W. D. Davies and Dale C. Allison, Jr., *Matthew*, ICC, vol. 2 [Edinburgh: T & T Clark, 1991], 168, 548). France perceives the geographic force of the commission but ignores that 1) Samaritan cities rather than all Samaritan territory are in view, and 2) the scope cannot include "the whole of

religious in the sociological parlance of our time would exclude Jews of the Diaspora from Israel, but surely such Jews remain Israelite. The time in which they will be touched directly by the gospel of the kingdom of Israel's God is coming, but it is not yet. The land of Israel, where a temple of the God of Israel still stands, is therefore implicated in Jesus' "saving his people from their sins." "House" is a term with territorial implications, and so "the house of Israel" is the remnant of the Judah-based kingdom of Israel, particularly as it finds itself gathered in the promised land.[36]

By designating twelve apostles and limiting the scope of their mission in this way, and by excluding visible, non-Jewish settlements in that land, the restriction of the mission publicly delineates the specific orientation and intention of the messianic mission to Israel. It does not seem to preclude all contact in the land with non-Jewish individuals (some of whom may reside in Jewish towns, as did the centurion of 8:5). It is not a mission exclusively to Jewish persons. It is an urgent mission to the visibly gathered Jewish *community* in the promised land, who has been forsaken by Israel's current shepherds there, and Jesus does not expect the Twelve to cover "the cities of Israel" before a proximate eschatological revolution (Matt. 10:23).[37]

The subtle, geographic distinction between ὁδὸν and πόλιν in 10:5 should not be reduced to a merely stylistic variation. For roads leading to gentile territory were avoidable, but the Twelve would normally travel through Samaria to reach Judea, which falls within

Israel" because it excludes dispersed Jews (R. T. France, *The Gospel of Matthew*, NICNT [Grand Rapids, MI: William B. Eerdmans, 2007], 381–82). As we'll see below, France quickly slips from geographic particularity to racial generalization.

36. E.g., Isa. 5:7; 14:1ff. Isaiah 5 is an especially important passage in Matthew (e.g., Matthew 21).

37. The formal separation of peoplehood from a homeland is a relatively recent phenomenon. Jesus and the writer obviously knew that many Israelites were dispersed throughout the world, and they no doubt considered these to be "lost." But in Matthew, Israel is regarded as a landed people and engaged as such. Towns of Jews living in the promised land count as "the lost sheep of the house of Israel" without excluding dispersed Jews from Israel, just as Jews who embrace Jesus as Messiah count as Israel without excluding Jews who do not confess Jesus as Messiah.

the scope of the commission. It is therefore the *cities* of the Samaritans that the Twelve are to bypass,[38] as Jesus publicly declares his claim upon the settlements and crowds of "the house of Israel." This of course has eschatological implications for Samaritans and gentiles, and the Jews living among them, but the prophets indicate that the light of eschatological blessing shines from Zion, and that God's covenant with Israel, centered in Jerusalem of Judah, remains the context of gentile (and Samaritan) participation in that blessing (e.g., Isa. 2:1-4).[39] With the other use of the phrase "the lost sheep of the house of Israel" at 15:24, this point will be driven home with scandalous clarity.

I have said that definitive opposition by Israel's key, current shepherds in the land is part of what has induced the appointment of twelve apostles and Jesus' sending them out as his apostles of the kingdom. That claim is supported by how the Mission Discourse then unfolds, for it stresses the opposition the Twelve will meet

---

38. That the Twelve are not to enter a *city* of the Samaritans may also be significant since πόλις is used of larger urban centers in Matthew and distinguished from κώνη (e.g., 9:35; 14:15; 21:2), as it is just a few verses later in 10:11. There may have been Jewish villages in Samaria (Jer. 41:5; Josephus, *Ant.* 11:346–47), which the Twelve were to enter. The prohibition of entrance into Samaritan *cities* further clarifies that the concern is with the public profile of Jesus' delegation. That Matthew does not relate any activity by Jesus or the Twelve outside Galilee, with the exceptions of Jerusalem and Bethany, does not imply the restriction of the mission to Galilee or the northern kingdom of Israel of old (centered in Samaria), for "you will not cover the cities of Israel until the Son of Man comes" (Matt. 10:23). Here Israel is the whole land of Israel rather than only that of the northern kingdom (cf. the similar use of "the house of Jacob" in the Tanakh). Matthew also hints that Jesus was known and embraced outside Galilee (e.g., Matt. 21:3, 11), and Jerusalem (and Judea) is hardly secondary to Jesus' kingdom mission (against Joel Willitts, "Matthew's Messianic Shepherd-King: In Search of 'The Lost Sheep of the House of Israel,'" *HTS*, 63, no. 1 [March 2007]: 365–82. I am nevertheless in sympathy with Willitts's more important insight that the scope of the kingdom mission in Matthew 10 is geographic.).

39. The eschatological return of YHWH is to Zion (e.g., Isa. 31:4; 52:7-8; 59:20; 62:11-12; 64:11-12). The Samaritans are distinguished from gentiles because they remember the God of Israel as their own (and apparently hail from the otherwise disintegrated Israelite society of the northern kingdom). But the public mission of the kingdom begins with the remnant of Judah settled in the land of Israel, and centers on those lost sheep associated with David as the king of a united Israel (cf. Hos. 1:11; Ezek. 37:15-28) per the hope of the prophets, those sheep who have lived by the hope of the coming of his Son. These Jews are the lost sheep of the house of Israel. Cf. Jn. 4:22.

from Israelite authorities and describes their work as a winnowing of Israel (10:16-42, esp. v. 25), sifting populations that will go the way of the current regime in the coming judgment from those that will be sustained through that judgment.[40] Note also that in 10:18, it is precisely the apostles' encounter with this opposition that has as its goal "testimony . . . to the gentiles" (εἰς μαρτύριον αὐτοῖς [i.e, "to rulers and kings"] καὶ τοῖς ἔθνεσιν).[41] Even here, in the mission exclusive to the lost sheep of the House of Israel, the gentiles are in view.

Gentile Participation in Israel through Messiah: Matt. 15:21-28

We meet a jarring Jesus indeed in Matt. 15:21-28. The First Gospel has portrayed Jesus as compassionate and particularly generous toward the broken outsider thus far. Yet, to a poor mother's persistent pleas for the mercy that he has so liberally and characteristically granted to others, Jesus here responds with an apparently cold shoulder of silence, leaving unabated the torment of the woman's helpless daughter. The dramatic effect is hard to miss. A few moments before, we have read of Jesus' first direct clash with "Pharisees and scribes . . . *from Jerusalem*" (15:1), the first time a provenance of these opponents is so named. In chapter 15, the story has depicted Jesus as contending for the honor of the mothers and fathers of Israel and the emissaries from Jerusalem as authorities who justify the denigration of

---

40. The mission of the Twelve also elicits "this generation" for the first time in 11:16.

41. In 10:16-42, we see that Jesus has come to heat the people of Israel, as it were, so as to bring the dross to the top, for it to be skimmed off (cf. Matt. 3:11-12 and chapters 24–25). The deep division he causes in Israel (Matt. 10:32-42) will allow some Israelite communities in the land to alloy with the dross of Israel's current, unfaithful shepherds. Many, however, will sympathize with Jesus and honor Israel's prophetic heritage (even if they do not confess Jesus to be the Christ); they will receive the reward of the righteous. Those who resist being alloyed to Israel's current shepherds can survive the fires of Israel's purging and figure among the remnant of Israel that will remain after the coming destruction. This whole shakeup of Israel is the judgment God brings upon God's people through Jesus. Something like it has happened before (e.g., "at the time of the deportation to Babylon," Matt. 1:11-12).

Israel's God-given trust. Jesus has called the lost sheep of the house of Israel back to the holiness of obedience to the commandments of the covenant, rather than the peculiar traditions of the house of Israel's current shepherds, who have led them astray.[42] To this clash with the authorities from the holy city (cf. Matt. 4:5; 27:53) over the holiness of Israel is adjoined the approach of "a Canaanite woman," who has "come out" (ἐξελθοῦσα) of an area in the district of Tyre and Sidon, to which Jesus has withdrawn following his ill-boding confrontation with authorities from Jerusalem.

Tyre and Sidon have emerged recently in the narrative, after the sending of the Twelve. They will fare better in the coming day of judgment than several towns of Israel in the north that have rejected Jesus and thereby the way on which he is leading Israel (11:21-22). Jesus is now apparently in the border lands of this historic and prestigious gentile region, one also associated traditionally with gentile faithfulness to the God of Israel in times of Israelite rulers' unfaithfulness (1 Kgs. 17:8-24; Luke 4:25-6). The conspicuous juxtaposition of a discourse on holiness (15:1-20) and the approach of the Canaanite mother from Tyre and Sidon suggests that the holiness of Israel and the participation of gentiles in Israel's messianic blessings go hand in hand.

---

42. In the discourse, Jesus follows the order of the latter commandments of Exodus 20 exactly, beginning with "Honor your father and your mother" (15:4)—the commandment the emissaries from Jerusalem disobey through "evil intentions"—followed by "murder, adultery, fornication, theft, false witness, and slander" (Matt. 15:19; cf. Exod. 20:12-17). By beginning the list of Matt. 15:19 with "murder" and finishing with "slander" rather than the final commandment against coveting (i.e., listing the commandments *between* "Honor your father and your mother" and "You shall not covet"), the accusation may in fact be that the emissaries of Jerusalem are guilty of far more than breaking the two commands which, in Exodus, bracket the list given in Matt. 15:19, and, in Matthew 15, are the flashpoint of the controversy. They have indeed authorized the coveting of what belongs to one's neighbor (Exod. 20:17), who in this case is one's parents, thereby dishonoring them (Exod. 20:12). But listing what lies between these commands in 15:19 implies a much more far-reaching unfaithfulness than simply voiding the word of God for the sake of a tradition in the case of a single command: Israel's shepherds in the land are leading Israel in unfaithfulness to the whole law of the covenant.

Matthew introduces the woman with the *hapax legomenon* Χαναναία, proverbially invoking the assault of idolaters on the holiness of the land, and the threat to Israel's holiness as the people of God when Israelite men married Canaanite women and their gods.[43] These are nuances screened out by readings that construe Matthew as a conflict between Judaism and the gentile-embracing church. But they should not be screened out. As we saw in the previous chapter, not all gentiles are the same. If the characters are dehistoricized and departicularized so as to represent timeless differences as construed by modernity (e.g., race, gender), we cannot avoid finding here a racist and sexist Jesus. But Canaanites from Tyre and Sidon were not simply gentiles; they were Israel's foremost idolatrous enemies when it crossed the Jordan to taste of its God's promises.[44] And it was Israelite men marrying Canaanite women, with all that such idolatrous alliances implied for life in the land, that invited the curses of the covenant, which in turn culminated in exile. The differences here are historical rather than timeless (i.e., they emerged in time).[45] But through King David the God of Israel promised Israel a future not of dissolution among its idolatrous gentile enemies, but of gentile nations' coming under the rule of Israel's king, the Son of God (Psalm 2). The house and kingdom of David would be made sure forever, his throne established for all time (2 Samuel 7). So here in Matt. 15:21-28 we have the promised Son of David confronting one who

---

43. But cf. Σίμων ὁ Καναναῖος of 10:4.

44. I do not mean to imply that anyone was known as "Canaanite" at the time of Matthew's writing. But this is how people who are known otherwise (e.g., Syrophoenician) can be situated by the language and story of Israel's Bible, and there are no doubt various historical lines to be drawn between the more ancient inhabitants of Canaan and this mother from Tyre and Sidon.

45. France, for example, conceives of the enmity between Jesus and the Canaanite woman as "racial," reading the encounter as finally Jesus' vision for a "multiracial people of God" (590). This is a good example how readings in the interest of racial reconciliation unwittingly inscribe the power of race into the text. Besides the epic biblical tension to which I have pointed above (i.e., the threat of idolatry), Matt. 15:1-20 configures the tension of Matt. 15:21-28 as a matter of *practice*, particularly that of sharing the meal table with Israel's historic enemies, with all that this implies for political economy.

has borne in her body and name the history of idolatrous enmity with Israel, one that threatened to blot the name of Israel—and with it its God's—from the earth.[46] Furthermore, that she does this as a mother, since it is for her daughter that she begs healing, indicates that the story is concerned not only with the Israel-Canaanite past but with the Israel-Canaanite future.[47]

The condition of the Canaanite woman's daughter is among the most characteristically tended by Jesus in the First Gospel, although the drama is heightened here by its particular severity (κακῶς δαιμονίζεται—"badly demonized," Matt. 15:22). More remarkably, the Canaanite mother addresses Jesus reverently, as so many of Jesus' patients and disciples have—"Lord"—and she even adds "Son of David," invoking the name of Israel's great king, and a title freighted with maximum weight by the opening genealogy and its dramatic occurrences in the narrative.[48] Surely this is enough faith for the healing of this mother's daughter! Surely confessing Jesus as lord and king is enough for deliverance! Yet Jesus ignores her, and for so long that his disciples are finally driven to plead that he give her what she wants.[49] But the language in which they do this is chosen carefully. "Release her, for she keeps calling out after us" (ἀπόλυσον

---

46. Josh. 7:9; 23:6-16; Judges 1. Note, too, that this encounter seems to come in the narrative upon the occasion of another withdrawal by Jesus, in this case from a clash with "Pharisees and scribes . . . from Jerusalem." Conflict within Israel is not equivalent to Jesus' tense encounter with the Canaanite mother but is instead the occasion and context of that encounter (as in 10:18).

47. Cf. the παῖς of the centurion in 8:5-13.

48. Only the two blind men of 9:27 have hailed Jesus as such, immediately prior to the description of the awe of the crowds and the anticipation of Jesus' decisive divergence with the Jewish authorities of the people in the land discussed above. In the midst of that divergence in ch. 12, the crowds, amazed at another exorcism, ask, "Can this be the Son of David?" It is this title that the narrative leaves ringing in our ears for Jesus' entry into Jerusalem and the temple (20:30—21:16), and from his last (silencing) exchange with Pharisees (22:21-46), through his final discourses (chapters. 23–25) and passion.

49. If they are telling Jesus to send her away without giving her what she wants (taking ἀπόλυσον as simply "send her away"), then Jesus' response (v. 24) does not make sense. Instead, they invite Jesus give her what she wants to get rid of her, and, in v. 24, Jesus refuses to grant the woman's request on the terms established thus far in the story and assumed by the disciples. Jesus presses for terms that go deeper.

αὐτήν, ὅτι κράζει ὄπισθεν ἡμῶν).[50] This is what the burdensome Canaanite past continues to do to the Israelite present—"calling out after us." In light of what Jesus says in v. 26, it appears that the disciples are ready for Jesus to give the Canaanite mother what she wants on the terms of her pitiful stubbornness and acclaiming Jesus Lord and Son of David. They wish simply to be done with the debt between the Canaanites and Israel. Perhaps these are the "merciful" terms on which Israel's rulers have entered into "beneficial" alliances with Canaanites in the past, thus securing their tribute. But Jesus has not come to exploit the Canaanites with his power and merely push them back to Israel's border again, pending a future clash or claim. He has not come to prey upon their weakness and receive such tribute. He has come to save Israel from their sins—which is to save Israel once and for all from Israel's enemies; the disciples must not be tempted by Jesus' power into compromising the salvation of Israel by settling for a temporary reprieve of the Canaanite burden under the cover of mercy. So Jesus draws the mother and the disciples in still closer.

In response to the disciples' pleas here on the border of the promised land, Jesus repeats the phrase of 10:6, but this time with added emphasis: "I was not sent to anyone but the lost sheep of the house of Israel" (οὐκ ἀπεστάλην εἰ μὴ εἰς τὰ πρόβατα τὰ ἀπολωλότα οἴκου Ἰσραήλ). Not only has the limitation of 10:5 been intensified with the negative εἰ μὴ εἰς in 15:24; Jesus here defines the entire scope of his commission from the Father of Israel as "no one except the lost sheep of the house of Israel." Should he release the mother on the terms expressed thus far, he is only a messiah and not

---

50. Ἀπολύω is the term for divorce, dismissal from a place, and releasing a captive. One need not read one of these senses to the exclusion of the others, given the history of Israelites and Canaanites and the condition of this mother and daughter.

the Messiah. The Messiah brooks no alliance with Canaanites, but delivers the lost sheep of the house of Israel once and for all.[51]

The scene has not yet reached its maximum pitifulness or dramatic apogee. The already thoroughly humiliated mother now prostrates herself before Jesus, begging, "Lord, help me." Jesus replies, in effect, that he should not take the salvation that belongs only to the children of the house of Israel and throw it to gentile dogs like her![52] And yet, this bereft mother is still not put off! She even concurs with Jesus but claims that there is a place in the house of Israel for gentile enemies like her, where they "eat of the crumbs that are falling from their lords' table" (15:27). At this—on these terms—Jesus calls this mother's faith "great" and gives her what she has so desperately sought: "Her daughter was healed at once" (15:28). As Jesus continues such healing, he draws the following response from the crowds just a few verses later: "They glorified the God *of Israel*" (15:31).

What does Jesus' encounter with the Canaanite mother tell us? The time for Israel's victory over its enemies has come. It is not a model for how Jews should treat gentiles. Nor is it a model for how men should treat women. It is how Israel's history of enmity with the Canaanites is coming to an end in and through Jesus. This indeed has implications for other gentiles, for if Jesus can deliver Israel from the Canaanites forever, then what can it mean but peace between Israel and the rest of the gentiles?[53] But let the terms of this peace be understood. There is for these gentile enemies of Israel, as well as less threatening gentiles, no Son of David, no Christ, no being

---

51. My reading of this encounter resonates somewhat with that of Howard Thurman in *Jesus and the Disinherited* (New York: Abingdon-Cokesbury; Boston: Beacon, 1996 [1949, 1976]), 90–92. The pagination is that of the 1996 publication by Beacon.

52. Note the subtle similarity in sound of the words Χαναναία and κυναρίοις/κυνάρια (15:26-27).

53. Besides inscribing a timeless Israel-gentile difference into the story, reducing this Canaanite mother to a representative of "gentiles" misses the "how much more" hope of the story. To read "gentile" here is simply not enough. The force of the passage depends on which gentiles are in view.

Christian, no holy people, apart from the covenant people of Israel. The eschatological blessing of gentiles—their salvation—obtains only at the table of Israel and its God, only within the covenant of the one true God.

This is to say that gentiles participate in the material blessings of Israel's healing only in their (mutual) dependence upon the (morally mixed) Israelite people of God in the flesh who have preceded them, who are their contemporaries, and who will come after them. Because Jesus "will save his people from their sins" (Matt. 1:21) and die as "the King of Israel" (Matt. 27:42), he is of full benefit to Israel and gentiles—he is their peace—only as gentiles are in solidarity with the people of Israel, knowing Israel's God as their own and themselves as fellow adoptees. Thus, the work of Jesus the Messiah not only allows gentiles to number themselves among God's people Israel (which has been happening for a long time) but brings final peace between Israel and the gentile nations, drawing them into one house, to one, overflowing table. Jesus does not eliminate the gentile threat with the sword but with mercy. This is not "mercy" that exploits gentiles' weakness. It is mercy that is revealed in their faith, that is, in abandoning their divisive gods and embracing the one God of Israel as their own in the name of the Lord Jesus.[54] They have been adopted by and into God's living election of Israel, and thus find a future of healing through Israel's Messiah, as Jesus brought healing to the daughter of this Canaanite mother in whom he inspired faith. As revealed in Messiah, this is what Israel's election means for Israel's most historic and bitter gentile enemies. And if this is what it means for the Canaanite future, what can it mean but healing and peace for all the nations that are the inheritance of the Son of David (e.g., Psalm 2; Matt: 15:22)?[55]

---

54. In other words, they are justified by faith.

To All the Nations: Matt. 28:18-20

Jesus' words to what is left of his delegation of twelve in 28:18-20 differ noticeably from his words to them at their first commissioning in 10:5-6. But exactly how they differ is not as obvious as has often been thought. These are the first words Jesus speaks to the apostles after pouring out his "blood of the covenant for many for the forgiveness of sins" (Matt. 26:28) and being raised from the dead. It is to this apocalyptic rupture, rather than the "rupture" of the Jewish-Christian schism, that the words of 28:18-20 respond. Anticipated throughout the First Gospel in and through Jesus, the time of the eschatological blessings *of and for Israel* has come. Nevertheless, Matthew has also insisted in chapter 16 and the Olivet Discourse that those blessings will unfold in the midst of Israel's ongoing judgment (e.g., Matt. 16:24-28; 24:1–25:46). Forgiveness does not spell the end of all judgment but eschatological blessing in and through the judgment that remains, culminating in resurrection. But the end of judgment is now in view in the body of the risen Jesus, and it will unfold as peace between Israel and the gentile nations under the worldwide rule of the Lord Jesus. Roads that lead to gentile territory and Samaritan cities now lie within the purview of Jesus' kingdom delegation, as the kingdom revolution has now taken place in the holy land of Israel and will begin to bleed into all the world.

---

55. This implies neither conforming to a pure Israelite identity nor remaining the gentiles that they were. Israel's identity is unfolding in time because it is always compromised and constituted by its God. Because God exceeds Israel in this way (i.e., in Christ), Israel is hospitable to a certain kind of difference. It is not to be a homogenizing agent or the police of an internal purity. In fact, it is called to engage this difference in a way that is transformative for Israel itself and enables it to become who it is called to be. This is what it means for Israel to be a living people. Yet, as the God of all, the God of Israel refuses to tolerate the divisiveness of idolatry indefinitely. It is the testimony of Israel that the creation is one as the God of creation is one, calling the world to serve the one true God, i.e., calling the world to peace. Christians say that that peace, that Messiah, is Jesus.

What introduces the expansion of the apostles' mission beyond the promised land is Jesus' pronouncement of Matt. 28:18. "All power in heaven and on earth has been given to me" (ἐδόθη μοι πᾶσα ἐξουσία ἐν οὐρανῷ καὶ ἐπὶ [τῆς] γῆς). All creation has become Jesus' dominion, and so Jesus commands his apostles to disciple "all the nations" (πάντα τὰ ἔθνη). We should probably hear the echo of Dan. 7:14 in Matt. 28:18. Dan. 7:13-14 (LXX) envisions one

> ὡς υἱὸς ἀνθρώπου ἤρχετο . . . καὶ ἐδόθη αὐτῷ ἐξουσία, καὶ πάντα τὰ ἔθνη τῆς γῆς κατὰ γένη καὶ πᾶσα δόξα αὐτῷ λατρεύουσα καὶ ἡ ἐξουσία αὐτοῦ ἐξουσία αἰώνιος, ἥτις οὐ μὴ ἀρθῇ, καὶ ἡ βασιλεία αὐτοῦ, ἥτις οὐ μὴ φθαρῇ
>
> like a son of man [who] was coming forth . . . and power was given him, even all the nations of the earth by family, and all glory rendered him, and his power is an eternal power, one which shall not pass away and his kingdom one which shall not be despoiled.[56]

A long Israelite tradition connects the rule of the eschatological Son of David with both the healing of the people of Israel and the extension of Israel's authority to the gentile nations (which go together).[57] Isaiah's contribution is noteworthy. In the same passage of Isaiah that Matthew has quoted at the beginning of Jesus' kingdom proclamation and healings (Matt. 4:15), we find the following regarding the child born to Israel, upon whom the rule shall rest:

> His rule is great and of his peace there is no limit. [I shall bring peace] upon the throne of David and his kingdom, to establish it and to uphold it in righteousness and in judgment from this time onward and forevermore. (Isa. 9:6 LXX)[58]

56. Compare ἐδόθη μοι πᾶσα ἐξουσία ἐν οὐρανῷ καὶ ἐπὶ [τῆς] γῆς (Matt. 28:18) and καὶ ἐδόθη αὐτῷ ἐξουσία, καὶ πάντα τὰ ἔθνη τῆς γῆς (Dan. 7:14a). Thanks to Richard Hays for pointing out this striking parallel to me.
57. E.g., Amos 9:11-15; Hosea 3:4-5; Isa. 16:4-5; Jer. 23:5-8; 33:15-22; Ezek. 34:20-31; 37:24-28; Zec. 12:7-10 (Cf. Ps. 2:8; 71:11).
58. Isa. 9:6: μεγάλη ἡ ἀρχὴ αὐτοῦ, καὶ τῆς εἰρήνης αὐτοῦ οὐκ ἔστιν ὅριον ἐπὶ τὸν θρόνον Δαυιδ καὶ τὴν βασιλείαν αὐτοῦ κατορθῶσαι αὐτὴν καὶ ἀντιλαβέσθαι αὐτῆς ἐν δικαιοσύνῃ καὶ ἐν

Similarly,

> Give heed with your ears and follow my ways. Listen closely to me and your (ὑμῶν) life will abide in good conditions, and I will make with you (ὑμῖν) an eternal covenant, the faithful devotion of David. Behold, as a witness among the nations I have given him as ruler and the one commanding the nations; nations that had not known you (σε) will appeal to you (σε), and peoples that do not learn of you (σε) will take refuge in you (σε) because of your God, the holy one of Israel, for he has glorified you (σε). (Isa. 55:3–5 LXX)[59]

We have already noted the crucial place of David in the opening genealogy and elsewhere in the narrative.[60] The worldwide power of Jesus expressed in Matt. 28:18 seems to be what the Son of David and Son of Man motifs of the Gospel have been leading to throughout the narrative.

"All the nations of the earth" (πάντα τὰ ἔθνη τῆς γῆς), of course, did not first appear in Dan. 7:14. These are the exact words used to describe the ultimate scope of the blessing of Abraham (Gen. 18:18; 22:18),[61] the other ancestor of reference in Matthew's opening

κρίματι ἀπὸ τοῦ νῦν καὶ εἰς τὸν αἰῶνα χρόνον. In my translation I have taken ἐπὶ τὸν θρόνον Δαυιδ to continue the thought of ἐγὼ γὰρ ἄξω εἰρήνην ἐπὶ . . . (9:5), thus extending the string of ἐπὶ-prepositional phrases begun in 9:5. We should surely connect this passage to the streaming of the gentiles to Zion in Isa. 2:1–4.

59. Προσέχετε τοῖς ὠτίοις ὑμῶν καὶ ἐπακολουθήσατε ταῖς ὁδοῖς μου· ἐπακούσατέ μου, καὶ ζήσεται ἐν ἀγαθοῖς ἡ ψυχὴ ὑμῶν· καὶ διαθήσομαι ὑμῖν διαθήκην αἰώνιον, τὰ ὅσια Δαυιδ τὰ πιστά. ἰδοὺ μαρτύριον ἐν ἔθνεσιν δέδωκα αὐτόν, ἄρχοντα καὶ προστάσσοντα ἔθνεσιν. ἔθνη, ἃ οὐκ ᾔδεισάν σε, ἐπικαλέσονταί σε, καὶ λαοί, οἳ οὐκ ἐπίστανταί σε, ἐπὶ σὲ καταφεύξονται ἕνεκεν τοῦ θεοῦ σου τοῦ ἁγίου Ισραηλ, ὅτι ἐδόξασέν σε. These words are directed to "those who thirst for water and as many as do not have silver" (Isa. 55:1a), who appear to be those laid low by covenant curses, the "many" whose sins the servant bore and because of whose sins he was handed over (Isa. 53:12).

60. We might add the invocation of "Son of David" as Jesus concludes his approach to Jerusalem (20:30–31), on the lips of the crowds ushering Jesus into Jerusalem (21:9), including the cries of the children in the temple that anger the chief priests and scribes (21:15), and in the closing disputation with Israel's unfaithful shepherds (22:42–46), where Jesus' relation to David is the explicit subject of the passage and the opening question is posed by Jesus himself.

61. Gen. 22:18 is the last time the promise is rehearsed for Abraham in Genesis, after his faith regarding God's provision of descendants has confirmed it. It is present in similar forms throughout Genesis, already in 12:3 (πᾶσαι αἱ φυλαὶ τῆς γῆς).

genealogy. How might this affect a reading of Matt. 28:18-20? Abraham has not figured prominently after the opening genealogy. But one characteristic of the blessing of Abraham does crop up in the First Gospel in such a way as to confirm my reading of its conclusion. The centurion of Matt. 8:5-13 does not foreshadow an eschatological blessing that has merely passed through Abraham and his descendants to reach the distant east and west. The "many" (8:11; cf. 26:28), rather, come and recline to eat *at the same table with* Abraham, Isaac, and Jacob (8:11).[62] Like the Canaanite mother, they take their place *within* the house of Israel (whose porous borders may expand). This is how the First Gospel reads the common "in you," "in him," or "in your seed" (ἐν σοὶ, ἐν αὐτῷ, or ἐν τῷ σπέρματί σου) of the blessing of all the nations in relation to Abraham.[63]

Reading Matt. 28:19 in light of the promise repeated to Abraham, Isaac, and Jacob in Genesis, we see that Abrahamic sonship brackets the Gospel narrative (1:1 and 28:19). The discipleship of 28:19-20 is a being "in Abraham," by being baptized into the name of the Father, of the Son, and of the Holy Spirit and taught to obey all that Jesus commanded. This is not to suggest that all Israelites who are not disciples of Jesus are thereby rendered not children of Abraham, for Israel remains a complex people whose shape is being worked out over time in the flesh through the ruling power of Jesus. It is to suggest that being children of Abraham is not simply a static rank but a calling with an eschatological bearing.[64]

---

62. Cf. "Eine Tischgemeinschaft mit Abraham, Isaak und Jakob" (Nils Alstrup Dahl, *Das Volk Gottes: Eine Untersuchung zum Kirchenbewusstsein des Urchristentums* [Oslo: J. Dybwad, 1941], 147).

63. Gen. 12:3; 18:18; 22:18; 26:4; 28:14. In relation to "the many" for whom Jesus' blood is shed, note also Abraham's fatherhood πολλῶν ἐθνῶν (e.g., Gen. 17:5) and the growing "many" of Exod. 1:9; 12:35-39; Hosea 1:10-11; Isa. 52:14; and esp. 53:12. See also Isa. 25:6-7; 56:7.

64. Matthew seems to indicate something like this with the two other incidents of "Abraham" after the genealogy. To Pharisees and Sadducees, John the Baptist says, "And do not consider saying to yourselves, 'We have Abraham as father,' for I say to you that God can raise from these stones children to Abraham" (Matt. 3:9). The idea is not that these figures are relying on their

In light of the geographic force of 10:5-6 and 15:24, translating
πάντα τὰ ἔθνη as "all the gentiles" is too restrictive.[65] If we are to
take our cue from the exaltation of the "one like a son of man" in
Daniel, in view are all the communities of the earth, among whom
many Israelite exiles continue to dwell. The scope of the apostles'
mission, in other words, now extends to all of the world's inhabitants
as they have come to be grouped through time according to place

"blood" or "ethnicity" but that they claim to live in a way (and lead Israel in a way) that will
inherit the blessings promised to Abraham and his children of promise. They claim to embody
Abraham's righteousness and anticipate the blessings promised for it. To Sadducees Jesus says,
"But regarding the resurrection of the dead, have you not read that which was said to you by
God? 'I am the God of Abraham and the God of Isaac and the God of Jacob.' He is not God
of the dead but of the living" (Matt. 22:32). Thus, Abraham is not simply the one from whom
Israelites hail, one who survives in but the memory and covenantal status of his children of
promise. Abraham's own life persists and awaits consummation at the resurrection of the dead,
thus summoning his children to fulfill their calling to faithfulness, which has been ordered to
the blessing of all the communities of the earth and the resurrection of the dead.

65. In *The Social and Ethnic Dimensions of Matthean Salvation History*, Amy-Jill Levine argues for
the translation of πάντα τὰ ἔθνη as "all the gentiles," and suggests that, with Matt. 28:18-20,
gentiles have been elevated to the soteriological status of Jews and that the prerogatives of (and
promises to) Israel have been fulfilled, calling this soteriological resolution "christological" (42).
Besides the problems with this contention mentioned above in the body of the argument, one
might also ask if this Christology takes the election of Israel seriously enough and whether
the First Gospel shows any clear support of it. While certainly embodying the consummation
in nuce, the death and resurrection of Jesus, with his consequent worldwide authority, hardly
satisfy the prerogatives of the covenant people of Israel or fulfill all the promises of the prophets
regarding the salvation of Israel (e.g., a new heavens and a new earth, Isa. 65:17).

The prophets Matthew has drawn upon for his Gospel, especially the tradition of the
eschatological Son of David, universally uphold the integrity of the elect people of God and
describe the Son of David always in relation to that people. The judgment of Israel is always
ordered to the salvation of Israel as well as gentiles in Israel, and Matthew shows every sign
of standing upon this traditional bedrock (e.g., Matt. 13:17, where the prophets and righteous
surely did not long to see an ethereal exaltation of the Christ but his rule of the people of Israel
and the world. What other exaltation is there?). In short, the Christology of the First Gospel
cannot be extricated from or made finally competitive with the people of Israel.

Furthermore, the First Gospel knows nothing of invisible, general/immediate changes of
"status," whether with respect to Israel or gentiles. The existing covenant people of Israel is in
no way diminished as such in the story, and gentiles acquire new "status" only by means of
material association with Israel, particularly through Jesus now that the eschaton has dawned.
Those Jewish shepherds for whom Israel's judgment means being cast out to the darkness
outside (e.g., those who blaspheme against the Spirit) are excluded over time through the
destruction of Jerusalem (and other parts of the promised land) and the resulting dispersion, as
their authority and even participation in the people of Israel dissipates with death and the grind
of time across generations.

and generations (i.e., as ἔθνη).[66] This scope thus includes the Israelites of the promised land, many of whom have already shown hospitality to the kingdom of heaven.

The closing words of the First Gospel thus underscore that Jesus is the son of Abraham in whom is fulfilled the promise to Abraham, that all the nations of the earth will be blessed *in him*. The expansion to "all the nations" does not relativize Israel, but follows Israel's own vocation under the cosmic, eschatological rule of the Son of David. Πάντα τὰ ἔθνη is also where Israel's remaining exiles continue to reside.[67] Thus, what we find in Matt. 28:18-20 is not the moving beyond the people of Israel. Nor is it a move from the particular to the universal, or from ethnicity to spirituality. That is not how Matt. 28:18-20 differs from Matthew 10:5-6, which restricted the apostles' mission to Jewish settlements in the promised land and excluded Jews living among the Samaritans and the gentiles. Rather, we find at the close of the First Gospel an extension of Jesus' mission to the furthest reaches of Israel's exile and beyond, whence Israelites are called to be disciples of Jesus and their gentile hosts to be gathered together with them to share in the one covenant people in the flesh under the rule of the Son of David and Son of Man.[68] [69]

---

66. If indeed Matt. 28:18-20 echoes Dan. 7:13-14, then Matthew suggests that the exaltation of "the one like the son of man" of Dan. 7:13-14 has taken place. Apparently, as of the time of Jesus' trial before the high priest, the coming of the Son of Man is "from now on" (Matt. 26:64).

67. Deut. 4:27; 28:37, 64; 29:23; 30:1-3; Jer. 32:15; 51:8; Ezek. 39:23; Amos 9:9; Joel 4:2; Zech. 7:14. My point here is not to limit the scope of the commission to Israel absolutely but to insist that it reaches beyond Israel only as it reaches with and for Israel. That is the relation between Israel and "all the nations" according to Daniel 7. The implication is also that the messianic mission "beyond" Israel empowers participation in Israel.

68. Thus the expectation of Isaiah is that gentiles will stream to Zion to learn the ways of the God of Jacob, the ways of peace (Isa. 2:2-4), bringing the exiles of Israel along with them (Isa. 49:22-23). In Isaiah 49, we are told that the gentile nations will be the ones to restore the children of Israelite exiles. Gentile "kings" and "queens . . . shall bow to the face of the earth before you and lick the dust of your feet" (Isa. 49:23 LXX). Nevertheless, to characterize the baptism of 28:19 as "baptism into Israel" flattens out two important distinctions. First, insofar as some in the purview of this apostolic commission are already Israelites, such would make discipleship redundant. Not all Israelites are disciples of Jesus, and not being a disciple of Jesus or even rejecting Jesus does not suddenly exclude one from Israel. Second, for Gentile nations

Judgment according to the Gospel of Matthew

The mission to all the nations in Matt. 28:18-20 does not respond to a failed Christian mission to Israel, consigning Israel to judgment and giving up on peace between Israel and the gentiles.[70] Quite the contrary: it responds to the fact of that peace. Through his life as consummated in his death, the Son of David and Abraham has won reconciliation, embodied in his resurrection. The time has come for gathering Israel among the gentile nations and welcoming those gentile nations into Israel's house to become one covenant people in the flesh. According to the First Gospel, the time for peace in Israel—which would be empty apart from peace with the gentile nations—has dawned with Jesus' enactment of the kingdom of Israel's God in the promised land. Jesus' disciples are now to train all the nations to live this peace by baptizing them in the Triune name and teaching them all that Jesus has commanded. The life of Israel is determined by the time in which it lives according to God's election,

to be discipled is not only for them to "join Israel" but to join in Jesus' way of being Israel, the way that responds in faith to the dawn of eschatological blessing, i.e., the resurrection of the dead. To be discipled in this way is to become part of Israel as it is moving toward resurrection along the way of the cross.

69. A brief word on the Parable of the Vineyard (21:33-46) since it may be thought to upset the reading of 10:5-6, 15:24, and 28:18-20 that I have offered: I understand the parable, like similar ones in Matthew, to be directed primarily against the Jerusalemite temple establishment, not the whole people of Israel. We are told that the chief priests and Pharisees sought to seize Jesus because he spoke the parable *against them* but that they feared the people, who apparently were not so offended by the parable (21:45-46). It is thus the Jerusalemite temple establishment that will lose its inheritance of the kingdom of God, not replaced by a sudden change in its formal status but dissolved in time just as similar regimes have been judged throughout Israel's history, i.e., "cut off," especially as a consequence of the coming civil war and war with Rome. The inheritance of the kingdom, the compass by which the people of Israel will be directed, will pass instead to any community (anarthrous ἔθνει in 21:43) producing the fruit of that kingdom. Such a community will mark the way to Israel's promised blessing. This reading is against that of Stanton who, like many others, identifies 21:43 as one of the most important verses of the Gospel, and reads it to announce the rejection "of Israel" or the removal of the kingdom "from Israel" and its being given "to the gentiles" (Stanton, *The Gospels and Jesus*, 65, 74).

70. Against Luz, *Matthew 1-7*, 50. "The church . . . failed in its mission to Israel, experienced the divine judgment of the destruction of Jerusalem, and now in Syria is called by the evangelist to a new task."

330

and Israel now lives in the time in which gentiles will abandon their divisive gods and stream in eschatological numbers to embrace the God, people, and law of Israel as their own. This can only mean that in Jesus' resurrection Israel has encountered the end of the course of God's judgment upon its sin, that is, the forgiveness of sins, which is the full material blessing of Israel (see, e.g., Jeremiah 31, Ezekiel 36, and Daniel 9; cf. Isaiah 43–44). This end of covenant curses is what the First Gospel has displayed in the passion of Jesus, who is God with us.

A shadow of judgment has hung over the entire story of Matthew. To understand it, we have to follow its lengthening through the Gospel until the night of the cross. The opening genealogy is laced with God's judgment, its last third devoted to the royal generations of the Babylonian exile. The news of "the one born king of the Jews" on the lips of magi from the East (the land of the judgment of exile) then fills Herod and Jerusalem with fear. What can it mean but a devastating war and finally the siege of Jerusalem in a struggle for the throne?[71] We glimpse the political powers at work, and the violence that is coming, in Herod's slaughter of Bethlehem's sons. With this story of slaughter in chapter 2, we might be tempted to conceive of Jesus as the one who averts God's judgment against Israel and leads a community who escapes it. But Jesus escapes to Egypt of all places, and the dead Jewish sons of Bethlehem are not an Israel that Jesus leaves behind. They are the children of Rachel, for whom she weeps only to hear these words:

71. Luz puzzlingly calls the fear of Herod and Jerusalem at the news of a non-Herodian, Jewish king a "historical absurdity," forgetting that in the history of Israel these are tidings of war to Herod and Jerusalem. Such war is in fact what the Gospel tells us is coming (esp. chapters 24–25). Moreover, Josephus tells of Herod's systematic and compulsive elimination of threats to his rule, a ruthless career that struck fear into any near his path and especially in the capital. Luz claims that Matthew has included such "historical absurdities . . . in the interest of the historical drama that led to the separation of the church from the rest of Israel" (*Matthew 1–7*, 54). Thus, in an effort to be more historically sensitive by way of the two-level-drama hermeneutic and the imagined Jewish-Christian schism, Luz's reading becomes less historically sensitive.

331

> Thus says the Lord: Let your voice cease from weeping, and your eyes from shedding your tears; for there is a reward for your works, and they shall return from the land of enemies. There will be a home for your children. (Jer. 38:16-17 LXX)[72]

These children cannot be mourned as Israel's exiles of the past have been, for now their savior, their future beyond the violence of Jerusalem's last corrupt king, is among them. And the son soon to return from Egypt, like Israel before him, has not escaped the fate of Bethlehem's sons; he has moved along the line of that fate towards its horrific culmination at the end of the Gospel. The judgment that Jesus escapes here at the beginning of the First Gospel only increases the judgment that he will endure, because he has come to lead Israel through the depths of judgment to deliverance. Thus, Jesus joins a gathering of Israel at the Jordan that is not simply praying for their deliverance from covenant curses but "confessing their sins" (3:6). Jesus joins this gathering in repentance because he knows Israel's sins only as his own. Already at his baptism by John, Jesus is numbered with sinners (cf. 9:13; 27:15-23), and it is precisely as such, rather than as one aloof from Israel's judgment, that he is anointed as God's Son (Psalm 2), as chosen ruler, as the elect one. This messianic solidarity with the sin of Israel is the way "to fulfill all righteousness" (Matt. 3:15),[73] and it is this solidarity of Jesus with his people that occasions the heavenly voice, "This is my Son the beloved, in whom was my pleasure" (Matt. 15:17).

At the end of his first discourse, Jesus announces judgment upon his listeners, righteous and unrighteous alike: a storm is coming upon all (Matt. 7:24-27; cf. Matt. 3:11). Those who do not heed his words will be swept away, destroyed in the coming hostilities.

---

72. These words of Jeremiah immediately follow those quoted in Matthew; the whole chapter breathes Israel's hope.

73. John the Baptist himself is taught this in Jesus' urging him to baptize the Messiah (Matt. 3:14).

Those slated to inherit the awaited kingdom of God, the current rulers of Israel in the land, "will be thrown into the outer darkness, where there will be weeping and gnashing of teeth" (Matt. 8:12; cf. Matt. 3:12). They will find themselves excluded from the healing Jesus is bringing to Israel as the coming age begins to open; they will bemoan their loss of power and enviously detest those who come to guide Israel's course into the future (i.e., those who come to rule).[74] In the face of the corrupt ways loose in Israel, only the Son of Man can calm the stormy seas of the nations that have been engulfing Israel and are about to assault the house of Israel with terrible violence (8:23-27).[75] Israelite towns in the promised land who do not heed Jesus' call to be peacemakers faithful to the law of the covenant will meet a fate worse than Sodom and Gomorrah's at the coming of the Son of Man (10:15). Jesus has come to shake Israel to its foundations so that its entire order will be upset in the course of its judgment and salvation, that is, in the course of its healing. Certain ways of publicly maligning the Spirit of justice by which Jesus is bringing forgiveness to Israel, and through Israel to the gentiles, will not participate in that forgiveness, whether in the approaching judgment or the age of resurrection to follow (12:15-21, 31-32). In other words, these Israelite ways will not survive, and the names of the rulers who practiced them will become shameful if not blotted out altogether. Their only hope is the judgment of Jonah (which is indeed hope, if through the most terrible suffering) (12:38-42), that is, to be redeemed by that judgment.

Upon the maligning of the Spirit by the most trusted authorities in the land, Jesus speaks in parables to keep the people from duplicity

---

74. See, e.g., Ps. 37:12; 112:10 for the meaning of "weeping and gnashing teeth."

75. Note how "Son of Man" is introduced in 8:18-22, and the scene of 8:23-27 plays out on the stormy sea to which the Son of Man comes in Daniel 7. Accordingly, Jesus is this empowered Son of Man who brings peace to the raging waves of gentile domination precisely as one who "has no place to lay his head" (Matt. 8:20).

in the face of their corrupt shepherds (13:13-16). He calls them to his discipleship, the way to Israel's deliverance where the mystery of the parables is revealed. In this context of judgment, the death of John the Baptist is but a shade of the death that is looming over the land (14:1-12), and so Jesus withdraws from the center of conflict for a final sweep of the house of Israel (14:13).

But after showing his royal power to rule over Israel and the gentile nations—to feed them and unite them in peace in honor of Israel's ancestors[76]—Jesus makes a revelation that is stunning to the disciples, even if it deepens his intimacy with the coming judgment. At the northernmost tip of the promised land, in the shadow of gentile empire in Caesarea Philippi, his disciples finally confess him the anointed Son of the Living God. In response, Jesus reveals to them that what it means for him to be Messiah, the elect one who shepherds his people and saves them from their sins, is to endure the terrible violence of the judgment to come (16:13-28). His church must point the way in and for Israel by showing that only this kind of death—taking up a cross—can withstand the fires of Hades that burn branches of Israel away and gentile peoples into oblivion. Only this way of living and dying leads to forgiveness, to resurrection life for all Israel, to peace with the gentile nations. Jesus will remain in solidarity with Israel to the very depths of its judgment. He will die for his people, and his disciples are to be a community that witnesses to the life that comes in and through that death. As they move toward the heart of Israel, then, Jesus trains them to be this church (chapters

---

76. In the chiastically structured narrative of 14:1—16:12, Jesus signals his power to feed the twelve tribes of Israel (12 baskets) and the Gentile nations (7 baskets for the seven Gentile nations hostile to Israel in the land, e.g., Deut. 7:1). His faithless shepherd Peter (14:22-33) is countered by the faithful Canaanite mother (15:21-28), in the middle of which Jesus teaches corrupt shepherds from Jerusalem the commandments of the covenant, and thus how to honor Israel's mothers and fathers (15:1-20). The power of Jesus as teacher of the law draws faith in the God of Israel from Israel's enemies (15:21-28; cf. v. 34) and so puts an end to that enmity. He is the promise of provision for all (cf. Gen. 22:14).

17–20). By the third prediction of Jesus' death on the way up to Jerusalem (20:17-19), it becomes clear that he will die not only at the hands of the corrupt rulers of the house of Israel, but humiliatingly at the hands of Israel's gentile overlords, on a Roman cross. These are indeed, as we've seen in chapters 4–5 above, the depths of the curses of the covenant—Israelite corruption and deterioration, gentile invasion and dominance, and now the destruction of the Son of David who bears Israel's promise.

We may think that to reject Jesus' way is to be separated from him. But as the story draws near to Jerusalem, we see that Jesus identifies the house of Israel's future of judgment with his own future, with the cross that he has told the disciples he himself will endure. The fruitless fig tree of the temple will wither and die. The current regime will be destroyed, and new tenants will be raised to cultivate Israel (chapters 21–22). The blood that Jerusalem has shed will be on its own head. But in all of this, Israel can only go the way of Jesus by God's election. Thus, in chapters 24–25, the lengthening shadow of judgment cast throughout Matthew by the light of Jesus begins to take clearer shape. It is the coming destruction of the house of Israel and the razing of its temple through civil war and the assault of Roman legions. Israel will be dramatically reordered and yet renewed. This will culminate the coming of the Son of Man in power, which begins with his enduring in his own body the approaching judgment upon the house of Israel (26:64). This coming of Jesus is thus the light that casts the shadow of Israel's judgment. As a death through Jewish infighting and by Roman power, his crucifixion (between two λῃσταί[77]) is the future of Jerusalem, but that means that Jerusalem's

---

77. For the sense of λῃστής, see Josephus, *Jewish War* 2:57; 2:253–54; 2:431; 2:434; 2:441; 2:541; 2:587–93; 2:653; 4:138; 4:199; 4:242–45; 4:409–10; 4:504; 4:510; 4:555; 5:448; 5:515; 5:524; 5:546.

future is finally what is future to his cross: "On the third day he will be raised" (20:19).

Nevertheless, in the loving mercy of his royal death as the final King of Israel, Jesus will make certain ways of ruling Israel no longer possible, "cutting them to pieces" (24:51). By the light of Jesus, their ways will simply fail to be compelling or worthy of remembrance, and so their place as rulers will be taken by others, by those producing the fruit of the kingdom (21:43). In his remembrance throughout the cosmos, that is, the power of his resurrection as crucified Lord, Jesus will rule "all the nations" as the King of Israel for the God of Israel. He will preserve the sheep—people who show mercy. But he will cut off the goats—those who refuse to be merciful as he is merciful, leaving behind only a memory of shame, if they are remembered at all.[78] Their inability to measure up to the mercy of Jesus—which is the power of his name, his story—will deprive them of power, and in this way Jesus will rule by his mercy.

"All the nations" that Jesus will rule are "all the nations" Jesus' apostles will disciple (28:18-20), thereby enacting his rule. In doing so, they will be "sitting on twelve thrones, ruling the twelve tribes of Israel" (19:28), as these "nations" will swell with people who join all Israel in remembering the God of Israel as their own. No one will be able to rule the people of the God of Israel without reference to the impression that Jesus has left and continues to leave on its history. That is simply the time in which Israel will find itself. This is hardly what the cross and destruction of Jerusalem will look like to most, hardly the future that the coming of the Son of Man seems to promise; the threat to Israel's life, particularly the destruction of the

---

78. There is no indication in Matthew 25 that the judgment in view is postresurrection, that is, after the gathering nations have been raised from the dead. It is instead the judgment of the risen Jesus upon the nations being gathered through time before the completion of the resurrection of the people of God (which has begun with Jesus and shall include the many and diverse people that Jesus has been judging).

temple, will seem to utterly flood the people rather than save it. So Jesus urges his disciples not to be deceived in the coming judgment and carried away by the violence of false messiahs. They are to rule as Jesus has taught and empowered them to rule, building their houses on rock (Matt. 7:24-25). They are to rule by mercy, for Jesus will be vindicated and revealed as king.

What is the name of this dramatic change in the time of Israel, the fulfillment of Israel's Messiah? Jesus calls it the "forgiveness of sins" (26:28). The shadow of the coming judgment deepens as Jesus plunges into the darkness of the Passover, when "the Son of Man will be handed over to be crucified" (26:2) after he has framed his death with the destruction of Jerusalem and its temple. Betrayed by his own, the sheep scattered, Jesus sheds "the blood of the covenant, which is being poured out for many for the forgiveness of sins" (26:28).

The covenant is the creator God's irrevocable marriage with Israel; Israel bears God's name for better or for worse. And Jesus' death is the love of this marriage covenant in its fullness, the Passover of all Israel's Passovers. It is not blood shed for only some of Israel, not for only those who embrace Jesus as Messiah. All have abandoned him. It is blood shed for the whole people of Israel (πᾶς ὁ λαὸς), the many who are enduring the curses of God's covenant love. The love of God in Messiah takes up, and is therefore stronger than, the deepest resistance Israel can offer: even when all the people (πᾶς ὁ λαὸς) gathers to choose the violence of the lawless way of Jesus Barabbas and call this blood of Jesus Messiah upon themselves and their children (27:25), they have found themselves declaring in their defiance their very own coming forgiveness. The depths of God's covenant love are not exhausted but revealed in the depths of this defiance. In Jesus' death on a Roman cross, he embodies the fullness of the curses of the covenant, but this turns out, by the light of the resurrection, to be the fullness of God's covenant love. Thus, this blood of Messiah cannot be a sacrifice that pushes gentile enemies back to the border of the land once more, pending yet another gentile invasion in response to Israel's unfaithfulness. Messiah is not only a son of David but is *the* Son of David and as such David's Lord (22:41-46). He is therefore the one whose blood draws the cry from the mouth of Israel's gentile overlord, "Truly this man was Son of God" (27:54). This is the blood that purifies the land once and for all and then bleeds into all the nations. Just as Israel had gathered to find in its defiance God's true words of forgiveness upon its lips, so the Roman centurion has found himself declaring the very words of God the Father of Israel (3:17; 17:5).

The centurion of 27:54 does not "represent" all gentiles. As the presence of the gentile rule of covenant curses (e.g., Deut. 28:25-26), he is the particular opening of Israel's promised future, as God is making the nations the inheritance of the Son of David who is Son of God and King of Israel, the ends of the earth his possession. This Son has begun to break them with a rod of iron, and dash them to pieces like a potter's vessel (Ps. 2:8-9). Such is the power of his mercy. That Jesus' blood is for the forgiveness of sins means that it moves the gentile nations to abandon their divisive gods and to serve the one God of Israel as their own, to obey the law of the covenant revealed in the merciful love of Israel's Messiah. That is what the death of Jesus and the consequent destruction of the temple in Jerusalem will do—move Israel's gentile enemies toward the temple of Messiah's body. That is the course of God's judgment according to Matthew. The catholicity of Jesus has embraced all Israel, rather than only the righteous. And it is precisely as such that his catholicity is enough to embrace the gentile nations as well, for he has come to call not the righteous but sinners (Matt. 9:13; Hosea 6:6). This peace is where the many contingencies of the election of Israel in time have led. As the cornerstone (Matt. 21:42), the elect one who is the culmination and order of those contingencies, Jesus leaves none of Israel's flesh behind, and draws the gentile nations to Israel's table of blessing and peace, the table of Israel's final Passover. Thus, election is the power of God to make of the entire world one Israel of peace. Such are the dimensions of the catholicity of Jesus the elect one and the election of his people Israel. It is the merciful death of Jesus that finally makes this one people.

We could hardly sustain this claim at the end of chapter 27 without chapter 28. It is Jesus' resurrection that makes the centurion's cry worthy of remembrance and the inauguration of Israel-gentile reconciliation. It is only because death itself has been defeated—the death that limited the sin of both Israel and the gentile nations, but was also their division according to the curses of the covenant. Without the resurrection, we cannot name the future of Israel in Jesus. We could find only another prophet or another king. But because Jesus has been raised from the dead, it cannot be said that he is only another prophet or another claimant of David's throne. It must be said that all power in heaven and on earth has been given to him (28:18). His now risen life is the salvation of his people from their sins, their peace with one another and the gentile nations, who will give up their idolatrous gentile ways as they are baptized in the name of the Father, Son, and Holy Spirit and learn the Israelite way of Jesus.

What has changed with Jesus, then, is not primarily the way that Israel lives in time but the time in which Israel lives, for all heaven and earth has been changed by the death and resurrection of Israel's Messiah. That change in time will indeed work itself out in the way that all of Israel lives in time, but we must not invert the time that determines the way Israel lives and the way Israel lives in time. Israel does not constitute itself but is constituted by God's election.

This does not mean that there is any future of steady progress to be imagined here. It will be tumultuous rather than steady, as the sea of the nations is stormy. The people of God will not be in control but can only follow the lead of Jesus by the Spirit. But because of the resurrection, it is a sure future, only a matter of time. Along the way, those who gather to worship the God of Israel under Jesus' name are to point the rest of Israel and the world to its future. They are to do this as Jesus has taught them, by the discipline of inexhaustible—that is to say catholic—forgiveness (chapter 18). That is the direction of the election of Israel in time, and that future will become fully visible when the people of Messiah—all Israel—is raised from the dead, when we will see him as he is.

The above rehearsal of judgment according to Matthew leaves one important desideratum (among many others, to be sure). What are we to make of those cut up and cut off over time by the power of Jesus' name? The future of those "cut off" in the Tanakh remains dark, and the First Gospel has not given us a theory or mythological mechanism of universal salvation. The Gospel story has insisted on the judgment of the unjust; there is no cheap grace. And yet Matthew has also deprived us of an argument for their permanent exclusion, for Jesus died the death of those "cut off." This accursed end is precisely what enshrouds a life—its name, its legacy, its teaching, its descendants, its influence, its flesh—in shame. It is what turns a particular name into a byword among future generations, and eradicates the place of that name in the land to be inherited.[79]

And yet, it is this accursed death that Jesus died and that led to his resurrection, and it is his cheapened, "innocent blood" that spelled the destruction of the temple and bought the field of the future for

---

79. Deut. 21:22; Josh. 8:29; 2 Sam. 4:12. The Philistines attempted to enact this curse on Saul and his house per 2 Sam. 21:12, but David refused to give the curse the final word because of God's election (e.g., 2 Sam. 4:12; 9:1-13).

those without a name or a place.[80] The future of crucified Jesus was to be cut off, but by the light of his resurrection we are unable to consign those cut off to eternal darkness. We are opposed by God in any attempt to define a reserve of judgment for those we despise. We can only forgive as our Father has forgiven us. Moreover, both Jesus' solidarity with the sin of Israel and the many contingencies that constitute Israel's history of election across generations warn us against attributing the injustice in a life to the agency of one person. Jesus cannot remain an utter stranger to such a one, and there is always more than the self (though not less) of that person to be adduced in accounting for how he came to live the way he did. We can only go on loving all of the flesh of Israel and living in the hope that Israel's election, as revealed in Christ, will in time embrace the whole world as one.

The First Gospel thus deprives us of a foil of peoplehood. Wherever we might want to find that foil in Matthew, Jesus has taken that place in his accursed death. The closest we come to it in the story of Matthew is not a certain population of the world, and certainly not "the Jews" or "Judaism," but the idolatrous ways of gentiles that lead only to oblivion. Yet even these ways meet their end at the foot of the cross: "Truly this man was Son of God."

Against Yoder (chapter 1 above), Matthew shows us that the people of God is not the people that is faithful rather than unfaithful, but the people whom God has formed by election over time. To be faithful to the God who elects, then, is to be in solidarity with the unfaithful, as revealed in Jesus, the elect one. This catholicity of election is at the heart of the politics of Jesus. Against Luz, the First

---

80. Matt. 27:1-10; Zechariah 11; Jeremiah 32 (cf. Jeremiah 19). The Zechariah passage from which Matthew quotes denounces the cheap price at which Israel has come to value its God and for which it is divided for slaughter, while the Jeremiah passage(s) to which Matthew alludes promises the future of Israel's name and place on the other side of the death of exile. Thus the betrayal of Messiah avails for Israel's blessing in and through its judgment.

Gospel tells a story not of the church's departure from Israel but of Jesus' irrevocable commitment to Israel and to the world's future in Israel. While the church is urged to avoid the false messianism that will stimulate devastating civil war and war with gentile empire, the church is not the community spared God's judgment against Israel. It is the community called to oppose injustice by taking up the cross in the midst of its sins and of those of the rest of Israel, to live by the discipline of inexhaustible forgiveness of sins, by the blood of the covenant.

Where does this leave us historically in the Jewish-Christian schism? It is difficult to "locate" the First Gospel in that development. The story certainly depicts tremendous tensions with Jewish authorities in the land. But it can hardly imagine two separate things known as Christianity and Judaism. It knows only one people of the God of Israel that is held together not by Israel's faithfulness but by God's election and the forgiveness of its sins. It resists a schism between Jews and Christians and refuses the possibility that such divisions are foundational or final. This is not to say that Jesus' Messiahship is secondary. It is essential. The First Gospel calls upon Israel and the rest of the world to follow the way of Jesus, and it certainly warns against the violence and injustice of corrupt shepherds in Israel. But Jesus' Messiahship does not immediately redraw the border of Israel according to the adequacy of Israel's response; the shape of the people is a matter of the time in which Israel and the rest of the cosmos are living. No one can help but respond to the presence of Jesus, and Jesus' death and resurrection spells hope for the adequacy of that response, for a love that corresponds to God's love. What is more, far from giving Christians an argument against their Jewish sisters and brothers, the covenant commandments of Jesus in Matthew invite Christians to ask how it is that we have become so law-less and whether that has something to do with our alienation from law-abiding Jews.

The Election of Israel according to the First Letter

Romans 9—11

We come finally to the *locus classicus* of the election of Israel in the New Testament. Having exposed in the previous chapters some of the snares awaiting the modern reader in Romans 9–11,[1] I aim here to offer a reading of this key text that points to a better understanding of what the election of Israel means for the Christian life, that is, the messianic life.[2]

---

1. I have kept my very selective engagement with the vast secondary literature on Romans 9–11 to the footnotes in the service of the flow of my exegesis in the larger theological argument of this monograph. That has made for some lengthy footnotes that I hope are nevertheless useful for addressing some technical exegetical matters and situating my reading in relation to several key voices in that literature. All translations of the Greek are mine.

2. In his commentary on Romans, which focuses on the Greek words of the first verse as the seed of the entire epistle, Giorgio Agamben signals the place of the letter's subject matter in the development of peoplehood, particularly the modern discourse of peoplehood: "The principle of the law is thus division. The fundamental partition of Jewish law is one between Jews and non-Jews, or in Paul's words, between *Ioudaioi* and *ethnē*. In the Bible, the concept of a 'people' is in fact always already divided between *am* and *goy* (plural *goyim*). *Am* is Israel, the elected people, with whom Yahweh formed a *berit*, a pact; the goyim are the other peoples. The

9:1-9

Paul opens with Christian words of solidarity with those in Israel who are his relatives according to the flesh, particularly those who, we will learn later in the argument, are hostile to the Christian gospel:

> I am speaking the truth in Messiah. I am not lying, my conscience bearing me witness in the Holy Spirit that it is a great sorrow to me and unceasing distress to my heart. If only I myself could be accursed from the Messiah for my sisters and brothers who are my relatives according to the flesh, who are Israelites, of whom are the sonship and the glory and the covenants and the giving of the law and the service of worship and the promises, of whom are the ancestors and of whom is the Messiah according to the flesh, who is God over all blessed forever, amen. (Rom. 9:3-5)[3]

Paul would sooner leave behind a legacy of shame and derision for himself, a name perceived only as a betrayal of Israel's messianic promise, than disown any of his Israelite family according to the flesh.[4]

Septuagint translates *am* with *laos* and *goyim* with *ethnē*. (A fundamental chapter in the semantic history of the term 'people' thus begins here and should be traced up to the contemporary usage of the adjective *ethnic* in the syntagma *ethnic conflict*)" (Giorgio Agamben, *The Time That Remains: A Commentary on the Letter to the Romans*, trans. Patricia Dailey [Stanford, CA: Stanford University Press, 2005], 47, emphasis his). What Agamben does not note here is that the reduction of Israel to *Ioudaioi* is itself part of the discursive development to which he refers.

3. Jacob Taubes: "Krister [Stendahl] says to me that his deepest worry is whether he belongs (we were speaking English) to the 'commonwealth of Israel.' So I said to myself, Krister, you super-Aryan from Sweden, at the end of the world, as viewed from the Mediterranean, other worries you don't have? No, he had no other worries! There I saw what Paul had done: that someone [Krister Stendahl] in the jungles of Sweden—as seen from where I'm standing—is worrying about whether he belongs to the 'commonwealth of Israel,' that's something that's impossible without Paul. (I was able to reassure him: as far as I'm concerned he's in.)" Jacob Taubes, *The Political Theology of Paul*, trans. Dana Hollander (Stanford: Stanford University Press, 2004), 41.

4. "As the apostle of the Church, Paul can be, and means to be, more than ever a prophet of Israel—in the Old Testament meaning of the concept. Only in this unity of his office does he wish to gather the Church, and only in its unity with Israel does he wish to see the Church gathered" (Barth, *Church Dogmatics*, ed. G. W. Bromiley and T. F. Torrance, 4 vols. in 13 parts [Edinburgh: T & T Clark, 1956–77], II/2, 202; cf. Taubes' similar remark in *The Political Theology of Paul*, 14). See Taubes's comparison of Paul's situation to that of Moses (via the

"According to the flesh" in v. 3 cannot be reduced to the modern superstition of ethnicity or biology, of "merely physical descent."[5] There is no pure bloodline in view here, no automatic history. "According to the flesh" in the present context is the gracious continuity—everywhere contingent and subject to decay—by which the living relatives of Paul in view have emerged as such from the long past of Israel, and by which the Christ himself is Israelite (cf. Rom. 1:3; 8:3). It certainly involves Israelite procreation, but it also involves "mixed" marriages, adoption, a constellation of institutions and practices, and innumerable other contingencies, as we saw in chapter 5 above.[6] It is the history of Israel as measured by the power

Jewish liturgical rehearsal of the situation of Moses at Yom Kippur), in which Moses refuses to start over and instead prays (28–47).

5. Against N. T. Wright, *The Letter to the Romans*, in vol. 10, *The New Interpreter's Bible: A Commentary in Twelve Volumes* (Nashville: Abingdon Press, 2002), 626 (hereafter *Romans*). My main interlocutors in the exegesis to follow are N. T. Wright and Karl Barth. More than any other recent New Testament commentator, Wright has sought to restore the language of the New Testament to its Israelite context. My debt to him is incalculable. Nevertheless, I suspect it will be more helpful to the reader for me to engage his reading of Romans 9–11 primarily where we differ than for me to note the many places where I'm consciously building on him. In particular, I will criticize his embrace of the modern myth of ethnicity, and thus his taking Romans 9–11 to be dealing with "ethnic Jews" or "ethnic Israel" or Israel as a "race" (ibid., e.g., 623, 625, 631). For example, the foil to descent by election for Wright (as for many others) is "merely physical descent": "'reckoned as seed' . . . means being part of the elect group, *as opposed to merely physical descendants*" (636, my emphasis). But the Bible, including Paul, knows nothing of "merely physical descendants." There is in fact no such thing, for there is always more to bodily descent than the abstraction, "mere physicality."

I completed this final chapter before the publication of Wright's *Paul and the Faithfulness of God* (Minneapolis: Fortress Press, 2013), hereafter *PFG*, so that I was unable to include detailed engagement with its exegesis of Romans 9–11. Wright has subtly revised his understanding of Paul's argument at a few key points, some of which I will note, but such revisions are minor and do not invite me to alter the engagement of this chapter with his previously published exegesis of Romans 9–11. To some extent, my criticism of Wright follows that of Richard Hays, who claims that at key places in Romans 9–11, "Wright's grand theory causes him . . . to overlook entirely what Paul is actually saying" ("Adam, Israel, Christ—The Question of Covenant in the Theology of Romans: A Response to Leander E. Keck and N. T. Wright," in *Pauline Theology*, vol. 3, *Romans*, ed. David M. Hay and E. Elizabeth Johnson [Minneapolis: Fortress Press, 1995], 83). Hays points out in several places in this essay that Wright's neat story of Israel, i.e., his "grand theory," is suspect, particularly as it reduces Israel to a "bomb squad."

6. Because Israel does not have a pure beginning in time and does not constitute itself, fundamentally every Israelite marriage is mixed and every Israelite is adopted. The father of Israel was a wandering Aramean (Deut. 26:5). But this does not preclude that a significant part

of what is passing away, such as decaying Israelite bodies and a temple in Jerusalem for blood sacrifice (cf. 1 Cor. 10:18). According to the preceding argument of the epistle, these present-age organs of Israel's life—themselves bearers of Israel's promise as well as temptation—are giving way to the Israelite life of resurrection (i.e., life κατὰ πνεῦμα ἁγιωσύνης, Rom. 1:4) now that the age to come has dawned in the resurrection of Jesus and the coming of the Spirit of resurrection (Rom. 8:1-17). "According to the flesh" thus evokes the history of Israel's striving against death and disintegration in hopes of reaching its promise, the history of what Israel itself has ephemerally done and been in response to God's eternal electing presence, particularly to God's covenant commands (Rom. 4:1). As such it is not the whole story of Israel. But nor is this history according to the flesh immaterial to who the Israelite people of promise is, and by it Paul finds himself numbered among certain Israelite sisters and brothers for whom his heart aches.

At this point, it is not clear exactly which Israelite relatives of Paul's are in view, only that they are for him a cause of great sorrow and unceasing distress to his heart.[7] But his sorrow and distress do not

---

of Israel's continuity through time was a matter of Israelite procreation. It implies simply that procreation must be understood within the thicker unfolding of the life of Israel down through the ages.

7. Wright follows the tendencies of traditional theopolitical "representation," taking Paul to be addressing "Israel's refusal (as a whole) to believe the gospel of Jesus" (Romans, 621, emphasis mine). Throughout his commentary on Romans 9–11, Wright totalizes as simply "Israel" or "ethnic Israel" or Israel "as a whole" the Israelite relatives of Paul introduced in 9:1ff and in view throughout Romans 9–11. But these relatives are nowhere thus totalized in Romans 9–11 or elsewhere in Paul. Nor are they generalized as "unbelieving Israel" or the like. Barth also tends to totalize these relatives as "Israel" (e.g., CD, II/2, 224, where "Israel in itself and as such is the 'vessel of dishonour'"), though on formal rather than ethnic grounds, and in a way that refuses their separation from the Christian community. For Barth, what unites the Israelites in view to Paul according to the argument of Romans 9–11 is not ethnicity but this: "His faith, the Church's faith in Jesus Christ, unites him with them. Whilst their unbelief creates this suffering for him his faith cannot let them go. Faith is possible for him only as he holds fast to them, only as he reaches out to them again and again, only as he prays for them (Rom. 10:1)" (CD, II/2, 202; cf. 280, 302, where Barth rightly denies any solidarity of "blood" at work in Paul's argument). What Barth says here is true, but it doesn't offer an adequate reading of ὑπὲρ τῶν

arise, he contends, from the withering of God's word of promise, for the word of God lives on even in these Israelite relatives who grieve him. With respect to these relatives Paul declares,

> But it is not the case that the word of God has withered, for not all who are of Israel are themselves Israel. Nor is it the case that all children are seed of Abraham but rather "by Isaac shall seed be named to you."[8] This means that the children of the flesh are not themselves the children of God, but rather the children of the promise will be determined for seed. For the word of promise is this: "At this time I will come and Sarah will have a son."[9] (Rom. 9:6-9)

Readers often understand the distinction here in 9:6-9 to differentiate between the relatives of Paul for whom he is sorrowful (supposedly οἱ ἐξ Ἰσραὴλ of 9:6b) and those who have responded to the gospel in faith (who are, in fact, nowhere in sight at this point but are nevertheless putatively and exclusively οὗτοι Ἰσραήλ of 9:6b). In other words, the relatives of Paul in view are supposedly among οἱ ἐξ Ἰσραὴλ but not οὗτοι Ἰσραήλ. But I will argue that the opposite is true: The distinction between οἱ ἐξ Ἰσραὴλ and οὗτοι Ἰσραήλ is precisely what has made Paul's relatives according to the flesh in view figure *among* οὗτοι Ἰσραήλ and thus the children of God

---

ἀδελφῶν μου τῶν συγγενῶν μου κατὰ σάρκα (9:3). In any case, while for Wright Paul's sorrow reflects a fundamental division between Paul and his Israelite relatives in view, for Barth "it is palpable [here in Romans 9-11] . . . that this [Paul's] is a zeal which includes rather than excludes, which seeks rather than rejects, which loves rather than hates" (*CD*, II/2, 204). In my view, Barth has grasped Paul's rhetoric, and Wright has not.

8. Gen. 21:12 (LXX). Note that the double conjunction that begins v. 7 (οὐδ' ὅτι) makes the sentence that follows it the resumptive parallel of the first sentence of 9:6 and not of the second sentence of 9:6. The antecedent clause on which the ὅτι of v. 7 is dependent, then, is οὐχ οἷον of v. 6a. Thus, v. 7a (which obviously does not begin with γὰρ or an equivalent as v. 6b does) is not an explanation or implication of v. 6b as is typically inferred by exegetes; rather, v. 7 is epexegetical relative to all of v. 6 following οὐχ οἷον (against Gadenze, who takes v. 6b as a rhetorical *ratio* that begins the *probatio* of v. 6a, which in turn he takes as the *propositio*; in Pablo T. Gadenz, *Called from the Jews and from the Gentiles: Pauline Ecclesiology in Romans 9-11*, Wissenschaftliche Untersuchungen zum Neuen Testament 2/267 [Tübingen: Mohr Siebeck, 2009], 89).

9. Gen. 18:10 (LXX).

and children of promise. They are not only οἱ ἐξ Ἰσραήλ, τέκνα [Ἀβραάμ], and τέκνα τῆς σαρκὸς (although they are indeed each of these) but *also* οὗτοι Ἰσραήλ, σπέρμα Ἀβραάμ, τέκνα τοῦ θεοῦ, and as such among τὰ τέκνα τῆς ἐπαγγελίας.

Particularly as shaped by the modern sensibilities exposed in chapter 3 above, we are tempted to construe "children of the flesh" (9:8) as the "genetic descendants" of Abraham, and "children of the promise" (9:8) as the "spiritual descendants" of Abraham, that is, as those who respond faithfully to God's call. But both Ishmael and Isaac are "genetic descendants" of Abraham, and how they responded to God's call is immaterial to that call or the argument at this stage (in fact, it will be explicitly excluded in 9:11-12). The root distinction that is material here is between one child of Abraham's body and another, and it is independent of how each lived and yet therefore determinative of how each lived. Thus, the formation of the people that is Abraham's children of promise (i.e., οὗτοι Ἰσραήλ) passed through the life of Isaac and not Ishmael.

We should not read into this simple observation of Paul's that the formation of the people of promise was merely a matter of the endogamous conception of children and of the election of some children thus conceived rather than the others. Israel's history, not least that of Jesus' ancestors within it, is manifestly full of intermarriage and the adoption of gentiles, and the people has been formed through time by far more than the mere birth of children (see chapter 5 above). The naming of Abraham's descendants of promise in view here was not only through the conception and birth of Isaac but through his whole life (from which came Jacob, etc.). Nevertheless, there was no Isaac without the conception and birth of Isaac. Thus, the conception and birth of children has of course been a key way that God has continuously provided the promised future of the people, as remembered with particular emphasis in the stories of its early generations in Genesis. But what is crucial here in Romans 9 is that since the future of some children born into the people was weaved out of Israel and into that of other, gentile peoples (while the future of certain gentile persons/communities was weaved into the people of Israel), the formation of the people of promise has unfolded as the future of some of its children and not others. Thus, the formation of Israel across generations as a tortuous history, which cannot be reduced to any law of genetics or biology or ethnicity, is the work of God's naming word, God's calling, or God's election. From Abraham, God's naming or election formed the people of promise in and through Isaac rather than Ishmael, embodied as that one gnarled and unfolding branch of the family, not the other. It unfolded *in*, rather than at some remove from, the flesh.

The distinction between "of the flesh" and "of the promise" in 9:8 is therefore not that between a timeless law of genetics and something else more "spiritual" or "true." It is not that between the continuity of "mere procreation" and that of adequate Israelite subjectivity (e.g., faith, obedience, spirituality).[10] The modern discourse of peoplehood—particularly its biologization and subjective constitution of "the people"—encourages many to see such a distinction in 9:6-9.[11]

---

10. There is no such thing as "mere procreation," just as there is no such thing as "merely physical descendants."

11. E.g., a "biological people" or "physical people" is the foil to the "true" people of God, which in turn is "true" (or simply "the people of God" proper) in virtue of its adequate subjective response to God (e.g., faith or belief). That adequate response is conceived as ontically equivalent to God's election, which nevertheless seems to require for many exegetes a sample of the "physical" people among the "true" people even as this "physicality" itself supposedly counts for nothing. So Wright, *Romans*, 636, and J. Ross Wagner, *Heralds of the Good News: Isaiah and Paul in Concert in the Letter to the Romans*, (Leiden, The Netherlands: Brill, 2002), 47–51. Similarly Fitzmyer, according to whom Paul is saying, "The OT promises were not made to the ethnic or historical-empirical Israel, those of physical descent or of flesh and blood, but to the Israel of faith" (Joseph A. Fitzmyer, *Romans: A New Translation with Introduction and Commentary*, The Anchor Bible [New York: Doubleday, 1992], 559–60).

Besides introducing two Israels (one "ethnic or historical-empirical" overlapping with the other "of faith"), Fitzmyer's reading has the disadvantage of flatly contradicting what Paul does in fact say in 9:4-5, namely, that the promises belong precisely to those unfaithful relatives for whom he is sorrowful and distressed. Fitzmyer worries that God's freedom is undermined by a

Ironically, it encourages some of the same readers and others to reduce God's election to Israelite procreation or ethnicity.[12] Somehow, Paul is supposedly implying two Israels here, one of "physical descent" and the other of faith—a distinction alien to the Tanakh.[13] On the assumption of two Israels, standard translations and many commentators attempt to name the distinction here as that between those who are "truly" Israel and those who are not "truly" Israel.[14] But such translations and glosses are textually baseless, and the

commitment to Israel in the flesh. Such would be the case only if flesh were a dead, enclosed principle like ethnicity. But the flesh of Israel is in fact a living, open history. With Chalcedon as our guide, we see that the flesh of Israel is not a straightjacket for God but God's very own skin, the way of God's freedom. And as we have learned from Barth in ch. 4 above, God's freedom is not God's ability to choose among alternatives but God's unconditioned power to be God's self. God simply is the one who will not abandon the flesh of Israel but inhabits and shapes it. Moo also resorts to two Israels, one of "ethnic descent" or "in a physical sense," the other "spiritual" (Douglas Moo, *The Epistle to the Romans*, NICNT [Grand Rapids, MI: William B. Eerdmans, 1996], e.g., 573).

Dunn is the best at this point (on Rom. 9:6), patiently refusing every groundless dichotomization of Israel (James D. G. Dunn, *Romans 9–16*, Word Biblical Commentary, vol. 38B [Dallas: Word Books, 1988], 538–40). But he finally yields: "The true heirs of Abraham are to be reckoned in other than national (physical or legal) terms" (540; in view throughout, Dunn says, is "ethnic Israel," e.g., 562). Dunn detects the rhetorical problem with his reading, however: "It is important to recognize that the antithesis here describes the mode, not the objective, of the promise" (540). He sees that Paul's excluding from some "true" Israel the relatives for whom he is sorrowful would undercut the entire appeal that he is making to the readers in Romans 9–11. But without a rhetorically coherent way of reading 9:6-8, Dunn is driven to salvage 9:6-8 with this assertion: "Paul's argument concerns the character and mode rather than the fact of election" (540). The problem with this is that the character and mode of election are part of the fact of election, and such arbitrary and overly subtle distinctions don't fit Paul's rhetoric or its purpose.

12. E.g., the elect people of God is "ethnic Israel," "ethnic Jews," or "Jews by birth." If anyone else participates in the elect people it is as once removed from the ethnic purity of the elect people proper (i.e., the Jews). For "ethnic Israel" as a superstition or myth, see ch. 5 above. Barth seems to fall into this in *CD*, II/2, 296. See also Dunn, *Romans 9–16*, 560, 562; Moo, *Romans*, 569, 738. For the way Wright lets this ethnic foundationalism in through the back door, see below. For Moo, elect Israel proper are individuals rather than a collective. Not incidentally, this is a supersessionist distinction as baseless as that between physical and spiritual Israel.

13. Those who recognize this distinction to be alien to the Tanakh or worry about Christian supersessionism then try to retain a place for the Israel that is "of physical descent" in the economy of God's revelation (see ch. 5 above). On the sense in which "a remnant" is distinct, see below.

14. For example, the NRSV renders 9:6b-7a as "For not all Israelites *truly* belong to Israel, and not all of Abraham's children are his *true* descendants" (my emphasis). Barth does not escape this misreading ("They are not the true Israel, i.e., the Israel which realises Israel's determination by

inference of two Israels at this point introduces intractable exegetical problems into the argument of Romans 9–11 and beyond, problems whose "solutions" only further muddle things. Like other readings promoted by the modern discourse of peoplehood, these ignore the history of God's electing activity in the flesh according to Scripture.[15]

Discerning that activity, as Paul bears out in what follows, requires time and can be traced and named only in retrospect. This is to trace the history "of the promise" within the history "of the flesh" (i.e., the sprawling flesh of Abraham). Thus, in 9:7, Paul effectively says this: the children of the flesh of Abraham sprawled in various directions, but the formation of his promised seed passed through Isaac. Filling in the story some, we might say that children of Abraham who came in and through Isaac went on through a particular history to be the promised people of Israel; meanwhile, the children of Abraham through Ishmael went on through a related history to be a people, *but they did not go on to be Israel*. The twelve tribal princes of Ishmael became another people that settled not in Canaan but from Havilah to Shur (Gen. 25:12-18).[16] The God of Israel blessed Ishmael, but the people descended from him as their named ancestor (through the same kind of sea of contingencies that connects the people of Israel to Isaac, i.e., the flesh) came in time not to know

accepting its proper place in the Church" [*CD*, II/2, 214; cf. 230]) and opens the door to the myth of ethnicity, though to less detriment than Wright's use of the same myth. Barth: "For it is (vv. 6b-7a) not at all the case that according to the Word and will of God all who belong to the race of Abraham, all bearers of the name Israel, were appointed to become members of the Church. They were certainly appointed members of the one elected community of God. This is something that none of this race [*Stamm*] can be deprived of. . . . This is what Jews, one and all, are by birth" (*CD*, II/2, 214). Barth's choice in German of *Stamm* rather than *Rasse* makes the consistent rendering of *Stamm* as "race" in English translation unfortunate, even if *Stamm*, too, is problematic. On this, see the helpful footnote in Katherine Sonderegger, *That Christ Was Born a Jew: Karl Barth's "Doctrine of Israel"* (University Park, Pennsylvania: The Pennsylvania State University Press, 1992), 107n31–108n31.

15. On the modern discourse of peoplehood, see ch. 3 above. On the history of God's electing activity in the flesh according to Scripture, see ch. 5 above.

16. Note how this has become a land of Amalekites by 1 Samuel 15.

the God of Israel as its own. Instead, the Ishmaelites served other gods and as such became a threat and stumbling block to Israel (e.g., Judg. 8:24).[17] The psalmist knows them as a people allied to the Edomites, Moabites, Gebalites, Ammonites, Amalekites, Philistines, Tyrians, and Assyrians—all against Israel (Ps. 83:6-8).[18] As we see here and elsewhere in the Bible, what readings committed to a timeless law of ethnicity cannot perceive is that many of Israel's perennial gentile enemies are themselves "biological" children of Abraham![19]

---

17. The Midianites (Abrahmic children through Keturah) appear to have united to some extent with the Ishmaelites (Gen. 37:27; Judges 7–8). See also the presence of Ishmael in the threat to David's kingdom (2 Sam. 17:25; 1 Chron. 2:17) and the service to David's kingdom (1 Chron. 27:30).

18. Together these peoples are the threat to the people of Israel (and to other peoples) that pervades the biblical history: "Come, let us wipe them out from among the peoples; let the name of Israel be remembered no more" (Ps. 83:4). We are prone to forget that the Ammonites and Moabites are peoples descended from Abraham's nephew Lot and thus "genetic" relatives of Abraham and relatives of Israel. If we go further back, we find that Abraham's ancestors are also the ancestors of other enemies of Israel (e.g., Canaan). Ezekiel knows Israel as sharing a common ancestry with the Canaanites, Amorites, and Hittites (Ezekiel 16). There is simply no pure Israelite ancestry, a fact about which the Bible is neither ignorant nor concerned. Yet, many moderns have consistently imported the superstition of pure ethnicity as the basis of certain theological commitments, whether such ethnicity is conceived theologically as foundation or foil.

19. The beginning of the postexilic historiography of the fall of the kingdom of Israel records these children of Abraham genealogically, among them the Ishmaelites, the Midianites, the Edomites, the Amalekites (1 Chronicles 1). First century Jews were not naïve to this fact. It is the modern discourse of peoplehood with its falsely pure notion of ethnicity that has made us naïve to the diversity of Israel in and according to the flesh. Readers such as Wright, Dunn, and Moo imagine that here Paul is countering an opponent's view that claims exclusive Abrahamic sonship on the basis of ethnic or "carnal" descent from Abraham, i.e., that putatively claims that the family of Israel was and is automatic across time/generations (Wright speaks of "what Israel had come to expect, had come to take for granted as its automatic right" [622]).

But there is no indication here, anywhere in Romans 9–11, or in the rest of Romans or Paul's other letters that Paul would need to oppose such an understanding. The debate in Romans is about what constitutes covenant righteousness or justice as this informs the politics of the covenant people, not who automatically counts as Israel or whether endogamous procreating is enough to make Israel. The Jewish opponent view from earlier in the letter is a matter of "works." No one is claiming that being born into Israel is the exclusive condition of inheriting what God promised to Abraham. It is hardly the case that Jewish opponents of Paul, with their insistence on works, held that the people of Israel could "look to their birthright as a guarantee of salvation" Moo, *Romans*, 573, for people do not have to work for what is theirs by birthright; see Dunn, *Romans 9–16*, 539, for a supposition similar to Moo's. The understanding of Abrahamic descent that Paul opposes earlier in Romans claims that Israel must secure its own "promised" future by works, that to be heirs of Abraham is Israel's work rather than what it is according to Paul's gospel: God's work in Messiah before, in, as, and for Israel.

But as such they are not the children of promise; they are not peoples who will live forever. They are not Israel but only children of Abraham "of the flesh," of which Israel names just one branch.

Paul now goes on to name this distinguishing formation of Abraham's family in the flesh by God's election through the next generation of Abraham's children—that of Jacob and Esau, of the Israelites and the Edomites (9:10ff). Here the people of Israel received its name and from here the differentiating ramification of election continued, bequeathing to only some—including those of 9:4—the name Israel, leaving others with names like Edom. The mythical purity of modern biology or ethnicity disappears this tangled weave of God's electing activity in the flesh, whereby, through a history everywhere contingent and "ethnically mixed," one messy line of

What Paul is hedging against here in the opening of Romans 9–11, as we will see, is not a false Israel of Jewish works but a tendency among his non-Jewish readers to disregard God's election by disowning and despising certain Israelite enemies (whom Paul claims as family). This is, however, and not incidentally, a mirror reflection of the understanding of certain Jews that Paul opposes earlier in the letter, one which despises Christians from among the gentiles who do not exhibit typical works of the law. Thus, we should not overlook the subtle intimation of 9:11-12 (particularly the phrase "not of works but of the naming/calling") in light of the subsequent argument (particularly 9:32): In 9:6ff Paul is opposing the "works" politics of certain non-Jewish readers, who are apt to despise Paul's Israelite relatives in view for their hostile lack of the faith they themselves have, much as he has earlier opposed the "works" politics of certain Jews, who demand of non-Jews works they claim as their own justification. In Romans 9–11, Paul opposes to such "works politics" the politics of God's election. To a peoplehood of policing the community according to some "covenantal" human adequacy Paul opposes one of hospitality according to God's uncontrollable covenant election. This is a matter both of the border of the community and its internal dynamic. The dispute, then, is not over who counts as Israel but over what makes the one Israel that is tick, what leads it to its promised blessing, its righteousness.

One change in Wright's most recent exegesis of Romans 9–11 is his sound insight that "*what Paul says in 9.6-29 would not have been controversial*" to non-Christian Jews (*PFG*, 1184-85, emphasis his), yet such Jews would hardly have accepted (or been able to imagine the meaning of) Wright's reading of 9:6-9, i.e., that, because of some revealed criterion, they were not in fact Israel. Wright has also come to recognize that the rhetoric of Rom. 9:6-29 is not directed against "Jewish unbelievers" but against non-Jewish readers who boastfully despise "Jewish unbelievers" (*PFG*, 1184-87; 1201; "the negative side of 'election'...had strongly positive intent," ibid., 1193; "... nothing to do with any special virtue in being Gentiles and everything to do with the surprising mercy of the God of Israel," ibid.). Yet, he still does not take the election of these "Jewish unbelievers" seriously. For Wright, it is not they who "stand firm" but "their story" (ibid., 1186–87).

Abraham's children came to be known as Israel, and many other messy lines of Abrahamic children became other peoples of other names. Thus, here at the beginning of the argument of Romans 9–11, Paul simply registers an obvious fact for those acquainted with the Scriptures of Israel (or who are observant of the history of any other people). It is the fact that not all flesh that hails from Israel is Israelite flesh. Not all the children of Abraham are the children of promise. What happened in the initial three key generations from Abraham to Isaac to Jacob anticipated what happened throughout the subsequent generations of the children of Israel. Abraham's children sprawled into a variety of peoples who went on to serve a variety of gods; many children of Israel (e.g., many from the ten tribes of the northern kingdom) have been assimilated through time by other peoples (some of them Abrahamic). Only some were and are the promised seed: Isaac, Jacob/Israel, and the people that has since borne the name Israel and remembered the God of Abraham, Isaac, and Jacob as its own. Among that people Israel, the elected seed, are the Israelites whom Paul has introduced as such in 9:4, and because of whom he is distressed.[20]

20. The effect of the myth of ethnicity is to make Israel or even "the Jews" the singular "race of Abraham" (even for Barth, *CD*, II/2, 214). But notice here in 9:6ff that Paul is concerned to trace the life of God's *promise* in the flesh from Abraham through the life of some of his children and not others, not to invoke Abrahamic blood, whether as essential to Israel or as insufficient in relation to something like the obedience of faith as the basis of Israel proper or "true" Israel (in any case, even if "Abrahamic blood" were a discrete, transmittable and traceable entity, it would ramify in many directions besides Jacob/Israel). Paul is concerned with Israel in a way that is innocent of the later distinction between the visible and the invisible church and of modern identity politics, in a way that is more publicly and uncontroversially understood, we might say. And so he simply draws the (esp. non-Jewish) readers' attention to this undeniable fact: not all of Abraham's sprawling children in the flesh are Israelites. Only some of them are. Others are Ishmaelites. Still others are Edomites, and so on. Those who are Israel are therefore the people of promise by the electing word of God, which has not withered.

Thus, in 9:6-13 Paul simply observes the divergence of Ishmael and Isaac and then of Esau and Jacob, who is named Israel, the "Israel" of 9:6. This is the primary "Israel" not all those out of whom are themselves "Israel," the son of Isaac whose name has named (only) his children of promise, Israel the children of Israel. Like Ishmael/Ishmaelites and Esau/Edom, who each hail from Abraham but are not the child/people of promise, many since Jacob hail from

What is the force of Paul's registering this obvious fact at the outset of the argument?[21] It is clearly not this: "The word of God has not withered because my Israelite relatives according to the flesh whom I have just mentioned are not truly Israel and thus do not constitute

Israel of generations past but are not themselves Israel, i.e., not a part of the people variously gathered through time under the name Israel. The future of many Israelite communities and persons since Jacob, it turns out, led out of Israel into other peoples (through migration, slavery, assimilation, etc.). Those who have found themselves part of the people named Israel and have thus continued as Israel, then, are the twisting life of God's promise in the flesh, the people who are οὗτοι Ἰσραήλ according to 9:6-13. Those who find themselves named Israelites in the present (9:4), passing as simply part of the diverse people commonly known as Israel rather than some other people, have therefore been chosen into existence as such. They are themselves Israel by God's election according to the promise.

The point of remembering this history of election *in nuce* is not to introduce a criterion by which Israel is divided into two but to show that the one people commonly named Israel, including both its faithful and its faithless, is a matter of God's naming word, God's election. It is thus to claim that Paul's Israelite relatives according to the flesh of 9:1-5 do not indicate the withering of God's word but its vitality, as they remain part of the one Israel that has branched across time and the face of the earth by God's election. This distinguishing history of God's promise to Abraham in 9:6-13 is the way Paul substantiates the claim that not all who hail from Israel are themselves Israel.

Paul is therefore not reading contemporary Israel and finding it divided into the true and the false according to some fictive and arbitrary criterion of adequacy to the name Israel (which he might cull from the Bible). He is reading Scripture's witness to the history of Israel by God's election. And then he is allowing that witness to read the current scenario in Rome and beyond and urging his readers to be read and to read accordingly (i.e., to relate humbly to those of 9:1-5 as irrevocably part of the family of Israel by God's election). That is how he will proceed throughout Romans 9–11.

The myth of race (or its derivative ethnicity, see ch. 3 above) renders Abraham and Jacob/ Israel indistinct, since they supposedly belong to the same race or ethnicity, which is imagined as the determinant of who/what Israel is (or is not). But Paul's argument turns not on the equivalence of Abraham, Isaac, and Jacob/Israel as bearers of the same magical blood or genetic inheritance of Abraham (in which case the biblical passages adduced are at most illustrative of a timeless and utterly hidden principle of selection). It turns on the particular way Jacob came from Abraham through Isaac and thus how the people of Israel has since been formed across time in like manner as the promised seed of Abraham, i.e., his argument turns on the history of Israel. The life of the name "Israel" is not incidental to this history but its remembrance.

21. Rom. 2:28-29 seems to me a similarly obvious and uncontroversial fact rather than the introduction of a polemical criterion that distinguishes "true Jews" from the mass of people commonly known as "Jews." Everyone knows that there is more to being Jewish than being circumcised or belonging to a family of circumcised males, that the bodily sign of circumcision is to indicate a life of loving God and neighbors as the law commands. Since all Jews know this, Paul says, Jews cannot order community life as if they were distinct in a way they are not, i.e., "by works," since non-Jews sometimes do such works and Jews often don't. As he goes on to say, such indistinguishability by works requires a particular, christological account of the God-given life of the covenant community and a corresponding hospitality.

a failure of the life or trustworthiness of the word of God."[22] Nor is it this: "The word of God is not about ethnicity or biology but something more determinative (e.g., faith, obedience, the obedience of faith)." There is not a whisper of Israelite genes here, nor is there any rhetorical appeal to Israel's (inadequate or adequate) response to its God. The force of registering the facts of the history of God's electing activity is this, as Paul will now argue: the word of God—its life and trustworthiness—is not a matter of Israel's response but of God's election, which is in turn *in* Israel's response even when part of Israel responds unfaithfully (as we saw in chapters 4–5 above and will see below). Whoever Paul's particular Israelite "relatives according to the flesh" are (introduced in 9:1-5), Paul begins by saying in 9:6ff that they are among the children of promise by the history of the electing word of God. The history of God's election or naming has made them Israelite, a fact with which the readers must reckon.

The sense of this opening claim is therefore not "the word of God has not withered because not all Israel is truly Israel" but this: "The word of God has not withered because my Israelite relatives of 9:1-5, unlike many others who hail from Israel of old, are themselves Israel." Over generations, they have been formed to be part of the people named Israel, while others who come from some stage of the Israelite past in the flesh have since been woven out of Israel into gentile

---

22. This is the force assumed by Wright, *Romans*, 634ff, and Moo, *Romans*, 572ff; Dunn realizes that this cannot be the force of the claim of 9:6-8, but he is unable to read the verses as indicating anything other than a division of Israel into two (*Romans 9–16*, 540–41). Barth not only perceives that this cannot be the force of 9:6-8 but also recognizes something of what 9:6-8 must say given the flow of the argument, namely, that the distinction of 9:6-8 cannot be a matter merely of not threatening the word of God but must *establish* the word of God. Nevertheless, he supposes that the division of Israel into two in itself somehow does this: "The Word of God (9:6) is not proved false but established by the phenomenon of the unbelieving Synagogue. According to the testimony of Scripture, God has from the first chosen, differentiated and divided in Israel. He has from the very beginning separated the Church and Israel, Israel and the Church. And in so doing He has confirmed the election of Israel" (*CD*, II/2, 216). Barth does not say here how this division establishes God's Word or confirms the election of Israel.

peoples. The Israelites of 9:1-5 for whom Paul aches do not suggest that the word of God has withered, then, but that it is very much alive.

What is more, Paul's opening claim in 9:6-9 implies that the word *of God* has not withered because that is not up to Israel. This is borne out immediately by the way the argument continues in vv. 10ff., which show that the formation of Israel in and through time according to the promise is not determined by its willing or striving but the mercy of God's election. The life of Israel is not determined by the way that it lives in time, but by the time in which it lives by God's election. The moving shape of the people that bears the name Israel is not attributable to how that people is currently living but is the living inheritance of the past of God's electing word. It thus embodies the promise of its future, however unsightly it may currently be.[23] Paul's Israelite "relatives according to the flesh" in view find themselves at a point in which God's merciful election through time has made them part of Israel, even if they are now opposing the apocalypse of their God in the gospel. Israel is their name however they live under it.[24]

---

23. Consider the extreme example of the shape of Israel before and after the civil war and war with Rome in the promised land in 66–70 CE. The shape of the people's life is not attributable to how they are living in the immediate aftermath of the war, though that is involved, but is what the living people has inherited from the past, particularly the past of the calamitous events of 66–70 CE that have so dramatically altered the life of Israel. The name for this shaping by inheritance through the drama of Israel's history, both broadly and in fine, is God's election (see ch. 5 above).

24. This is to say that God's election in the flesh, that is, Israel itself, is always a matter of the one people living visibly and diffusely as a community of communities under the name Israel rather than an invisible substance or power that distinguishes some of that people as "truly" Israel from the rest. What *is* invisible about Israel according to God's election in the flesh is not some underlying "biology" that unites Israel and distinguishes it from other peoples, nor is it an "inside" moral or spiritual quality that unites "true Israel" and distinguishes it from the rest of the visible people known as Israel. It is the past activity of God that has shaped Israel to be who and how it is in the present, having determined Israel's range of possibility. Living Israel cannot see any of that past activity directly because it is past, and it can remember only some of it. Also invisible is the future of Israel that God is making by election, which only future Israel will see directly and present Israel can see only in part with prophetic insight variously given by God.

Much of the Christian tradition and many readers today render the "according to the flesh" (9:3) of these Israelites immaterial to who they are in the economy of God's election (i.e., they are in effect deemed not Israel since only faithful Israel is meaningfully, truly Israel). But the flesh of Israel is no more immaterial to who Israel is than it is to who Jesus is (9:5; cf. 1:3). These Israelites are Israelite as the Christ was Israelite (see chapter 5 above). Perhaps such readers have been tripped up by the misleading resemblance of κατὰ σάρκα in 9:3 and τῆς σαρκὸς in 9:8. But the prepositional phrase and definite genitive noun are not semantically equivalent in the way the words of the argument run (although they do overlap).[25] What should immediately forestall the exegetical claim that only faithful Israelites are truly Israel (9:6-8) is that the force of 9:6-8 would undermine the litany of 9:4-5. Paul is not saying with 9:6-8 that none of 9:4-5 is true![26] 9:6-8 is the opening explication of *how* 9:4-5 is true!

To reiterate what I said above, κατὰ σάρκα is here (as in 1 Cor. 10:18) the way that Israel, like other peoples, has continued across time to the coming of its Christ in and through what is corruptible and passing away (cf. Eph. 6:5; Col. 3:22), particularly Israel's striving against death and disintegration, its striving for the fulfillment of the promise. While this has been a history of dying, it has also been a history of God's electing grace according to the covenant (i.e., God's electing grace *in* Israel's dying, for life κατὰ σάρκα without God's election cannot account for any of the history of Israel, not a single material particle of it). This Israelite way according to the flesh is not eternal. But Eternity has created and inhabited it as his own, and it is therefore constitutive of who Israel eternally is.[27]

---

25. They are certainly related, as what follows will show.

26. That would be for Paul to cut off the legs of his argument just as it begins to run.

27. Just as Jesus' corruptible flesh is not eternal but constitutive of who Jesus eternally is (cf. Rom. 8:3; 2 Cor. 5:16-17).

The children of Abraham τῆς σαρκὸς, however, are all those peoples whose past is traceable to Abraham (Israel being one of them): peoples of flesh who, likewise striving against death and disintegration, have taken shape and persisted under distinct names for a segment of time. In Paul's time, few if any of them besides Israel are left (e.g., apparently no living community claimed to be Ishmaelite; the Edomites had perhaps been reduced to the remnant of Idumea); primarily (or only) the Jews and Samaritans still trace their history to Abraham by name and remember the God of Jacob/Israel as their own (and they do so competitively). The flesh of Abraham, then, has been cut through time. Some of it continued for a time despite its divergence from the flesh of Israel—that is, from the seed of promise—but these peoples have found themselves finally on a course of disintegration, of being cut off, of being burned away.[28] Alternatively they have rejoined the rest of Israel.[29]

That the relatives of Paul in view are Israelite but κατὰ σάρκα means not that they have withered from the life of Israel—for they are children of promise in the same way that Jesus was the promised Son of David (i.e., κατὰ σάρκα, 1:3)[30]—but that their configuration within the elect people remains subject to death and decay. They remain in that condition because they are living according to what is passing away. Such living is manifest in their case, we will learn later in Paul's argument, in their hostility to the fulfillment of the

---

28. See ch. 5 above for the meaning of "cut off." That some known as Muslims have been formed in time as calling upon the God of Moses as their own and claiming to hail from Abraham by Ishmael is a most intriguing development in the history of God's electing activity. I cannot say much about it explicitly in the context of the present chapter, but I think we must say at the very least that such people have not been forgotten by the God of Israel; they have been claimed by that God and remain bearers of that God's revelation.

29. As some descended from Lot or from Esau did (e.g., Ruth the Moabitess, 2 Sam. 23:37; 1 Kgs. 11:1; 14:21; 1 Chron. 11:39, 46; 2 Chron. 12:13; 24:26; Neh. 13:1-3; a remnant of the ten tribes of the northern kingdom according to 2 Chronicles 30).

30. That is, it does not mean that they have become some Abrahamic people other than the people of promise.

promise, that is, to the gospel borne witness by the Jews and non-Jews of the churches in Rome.[31] This is to say that, among other liabilities of life according to the flesh, they remain vulnerable to Israel-gentile enmity in a way that living according to the promise fulfilled—what is not passing away—does not (cf. Rom. 4:1). They exhibit the corruptibility of the flesh, which is what allows the subjective lag in Israel's response to God's election (a lag not unknown to the ongoing life of the Christian readers per, e.g., Rom. 13:14).[32]

Whatever sense is to be given to the relation between τῆς σαρκὸς and κατὰ σάρκα, or to the assertion "not all who are of Israel are themselves Israel," it must fit the conclusion of the argument in chapter 11. That conclusion is quite unambiguous, as we shall see, corresponding to the litany of 9:4-5 and echoing 9:7. In other words, we cannot say that in the course of the argument of Romans 9–11 Paul disowns his Israelite relatives in view in 9:1-5, only to claim them in the end as elect children of promise worthy of the readers' Christian solidarity and patience. Paul's Israelite "relatives according to the flesh" in view in 9:1-5 are in 11:28 "according to election beloved because of the ancestors."[33]

---

31. There are of course many ways to engage in this hostility, and it is not primarily a matter of "beliefs."

32. The bodies of Israel to be raised from the dead are therefore not of corruptible flesh but the incorruptible material of the Spirit, who by resurrection completes the healing of the body.

33. Wright and Moo do not seem to notice that any opening claim here in 9:6-8 to the effect that the relatives of Paul in view are not truly (or "spiritually") Israel is at cross-purposes with the whole rhetorical momentum of Romans 9–11 and so would undermine the entire argument for the readers' patience with God's election. While each recognizes that the readers' relation to such relatives is the abiding concern of the whole of Romans 9–11, each imagines that Paul first deals with the apparently separate question of whether their hostility to the gospel and the readers implies the withering of the word of God. Paul can supposedly answer that it does not because "Israelites" like Paul's unbelieving relatives are not really Israel anyway, and he can supposedly do this in the course of arguing for the readers' patience with them according to their election by God (i.e., the election of those of 9:4-5 who have become enemies of the readers according to 11:28). But whether the relatives of Paul in view are the withering of the word of God and how the readers are to treat them is one question, not two.

> According to the gospel they are enemies on your account, but according to election they are beloved on account of the ancestors. For irrevocable are the gifts and naming of God. (Rom. 11:28-29)

These Israelite enemies disobedient to Christ, who are among those "dulled" per 11:7, remain Israelite with all of the promise of Israel. Like the rest of Israel, they find themselves in the middle of the cutting of the people through time, of God's circumcision of Israel (see chapter 5 above). But so long as they simply *are*, so long as they find themselves among those who remember the God of Israel as their own and thus constitute a trace of Israel—however slight that trace may seem—they are beloved according to election on account of the ancestors to whom God gave the promise. In fact, Paul will argue in Romans 9–11 that the enmity and unfaithfulness of these Israelites have, according to the gospel, embodied the occasion of God's mercy upon the non-Jewish recipients of the epistle. And this is not a gospel about how such Israelites have served the readers of Romans finally to their own detriment. It is about the fulfillment of God's election in Christ, such that even those bleeding under the knife of Israel's cutting are claimed by the unassailable hope of election, "for the gifts and calling of God are irrevocable." The gospel means that mercy upon the non-Jewish Christians in Rome must avail for mercy upon these Israelite enemies and that Christians must engage such Israelites as family in the Spirit of forgiveness rather than as reprobate to be disowned.[34] From the disobedience of all to mercy upon all is the movement of God's election of Israel through time. In this way, the word of God never withers but lives until it has grown to fulfill its purpose: mercy for all.

---

34. "It is to be noted that these passages also speak of God's steadfastly continuing grace towards Israel" (Barth, *CD*, II/2, 232). Note the "through line" of κληθήσεταί σοι σπέρμα, 9:7b, ἐκ τοῦ καλοῦντος, 9:12a, ἐκάλεσεν ἡμᾶς, 9:24, and ἡ κλῆσις τοῦ θεοῦ, 11:29, the last of which is explicitly the calling of the Israelites of 9:1-5 and should be interpreted as having the same force as the previous instances of "calling."

9:10-29

Everything between 9:1 and 11:28 must serve the correspondence of 9:1-5 to 11:28-29 and the merciful purpose of God's election. In Romans 9–11 Paul is not "explaining" the curious development of Jewish opposition to the gospel with some pathetic theodicy. Nor is he seeking "to legitimate the new congregation."[35] He is teaching non-Jewish Christians the politics of election as the politics of the cross. Paul is teaching the election of Israel as the catholicity of Jesus, the death that is forming the broken people of Israel into one people of peace by the Spirit of his resurrection, refusing to disown any of the lost sheep of Israel, reconciling Israel according to the flesh with the gentile nations. The church is to be the witness and taste of this refusal and reconciliation, and to that end it must insist that even opposition from within Israel serves the merciful purpose of God's election for all Israel. Such opposition cannot justify any Christian separatism.

The force of Paul's initial, historical claim that "not all who are of Israel are themselves Israel" is, as I've said, borne out by vv. 10-18. Israel is a history of God's promise rather than of Israelite faithfulness (and that promise is therefore the basis and power of any Israelite faithfulness). The way in which that history passed from Isaac to Jacob clarifies this. While it is not Paul's point, but an implication of the argument given the exegetical constraints of the modern discourse of peoplehood, we must note that there is no distinction to be made between Jacob and Esau on the basis of ancestry or descent (i.e., myths of biological, genetic, ethnic, or racial continuity, purity, discontinuity, or impurity); they were children of the same mother and father, in fact of the same act of sexual intercourse, and yet became two different peoples. Paul's point is

---

35. Against Taubes, *The Political Theology of Paul*, 41.

that there is no distinction to be made between Jacob and Esau (or Israel and the Edomites) on the basis of human activity (even passive "activity"), for according to 9:10, Rebecca, in a single instance of sexual intercourse with Isaac our father ('Ρεβέκκα ἐξ ἑνὸς κοίτην ἔχουσα, Ἰσαὰκ τοῦ πατρὸς ἡμῶν), conceived two children who were distinct by election before they had been born or done a thing. Neither the way they lived nor the way any of their ancestors or descendants lived could be called upon to "explain" that one is the father of Edom and the other the father of Israel. Rather, that "the purpose of God according to election might remain—not of works but of the naming"[36] (9:11b-12a), Rebecca was told before they were born or had lived, "The elder shall serve the younger" (9:12b).[37]

The scandal of this scriptural claim then induces the question of 9:14, "Is there injustice with God?" Why should Esau serve Jacob and be "hated" by God? Paul's answer is that there is no injustice, because this election is not a matter of God's refusing anyone their due but of God's mercy and compassion. Not only Esau's noninvolvement but even the outright opposition to God of the likes of Pharaoh can only serve the mercy of God (9:14-18). Esau's subordination by the election of Jacob, like Pharaoh's hostility to Israel as prompted by God, can only serve God's mercy. Mercy for whom? For Jacob and not Esau? For Israel and not Pharaoh? That is not yet clear, but

---

36. I translate ἀλλ᾽ ἐκ τοῦ καλοῦντος as "but of the naming" to emphasize that the call of God operates in and through, inter alia, the naming of peoples and persons, and that it is thus a matter of "the word" of God (cf. Eph. 2:14-15). Note that it is here with the naming of Israel that the term ἐκλογή is introduced into the argument. Also note the correspondence between κατ᾽ ἐκλογὴν here in 9:11 and κατὰ τὴν ἐκλογὴν in 11:28.

37. By trying to hold together his exegetical commitment to God's having "elected Abraham and his whole race" and the purchase of this part of the argument on the readers' embrace of those of 9:1-5 and 11:28-32, Barth loses the thread of the argument here. He takes the argument to be about how God unites the elected and the rejected because Jacob and Esau are of Abraham's race and God is the subject of all the action. It is the action of God "within the community," Barth says. He then has to concede a conflicting emphasis: "But all the same the emphasis rests on the fact that it is something different which occurs, that the Church and Abraham's race are not identical, that the Church is founded and built by a separation which operates right from the beginning of the history of this race . . . which repeatedly means exclusion" (CD, II/2, 217).

Paul is working toward the answer, adumbrated in the declaration of Exod. 9:16 in Rom. 9:17: God raised Pharaoh up for the very purpose of revealing God's power in him so that God's name might be proclaimed *in all the earth*. The answer will be mercy for all.[38] The present point is that election through time is not conditioned by human willing or striving, and that God has preempted any consequent charge of injustice, insofar as God's purpose in determining such willing or striving is mercy rather than mere differentiation or some "glorification" of God at the expense of the hardened.[39]

---

38. Even those "hated" according to election? Barth gives us good reason to think so (*CD*, II/2, 217, citing Gen. 21:17 and the genealogies of Genesis 36 and 1 Chronicles 1), invoking the mercy in Christ on 219. He rightly emphasizes the mercy of the name of God in 9:15 as the determinant of the entire movement of God in the argument, culminating in 11:32. "The twofold θέλει [of 9:18] cannot possibly be regarded neutrally, i.e., as an indeterminately free willing which now takes the one direction (mercy) and now the other (not mercy). To be sure, this willing of God is free. But it is not for that reason indeterminate. It is determined in the sense given by God's name (v. 15). . . . The one purpose of God in the election of His community. . . . This purpose is the purpose of mercy" (*CD*, II/2, 221; cf. 231–32). This is important for making sense of 9:19ff.

There is no trace of human subjectivity in all of this in Romans 9, yet Barth cannot resist letting it into his description of God's election as twofold here, i.e., the "voluntary" service of Moses as God's friend and the "involuntary" service of Pharaoh (*CD*, II/2, 222). He also opens the door to a textually baseless distinction between Israel as a whole and Israelite individuals (*CD*, II/2, 232).

39. The point, then, is not this: "Paul's relatives in view are not truly Israel but those excluded by God's election like Esau and Pharaoh, and this exclusion is not unjust because it means mercy for the elect church." Paul has moved from the first phase of the argument, i.e., whether the word of God has withered (9:6ff), to the second phase, i.e., whether God's purpose of election is unjust (9:14ff). In this second phase he is no longer substantiating directly the claim that not all of those out of Israel are themselves Israel but addressing an anticipated objection to his claim that being οὗτοι Ἰσραήλ does not depend on those who are οὗτοι Ἰσραήλ (9:11-13). The unconditioned election of Jacob over Esau, God's loving Jacob and hating Esau before they were born or had done anything, is the segue from the first phase to the second. With the drama of the exodus—the foundational moment of the people of Israel—he is now building on the life of the word of God in his relatives in view by arguing that the differentiating way in which Israel has come to be Israel is not unjust but merciful. The life of the word is merciful.

The word for the hardening of Pharaoh (σκληρύνω, 9:18) is simply the word in the corresponding refrain in the Exodus story (LXX). It is different from the word Paul will use for the dulling (πωρόω, 11:7) of "the others" (οἱ λοιποί) who oppose Jesus and the readers like those who opposed Elijah and bowed the knee to Baal. It is not wrong to see a relation between the hardening of Pharaoh and the dulling of those "others" (note the use of φύραμα in 9:21 and 11:16), but the relation is not that they belong to the same category, i.e., those excluded by election. As becomes clear in 9:19ff and 11:11ff, it is the familiar Pauline "How much more?"

Another layer of scandal then emerges: How, then, can God find fault in any such human willing and striving (9:19)? If even opposition such as Pharaoh's conforms to God's purpose, is not such opposition inculpable, rendering God's judgment capricious on Paul's reasoning? Paul replies that this accusatory question is baseless, with no place to stand for the human person who poses it, since the relation in view is between human beings and God, who creates and shapes them as a potter does clay. We might expect Paul's argument now to insist on the culpability of human opposition to God even if it conforms to God's purpose or despite its resulting from God's hardening, but that is not Paul's concern or the way his argument runs. His concern is the readers' neglect or defiance of the unfolding,

relation: If the hardening of Pharaoh meant mercy for Israel and cosmic glory, how much more does the dimming/dulling of "the others" in Israel—which has meant mercy for gentiles and cosmic reconciliation—mean mercy for "the others" in Israel, i.e., the resurrection of the dead, the salvation of all Israel?

Insofar as Wright tells a history of Israel as God's action at the expense of Israel in the flesh and uses such a history to make sense of Romans 9–11, Douglas Harink is right to criticize him in *Paul among the Postliberals: Pauline Theology beyond Christendom and Modernity* (Grand Rapids, MI: Brazos Press, 2003), 176–84. As Harink insists, Romans 9–11 invokes God's action rather than Israel's disobedience, and this is to inform the Christian life of mercy. But Harink is wrong that "Israel's history remains for Paul a series of fragments and figures which testify to God's election" (179). Again and again, Paul's Bible rehearses Israel's past as a coherent and continuous, if also unpredictable and tortuous, narrative, even as it is under constant revision (Genesis–Deuteronomy; Deut. 26:1-11; the Deuteronimistic History, esp. Josh. 24:1-13; 1 Sam. 12:6-18). Although Wright does not give an adequate reading of that narrative, Wright is correct that the apocalypse of Israel's God cannot be extricated from it or understood without it. Harink leaves us with a God whose "action" is always invading and then leaving off from Israel's flesh rather than working ceaselessly in the flesh. And while Wright is wrong to allow the story of Israel to remain aloof from the flesh of Israel, Harink is wrong to imagine that the intimacy of God's election of Israel can be told as "primarily biological descent" and "ethnicity" (182).

Here we see that "primarily biological descent" and "ethnicity" are mythological categories that are simply inadequate to the history of God's election of Israel. Tellings of Israel's history that are predicated on such categories, whether to justify them (Harink) or to claim them as a foil and therefore their supersession (Wright), cannot help but reinscribe the violently impatient tendencies of the modern discourse of peoplehood into the very telling of Israel. Notice that rehearsals of Israel's history in the Bible, as here in Romans 9–11, always segue directly into an imperative already implicit in the rehearsed history. That imperative is never something to the effect of ("So don't compromise your biological integrity" or "So overcome your ethnic limitations"). It is always, "So be faithful to the God of your ancestors by refusing idolatry and loving your neighbor." On the biblical concern with intermarriage, see ch. 5 above.

merciful purpose of election by presuming to find God's judgment intelligible, justifiable, and complete as simply the wages of some discernible segment of human activity, the calculable due of some measure of human willing or striving (i.e., wrath for the unrighteous, mercy for the righteous; specifically, wrath for the unrighteous enemies in view in Romans 9–11 and mercy for the righteous readers).

Such presumption is impatient with the scandalous compass of God's merciful election and arrogates to itself God's authority to shape human communities and persons. This shaping work of God is not conditioned by those God is shaping, such that differences among them could be attributed decisively to their willing and striving as the condition of God's shaping them and thus the basis of human policing in God's name. Rather, their decisive differentiation as far as the readers are concerned (which is not to say all their differentiation without qualification) is the unconditional shaping work of God the potter. And this work is not a matter of caprice but is governed by mercy. "What if, willing to evince his wrath and make known his power, God molded with much patience clay vessels of wrath fitted for destruction (e.g., vessels of wrath like Pharaoh)[40] in order to make known the riches of his glory in clay vessels of his mercy, which God prepared beforehand for glory (e.g., the liberated people of God) (9:22-23)? Then human willing and striving as the condition

---

40. Barth is no doubt right to look back to 1:18ff and 3:24-26 and read this destruction for the sake of others as precisely what Jesus endured, and therefore "not according to the caprices of omnipotence but in the determinate purpose" of mercy fulfilled in the cross and resurrection of Messiah (CD, II/2, 223). There is a disequilibrium to the twofold action of the potter (i.e., destruction and giving life), rather than a symmetry with equally ultimate sides. Unfortunately, Barth conceives Israel as such as the "vessel of dishonor" and only the church in Israel as the "vessel of honor," i.e., only the church in Israel is "the witness to the divine mercy, the embodiment of the divine goodness which has taken the part of this [Israelite] man" (CD, II/2, 224; cf. 227, 229, 259). This is one place where Barth is driven to darken Israel in contradistinction to the church, so as to brighten God (for Israel). On the mistake of this race to the bottom of the depravity of Israel, see ch. 5 above. Consider how even obeying the law falls prey to this Barthian race to the bottom in CD, II/2, 241–42, 244.

of the curses or blessings by God that they invite (i.e., as retribution) does not adequately tell the story of God's shaping word. Then a merciful purpose of God underlies and inhabits God's wrath (which is thus revealed as "patient"), a purpose that culminates in a mercy that is more determinative of that purpose than the wrath (9:20-23). And what if among those in whom God has made known the riches of God's glory, continues Paul, we find ourselves, "whom God also named ('called'), not only from the Jews but rather also from the gentiles" (9:24)?

The rhetorical point of 9:20-24, then, is not that some Jews (i.e., the relatives of Paul in view in 9:1-5) have been justly excluded from such mercy but that the purpose of God's election is merciful, and as such beyond contestation by human calculations of justice (cf. Mt. 20:1-16). The emphasis of v. 24 in this context is the testimony of Paul and his readers to this merciful purpose, namely, that God's election has embraced *not only* Jews but people from among the gentiles *as well*.[41] The sense is this: "That people like you (cf. 1:5-6) from the idolatrous gentiles (probably to be understood as those who were vessels of wrath) are among the called of God with Jews like me (ἐκάλεσεν ἡμᾶς, 9:24; cf. κληθήσεταί σοι σπέρμα, 9:7b, ἐκ τοῦ καλοῦντος, 9:12a, ἡ κλῆσις τοῦ θεοῦ, 11:29)—among οὗτοι Ἰσραήλ—attests to the merciful purpose of God's election of God's people." The unconditional election of Israel might otherwise be thought to destine idolatrous gentile enemies only for destruction.[42]

---

41. Against Wright, who takes the rhetorical point to be that the word of God is uncompromised because God has elected some, albeit not all, Jews (*Romans*, 642). Note that 9:20-24 is a response to the scandalized question of the Christian reader (particularly the non-Jew), not to a scandalized question of a Jew opposed to non-Jewish Christians. It is an articulation of the mercy of God irrespective of human obedience or disobedience, not the justification of the exclusion of some Jews.

42. So Barth, *CD*, II/2, 228–30, 232. "Called and gathered with them and justified by the same faith there is a whole abundance of manifest 'vessels of wrath,' a horde from among the Gentiles, from the realm of Moab and Ammon, of Egypt and Assyria" (228). "Thus the death of Jesus unites what was divided, the elected and the rejected" (229). I might add that this calling and

That God's electing and calling Israel into being has claimed a mix like us, says Paul, including people from among the gentiles headed by vessels of wrath like Pharaoh, is a testimony to the mercy of God's election if ever there was one. Such is the justice of God. Such mercy is God's glory.[43] The emerging message to the non-Jewish readers in particular is that the election by God that scandalizes, because it is not conditioned by human willing or striving, is the very election that has seized them in mercy. They can therefore be scandalized and merciless toward Paul's elect relatives in view in 9:1-5 only in defiance of their own place according to the mercy of God's election.[44]

gathering from among the gentiles is itself the activity of God's election of Israel. "If according to v. 24 the Church is now called from both Jews *and* Gentiles, this casts over the past and present of Israel, not new shadow, but a new, surpassing light" (230, his emphasis).

43. "We now learn explicitly [9:23] that God's mercy is His glory" (ibid., 227).

44. The way that Paul has invoked election to this point invites Barth to concentrate the power of election in the idealist realm of forms rather than in the flesh. Ishmael, Esau, Pharaoh, and the Israelite "relatives according to the flesh" in view in 9:1ff correspond to the form of rejection, while Isaac, Jacob, and the church of Jews and gentiles correspond to the form of election (*CD*, II/2, 219-21, 228, 231, 286-87, 291). To be sure, for Barth these forms are not absolutely, only ineffaceably, distinct (a nuance that is too subtle, no doubt). They are finally one, Barth claims, for he perceives the underlying claim of mercy for all in the oneness of Christ, and so insists that the rejected are being elected in their rejection, being united with the elect. Ishmael, Esau, Pharaoh, and the dimmed/dulled part of Israel are therefore all elected in and by their being rejected. Their being elect is their participation in the "history" of election in the world, i.e., the history of unequal encounter between the form of God's election and the form of God's rejection, unequal because God's rejection is subordinate to God's election and finally the servant of it.

The spirit of Barth's reading is right, but it has drifted from the grain of Paul's argument. Paul is not urging patience with Israelite enemies upon his non-Jewish Christian readers by defining such enemies as rejected and appealing to God's election of those rejected, such as Ishmael, Esau, and Pharaoh. Ishmael and Esau are not Israelite, and grouping Pharaoh with Israel by virtue of their participation in the same history of election underplays the way election has differentiated them in the flesh (i.e., as Israel and its gentile enemy), even if Barth is right to highlight the underlying merciful purpose of that differentiation. The effect is to obscure how the argument situates the readers and their Israelite enemies in view, allowing those enemies to be cast as a latter day Pharaoh (via election by rejection) and the readers as the new Israel. But the preceding argument has shown God's election to embrace those enemies as part of Israel rather than exclude them with the rest of Abraham's flesh and appealed to the merciful purpose of God with Pharaoh specifically to rule out the injustice of that embrace (Barth begins to see the problem on *CD*, II/2, 286). Paul has appealed to the difference *between* Ishmael and Isaac and that *between* Jacob and Esau to show that the Israelite enemies of the readers *are part of* the

The Hosea quotation of 9:25-26 indicates that the mix of Paul and his non-Jewish readers belongs to the Israelite future promised by Hosea. That is not simply because Christians from among the gentiles were once "not my people," for Hosea speaks of the conclusive doom of the northern kingdom of Israel, not of gentiles. But the people of this once Israelite kingdom became largely gentile over generations through war, exile, and assimilation; their subsequent generations ceased to remember the God of Israel as their own and so no longer figured among the people of the God of Israel. Under the power of God's wrath, they became as the non-Jewish Roman Christians used to be—servants of others gods.[45]

But Hosea envisions the work of this wrath as subordinate to God's underlying mercy, for the remaining people of Judah and of Israel were to be regathered. The wilderness of God's wrath would also be the wilderness of God's speaking tenderly to Israel. In and through that wilderness God would move to heal Israel, eliminating the threat of idolatry and violent enmity with gentiles (Hosea 2:14-23). This is the promised future in which God has placed "us, not only from the Jews but rather also from the gentiles" (Rom. 9:24), called in,

children of promise in the flesh. They belong with Isaac and Jacob, not with Ishmael and Esau. Pharaoh is not yet another instantiation of the form of God's electing through rejection. The reference to Pharaoh substantiates the claim that Israel's history of promise is not a matter of human willing or striving but of God's mercy, in this case, God's hardening Pharaoh in order to have mercy primarily upon the people of God independently of the subjectivity of either.

God's merciful purpose with Pharaoh does go to the later point of the dulling of some in Israel and so relates them to Pharaoh, as noted in the body of my argument above. But this does not ignore the election of Israel in the flesh through time by making it formally equivalent to God's way with Ishmael, Esau, and Pharaoh. Such a "form" of election cannot be invoked as more determinative than the history of Israel in the flesh with the result that the Israelite "relatives according to the flesh" in view become indistinguishable from Ishmael, Esau, and Pharaoh. If we must speak of a form of election, it must determine the flesh of Israel itself through time rather than thinning it out so that it is formally rendered indistinguishable from other flesh. Furthermore, a form of election must determine other flesh only as derivative of the history of the election of Israel.

45. This history is often truncated by reading Paul to reduce unfaithful Israel to something gentile (e.g., Wright, *Romans*, 643).

through, and from a past of wrath to be a vessel of mercy, from "not my people" to "children of the living God" (Rom. 9:25-26).

The theme of unconditional mercy as attested by Paul and his readers continues from the Hosea quotation, as Paul now shifts to Isaiah.[46] The wrathful judgment of God does not rival or trump God's mercy. The judgment that befell Israel would culminate in a remnant saved by God (Rom. 9:27; Isa. 10:22). Only by the mercy of the electing God (and this includes the mercy of God's wrath) is Israel spared from the fire and brimstone of Sodom and Gomorrah: cities blotted out, a people without a remnant (9:29). What remains of Israel can therefore be only the work of God's electing word: "For the Lord will perform a word of closure and cutting off" (9:28; Isa. 10:23). The point, then, is not that those with Paul "called from not only the Jews but rather also from the gentiles" are the remnant, and that Paul's "relatives according to the flesh" in view in 9:1ff have been burned away.[47] It is that all that persists of Israel remains not by

46. The same verse in Hosea from which Paul has quoted in Rom. 9:25-26 (i.e., Hosea 2:1 [LXX]) prophesies that the children of Israel will become like the sand of the sea, the very language that Isaiah invokes in Isa. 10:22-23, which Paul quotes in Rom. 9:27-29. What links these quotations in the argument in Romans 9 is not the way Isaiah qualifies Hosea but the mercy of God at work in both. Nevertheless, the introduction of "remnant" here is a noteworthy development. The subtle claim is that any remnant is the product not of its own faithfulness but of God's mercy.

47. Against Wright, *Romans*, 643. They haven't been burned away but remain with the rest of Israel in the flesh. Wright and the NRSV miss the point of the quotation from Isaiah by inserting "only" at the beginning of the apodosis of Rom. 9:27; Isa. 10:22. The concessive force of ἐάν in the protasis does not imply this, and there is of course no explicit basis in the LXX for "only." The point in the present context of Romans (rather than Isaiah) is not that *only* some are saved but *that* some are saved, i.e., by God's mercy.

Wright has preempted the following section of the argument (9:30ff) and assumed that the point here is to identify the remnant church in contradistinction to rejected Israel in order to justify God. Wright: "Has Israel failed to believe the gospel? Well, maybe, but it is not as though God's word has failed; for God had always specified . . . one small group while the rest fell away, one tiny remnant while the rest were lost to view, exiled apparently forever" (*Romans*, 634). The whole Bible seems to me to cry out against Wright's reading of Israel's story and of Romans 9–11 here (and here his reading is similar to Yoder's [ch. 2 above] and even Barth's to some extent [e.g., *CD*, II/2, 226-27], though for Barth the lost are never "lost to view"). The remnant cannot be played off against the exiles. It is precisely those who are "apparently exiled forever" whom the God of Israel refuses to forget or lose from view (e.g., Jer. 31:35-40; Isa.

escaping God's wrath through righteous striving (or believing) but by receiving God's mercy as it has emerged through God's wrath.[48] And it is to this mercy that those called with Paul "not only from among the Jews but rather also from the gentiles" bear witness as "a vessel of mercy" (9:23).[49] They are a witness of hope for the judged according to God's election.

9:30—10:21

The reader must not infer that the subject of the argument has changed in 9:30—10:21 (i.e., from God's unconditional election of Israel in 9:1-29 to a new subject of how "Israel" has gotten God wrong by works and the church has gotten God right by faith).

49:14-18), precisely the judged whom God will save. By reducing God's elect to those who elect God, Wright has made God's election empty, and the problem is that a theology of God's disowning some promotes a politics of our disowning one another. One can imagine what kind of political economy flows from imagining the chosen as one small group while the rest have fallen away, "lost to view." Recall (in chapters 4–5 above) that any election within Israel is in service to God's election of all Israel, who are never lost from view but an open "many" that we seek to enclose or count only by the wiles of Satan (1 Chron. 21:1ff). See also Barth, *CD*, II/2, 232, for the remnant of 9:27-29 as positive witness to God's purpose for all Israel, rather than the justification of God's burning some (or much) of Israel away.

48. Wright infers that Paul's point is that his relatives in view since 9:1-5 are not saved (*Romans*, 654) and later assumes that being not saved is coterminous with being not elect. But the election of Israel precedes and is the basis of the salvation of Israel; election is not the equivalent of salvation. Election therefore embraces the many in Israel who will be saved; it does not leave out any of those Israelite many who are not yet saved (Rom. 8:28-32). Note, in this connection, the future tense and passive voice of σωθήσῃ in Rom. 10:9.

49. I am sympathetic with Wright's claim that "the story Paul has told in vv. 6-29 is the story of what it means for Israel to be the people of the crucified Messiah" (*Romans*, 643), but this is precisely why it should be understood as the story of God's embracing all of Israel in the flesh, and as such a story that is calling upon the readers to embrace their Israelite enemies. All of the crucified Messiah was raised from the dead, not just some of him. "Paul has clearly in view that at the goal of Israel's history God will not say No to man but that veiled under the No He will say Yes; that He will not leave Jesus in the grave after being put to death but will raise him from the dead" (Barth, *CD*, II/2, 226; see on this page the Christology of Jeremiah's potter parable according to Barth). "If God's mercy is so rich and powerful even upon Gentiles who were standing wholly under His curse and sentence of rejection, how much more so upon those to whom He has already promised it! Indeed we must even read and understand the Hosea quotations quite simply as a repetition of the prophecy originally—and as established by its comprehensive fulfilment, definitively—addressed to *Israel*, namely to that other, *rejected* Israel" (ibid., emphasis his).

The subject remains God's unconditional election according to God's mercy. Any exegesis of Israel's Scriptures, anything Paul says against his relatives in view, any claim he makes about the messianic life—all this—serves rhetorically to substantiate the mercy of God's election and the embodied witness of the readers to that mercy.

Picking up from 9:24 now that he has situated himself and the readers in Israel's history of election with 9:25-29, Paul notes in 9:30 that the mercy of God's election has taken another scandalous turn: whereas Israel of old, pursuing a law of righteousness, did not attain to that law, law-less gentiles, not pursuing righteousness, have obtained it because it is the righteousness of faith (9:30-31).[50] Righteousness here is not so much a status of rightness as a manifold and concrete life of promised covenant blessing. 9:30-31 are not about rival systems of salvation (i.e., law and faith, with an implied premise that the law is essentially undoable) but commentary on the history of Israel and gentiles as shaped by the merciful activity of God's election. But before invoking the activity of God's election (as he will in 9:33) to account for this strange development in the history of Israel, Paul claims that through its history Israel did not attain the righteousness it sought (i.e., by a law of righteousness), because it understood it as stemming not from faith but from works (9:32).

The works in view here are no doubt particular (e.g., circumcision as violently policed by the Maccabees), but they are nevertheless a matter of the broad willing and striving of the community that Paul has been addressing in the preceding argument. There he has

---

50. "Israel" here is not a timeless entity or category (i.e., to be opposed to the church or reduced to the dimensions of Paul's relatives of 9:1-5). It is the scriptural Israelite generations of the past that Paul has just been writing about in 9:25-29 (i.e., quoting Hosea and Isaiah). Paul will go on to say that his relatives in view from 9:1-5 find themselves continuing in ignorance of their God's ways like these generations of the past (10:1ff), but it is the fate of the Israelite generations of Hosea and Isaiah that directly induces the question of 9:30, not the faithlessness of Paul's relatives in view. The temptation to totalize and dehistoricize Israel, as if Paul here described "what Israel has always done" or "who Israel essentially is" must be resisted.

excluded them as conditions of God's shaping the people of promise across time (and therefore conditions of participating in the blessings of that family) by insisting that that people has always been fundamentally a matter of God's unconditional election ("not by works but by God's call/naming," 9:12). There is of course no hint that such works are a matter of ethnocentrism or ethnic pride.[51] They are the works by which Israel according to the flesh has willed and striven to survive and thrive as a people, to reach its promised future, whether in the interest of integrity and resisting assimilation or of expansion and assimilating others.[52] Paul claims that Israel endeavored

51. Wright (and Dunn, *Romans 9-16*, 582-83) lifts v. 32 from the flow of the passage so as to narrow the sense of "works" from Israel's willing and striving to supposedly ethnocentric practices that set "Jews" apart from gentiles. "What Israel has sought, and what 9:6-29 has been at pains to deny, is an inalienable identity as God's people for all those who possess Torah, for (that is) ethnic Israel as a whole" (*Romans*, 649). While Wright is correct that the Torah was in fact always destined for gentiles (i.e., to Israelize them—but this was not a matter of controversy with Paul's relatives in view) and that the way in which this happens has changed with the coming of Messiah and his Spirit (this, on the other hand, was the matter of controversy), there has been not a whisper of any ethnic exclusivism among the relatives of Paul for whom he is sorrowful.

In Paul's debate with his opponents, *Torah is not a matter of ethnic purity but of practice.* As his recognition of the Judaization of gentiles through proselytism implies (655), Wright's claim here in 9:32 that Paul is arguing against Jewish ethnocentrism and Abrahamic sonship as "automatic" is exposed as untenable. The problem is not what Paul's relatives in view claim is automatic, but what they claim people must do (or rather, simply *that* they claim people must do anything). Wright has concocted their ethnocentrism in the service of his (sound) claim, so far as it goes, that the election of Israel is not ethnically exclusive ("the attempt . . . to confine grace to race, to create a covenant status for Jews and Jews only," 650; cf. 676). But the understanding/practice Paul opposes does not deny this. In 9:6-29 he has not been at pains to deny any inalienable ethnic rights of Israel but to deny that Israelite works in Israel's history have been determinative of God's election (or to deny the ontic equivalence of those works and God's election). Such works can only *serve* God's election and are faithful only to the extent that they are undertaken as such. Accordingly, Israel's calling is to remain hospitably open to its God's simply seizing people and bringing them to Israel's table. Any works of covenant obedience can only follow such acts of God's election and cannot condition God's election. For this reason, the readers cannot regard the hostility of Paul's relatives in view as disqualifying.

52. So Wright is correct to understand Torah as regulating the Israel-gentile difference. But he is wrong to identify that difference as ethnic, whether in Torah itself or among Paul's relatives in view. The difference is rather that between Israel's remembering the God of Israel as its own and forgetting the God of Israel in favor of false gods (i.e., becoming gentile through total assimilation to a gentile society). Barth is better here: "What it lacked was that it did not want to rely on the promise, on the mercy of God, but on itself, on its own willing and running in the direction of the promised fulfilment; that it sought by its own willing and running to bring

to secure its own future of righteousness but that in this way it could not reach that future, which was and is fundamentally a matter of unconditional promise rather than conditional compensation. Attempting to secure its own future of blessing led Israel to the curses of the covenant, to insecurity, to unfaithfulness, and to violence, as the biblical history attests. The promised future could be reached only by faith, only by clinging to the faithfulness of the God of Israel to provide for Israel, despite and even through Israel's unfaithfulness (e.g., 1 Sam. 12:20-22; Daniel 9). Such is the trusting, nonviolent politics of faith.

This faith is what has led unrighteous gentiles to righteousness, to eschatological peace at Israel's table of blessing. Faith is of course not a matter of doing nothing, and Israel could have performed works such as circumcision by faith, as some no doubt did. Paul's claim is not that no one in Israel lived by faith, but that Israel did not attain righteousness as it sought it. It tended to seek its future of blessing amidst both domestic and foreign threats as a product of its own striving rather than the work of God's mercy, as a matter of its works of the law rather than the gracious gift promised in the law.[53] Paul is working toward his coming appeal to the mercy of God's election,

---

about the fulfilment of what was promised" (*CD*, II/2, 241). But Barth imagines that lacking faith they "lacked all" (241) and that "All its works . . . the temple cultus and service of the Law, become sin and guilt" (242). This is a non sequitur with respect to the lack of faith.

53. Daniel 9 (like 1 Sam. 12:20-22 and Psalm 79) expresses exactly the prayer that Israel should always have uttered and should continue to utter, according to Paul. Ordering the community by striving rather than faithful waiting upon its God militated against Israel's being a people of faith, a people of mercy (Isa. 1:10-17; Hosea 6). See Wright's helpful argument that the law itself is what Israel did not attain to (649). The Messiah himself is finally the gift of the law. Cf. Michael Wyschogrod, *The Body of Faith: God in the People of Israel* (Northvale, NJ: Jason Aronson Inc., 1996 [1983]): "In the context of the messianic future, the prophets speak of a circumcision of the heart that will complete the circumcision of the flesh, which seems to have left the heart insufficiently transformed" (19); "Messianism is . . . the Jewish principle of hope" (255); "the messianic vision" is for "the abolition of war" (243). This last quotation is especially important for understanding Ephesians 2 in relation to the law's sentence of divisive death between Israel and the gentiles, to the peacemaking work of Christ, and to the derivative nature of the works of the ecclesial body of Christ.

as opposed to the willing or striving of God's covenant partner, as the basis for his readers' treatment of their Israelite enemies in view (9:1-5; 11:28-32). It is the pursuit of righteousness as a matter of willing and striving that is leading the Israelite enemies of the readers to reject them, to refuse them hospitality at their Israelite table in the name of the law.[54] And the readers' understanding of their own place as the product of their willing or striving (e.g., of being "faithful" to Jesus) will lead them to similar inhospitality; they must therefore engage these enemies with and from the mercy in which they the readers stand by God's election, the mercy that has not disowned their enemies and to which their enemies, like the readers, are also destined.[55]

54. We are apt to assume that the recipient community of Romans are the "insiders" deciding what to do about Jewish "outsiders." But, as we saw in ch. 1 above, Jewish communities in places like Rome were populous and well-established. What we have here is more a case of some minority churches, composed of Jews and non-Jews, struggling with what to do in response to their exclusion/mistreatment by some from powerful communities composed of Jews and proselytes.

55. In naming the inadequacy of the understanding of his relatives in view, Paul has not suddenly departed from his argument for their place within the elect people of promise by God's mercy in order to "explain" their behavior. The way in which Paul names the inadequacy of their understanding in 9:32-33 serves his larger argument for his readers' patience, and prepares the way for Paul to claim that such inadequacy is subordinate to God's merciful purpose of salvation for all. Wright has lost sight of the larger argument, which calls for patience with God's election. Instead, he discerns a distinct purpose here: "To develop the theme that was already bound up within the earlier arguments [of Romans]—namely, the inclusion of Jews and Gentiles together in the single family promised to Abraham" (*Romans*, 647). This problem is aggravated in *PFG* by Wright's beginning with 10:1-17 as "the heart" of Romans 9-11 and trying to build the sense of the argument of the three chapters around it (1164ff). His reading of 10:1-17 thus misses the rhetorical thread of the section, for which it is better to start at the beginning of the argument of Romans 9-11 and work to the end. He discerns the correspondence between chapters 9 and 11 (more clearly in *PFG* than in *Romans*) but cannot articulate the sense of ch. 10 that links them, and he tends to bend parts of chapters 9 and 11 to fit the center of ch. 10 that he has imagined. Furthermore, by imagining "works" like circumcision as the "badge" or "marker" of covenant peoplehood for those Paul is supposedly opposing and making "faith" the "badge" or "marker" of Israelite Christian "identity" or "status" (i.e., of being "the Messiah people") throughout his exegesis, Wright imposes a form of modern identity politics on both Paul and his opposing relatives, locking the Christian gospel in the logic of that identity politics, simply trading one "badge" or "marker" for another ("Abraham's family…was defined not by the marks of Jewish ethnicity but by 'Messiah-faith'" (*PFG*, 1169). This kind of identity politics simply refuses the mercy of God's election, which troubles the use of such "badges" and "markers" to distinguish a people's "identity" and insists on solidarity in the flesh.

Now in 9:32-33, quoting from Isa. 28:16 and 8:14, Paul makes explicit the electing activity of God in the midst of Israel's pursuing a law of righteousness, a law to which it could not attain as a product of its works because the manifold blessings of righteousness come only by awaiting them in faith as God's gift. The stumbling of some in Israel (i.e., his relatives in view) is on a stone *that God has laid* in Zion, and such stumbling will move Israel to seek righteousness by faith rather than by works. In each of the quoted Isaiah passages, the stumbling of Israel is a prelude to the deliverance of those who endure that stumbling, of those of Israel who remain. The stone itself has been placed before Israel that it might find faith: the one who believes in the stone will not be put to shame. The stone of stumbling is thus itself the presence of God's stubborn mercy for Israel.[56]

---

56. Again, Wright seems to have lost the thread of the argument. He has taken the preceding argument to have drifted away from 9:1-5 and moved to the subject of what it means to be the true Israel, i.e., the church (Barth falls into the same trap, *CD*, II/2, 217.) Now, he surmises (in 9:32-33), Paul must resume explaining away the threat of Israelite unbelief to the word of God: "Ethnic Israel as a whole has failed to believe in the Messiah, because his crucifixion is a scandal to them" (*Romans*, 650). There is, of course, no mention of the cross at this juncture of Romans 9–11. The subject of the argument is not the scandal of the stone that has made some in Israel stumble. It is that the stone of stumbling has been placed *by God*, that the elected and electing stone of God's Messiah is the occasion of some of Paul's relatives' rejection of Messiah (as Wright recognizes in *PFG*, 1179), and that God thus claims and embraces them even in that rejection. Consequently, the readers cannot simply blame the relatives of Paul in view for their hostility. God's electing work is in it. Paul's response is prayer for them (10:1), and the readers' response must be merciful patience.

Here at 10:1 Wright suddenly (653) recognizes that the argument is picking up 9:1-5, and he rightly discerns its purpose ("[Paul] wants to draw his largely Gentile audience in Rome ... to share his earnest desire for the salvation of Jews.") But because he has read 9:6-30 in a way that is at cross-purposes with chapters 9–11 as a whole (somewhat less so in *PFG*), he must say that 10:1 "has the effect of curbing any false impressions that might be received from chap. 9," (i.e., the false impression that God has been unfaithful to some of Israel, an impression left by Wright's reading but not by Paul's argument). The same misreading leads him to take the γὰρ of 10:2 as explaining that Paul is praying for his relatives in view because they are unsaved (654), when the syntax indicates Paul's sympathy for them because their zeal is indeed for the God of Israel. While they are indeed not yet saved, they are elect and will be saved (so Barth, *CD*, II/2, 243: Paul "thus attests to them that their purpose is already set in the right direction, and indirectly that the right goal already lies before them, that they certainly do know the God of Abraham and Isaac and Jacob and in Him the Father of Jesus Christ, and hear His Word.")

We find in 10:4 that Christ is this stone of stumbling.[57] He is the gift of God that is the goal of the law. In him all those who trust the God of Israel with their future, as Abraham did before he was circumcised, come to enjoy the blessings that God has promised. While the relatives of Paul in view are indeed zealous for the God of Israel—perhaps as Phinehas and the Maccabees were and as Paul once was—they are not knowledgeably zealous, because they do not know that the blessings of God's faithfulness are predicated not on their zeal but on the mercy of God's righteousness (10:2-3), now fulfilled in the gift of Christ.[58] This knowledge induces a blessed politics of vulnerable hospitality instead of the scarcity and rivalry of hostile protectionism.[59]

The relatives of Paul in view have mistakenly inferred that the righteousness "which is of the law" is the only righteousness possible, identical with the righteousness promised, that Israel's faithfulness to the law is the condition of the blessings of the covenant (Lev. 18:5; Rom. 10:5). But this is only a subordinate part of the law rather than the whole story of the law. The whole story shows that blessings

57. So Wright, *Romans*, 650.
58. Here Wright puzzlingly generalizes the zeal of the relatives of Paul in view since 9:1 to be that of all "Israel according to the flesh," supposing that all of Paul's kinsfolk (i.e., "ethnic Israel"), rather than the particular kinsfolk in view in 9:1-5, were "ignorant" of "the entire sweep of covenantally loyal actions God has undertaken from Abraham to the Messiah" (ibid., 654–55). He has fallen into the same trap as Luz and Stanton as we saw in ch. 6 above, comparing all of Paul's kinsfolk to "the wicked tenants in Jesus' parable" (654), asserting that δικαιοσύνη is "a status that gentiles have come to share but which ethnic Israel as a whole seems, for the moment at least, to have forfeited" (646).
59. See Wright's sound exegesis of "zeal" and "knowledge" in 10:2 (ibid., 653–54) and of Messiah as the goal of the law (657). Also consider that Judaism did not canonize the Maccabean literature, as Rabbi Stephen Schwarzchild was keen to point out to Yoder (John Howard Yoder, *For the Nations: Essays Public and Evangelical* [Grand Rapids, MI: William B. Eerdmans, 1997], 67–68 and 68n40). Barth's reading is headed in the right direction but, following much of the Christian exegetical tradition, remains in a depoliticized idiom and thus does not speak clearly to the life of the covenant community as this passage does. Barth can say only that those who are zealous for God through works of the law "are reluctant to concede to Him His right to accept and receive them on His own initiative" (Barth, *CD*, II/2, 243) and that this is rhetorically a warning to the church not to despise their own election whereby God likewise receives them on God's own initiative.

given unconditionally by God are the condition of Israel's faithfulness and that God's covenant blessings are not only or primarily the reward of Israel's faithfulness. God's covenant blessings are always the work of God before and as they are the work of Israel. The conditional righteousness "which is of the law" can therefore operate only subordinately within the unconditioned righteousness of God, the electing faithfulness of God whereby God seizes Israel as God's own, shapes Israel through curses and blessings, and leads it to the gift of righteousness, which includes the blessing of Israel's righteous response.

Thus, Paul's claim about "the righteousness of faith" in relative contrast to "the righteousness which is of the law" (10:5ff) is simply commentary on the covenant history of Israel. It was chosen by God unconditionally (and continuously), given a life of blessings and curses as conditioned by its way of living in response, and was to be saved by the faithfulness of God who would finally bless accursed Israel with a heart of obedience (Deuteronomy 30; Jeremiah 38 [LXX]), a manifold salvation Paul claims has now dawned. The way in which Israel's life has been conditioned by the way it has lived is therefore not the basis of Israel's hope and life; the way God has provided the conditions and conditioning in and by which Israel has lived is the basis, continuous impetus, and promise of Israel's life. Israel's whole history from Abraham through Isaac and Jacob to the present, rather than an invisible and formless principle (e.g., ethnicity) or simply its shape when constituted as a people in the exodus or at some other point in time, is thus the elected shape of Israel as conditioned by its God. The fully grown tree of Israel was anticipated in its earliest seed, and the Messiah of Israel's salvation—the gift of God and goal of the law—is the sap of promise and hope that has given life to the whole and has now finally revealed the way of salvation.[60]

To explicate the righteousness of faith as commentary on the covenant history of the people of God, Paul turns, starting in 10:6, to a foundational moment in Israel's covenant story (Deuteronomy 30). Here, narratively on the plains of Moab, Israel is given again the law to live by in the promised land. And yet, it is told at once that it will not live but die by this law and then promised the life to which God will lead it under that law, even through the death of disobedience (which is finally exile). This is the life of God's righteousness that comes not by Israel's works but by God's provision for Israel's future, calling forth Israel's faith in that provision even when Israel's works prove empty.

The promised life of Israel Paul calls "the righteousness of faith" (10:6), and it is on display, Paul will soon say, in a Christian politics of hospitality according to election, that is, of loving enemies of the gospel who according to election are beloved because of the ancestors (11:28). Such hospitality, which refuses to be conditioned by the enmity of covenant family members, is the covenant answer to (and itself the gift of) the unconditioned righteousness of God.

60. Thus faith is not a "mark" or a "badge" (against Wright, *Romans*, e.g., 648, 655, 663) but a politics (as it is in Genesis 12, 15, and 22). It is a politics of people not pretending to constitute their own life or to secure their own future or to do what the reprobate fail to do, but of receiving their life by God's election and thus being merciful even with those who are disobedient and hostile. Wright does well to resist reading 10:5 and 10:6ff as opposing principles, but by supposing that 10:6 is simply epexegetical with respect to 10:5 (660), he misses the adversative force of 10:6 (with its δέ) and ignores the relation between the contrast of 10:5-6ff and that of 9:30-10:4 (which also uses "law" and "faith"). This contrast in 10:5-6ff develops the preceding argument that contends that works in Israel's history (e.g., Israel's doing the law) have not conditioned God's election, and therefore that the hateful works of the readers' Jewish enemies (or their not doing faithful works) cannot disqualify them, nor can the readers' works of obedience justify disowning such enemies. The contrast between 10:5 and 10:6ff is (as in Gal. 3:10-12) that 10:5 (Lev. 18:5) is not the whole story of Torah, which 10:4 has in turn evoked with the term τέλος. For a similar argument—that any bilateral conditionality to Israel's life remains subordinate to God's unilateral and unconditional election of Israel's life—see Galatians 3. Wright misses all of this by making faith a matter of our doing (i.e., the law, as also in *PFG*, 1175). Although he is right that all (including gentiles) are called to obey the law of the covenant (as Barth also affirms, *CD*, II/2, 203), it is God, rather than our doing, who fulfills the law in and among us (as Wright himself claims on the basis of Bar. 3–5 [661] but whose significance he does not discern).

The commandment of Deut. 30:11 is not too hard or far away (Rom. 10:6-8), what it seems in the conditions of exile, not because the law is easy to keep but because keeping it is not finally the work of Israel; it is the gracious work of God that will circumcise Israel's hearts so that they will love God with all their heart and their neighbors as themselves (cf. Jer. 38:31-40 LXX). Even when Israel is unfaithful and is exiled "from one end of heaven to the other" (Deut. 30:4 LXX), Israel's God will gather the people by God's blessing for the sake of filling it with that blessing.

The command of the covenant in Deuteronomy is therefore not an ambiguous word, whose goal is either curse or blessing depending on Israel's response. It is the word of God bearing the unconditional promise of election, whose goal is Messiah and the salvation of Israel in him, whatever path of curses and blessings might lead to him. Thus, in Deuteronomy 30, God has made Israel's promised future near, placing the word of command on Israel's lips and in Israel's heart so that Israel will not be able to forget it, whatever befalls the people for its disobedience. Even in the furthest reaches of exile, Israel will find itself speaking and believing the covenant word of God. It is an eternal word, a word that has not withered in the case of Paul's relatives in view (9:6ff), Israelite enemies of the readers in Rome (11:28) whom this word of promise and command continues to enliven and embrace as part of God's people by God's election.

This word is revealed in its fullness, according to Paul, in the cross and resurrection of Messiah, who is the promise that carries Israel along from beginning to end. The word of command has therefore grown to be the word of faith about Jesus that Paul and other apostles of Jesus proclaim (10:8b, thus the word of faith includes and orders the preceding covenant word of command). As such, the word of the gospel is the witness to the unfailing "word of God" of 9:6. To confess crucified Jesus as Lord, and believe him raised from the dead by God as the firstborn of Israel's promised future, is to find the fully grown covenant command of God on one's lips and in one's heart (Rom. 10:9-10).[61] This faith leads to the love sought by God's election, the love that zeal for God without the knowledge of God's merciful righteousness cannot attain. Consequently, every one who becomes loyal to the stone of stumbling that is Messiah will not be put to shame (10:11). Like anyone else who has done so, such a person has not come to participate in the promised blessings of the covenant by her own ephemeral righteousness but by the unshakeable mercy of God. The knowledge of this can only make her merciful.[62] Because

61. That Jesus does not raise himself from the dead, but was raised from the dead by God the Father (10:9), is not incidental to the argument. Jesus did not achieve his own resurrection by faith and obedience. It was not a matter of Jesus' willing or striving (which is not to say that Jesus did not desire it). The economy of God in Israel, according to Romans 9–11, is fundamentally a matter of God's election (see Barth, CD, IV/1, 300–4). The election of God the Father is indeed perfected in the Israelite Son—the τέλος of the law and the elect one—the one in whom God's election is ontically equivalent to his faith and obedience, the one who thus rules as Israel's final king, the Son of David. But the consummation of this election, i.e., the resurrection of Jesus, is the Son's receiving from the Father by the Spirit, not the Son's doing what the Father commanded (cf. Phil. 2:9-11). Jesus did not perform his resurrection.

Moreover, the rest of Israel (πολλοῖς ἀδελφοῖς, Rom. 8:29) is elect not in measuring up to Jesus' faith and obedience, but in being moved by him to faith and obedience, culminating in their own resurrection from the dead. This election is not at work only in the one who "confesses with her mouth and believes in her heart" but in all whom God has elected, even when that means jealousy, as Paul is about to show. What is key for the readers is that they recognize Israel's tortuous history in the flesh—even its divisions—not as a matter of the people's willing or striving but of God's election. Israel is a matter of its faith and obedience only as God *in* the people and the people *in* the Son by the Spirit, and the same God is at work in Israel's faithlessness and disobedience.

62. Hays draws attention to the quotation of Deut. 9:4 that introduces Paul's exegesis of Deut. 30:12-14. As Hays says, in that section of Deuteronomy Israel is warned not to regard its place in the promised land as its own doing, because that work of salvation (i.e., from "the house of slavery" in Egypt and from the gentile inhabitants of Canaan) has been God's: "Do not say in your heart, 'My strength and the might of my hand secured for me this great power'" (8:17). And then in 9:4, "Do not say in your heart when the Lord your God has destroyed these nations before you, 'Because of my righteousness the Lord has brought me in to inherit this good land'" (See Richard B. Hays, *Echoes of Scripture in the Letters of Paul* [New Haven: Yale University Press, 1989], 78–80).

Wright (*Romans*, 662–63) construes this subtle introduction of Deut. 8:17 and 9:4 as only making the point that the Israelites in view in 10:3 are doing precisely what Israel was warned against in Deuteronomy 9. But proving that they are in the wrong is neither the primary subject of the argument nor rhetorically what Paul must succeed in doing for his readers (who already believe them to be in the wrong). Within the larger argument for the patient politics

a place at the table of Israel's blessing comes only by God's merciful gift, there can be no distinction in the blessing of that table between the Jew who has striven to keep the law and the Greek who has found the law on her lips and in her heart as the name of Messiah Jesus risen from the dead (10:12).[63] For everyone who calls upon the name of the Lord God of Israel—now revealed as Jesus—will be saved (10:13; Joel 3:5 LXX). The way of Jesus is the unshakeable way of and to Israel's promised blessings.[64]

of God's election, the force of Paul's use of Deut. 8:17 and 9:4 (and then Deut. 30:12-14) here is that the readers must not respond in like kind to the hostile Israelites in view. Because the readers and their Jewish enemies find themselves shaped by God's election (rather than the readers' righteousness), the readers must respond to the hostility from their sisters and brothers with the mercy of patience. This is "righteousness of faith" (10:6). The point is not that the Israelites in view since 9:1 (including 10:1-4) do not have "the word of faith" (10:8); it is that the gospel of Deuteronomy is the word of faith in the merciful God that the readers *do* have, i.e., on their lips and in their hearts. Paul's prayer in 10:1 is not for the salvation of unspecified people to be saved, or for the Jew-gentile church, but "for them," i.e., the Israelite relatives of his in view since 9:1-5 (against Wright, *Romans*, 664, 666). The argument directed to the readers is "for them." Barth is therefore on the right track when he says of those who confess and believe in contrast to those who will and strive without knowledge, "Their solidarity with Israel is not effaced but established by what is now said 'against' Israel" (*CD*, II/2, 243).

63. Jewish teachers like Paul often summed up, as Paul does here, the whole of the Torah in one word or sentence, i.e., *kelal* (e.g., *b. Šabb.* 31a; *b. Mak.* 23b–24a). In Rom. 13:8, Paul will sum it up as "loving another." In 1 Corinthians 1 he sums up the whole of God's revelation in "the cross" (e.g., ὁ λόγος γὰρ ὁ τοῦ σταυροῦ). This is rightly how Barth understands Messiah as the τέλος of the law here in Romans 10 (*CD*, II/2, 245), though we should not miss the nuance of τέλος as fulfillment in time of the economy of the law. See also Taubes, *The Political Theology of Paul*, 24, especially the relation of Christ crucified as "the eye of the needle" to the election of Israel on 25.

64. The rhetorical thrust of 10:9-14 is not "so you who believe in Jesus are in the right and have hope," as Wright imagines (*Romans*, 666). It is that Jesus is not the hope of some but of all, the Lord not only of the non-Jewish readers but of their Jewish opponents as well, the "them" and "they" of 10:1-3, i.e., Paul's relatives in view since 9:1-5. That is why the opening question of 10:14ff is, "How, then, might *they* call upon one in whom they have not believed?" The argument is about and for "them." Wright notices that here in 10:1-13, 1) we have the heart of an argument (Romans 9–11) that is "about God," 2) that the participle πλουτῶν (10:12) looks back to 9:23 and ahead to 11:33, 3) the repetition of declensions of πᾶς in 10:11-13, and 4) the resemblance of 10:13b and 11:26a (665–66). But he does not discern the rhetorical implications of the very things he observes. The implications are the irrevocable election of the Israelite enemies of the readers and the imperative that the readers be patient with God's election. After identifying 10:13b with 11:26a, Wright waffles on the meaning of πᾶς, saying that it means "all sorts" (666, 667), which it obviously does not mean in 11:26a.

Against Wright's contention that Paul is advocating Christian works of the law with Deuteronomy 30 much as 4QMMTa enjoins certain works of the law on its recipients with

How will those for whom Paul prays according to 10:1 participate in this salvation, unless they hear the name of Jesus and become loyal to him as living Lord?, asks Paul starting in 10:14. Paul is one sent to proclaim that name as God's good news for Israel (10:15). But not all Israel have obeyed the gospel of God's mercy in Christ, just as Isaiah anticipated (Isa. 53:1; Rom. 10:16), and the relatives of Paul in view are among such Israelites. According to Isaiah, the faith of calling upon the name of the Lord is contingent upon the proclamation of the good news of that Lord. Faith, and therefore the righteousness that flows through it, is spread through that message (ἐξ ἀκοῆς), the message about Israel's glory, and salvation by God, in and through Israel's rejection and suffering (10:14-17). This message is transmitted

Deuteronomy 30 (661), it seems to me that "works of the law" are pejorative for Paul precisely because of how they are used in the politics of the likes of 4QMMTa. Thus, Paul is with the later rabbis that such sectarian arguments about works of the law are impatient with God's election of Israel as one people and led to the judgment that was the destruction of the temple and Jerusalem (see Shaye J. D. Cohen in "The Significance of Yavneh: Pharisees, Rabbis, and the End of Jewish Sectarianism," *Hebrew Union College Annual* 55 [1984]: 27–53). That Wright concludes that Paul advocates "the works of the law" in Romans in the same sense as 4QMMTa suggests he may be missing the meaning of Romans 9–11 by a lot. Wright: "For Paul, the thing that marks out members of the renewed covenant, the people envisaged by Deuteronomy 30, over against all others, Jews and pagans alike, is Christian faith" (661; Wright is then forced by the text to an inconsistent reading of "works" elsewhere, e.g., 11:5-6 [676]; he distances himself from this claim of the parallel between Paul and Qumran on *PFG*, 1224). But what constitutes all Israel for Paul is God's election, rather than some mimimum of subjective Israelite adequacy (i.e., works), and the new covenant is in fact not for any group smaller than all Israel, much less a new people altogether, as Jeremiah 31 makes clear. There is of course not a hint here in Romans of "opening the promise to those of any and every ethnic background" (662; cf. "opened up ... to people of every race," 673), for there has never been any ethnic or racial closure upon the promise or the people that has lived by it.

Agamben offers some corrective to Wright (and somewhat to Barth) in denying any new, stable identity to the *ekklesia* of Jews and non-Jews over against (non-Christian) Jews (or gentiles for that matter) (*The Time That Remains*, 51). But without a theological account of Christian oneness Agamben's conception of the *ekklesia* as non-non-Jews according to the "cut of Apelles" (i.e., a line that cuts the ever-so-thin line between Jews and non-Jews in half) cannot avoid unhinging the church from Paul's relatives of 9:1-5 much as Wright does. Without God's election of Israel in the flesh, Agamben has no way of holding together those of 9:1-5 with the Christian recipients of the letter (or with the remnant, on which see below). According to Romans 9–11, Apelles's cut must not be understood only to divide; rather it takes the cut Jewish flesh as its own and works reconciliation. "Paul, after all, if one tries to summarize it, speaks of nothing other than atonement [*Versöhnung*]" (Taubes, *The Political Theology of Paul*, 32).

(by Paul and others who are "sent," ἀποσταλῶσιν) through the word of Messiah, that is, through the Deuteronomic word of command fully grown as the story of the mercy of the God of Israel in the death and resurrection of Jesus.[65] Yet, that some in Israel have not obeyed this gospel is not a matter of their not hearing or of their ignorance, as if the gospel must be transmitted more loudly, more widely, or more informatively to occasion their faith (10:18); God's purpose of election is not held in suspense in their not obeying the gospel. Rather, as Paul will now argue, even their not obeying the gospel conforms to the merciful purpose of God's election, which is to bless the gentile nations at Israel's table of blessing and so make the disobedient in Israel jealous of what is indeed their own. The purpose of election for those disobedient, too, is mercy.[66]

The effect of the quotations from Deut. 32:21 and Isa. 65:1-2 in Rom. 10:19-20 is to claim that the opposition of those disobedient in Israel—among whom are the relatives of Paul in view—is anticipated by Moses and Isaiah. The current scenario is no hiatus. Moreover, that opposition arises from the favor of the God of Israel toward Israel's gentile enemies. And yet, in both scriptural texts—and here in Romans—such opposition can be only the prelude to the blessing of those in Israel who have been disobedient.

---

65. On "the power of the announcement," see Agamben, *The Time That Remains*, 90ff. "When thinking of the nearness of the mouth and heart, we have to venture something like a performative efficacy of the word of faith realized in its very pronouncement" (131), i.e., Jesus' very name is unforgettable and unrestrainable, burgeoning in weakness (cf. Phil. 1:18; 2:9-11).

66. The purpose of the catena of quotations of 10:18-21 is not to "explain" "the (partially successful) Gentile mission" and "the (mostly unsuccessful) Jewish mission" (against Wright, *Romans*, 667). There is no such gentile mission in view, nor has anything in the argument occasioned the need to "explain" a mission or its results. The purpose is instead to show how the opposition that the readers are meeting from some of Paul's Israelite relatives, for whom he prays, is already inscribed in the "Israel" of Scripture and thus operates as part of God's election of Israel (see Barth, *CD*, II/2, 258; Wright is better in *PFG*, 1180, where he recognizes that the quotation of Isa. 65:2 in Rom. 10:21 means "a continuing commitment" to Israel).

11:1-24

God's merciful purpose of election is hardly served by the final exclusion of those who have been disobedient from the table of blessing that is their own according to God's election. By no means did God repudiate God's people (Rom. 11:1-2). Paul is part of a remnant that is a testimony of God's faithfulness to Israel and therefore a token of the future God has promised for all Israel (11:1).[67]

67. By supposing that the remnant is small and the rest is great, we are tempted to retroject into the argument the later schism that resulted in "Judaism and Christianity" (e.g., Wright's "Israel has, by and large, not believed the gospel of Jesus the Messiah" [*Romans*, 672]; others such as Barth speak of rejection by "the majority of Israel" or similar [e.g., *CD*, II/2, 241]). But in fact Paul nowhere indicates how numerous the remnant or the rest is, and his argument does not depend on any ratio. We may surmise that the remnant is smaller and the rest substantial. But the difference between the two is not so clear as the Jewish-Christian schism has led us to imagine, and the Israelite relatives in view are not "all non-Christian Jews" nor "representatives" of the same, but primarily those relatives of 9:1-5 and 11:28-32, who are known to the church in Rome. They are Israelites, but we have no reason to totalize them by identifying them as all of "Israel according to the flesh" or some such.

   Without keeping this in mind, readers like Wright repeatedly understand the "they" and the "them" of Romans 9–11 as "Israel according to the flesh," "ethnic Israel," or the like. It leads Wright to paraphrase the questions of 11:1 and 11:11 in his *Romans* as "Can any Jews then be saved?" and "Can any more Jews then be saved?" respectively (cf. the *Judenfrage* in ch. 4 above). But such stingy questions, and the gloss of "saved," misconstrue Paul's assertion that God did not disown and will not disown any of God's people as an assertion that God might well save some while apparently disowning the rest—hardly the "riches" of 9:23, 10:12, and 11:33 (cf. Wright's extraordinary claim on *PFG*, 1213: Paul's "point, here and throughout the section [presumably 11:16-24], is that they are not automatically *not* saved. That is the rhetorical thrust of the entire chapter, and in a measure of the whole of chapters 9-11" emphasis his). Wright has simply collapsed the elect into the already saved, implying that those Israelites not yet saved are not in fact Israel and have been removed from "the single family of Abraham" (*PFG*, 1205; Wright then says on 1254 that "unbelieving Jews still belong...[to] the physical family of Abraham, Isaac and Jacob.").

   The sense of 11:1 is not "So this is the question I must raise at last" about contemporary "Israel according to the flesh" in general (against Wright, 675), but "How are we to read Isa. 65:2?" It is that scriptural verse rather than the current scenario of 9:1ff that directly induces the question of Rom. 11:1, as indicated by the aorist tense of μὴ ἀπώσατο. The relatives of 9:1-5 are not the whole of ὁ λαός αὐτοῦ (10:21-11:1). Moreover, Paul is ἐκ σπέρματος Ἀβραάμ (11:1), just as his relatives of 9:1-5 are σπέρμα (9:7-8); he is not ἐκ σπέρματος Ἀβραάμ to the exclusion of such relatives (against Wright, 675). Wright's reading gives Paul's claim of Rom. 11:1 a force opposite to the one it has (i.e., "Don't worry about the relatives in view because they don't count as seed like I do" vs. "As part of the same seed as my relatives of 9:1-5, I am a witness to the fact that God did not forsake God's people and so has not forsaken my relatives of 9:1-5."). Realizing that there must be some force in this direction rather than the one he has

This remnant is without grounds for boasting, for it has come to be according to an election of grace and therefore not according to works, whether its own obedient ones or the disobedient works of the rest of Israel (11:5-6).[68] The obedient remnant has not suddenly become the sum total of the elect people.[69] Rather, as we saw in chapters 4–5 above, God's election of Israel has always ordered the whole of Israel in the flesh as distinct from gentile peoples through internal distinctions (e.g., the election of David and the tribe of Judah over Saul and the tribe of Benjamin, or the seven thousand over the rest who bowed the knee to Baal [11:2-4]).[70]

Here again, Paul anticipates the upshot of his argument, for if the distinction of the remnant is by grace rather than by works, then its members (or their non-Jewish Christian sisters and brothers among God's beloved in Rome) have no place to stand in judgment upon the disobedient (i.e., they stand by grace rather than works, and even their Jewish enemies have stumbled by grace rather than by works).[71] The readers have no justification for attempting to disown them, to

taken, Wright adds what is nowhere in the text: some of Israel like Paul have come to faith "and many more will follow" (677).

68. See Barth's comments on the significance of Paul's emphasis on his being "Benjaminite" (*CD*, II/2, 268–69; cf. Taubes, *The Political Theology of Paul*, 50).

69. That is not the sense of Rom. 11:7.

70. See Barth's excellent description of the election that operates at once within and as the border of Israel, particularly the way that it is *in* time (*CD*, II/2, 271–72). See also ch. 5 above. The purchase of this description here is that election within Israel is for the sake of all Israel and is itself the working out of the election of Israel. Israel does not suddenly contract to the remnant, as Wright imagines.

71. Cf. Rom. 2:1ff. See Barth's comments on the remnant, not as preserved in recognition of their faith, but for God's own purpose and for the sake of all Israel (ibid., 271). Nevertheless, we should avoid Barth's recourse to the concept of representation (i.e., the remnant represents the whole of Israel). This preempts the history of Israel in the flesh and claims too much for the remnant (e.g., "the true Israel," ibid., 274). Barth is better when he says that faith is "the confidence that dares to wait" for the fulfilment of the promise to Israel (ibid., 272). It is the solidarity of this faith with the rest of Israel that allows the elect remnant to "stand also for the whole of Israel" (ibid., 272–73). "The Gentile Christians must consider that the very thing which they have against the unbelieving Jews, their attitude to Jesus repeated in their attitude to Paul and the Christian Church, in a most remarkable fulfilment of Isa. 2:2-4; 25:6; Jer. 3:17; Zech. 2:11; 8:20f, has become the presupposition of their own salvation" (ibid., 279).

exclude them from the table of Israel's blessing. They are to love them as their own according to God's election.[72]

Paul now reiterates in 11:7 what he stated in 9:31: Israel as a whole did not obtain the life of blessing (i.e., righteousness) it sought. But whereas earlier in the argument Paul followed the path of the gentiles (with some Jews) who have obtained it by God's mercy rather than by works in contrast to those Israelites who have pursued it by works (9:30ff), here he proceeds with the token remnant within Israel according to an election of grace. Likewise not by works, the remnant has obtained the life of blessing promised to Israel while the rest of Israel were dulled. The passive voice of ἐπωρώθησαν (11:7b) is crucial, for nowhere in what follows does Paul inculpate the dulled.[73] Instead, he adduces selections from the same texts with which he has been working in the preceding argument (Deuteronomy, Isaiah, and the Psalms) to claim that the current dulling is a work of God (Rom. 11:8-10), as it has been in Israel's past.

Paul emerges from these quotations hearkening back to the salvation of gentiles that he introduced with previous quotations from the same biblical sources (9:24-32). He claims that the disobedience of some in Israel has occasioned God's blessing the gentiles with salvation, so as to make the dulled in Israel jealous (Rom. 11:11-14;

---

72. Agamben's reading of the remnant evinces a neglect of the election of Israel. Key to the political legacy of Paul's letters, says Agamben, the remnant is what is continuously left by Apelles's cut (*The Time That Remains*, 53). "It allows for a new perspective that dislodges our antiquated notions of a people and a democracy, however impossible it may be to completely renounce them. The people is neither the all nor the part, neither the majority nor the minority. Instead it is that which can never coincide with itself, as all or as part, that which infinitely remains or resists in each division, and, with all due respect to those who govern us, never allows us to be reduced to a majority or a minority. This remnant is the figure, or the substantiality assumed by a people in a decisive moment, and as such is the only real political subject" (57). The problem here is the way the subjectivity of the remnant has been shorn from the rest of "the people" whom God has elected into being, the way that its living debt to the past in the flesh is relativized to become, if anything, a mere abstraction.

73. This is not to say that they bear no responsibility, only that that responsibility is not what determines their current condition according to the argument, which is concerned primarily with how the readers are to relate to them.

cf. 10:19).[74] Paul insists that the dulled did not stumble in sin with the result that they fell altogether. If through their transgression salvation has come to the gentiles, if their transgression means the riches of the cosmos and their shortage the riches of the nations, then how could their election culminate in God's repudiation of them? They can hardly serve so merciful a purpose only to be cast aside![75] God's merciful election of them means that this blessing of gentiles and their being dulled are also for their sake—their dulling and jealousy will eventuate in their embrace.[76] If their shortage has meant such tremendous blessing for the gentile nations, how much more does it entail their own being filled?[77]

---

74. Wright imagines that "jealousy" from the quotation of Deut. 32:21 in Rom. 10:19 "appeared purely negative" and is only now in Rom. 11:14 "turned to positive effect" (*Romans*, 680). But this is simply Wright's having lost the thread of the argument and now happened back upon it. The rest of Deuteronomy 32 of course goes on to describe the salvation that will eventuate from Israel's jealousy.

75. Throughout this section, Wright repeatedly compares the "casting away" of "Israel" to the "casting away" of Jesus the Messiah (e.g., ibid., 681–83, 685, 694), but he cannot see that this is precisely how Paul shows the Israelites in view to be inscribed in the messianic history of Israel, i.e., the history of promise (cf. Barth, *CD*, II/2, 275: "As a salvation-history it also embraces perdition"). Instead, Wright imagines that the cross and resurrection of Christ divide into two Israels: one that goes the way of the cross, the other that goes the way of the resurrection (and judgment and grace as competing principles in God or as a zero-sum game, i.e., judgment cannot be gracious and grace cannot include judgment). "Judgment must be judgment if grace is to be grace. . . . If God's covenant faithfulness has been revealed in the death of the beloved son, we should not expect the covenant to be effective for any who reject that son, and that death, as the long-awaited unveiling of God's saving plan" (678).

Here Wright misunderstands the Christology of Paul at its most basic. It is precisely because God's covenant by election is effective for those who have rejected that Son that there is hope for any, for our hope is not a matter of our adequate response but of God's gracious election of us. "While *we* were *still* sinners Christ died for *us*" (Rom. 5:8). Wright is better when Paul's rhetoric is unmistakeable (11:28-31): the likeness of the disobedient in Israel to Jesus (i.e., their being "cast away") means mercy for Israel (694; see also his insightful claim that the remnant does not escape the verdict of judgment but comes through it to new life on 675). And of course Wright is correct that this mercy for Israel is not only for some exotic end-time salvation but for the present (also on 683).

76. "According to this passage, hope in the revelation of Jesus Christ, which is the life of faith, stands or falls with hope for Israel" (Barth, *CD*, II/2, 284). The truth of this claim reflects very poorly on the "faith" of the Christian church that has not sustained this hope, to say nothing of those who denied it and sought to eradicate it (e.g., ibid., 292, where Barth says that losing this hope is losing our faith).

Paul pauses here at 11:13 to gather his readers for the pronouncement he has been working towards since 9:1. In the previous verses he has been speaking about the life of blessing in which his non-Jewish messianic readers along with a remnant of Jews like him within Israel find themselves only by God's gracious election. Now the apostle "acclaims" his own service of leading such gentiles to the obedience of faith in Israel's Messiah, in hopes that this glorifying of his service may somehow move his flesh—the relatives in view in 9:1-5—to jealousy, drawing some of them to the table of Israel's messianic blessing (Rom. 11:13-15).[78] Far from the withering

77. Wright misses the rhetorical force of the passage, inferring that Israel's dulling is ambiguous with regard to Israel's future, depending on whether Israel comes to faith in Jesus (*Romans*, 677). On his reading, the response to the question of 11:11 would not be μὴ γένοιτο but "Maybe . . . it's up to them." Cf. the self-constitution of the modern discourse of peoplehood in ch. 3 above. But the whole point, as Barth discerns (*CD*, II/2, 276–77, 79), is that if the transgression of some in Israel (i.e., their being dulled) has meant such riches for the cosmos and the gentiles, how much more does it mean τὸ πλήρωμα of them, i.e., their own enriching or filling? The antecedent of αὐτῶν in 11:12 is the dulled rather than a subgroup thereof.

To soften his reading that "unbelieving Israel is hardened permanently," Wright allows that "particular [Israelite] individuals" can come to faith (677). But there is no Israelite whole-individual duality here or anywhere else in Romans; Israelites like Paul do not come to confess Jesus as Messiah (or do anything else) only as individuals and not as Israel. Wright is working with a mythological Israelite form or whole that is excepted by individual Israelite faith. "The judgment is simply the other side of the coin of ethnic Israel's rejection of the crucified Messiah" (cf. "Israel as a whole" on 676; "Jewish unbelievers as a whole" on 686). Rhetorically, such claims by Paul could hardly inspire what is in fact the purpose of the argument: Christian patience with the Israelite relatives of Paul in view. There is no permanent dulling of Israel in the Bible, only a dulling that must run its limited course (see Barth on "the provisional nature of this divine measure" in *CD*, II/2, 278).

2 Macc. 6:13-16, which Wright regards as "suggestive" for Romans 9–11 (639, 677) and is the basis of his description of "hardening" (676–77, 683, 688), is explicitly about what God does to Israel's lawless enemies and does *not* do to Israel, "from whom God never withdraws mercy but, disciplining with misfortune, does not forsake his people (οὐδέποτε μὲν τὸν ἔλεον ἀφ᾽ ἡμῶν ἀφίστησιν, παιδεύων δὲ μετὰ συμφορᾶς οὐκ ἐγκαταλείπει τὸν ἑαυτοῦ λαόν, v. 16).

78. That Paul hopes to save "some" of his flesh does not imply that God will save only some of Israel (against Wright, *Romans*, 682). Israel's future is not limited to what Paul himself hopes to do. The sense of εἴ πως παραζηλώσω μου τὴν σάρκα καὶ σώσω τινὰς ἐξ αὐτῶν (v. 14) is that of Paul's desperately groping for whatever he can get, i.e., "if somehow, some way, I might make my flesh jealous and save some of them." Paul says self-mockingly—and thus to great rhetorical effect—that this is the glory of his apostolic service to gentiles like the readers (v. 13). He is like the shepherd who refuses to settle for the ninety-nine sheep already gathered and strikes out for the stray, however offensive this obsession is to the ninety-nine.

of God's word, their temporary deprivation of promised covenant blessing by God has meant cosmic reconciliation, in which the non-Jewish readers have been caught up. And since that is the case, what can God's fully embracing Paul's flesh mean but the consummation of Israel's election—life from the dead?[79]

Wright imagines that the prospect of saving some is what enables Paul to answer "No" to the questions of 11:1 and 11:11. "God will always be faithful to the promise to Abraham. ... There will always be some of Abraham's physical descendants who are included in the true 'seed.' That is all that the promise envisaged; that is the whole point of 9:6-29; and God will be true to the promise" (682). So Wright has now let ethnic purity as a constituent of the elect people of God in through the back door (he reverts to denying this on 684 and back again to asserting it on 693). And he takes Paul to be saying that as long as there is an ethnic sample of Abraham's descendants among the saved (two "full-blooded" Israelites? A hundred? A sizeable minority?) God will have kept all God's promises to Israel.

This is hard to reckon with any passage of the Tanakh, much less the whole. It renders empty God's promises and therefore God's salvation (including the life and hope of the Christian church). Here and elsewhere, Wright is concerned not to spoil what he imagines as the prescribed procedure of salvation of Rom. 10:9-10 (the "route" which he acknowledges he must "assume" in the present context of Rom. 11:13-15 [682]). He implies that only those who confess with their mouths that Jesus is Lord and believe in their hearts that God raised him from the dead will be saved. Besides excluding the many people in Israel and the rest of the world throughout time who did not hear about Jesus (unless they hear about him in death and can confess him in death), reading Rom. 10:9-10 as a prescribed procedure is a misconstrual. Moreover, as the argument proceeds, Paul does not attribute the unbelief of his relatives in view primarily to a failure to follow the procedure but to God's inhibiting them and making them stumble (11:8-10). This stumbling has served God's saving purpose and therefore anticipates their salvation (11:12, 16, 25-32), which in turn will unfold, as Wright correctly insists, as they obey the Messiah.

Paul's point in 10:9-10 is not that only those who follow this procedure will be saved but that the word and faith of the readers about Jesus is the Deuteronomic word that God has brought near to them to save them, i.e., their righteousness comes from God rather than themselves. It is not works—faithful covenant practices that some Jews might claim as the basis of their life of blessing, or a competing list the non-Jewish readers might similarly and mimetically claim—but the Lord that is the hope and life of the people of God and therefore makes the readers who they are. Christians must indeed insist (according to the grammar of the faith) that God calls everyone to confess Jesus as Lord (e.g., Phil. 2:10-11) and that no one is saved but by the God of Israel through the Lord Jesus. But this "through" is not exclusively confession and belief before death. That everyone who calls upon the name of the Lord will be saved does not imply that anyone who doesn't will not. The Christian confession is not the means by which anyone must save himself but the witness to the one by whom any are saved, i.e., the Christian witness to Jesus as Lord and savior. That Wright perceives the Christian procedure of salvation to be threatened by an unconditioned mercy of God suggests that he may be channeling the very threat that Paul is warning us against.

79. "In this very hardening He has really made them more than ever His main concern. This must be noted by Gentile Christians, too, who would like to regard the hardened as forsaken. God has so little forsaken them that it is for their sake that He has stretched out His hand to the

What does this mean for the way the readers are to engage the Israelite relatives of Paul that have been in view since 9:1-5? It means they are to regard them as holy.[80] If the "first portion" (ἀπαρχὴ) of the dough—that is, the token Israelite remnant Paul has just named—is holy, then so is the whole lump—that is, the whole of Israel (Rom. 11:16a).[81] And so Paul will now move explicitly to persuade his readers not to despise these relatives of his who have become their enemies because of the gospel, but to love them according to the merciful purpose of God's election. This purpose has seized the readers in mercy through the hostility of some of God's elect; the

Gentiles. The existence of Gentiles as recipients of salvation has the meaning and purpose of a summons to these hardened Jews and therefore of a confirmation of their eternal election" (Barth, *CD*, II/2, 279). "The Gentile mission and the Gentile Church have as such no δόξα of their own. They share in the δόξα of Israel by serving it. . . . This is the meaning of their baptism and their faith (Rom. 10:9-10)" (Barth *CD*, II/2, 281).

80. Wright acknowledges that "this section of the letter is an argument against Gentile arrogance" (*Romans*, 681) while he has variously claimed that previous parts of Romans 9–11 (all which he repeatedly says is one train of thought) are about something else. In the interest of his consistent appeal to the readers since 9:1, Paul here subordinates his entire mission to the gentiles (i.e., including the non-Jewish readers) to God's electing purpose for the dulled. Thus, Wright's foil of Jewish ethnocentrism or "automatic" salvation is further exposed as baseless. He supposes that Paul is warning "against Gentiles falling into the trap of assuming an ethnic superiority, the trap Paul sees the Jews having fallen into" (681).

This reading has the virtue of recognizing that what Paul has said about the life of righteousness in which the readers find themselves goes to the way in which they must treat Paul's relatives of 9:1-5. Its flaw is that it mistakes as a warning against ethnocentrism or some analagously secure "status" what is clearly a warning against righteousness by "works." And if "Jew" does not in fact name an ethnicity (see ch. 5 above), then "gentile" or "Christian" most certainly does not. On what basis would "Gentiles [of Rome] fall into the trap of assuming 'an ethnic superiority'" merely as gentiles? Wright is forced to thin out this false "status" or "superiority" even further on 686: "But they must 'remain in God's kindness,' in other words, maintain their position simply by trust in God rather than by reliance on their own social, cultural, or ethnic status."

81. I agree with Wright's reading of "the whole lump" on *Romans*, 683 (except that it should not be restricted to Israel according to the flesh any more than the subsequent tree metaphor should). But he does not allow this reading (nor his reading that "Jews, even unbelieving ones, belong to [the tree] by nature," 686) to inform the sense of the argument. Apparently for Wright, that "the whole lump" is holy and "not disposable" does not mean that God will not dispose of most of it. Wright does not see that God's election precedes, anticipates, and thus exceeds the presence of God's salvation. He therefore has no way of holding together as elect Israel those Israelites who are not yet saved and those Israelites who are. But the point in Romans 11 is not that "God is, after all, well capable of bringing them back again" (685) but that God has never let them go in the first place and so will deliver them.

same purpose therefore calls upon the readers as among God's elect to be merciful toward these now family members who are hostile to them.[82]

Paul changes metaphors in the middle of v. 16, and with the change he draws a subtle inference that segues into the final piece of the argument before its conclusion: if the holy first portion can be drawn only from a whole lump that is holy, then all the parts that issue from the holy base (i.e., not from the first portion offered but from the beginning of the batch) of that whole are holy. But here Paul has switched from sacrificial dough to a tree. The whole is now compared to a tree with a holy root, and its parts are the branches, which are therefore also holy. Thus, Paul is not saying that the remnant is the root but that the remnant and the rest of the tree share a common root (or base of the dough).[83] In 11:28, that this root is the ancestors of Israel (i.e., Abraham, Isaac, and Jacob) will be made explicit,[84] and from 11:16b to 11:28 Paul elucidates what he has been driving at since 9:1 and claimed in summary form in

82. Paul's claim is far stronger than that "God still wants and intends to save more Jews" (against Wright, ibid., 684).

83. Puzzlingly, Wright suggests that the remnant must be "branches that were broken off and then grafted back in again. Otherwise Paul's protestations about grace in 11:5-6 would be undermined" (ibid., 684). Assuming for a moment that the tree is to be identified with Israel, Wright imagines that the tree of Israel has effectively started from scratch with Jesus and that those of the remnant could have found themselves in the tree of Israel before Jesus only by "ethnic membership" and "Torah-observance" (i.e., not by grace). But Paul's claim in Romans 9–11—his reading of Scripture—is that from Abraham up, the tree of Israel has been a matter of God's gracious election and not of Israel's works, which remain secondary. He has of course said nothing for or against "ethnic membership." He implies that God's election has preceded and inhabited any Israelite continuity by procreation and socialization of children and only thus is *in* such procreation and socialization (Rom. 9:11). The problem here is that Wright imagines that grace is a "principle" (676) that could be violated, when in Romans 9–11 grace is a complex history, the history of God's election in the flesh that has seized and held in hope both the readers and Paul's relatives in view.

84. Against Wright (ibid., 684) and Barth (*CD*, II/2, 285) who regard the root as Messiah. The "root" recalls the beginning of the argument in Romans 9, when Paul rehearsed the history of election from Abraham by Isaac to Jacob/Israel, of whom the relatives of Paul in view are part. Nevertheless, the root of the ancestors should not be played off against the Messiah (and here Wright's and Barth's intuitions are right) because the Messiah is the life and promise by which the tree has grown, and continues to grow, from root to branches.

11:13-15: the non-Jewish Christians of Rome are without grounds for disowning any of the branches of the tree of promise into which they have been grafted. On the contrary, all such branches remain part of the very ground on which the non-Jewish readers stand. The non-Jewish Christians of Rome are therefore to regard the relatives of Paul in view—who have become hostile to them—as holy, beloved for the sake of the ancestors according to God's election.

The main (imperative) verb of Rom. 11:17-18 is μὴ κατακαυχῶ. This stands over the entire development of the tree metaphor (11:17-24) and is its point. Paul instructs the readers not to boast *against* other branches and concludes the image with its rhetorical aim: ἵνα μὴ ἦτε [παρ'] ἑαυτοῖς φρόνιμοι ("that you might not be wise in your own estimation").[85] This is not the first time Paul has warned against boasting in the letter. In Romans 2, he has warned against boasting in the law in such a way that non-Jewish, messianic believers in the God of Israel are wrongly (and fictitiously) deprived of a place at Israel's table (2:16-29; cf. 4:2). One can boast only in the God who gave Messiah while we were still sinners, with nothing of ourselves to boast in. This God who loves God's enemies calls upon us to love our enemies (Rom. 5:1-11). Correlatively, in Rom. 11:17-24 the inhospitality of non-Jewish Christian boasting is without basis because "you are not upholding the root but the root is upholding you" (Rom. 11:18). The rhetorical force of the tree metaphor, then, is not to give the readers a picture of who is in and who is out so that they might decide that difference or otherwise enact it. It is to move them to be patient and hospitable in the face of the inhospitality of the Israelite sisters and brothers in view since 9:1.[86] To disown such

85. Note the similarity of the construction in Rom. 12:16: τὸ αὐτὸ εἰς ἀλλήλους φρονοῦντες, μὴ τὰ ὑψηλὰ φρονοῦντες ἀλλὰ τοῖς ταπεινοῖς συναπαγόμενοι. μὴ γίνεσθε φρόνιμοι παρ' ἑαυτοῖς ("being of the mentality of unity with one another, not of the mentality of the proud, but rather being carried away with the lowly, do not become *wise in your own estimation*.").
86. So Barth, *CD*, II/2, 292.

family members would only be to forget who they the readers are, to forget and assail the very tree that sustains them.[87]

Paul anticipates an objection to his claim that all the branches of the tree are holy in 11:19: "Branches were broken off that I might be grafted in." "Very well," Paul answers,

> They were broken off through faithlessness, but you have come to be where you are through faith. Don't be of the mentality of the proud but fear, for if God did not exempt [i.e., from the breaking off that is God's judgment] those who are branches according to nature, neither will God exempt you. (Rom. 11:20-21)

Paul proceeds to claim that the current disparity of participation in Israel's promised blessings is nothing the objector to his argument can boast about; it has nothing to do with him. It is a matter of the kindness and severity of the God of Israel. The place of the objector at the table of Israel's promised blessing is no more secure than was that of the relatives of Paul in view: the objector will be cut off if he does not remain in the kindness of God, and the relatives of Paul in view will be grafted back in as they stop persisting in faithlessness.[88] In fact, if anything, the promise of the participation of these Israelite

---

87. "Precisely in its Gentile Christian members the Church would have to regard itself as forsaken if it tried to think and say this of Israel or even of the hardened in Israel" (ibid., 285). Also, that the obedient remain united to the disobedient shows that the life of the people is based not on its obedience but on the God who holds the obedient and the disobedient—all Israel—together.

88. This gives the lie to every modern nationalism, insofar as it is predicated on disowning part of the community and starting over as a supposedly brand new "people," as in "We the People...." For some reason Wright does not assign to Christian branches (as Paul does) the same precarious conditionality he does to the Jewish branches that have been removed (*Romans*, 686), taking such to run counter the argument of Rom. 3:21—8:39 (cf. his description of the μή πως variant of 11:21 as "appropriately reverent" [685n444]). Consequently, he resorts to a baseless distinction between individual Christian security and corporate Christian (i.e., ecclesial) insecurity, strangely adducing Phil. 1:6. Phil. 1:6 is in fact about the security of the Philippian church on the basis of God's work, rather than the security of its individual members (note the plural second person pronouns throughout Philippians 1, which appear to be semantically collective rather than distributive). Nowhere is the argument of Romans 9–11 predicated on any distinction between Israelites and Israel (or Christians and the church), which remain inextricable and mutually constitutive.

relatives of Paul in the table of Israel's promised blessings is less in doubt than that of the objector already seated at that table: "For if you were removed from a naturally wild [i.e., gentile] olive tree and were grafted against nature into a cultivated olive tree, how much more will these very ones [i.e., the Israelite relatives of Paul in view] be grafted according to nature into their own tree" (Rom. 11:24)?!89

11:25-36

Paul moves from the tree metaphor to his closing appeal to his readers to be merciful toward the Israelite relatives of his that have become their enemies and been in view since 9:1-5 (and before). He does not want his readers to be ignorant of the mystery at which he has hinted with his tree metaphor in order that they not be wise in their own estimation, that is, that they not disown his Israelite relatives in view because of their own supposedly superior politics.90 The mystery? "A dulling from a part of Israel has issued forth until the fullness of the gentiles comes in and thus all Israel will be saved" (Rom. 11:25-26).91 The dulling that is issuing from some in Israel

89. Notice how Barth criticizes the conventional Christian telling of the Jewish-Christian schism as pretending "to judge that God had left and forsaken His people": "How can they arrive at the obscure distinction between 'Judaism' and 'Christianity' as between two separate religions and worlds succeeding one another?" (Barth, *CD*, II/2, 293).

90. "Although the term 'mystery' is finally introduced with reference to the enigmatic delay in the conversion of Israel, it embraces the three chapters in their entirety, and the whole problem posed by them. The aim is to prevent them [the readers] from becoming . . . ἑαυτοῖς φρόνιμοι, i.e., from being wise with a wisdom of their own devising, from building on their own wisdom and in that way grounding themselves in themselves" (ibid., 299).

91. The salvation of all Israel includes all the branches added from among the gentiles as well as all the branches cut off and finally grafted in again. "It is in this way [of the first being last and the last being first] and only in this way that this deliverance of all Israel occurs as an act of the divine mercy and is characterised as such. . . . Only as it occurs in this inversion can this deliverance be the effect and fruit of the divine election which is itself that of God's mercy. . . . The last will be first because the Deliverer obviously takes the part of those who are lost, doing for them just what will help them" (ibid., 301). The danger here is regarding (non-Christian) Jews as somehow more primordial or original or first than others in Israel. The idea should be that some embraced by election all along (i.e., part of Israel) will be saved through their disobedience, consequent upon God's saving according to election those once excluded by election (i.e., gentiles) together with some of all-along-elect Israel such as Paul.

is but a moment in God's salvation of all Israel (i.e., including the dulled part), a moment that serves the welcoming of all the gentiles to Israel's table of promised blessings and can therefore only indicate mercy finally for all Israel.[92] This is how the enemies of Israel will be destroyed. They will give up their divisive gods and take their seats at Israel's table as fellow worshippers of the one true God, the God of Israel. Thus, the dulled in Israel will be left without gentile idolaters to oppose. As Paul's quotation of Isa. 59:20-21 and Isa. 27:9 attests, God's electing purpose for Israel is not to confirm part of Israel in its sins but, through the Deliverer of Zion, to remove the sins of all Israel, to save all Israel. That is God's covenant with Israel (11:26-27).[93]

92. And this welcoming of the fullness of the gentiles, itself induced by the dulling of part of Israel, is in service to that dulled part of Israel. Its purpose is to make the dulled part of Israel jealous and thus draw them to their seats at the table of Israel's salvation. This is how the non-Jewish Christian readers are to understand their role in God's salvation economy: they are servants of the jealousy, and therefore the salvation, of the dulled part of Israel. What a glorious role Paul assigns to readers who would disregard God's election and disown his flesh. Wright seems to miss the degrading irony here (*PFG*, 1203-04).

93. There is of course no justification for reading "Israel" in 11:26 as different from "Israel" in 11:25 (against Wright, *Romans*, 690). Wright articulately shows that Christians from among the gentiles have become Israelite, while denying the supersession of one Israel by another. He then rightly claims that Israel is "transformed, through the death and resurrection of Israel's own Messiah and the Spirit of Israel's own God" (690). But he conceives of this transformation not as healing—as the resurrection of the body that died—but as a redefinition. In fact, he goes so far as to say that Paul himself "was redefining 'Israel'" (690; cf. Wagner, *Heralds of the Good News*, 49).

This does not improve much upon traditional Christian supersessionism and plays right into the violent tendencies of the modern discourse of peoplehood (which has also had room for a "remnant," as long as it has been White). Wright has cut the πᾶς of 11:26 loose from (his own reading of) the holy φύραμα and κλάδοι of 11:16. The "dramatic irony" of this redefinition of Israel (so that "all Israel" is not all Israel but all of the right Israel, i.e., those who are like "us") is supposed by Wright to be the climax of the argument of Romans 9–11, which has been about God's irrevocable election of Israel, God's compassion, God's faithfulness, God's mercy, and therefore God's call upon the readers to be patient with the relatives of Paul in view throughout. A redefinition of "Israel" at 11:26a is not a climax but a case of the old bait and switch, not the triumph of a crescendo but the hollow discord of a botched finale.

Wright cannot read 11:26b as it is in Isaiah 59 (LXX). According to Wright, the Deliverer has not removed ungodliness from Jacob but from some of Jacob (or from one Jacob and not the other), leaving ungodliness in the rest and de-Jacobizing it. God's covenant, on his reading, is not to take away the sins of Israel but the sins of some Israel, leaving sin in the rest and de-Israelizing it. By reducing God's election of Israel to those who elect God according to the

Israel's sins invited gentile invasion and exile according to the prescribed curses of the covenant, but, as also promised in the covenant, the Deliverer has brought the forgiveness of sins to Israel, pouring God's love into Israel and turning the gentiles to worship the God of Israel in his name, thus making peace. Such is the power of the faith, obedience, and love of Israel's Messiah that have been thematic to Romans. Even Israel's sins have proven the occasion of God's mercy among the gentiles who were their enemies, and so now such non-Jews who serve the God of Israel in the name of Jesus must extend mercy to their Jewish enemies, who are their brothers and sisters. Such is the embracing movement of God's election of Israel. "According to the gospel they are indeed enemies for your sake, but

established Christian procedure, Wright has deprived the promise of election of its promise, including its promise for the Christian church (cf. the de-Israelization of non-Christian Israel, *PFG*, 540–41; de-judaization of non-Christian Jews, ibid., 545; "If Israel according to the flesh is now, for the most part, 'hardened', Paul sees this as the necessary placing of them in the same category as Gentiles…," ibid., 1254). But God's provision of forgiveness is not that of a "path" or a "means" to forgiveness to which we must then add our own work to secure. God provides forgiveness itself, walking the path for us in Christ and then in us as Christ by the Spirit (see Barth, *CD*, II/2, 244; IV/1, 219–83). God does not elect a path or a means but elects God's Son, and the covenant people and its persons in him.

Wright argues that if "all Israel will be saved" means what it says, Paul "could have saved himself a lot of heartache: 9:1-5 would be beside the point" (*PFG*,1213). "If, after all, Paul really did believe that those presently 'hardened' would sooner or later be rescued by a fresh divine act…then why the tears? Why the unceasing anguish of heart? Why the heartfelt prayer for 'their' salvation…" (ibid., 1238)? One can venture this dismissal from behind a desk where salvation is a matter of statistics and the afterlife but not from the pastoral and brotherly place of Paul where salvation is the drama of life in the flesh. Wright's rhetorical question here is akin to asking, Why were the prophets so grieved over the exile of their people if they knew Israel would eventually be delivered? Why did they pray for that deliverance? Why did Jesus pray what he did in Gethsemane? Why the heartache over the death of Christians' loved ones if they know they will be raised from the dead and reunited? Bafflingly, Wright unwittingly dismisses the horrific pain and loss that lie along the way of and to salvation, pain that moved Paul to call upon his readers to live in hospitable hope for the rest of his family, who, we should not forget in this context, have suffered much since the time of his writing. The assurance of their eventual salvation, like the sure hope of the prophets for Israel in exile, does not remove or numb the pain of the path to deliverance. Such assurance is the christological power of service to the death, when a hope without promise is prone to cut the losses and settle for the 99. At the root of the false and violent "sacrifices" of modern peoplehood lies this hope without promise, whereby "we the people" settle for the "life" that we can secure for ourselves at the expense of others, the "life" that we can imagine rather than the one we trust God to give.

according to election they are beloved for the sake of the ancestors. For irrevocable are the gifts and naming of God" (Rom. 11:28).[94]

94. It is not the case, then, that such enemies are "gaining no life from the root" (against Wright, *Romans*, 685). Also, note Paul's unusual way of addressing the letter in relation to the language of 11:28: πᾶσιν τοῖς οὖσιν ἐν Ῥώμῃ ἀγαπητοῖς θεοῦ (Rom. 1:7; cf. Rom. 12:1). Nowhere in his comments on 11:28-29 does Wright mention or exegete the crucial term "election," and he claims that the irrevocability of the gifts and calling of God means only that an ethnically Jewish sample must be among the saved, and thus applies only to those who follow the Christian procedure of 10:9-10 (ibid., 693–94; he offers some corrective to this in his reading of 11:31). He does not realize that such "irrevocability" bankrupts Paul's appeal to the readers to love the enemies in view for the beloved Israelite sisters and brothers that they are. To say that "unbelieving Jews" find themselves in the same place as the rest of the not-yet-saved, in the "same category as [non-Christian] gentiles," and to exegete 11:28 as "they are…well within distance of God's call to faith, because of the patriarchs" (*PFG*, 1254) is to empty the whole of Romans 9–11 of its force and misapprehend its rhetoric entirely. Wright's reading is that "unbelieving Jews" are simply not any worse off than anyone else, which is to imply that the patriarchs mean nothing for them. He makes "because of the patriarchs" ring hollow.

It is here, from 11:28, that we can look back and see the intractable problems with any reading of 9:6-8ff that discerns two Israels, particularly two timeless "categories of 'Israel'" (Wright, 688; note that he takes 9:6 as the basis for a change in the meaning of "Israel" between 11:25 and 11:26 on 690). The rest of the argument will always be pressed into the service of defining one Israel over another. But the argument is that God and only God has defined one and only one Israel of promise by God's election (in the flesh), such that those brought εἰς ὑπακοὴν πίστεως (Rom. 1:5; 16:26) must embrace as their own those characterized τῇ ἀπιστίᾳ. Because of God's election, even τῇ ἀπιστίᾳ they cannot help but participate in and witness to Jesus the Messiah of Israel (Rom. 8:32). Two Israels can only undermine the rhetorical purpose of the argument, only fight against its current of oneness by God's election. The basis for the dichotomization of Israel subsequent to 9:6-8 is the supposed inadequacy of one Israel (e.g., τῇ ἀπιστίᾳ) and adequacy of the other (e.g., πίστις), but as 9:9ff clearly indicates, the only fundamental basis for the defining of Israel and the internal distinctions within Israel is the electing activity of God. It is only a further push against the grain of the argument to read the faith of some as ontically equivalent to God's election such that those without faith are de-elected. Any faith or faithlessness is not immaterial, but it remains secondary, subservient to the salvation of all according to the unrelenting mercy of God's election. The Jew-gentile church is not the sole object of this divine mercy, but the witness to this mercy for all, a mercy that refuses to settle for Israel as it is but moves it to the faith of obedience, toward the life of promised righteousness that is finally resurrection from the dead by the Spirit at work in the church (and elsewhere, no doubt). The depths to which God leads Israel (e.g., by placing before it a stone of stumbling) can only be for the sake of all Israel as it is made hospitable for the world.

If Romans 9–11 is about two Israels, then Israel is a matter of Israel's doing rather than God's election, then Paul cannot say that God has not rejected God's people (11:1), then "they" have not only stumbled but fallen (11:11), then God enriches some by means of forever depriving others, then non-Jewish Christians can boast in the works of their faith, then non-Jewish Christians can disown non-Christian Jews and Christians can disown one another on the same basis, then we must decide who is elect and who is not and enact and police the difference, then we must forgive one another sparingly, then the people of God is elect in some one or some thing other than the crucified Jew Jesus, whom the Father of Israel raised from the dead

Thus, πίστις in the God of Israel as revealed in Jesus entails loving as one's own those characterized τῇ ἀπιστίᾳ, whom God has in fact elected/named into Israelite being.

We learn in 11:28 that the Israelite relatives of Paul that have been in view all along are not just any non-Christian Jews, as if we could subsume all such communities or persons under one neat category.[95] They are particular Israelites (presumably Jews) who are openly hostile to the readers he is addressing, a hostility that has apparently moved some of the readers to repudiate them and to attempt to sanctify that repudiation by regarding them as disowned by the God of Israel.[96] But such readers in Rome are not well enough acquainted with the electing God who has seized them with blessing, with the place that is theirs at that table of blessing. That blessing is what it is because Israel's God is unrelentingly gracious, because the

to be Lord. If Romans 9–11 is about two Israels, then the God of Israel is not faithful but duplicitous. While Barth too succumbs to a dualization of Israel according to 9:6-8, unlike Wright he refuses the dichotomization of Israel and is able to track better with the subsequent argument (and subvert his own misreading of 9:6-8), because the duality remains formal and as such subservient to God's singular election of one people in the flesh. Barth's material defiance of the modern myth of ethnicity (despite his formally caving to it here and there) makes his reading both more historical and more traditional. His reading is more rooted in the Tanakh and is more christological (which go together). He realizes that the oneness of God and the oneness of the Messiah entail the fundamental and eschatological oneness of the people of the God of Israel in the flesh.

95. Against Wright, for whom the broken branches are simply "Jews who have not believed the gospel" (Romans, 685). τῇ ἀπιστίᾳ (11:20, 23), as Wright has so eloquently argued elsewhere (N. T. Wright, Jesus and the Victory of God [Minneapolis, MN: Fortress Press, 1996], 258–564), is not a matter of naked and unadorned "unbelief." It is a politics of faithlessness rather than faith, of attempting violently to secure the promised future rather than trusting God to provide it, and it is attended by God's corrective judgment rather than blessing. Faith is thus self-humbling (see Barth, CD, III/1, 31–36; cf. Agamben, The Time That Remains, 90–104). Faithlessness, then, is more particular than simply "not believing the gospel" and cannot be neatly pinned on all "non-Christian" Jews. Moreover, assuming for a moment that the tree is simply the people of Israel as Wright says, what basis have we for supposing that the many faithful Jews who had not yet heard of the Messiah well after his death and resurrection had been "broken off" or that the tree did not preexist the incarnation?

96. Wright imagines that 11:28 says that "they" are enemies not because of the gospel but because of "you" (i.e., the readers, particularly the gentile ones), as if the gospel, which is about Jesus' lordship over all and embrace of the gentiles, were thus separable from the gentile Christian readers (Romans, 693).

gifts and calling of the God of Israel are irrevocable (Rom. 11:29), because the word of God cannot wither (9:6).[97] Because the faithfulness of the God of Israel is at stake in these Israelite enemies, the readers have no hope that is not the hope of these enemies; to regard them as anything other than elect family would be to attempt to cut off the branch on which they themselves are sitting. The gifts and calling of God thus show all to be loved, not because of their obedience, but because of God's election and therefore even through their disobedience, that God might be merciful to all and form of the world one people of overflowing mercy (Rom. 11:32).

The readers were once disobedient but have now received mercy through the disobedience of the Israelite relatives of Paul in view, who continue the ways of those who were hostile to Jesus (11:30). That hostility has been the occasion of mercy for the non-Jewish readers, who have been moved by the message of Jesus' faith to become faithful to the God of Israel in him. In the same way, the Israelite relatives of Paul in view "have now disobeyed through mercy upon you in order that they themselves might be shown mercy" (Rom. 11:31).[98] God's mercy upon the now Israelite readers from among the gentiles has inspired the disobedient hostility of the Israelites of 9:4-5 and 11:28ff so that these latter too, moved by jealousy, will receive that mercy. This is the hope by which we the readers must live. God's electing purpose is mercy for all (Rom. 11:32). It is not limited by or to those in Israel who prove subjectively adequate to God's revelation. The lag of the flesh in Israel's being formed by God's election is where the severity of the God of Israel

---

97. The statement of 11:29 "reminds us distinctly of 9:6: 'The word of God cannot fail of its effect.' We must certainly understand that more general statement, and indeed the whole of chapters 9 and 10, from the point of view of this saying in 11:29" (Barth, *CD*, II/2, 302).

98. That is, they have responded to their God's unconditional embrace of gentiles in the name of Jesus with envious hostility, and this is God's mysterious and merciful moving them toward salvation.

is revealed (as it also is within the church in Israel, per 11:21-22). But because the purpose of God's election is finally and unequivocally mercy for all, that severity is but a moment in God's kindness, a kindness that refuses our refusal to love as God loves.[99] What could this draw from us but an encomium like Romans 11:33-36?

Final Observations

1) The tree of Rom. 11:17-24 cannot be reduced to those of Israelite "status" or "identity," language and concepts that are foreign to Romans and the rest of the Bible. Throughout the Bible, Israel is a complex, unfolding political reality that is being shaped across time concretely in the flesh rather than one of many abstract realms of identities and statuses. Imposing such abstractions on the sense in which the tree is Israel invites readers to understand ἐκκλάω (Rom. 11:17-19) as the removal of branches from Israel such that they are no longer Israel in any meaningful sense.[100] But the argument of Romans 9–11 clearly insists that those who ἐξεκλάσθησαν figure among the promised descendants of the ancestors of Israel, for whose sake they remain beloved (in contrast to Esau in 9:13). Despite and even through their enmity, they are Israel by God's election—not because they are ethnic descendants of those ancestors but because, through a veritable sea of historical contingencies ordered by God's faithfulness (chapter 5 above), they have found themselves named Israel, calling out to the name of the God of those ancestors as their own. Consequently, being "broken off" does not mean being immediately severed from the people of Israel, as if it were possible for

---

99. In 11:32, Wright correctly reads the "all" whom God has enclosed in disobedience as cosmic in scope, i.e., the whole human race, but then reads the "all" five words later in the parallel as "all kinds," i.e., the two kinds of Jew and gentile (*Romans*, 687, 694). He is concerned that the cosmic scope of the latter would undermine the exclusive Christian salvation procedure of 10:9-10 (e.g., 683, 693). But exegetically (in 11:32), this is special pleading. The God revealed in Israel and as Jesus per Romans 9–11 invites us to live in a much wider, catholic hope.

100. Barth recognizes this problem (*CD*, II/2, 291).

an Israelite person or community to be declared illegitimately Israelite or alien by virtue of their subjective inadequacy.[101] Israel includes the branches broken off in Rom. 11:17-24. Such branches are not broken off into nothingness.[102] They do not immediately become gentile. They remain, as Paul argues, "holy." Recall that the whole rhetorical drift of Romans 9–11 is against non-Jewish Christian boasting in the face of Paul's hostile Israelite relatives in view and toward their loving such relatives as embraced by God's scandalous election, not toward a basis for such Christians to define Israel and exclude them.

While the tree metaphor must not be pressed to mean something beyond its use in the course of Paul's argument, I think we may venture the following description. The tree is the unfolding life of Israel. Not being broken off but remaining well placed in it at the present stage of its growth is to be enjoying the life of Israel toward which the mercy of God's election forms and moves Israel and incorporates gentiles, the still-transformative or saving life that we might call the Israelite table of blessing (i.e., righteousness). This salvation or blessing is the fruit of the kingdom of the God of Israel. It is a table too hospitable to be limited by the choice of food and drink (and the political economic restriction this implies). It is "righteousness and peace and joy in the Holy Spirit" (Rom. 14:17), the blessing or shared life promised to Israel's most ancient ancestors, who are the root of the tree, and to their descendants of promise ever since. As their being "broken off" implies, Paul's relatives in view since 9:1-5 have grown from this very tree as it flourished into the time of the past generation. But now in the dawning of the age of

101. Cf. Lev. 1:17, where ἐκκλάω is explicitly distinguished from severing. Breaking a stock branch in order to graft a scion branch into the stock tree in its place usually does not involve severing the stock branch altogether, but breaking it enough to insert the scion into the exposed flesh of the stock tree (see, e.g., Pliny the Elder, *Natural History*, 17:22–29).
102. Note that the word for the way that gentiles have been cut from their natural trees (ἐκκόπτω) is not the same as the word for what has happened to those dulled in Israel (ἐκκλάω).

resurrection, they find their branches broken and dangling from it, kept by God from enjoying the promised life that has for so long been the future of the tree and that God has begun to inspire into its present, yet held dangling from the tree in hope by God's election. The wounds of the tree and these branches where they have been broken off and are dangling are where the non-Jewish readers of Romans (and others) have been grafted into its life. Paul teaches these wild branches to live by the hospitable expectation that the broken branches by which they have found their own place in the tree will be restored to healthy sharing in the now eschatological life of the tree. He impresses upon them that if these natural branches have been broken off by their lack of faith, even more does their own future vitality in the life of the tree as wild branches depend on their own faith, which, as revealed in the faith of Christ, includes their solidarity with the natural branches now dangling near them.

We must not fail to recognize that while God's election of Israel is irrevocable (unconditional), neither faithless natural branches nor faithless wild branches will be spared in the pruning of this tree of righteousness.[103] Enjoying this Israelite table of eschatological blessing to which God's election draws all depends on the obedience of faith (cf. Matt. 8:11; 15:28).[104] It is conditional, as conditioned

---

103. Wright insightfully observes that God's "not sparing" (φείδομαι) natural or wild branches here in 11:21 is anticipated by God's "not sparing" (φείδομαι) God's own Son in 8:32, although he calls it a "strange echo" and does not exegete it (*Romans*, 685). The meaning is that even enduring the cutting of the tree is a matter of being determined by God's election of Israel in the elect one Jesus Messiah, a participation in his life (cf. the εἰς phrase and ἵνα clause of 1 Cor. 5:5). This is not what "happens if you regard yourself as automatically part of God's people" (685), but what happens if you live as if the life of the people of God were a matter of the people's works rather than God's election.

104. The reader may have noted that my reading of Romans 9–11 seeks to vindicate much of the exegetical tradition from Augustine to Calvin and to refuse the New Perspective to the extent that the New Perspective is locked in the modern discourse of peoplehood with its ethnicized and racialized imaginary. As the more traditional exegetical tradition maintains, Romans 9–11 is indeed about God's election over against the works of human willing and striving. On the other hand, I have been guided by the New Perspective—whose revision of our understanding of Second Temple Judaism is absolutely essential—to the extent that it rightly places in the

by God in and among human beings. The obedience of faith can therefore not be the condition or ontic equivalence of God's election but is the eschatologically-oriented work of that election, already growing in Abram and fully grown in Christ (who is the ontic equivalence of God's election and the human obedience of faith in one person). Thus, the tree remains the whole, visible/gathering people that God has elected into being under the name Israel, both broken and unbroken branches. And God moves Abraham's inheritance (finally the whole cosmos per Rom. 4:13) to the fullness of life in that tree through the obedience of faith, the life of salvation that is the irrevocably promised future of all Israel.[105]

2) We must not read into Romans 9–11 the bifurcation of the people of the God of Israel into two neatly distinct communities (much less "religions") known as the Jews and the church. Nor can we presume to be "the insiders" or to define "the outsiders" of the

foreground the oneness of Jews and gentiles at Israel's eschatological table of blessing (cf. Taubes, *The Political Theology of Paul*, 21) and problematizes the (Pietist) Protestant law-gospel distinction (which is quite alien to the likes of Augustine and Aquinas).

The trouble with much of the exegetical tradition from Augustine to Calvin (and with Moo), then, is not its concern with Pelagianism, but its (supersessionist) abstraction of God's election on the one hand, and human willing and striving on the other, from the history of Israel in the flesh as attested in the Bible (thereby undermining the covenant community as political community, as people). It is in this history in the flesh that God's election and human willing and striving have their sense in Romans 9–11. Thus, willing and striving are not primarily about individuals' working for the beatification of their souls, much less any general moral improvement, but attempting to secure for ourselves what God has promised to provide to Israel in God's own time. Thus, Romans 9–11 is indeed concerned with a politics that we might describe as Pelagian, i.e., attempting with our own willing and striving to supplement, police, and thus preempt God's election in the flesh.

105. In light of the explication of God's election of Israel in ch. 5 above, we might say that the future of the broken branches, those who learn from them and follow their ways over time, may be one of assimilation to gentile peoples, eventually with no human memory of their past in Israel. But that will be intelligible only in retrospect, and such a future is not necessary or present. It is therefore not a future for Paul or the readers (or the broken branches themselves) to fictitiously preempt by declaration or decision. What *is* for Paul and the readers is to respond with the Christian mercy and hospitality to the branches' current, broken presence by God's election. And should the future of their enemy relatives turn out to be lost in the sea of gentiles, the readers must remember that that is where they themselves have come from by God's election and where the future of God's election will continue to make its claim by the power of Jesus' name, by the Spirit of resurrection.

argument. I have already noted that the Israelite relatives of Paul in view are not to be totalized as non-Christian Israel much less as "ethnic Israel." They seem to be primarily Israelite relatives of Paul that are known to be openly hostile to his gospel and to the non-Jewish readers who have already benefitted directly from it.[106] They are no doubt part of a larger phenomenon of Israelite opposition of unknown proportions, which is touched by the argument of Romans 9–11 but not circumscribed by it. The immense and diverse Jewish community of Paul's time appears to have responded to his gospel in a wide variety of ways, many of which were simply ambiguous in their time. Accordingly, the tree does not correspond neatly to "the church" (for there is no ideal church), nor the broken branches to the non-Christian Jews of yesterday or today. I am not saying that the confession of Jesus as Messiah or the promise of life in his church is immaterial, for his is indeed the name of Israel's salvation and that of the rest of the world, in Israel and in him. But Christians cannot presume to be living more adequately to that confession or the calling of Israel than are non-Christian Jews. In fact, Yoder has given us good reason to believe that the Jews have been typically more adequate to that confession and calling than confessing Christians typically have (chapter 1 above). This is not to romanticize Judaism, only to say that Christians have a lot to learn about Jesus from many Jews and from Judaism, and it is to deny that confessing Christians are unambiguously the insiders and "non-Christian" Jews unambiguously the outsiders of Romans 9–11. In fact, according to the argument the Christian vocation consists partly in troubling such imposed borders and refusing the closure of an ecclesial "identity," as

---

106. Given the way that these relatives order (e.g., have the effect of dulling) part of Israel according to Romans 9–11, they probably include significant Jewish authorities in places like Rome. This is what Paul's encounters with synagogues in Acts would lead us to expect. Their power no doubt exerted pressure on more "conservative" members of the churches in Rome, as exhibited in various parts of the epistle (e.g., Rom. 2:17).

the church is made fundamentally of mercy. Its body is the work of God rather than the policing of the church. Faith that polices in this sense is not the faith of Jesus.[107]

3) Romans 9–11 knows of no "nature" (φύσις) that is timeless, changeless, and enclosed. It knows only of a "nature" that is open to formation by God's election in and through time. There is, for example, no essential Jewish nature (nor Christian nature nor gentile nature).[108] There is only the open history of each of these in the flesh, none of which is independent of the other, all of which are destined to converge in Israel's Messiah. The Jewish history and the Christian history are not safe from one another but mutually dependent and convergent. These histories are in fact mingled, remain vulnerable to one another, and are destined for one another. They are not so much histories as a history. That mingling, vulnerability, and destiny are not to be denied violently but negotiated peaceably. This means that the Christian confession that Jesus is the Messiah can no more leave Jews alone than it can leave Christians alone. It changes all of us.

4) My reading of Romans 9–11 is largely sympathetic with Barth's reading, certainly with the spirit of his reading. But whereas Barth has identified the mercy of God's election of the rejected in the realm of formal representation—where Ishmael, Esau, Pharaoh, and all non-Christian Jews (i.e., "the synagogue") are located in one group or form—I understand the mercy of God's election to be the shape of Israel's history in the flesh. Ishmael, Esau, and Pharaoh obviously have important places in the story of Israel, but the history of the flesh of

---

107. It is beyond the scope of Paul's and my argument to resolve for a suspect curiosity how salvation is in Christ alone and yet will embrace those who have not known Christ by name or even opposed him by name until the end of their dying. Suffice it to say that Paul's concern is with the way readers engage those from living Israel who oppose them until all living Israel is saved.

108. This means that we should beware of allowing differences derivative of a mythological Jewish-Christian difference to harden into a timeless something we imagine as "ethnic," to say nothing of a something we imagine as "national."

Israel did not include them, while it did include the Israelite relatives of Paul that are the occasion of Romans 9–11 (i.e., his flesh).

This is not to say that there is no analogy between the hardening of Pharaoh and the dulling whereby some branches of the tree of Israel are "broken off." Recall that the election whereby God distinguishes Israel from the gentile nations over time is of a piece with the election whereby God distinguishes some from others within Israel (chapters 4–5 above). Nor is this to say that there is no hope of resurrection for those not included in God's elect people in the flesh through time. Paul's claim that the purpose of God's election is mercy for all must be taken with due seriousness. But the election of Israel in the flesh (not according to the flesh) implies that the hope of such far-reaching mercy lives not in representations that we grasp with the mind (or that grasp our minds), but in the historical, bodily gathering of the people of God, whose beginning and end is the Son made flesh as Jesus the Messiah. Barth's christological representations remain abstractions of this gathering in the flesh. As such, they undermine our vulnerability to the people that God has in fact gathered, who remember the God of Israel as their own. Such representations encourage us to pretend that we can make a decision that corresponds to God's decision about who they are and who we are. But we must fix our eyes only on Jesus, on the oneness that he is as the Christ, on the oneness God has made us in him.

5) Yoder rightly tells us that the love of enemies is at the heart of who the church is. This requires, he insists, that it be a political community in its own right (i.e., a people) rather than a mere member association of some more determinative political entity such as the modern nation-state (e.g., the People of the United States). He also rightly understands this political vision to be that of many Jews since the time of Jeremiah. But he assumes that the political integrity of this people is predicated on its subjective adequacy to the love

God has revealed. In other words, Christians or Jews must embody a politics of adequate love in order to count as Christian or Jewish. Without this, Yoder supposes that there is nothing substantive to who the people of God is. But Romans 9–11 shows us that the love of God revealed in Christ is the love of God's election, which remains the only basis for who the people of God fundamentally is. Therefore, Christians cannot treat as foreign any of those whom God has elected into fellowship with us under the name of the God of Israel (in the sense clarified in chapter 5 above), no matter how opposed they are to the love of the cross. The love of election that culminates in the cross has already embraced them and compels us to embrace them in response. This means that we cannot disown Constantine even if we must oppose him. We cannot engage such enemies from behind a constructed wall of distinct identity, one that would make them "the false Israel" and us "the true Israel," them the foil and us the representatives. The past of God's election has left its indelible and irrevocable mark on who we are according to God's election in the present.[109]

We must therefore go further than Yoder and say not only that we are called to love our enemies but that we must love as "us" those people of the God of Israel who are unfaithful and hostile to us (and this may teach us to love others more faithfully as well). We must not engage in a politics (including our patterns of speaking and thought) of disowning them in the present, nor a historiography of disowning them in the past (e.g., by writing the history of those who are "truly" or "representatively" the people of God). In other words, our politics and historiography must be characterized by loving the first enemies that we meet—our parents. Not only the parents by whom God has given us our individual lives, but the many in God's people that bear

---

109. See Agamben's account of Walter Benjamin's *das Jetzt der Lesbarkeit* or *der Erkennbarkeit* in this connection (*The Time That Remains*, 145).

to us the past of God's election, who mediate that election to us, and whose old or corrupt ways might incline us to disown them in the spirit of revolution and false independence.[110] We love such enemies by remembering that they are we and we are they, for better or worse, as Jesus did with the Israelite gathering at the waters of the Jordan and especially on the cross. If our ancestors were unfaithful, they are among those that Yoder would have us regard as not the people of God. But we can hardly learn to love our enemies without naming as beloved according to election those enemies with whom God has already gathered us in and by God's name and naming, those whom God has graciously enabled us to remember as our own (e.g., 1 Cor. 10:1ff). By their presence, even if they are dead and seem to haunt us only by name, God calls upon us to be patient and, with the psalmist, to wait upon the Lord.

---

110. Attempting to disown, supersede, and thus blot out ancestors who have failed in the past is a recipe for a violent and vicious cycle of revolution. Honoring our parents, on the other hand, is the way to learn from our past as a gift, even when it is full of sins, and to promote forgiveness and peace in the present and future (cf. 1 Cor. 10:1ff). That is why the command that we honor our parents is the first to bear an explicit promise (Exod. 20:12; Deut. 5:16; Eph. 6:1-3).

Conclusion

In 1979, Jacob Taubes wrote the following to Carl Schmitt:

> Perhaps there will still come a moment at which we can speak about what is to me the most significant Jewish as well as Christian political theology, Rom. 9–11. The word "enemy" also appears there, in the absolute sense, but—and this seems to me to be the most decisive of decisive points—connected with "love."[1]

Taubes sees, with the help of the Apostle Paul, that the basis of peoplehood cannot be what Carl Schmitt theorized it to be under the violent spell of the modern discourse of peoplehood, namely, the difference between friend and enemy. Instead, the basis of peoplehood is the electing love of the God of Israel who holds friend and enemy together in the flesh with forgiveness (and this is a very Jewish thing to claim, according to Taubes).[2] That is the election of

---

1. Jacob Taubes, *The Political Theology of Paul*, trans. Dana Hollander (Stanford: Stanford University Press, 2004), 112. To the extent that Schmitt helpfully articulated the unconditional basis of political authority, Taubes insightfully called him the "apocalyptician of counterrevolution" (69). The problem was that Schmitt understood this apocalypse as a human decision rather than the decision of God (or a human decision ontically equivalent to God's and distinct from Christ himself) and the God of political theology as other than the God of Israel in the flesh (see ibid., 51, where Taubes recalls his exchange with Schmitt about Romans 9–11 and connects Schmitt's misunderstanding to racist theozoology).

2. The way in which this election is in the flesh names what is missing from Agamben's insightful comments on Romans. Without it, we are left with what must remain negative political theology that as such is more of an apophatic political philosophy. For example, the Pauline "call" (κλῆσις, as in Rom. 11:29) "is, above all, a nullification. . . . *The messianic vocation is*

413

Israel fully revealed in Jesus and still being worked out today. We can say that it is fully revealed in Jesus, who lived and died in loving solidarity with his people Israel, only because the God of Israel raised Jesus from the dead. Death names the coming apart of the collective and individual human body along with the rest of creation, a coming apart by which all of creation nevertheless lives (i.e., as food) and that it must fully endure to reach the healing of incorruptible life. In the specific language of the covenant, death names the manifold curse (affecting land, human community, animals, etc.) that Israel endures until it has run its course and God gives the people life that is no longer corruptible. The elect one crucified and raised thus embodies the life of the people of the God of Israel, whatever any part of that people may know of the way it is being transformed by that death and resurrection.[3]

---

the revocation of every vocation" (Giorgio Agamben, *The Time That Remains: A Commentary on the Letter to the Romans*, trans. Patricia Dailey [Stanford, CA: Stanford University Press, 2005], 23, emphasis his, cf. 41). While Agamben's warnings against a discrete and stable messianic identity are most welcome (and trouble Wright's and even Barth's readings), this claim of messianic nullification resembles too much the foundational political decision of Schmitt, which "emanates from nothingness" (Carl Schmitt, *Political Theology: Four Chapters on the Concept of Sovereignty*, trans. George Schwab [Chicago: University of Chicago Press, 2006], 32). Agamben offers us a compelling account of messianic time according to Paul, but we must not lose sight of the fact that that time is the time of Jesus, who is of the flesh of Israel. While it is true that we no longer know Jesus according to the flesh (2 Cor. 5:16), the Jesus that God raised from the dead is the same Jesus that died, and this identity is a body (which is always a relation of other bodies).

3. Note Barth's helpful observation to the effect that Romans 9–11 is not simply about a future hope, much less a mere idea, but a politics in the present: "The Christian axiom of v. 29 . . . according to the development of its meaning in vv. 30-32 . . . contains the consolation which the Church and the Synagogue have in common, but which also they can hear and receive only in common" (*Church Dogmatics*, ed. G. W. Bromiley and T. F. Torrance, 4 vols. in 13 parts [Edinburgh: T & T Clark, 1956–77], II/2, 303). He goes on to notice in Romans 9–11 that this consolation is not predicated on human subjectivity. Non-Jewish Christians might be tempted to invoke their obedience as their consolation—an impetus Wright's reading encourages—"Yet it is not stated [in vv. 29-32] that they have now become obedient. This might well have been stated, for now they have, in fact, become obedient. But this is only the consequence of their finding mercy, the mercy of the very God to whom they had previously been only disobedient" (ibid., 304). And thus comes Barth's Christian answer to the Jewish Question and the violence of modern peoplehood that grows from it: "What this striking second νῦν [of Rom. 11:31] makes quite impossible for Christian anti-semitism (he that has ears to hear, let him hear) is the

How can I say this when those of us confessing Jesus as Messiah have wreaked such havoc in the world on the backs of our Jewish sisters and brothers? I can only say that being Christian means we must confess this as sin and that our violent history is not closed but open, open to a future of peace. Christians must be committed to that future and confident in the promise of it so as to embody it in the present.

Modernity in the West has been at once a critique of the imperialist ambitions of Christendom and an attempt by some in the breakup of Christendom to make peoples themselves. Both have traded in an understanding of the election of Israel that is inadequate to the biblical witness. To the extent that it imagined itself as having replaced Israel, the "new Israel" of Christendom could not help but promote triumphalism and impatience with God's election. Likewise abstracted from the history of Israel in the flesh, modern Christian understandings of the election of Israel have been key to the construction of race and the derivative peoplehood of nationalism. This is to say that the idea of the election of Israel has been used to construct a mythological purity of identity that lies at the heart of modern peoples, a purity rightly named Whiteness (chapter 3 above).

The Bible deprives us of any such purity and insists that the backs of those on whom we might try to imagine and implement it are our sisters and our brothers, our very selves. Christian unity with Jews is therefore key to the peace the church is to seek with all. We have seen how the first Gospel and first letter of the New Testament canon declare the end of our vicious cycle of violent revolutions, for we do not choose ourselves into being as a people, nor is any group naturally the people of God (at least in the modern sense of

relegation of the Jewish question [*Judenfrage*] into the realm of eschatology. That Israel's hope is really the *hope* of Israel and the Church, and is therefore *future*, makes no difference to the fact that in relation to Israel the responsibility of the Church, which itself lives by God's mercy, is already a wholly present reality" (ibid., 305, emphasis his).

"natural"). The Israelite people we are by adoption (since Abram) has already been chosen by the God of Israel, and it includes those we have attempted to disown in order to constitute by violence our own national peoples.[4] God's election has thus preempted all our choosing and all our claims to what is natural.

Our shape as the people of God is also constantly coming to us from without, so we cannot meet those who lie beyond the covenant fellowship as alien, nor treat our "identity" as our possession. We can only expect to find our very self in Messiah in the vulnerable encounter with those who know nothing of the God of Israel or have practically forgotten that God. They, too, are to be recipients of God's mercy. It is the church's task to bear embodied witness to the one who is forming the people of God by the power of the resurrection through that ongoing encounter. It does this by a life of being conformed to the love of his death by the Spirit of that resurrection, by the power of his mercy.

We may repeat with comfortable enthusiasm that as Christians we are called to be a people different from that claimed by a modern nation-state like the United States. That is true as far as it goes, but I hope this book has helped the reader see how thinking that way may just be too easy. Too easy not because modern nation-states are "necessary" or "good," but because their roots in the West go very deep and they thoroughly shape our lives. Chapter 3 in particular should have clarified why "We the People" of the United States remains so immensely powerful, particularly why so many American Christians and others are content to go on killing and exploiting in its name, often with little idea of what they are doing. It has been

---

4. Accordingly, Taubes understands Paul to defy the docetic "as if" of modern political philosophy (targeting Adorno in particular, in whose writing "the whole messianic thing becomes a *comme si* affair," 74). Agamben traces the "as if" (or *als ob*) from Kant to the neo-Kantians and beyond (*The Time That Remains*, 35–37). But the messianic redemption is not an "as if" on which to build a new people but the historic redemption of Israel, the forgiveness of its sins.

formed through a mighty and dynamic mythology. Christians so inclined can say we're different all we want, but the fact remains that the theologically derived power of modern peoplehood deeply shapes our imaginations, associations, sociopolitical structures, economic patterns, and habits of mind and body, including of course the way we are church. The extent to which it has determined basic institutions, the landscape, and our manifold affections is simply mind-boggling. Moreover, our exegetical and theological habits are implicated in this formation of modern peoplehood and continue to contribute to it. So there is no criticizing something like "We the People" of the United States or another modern nation-state—and there have been worse political orders—from some safely distinct theological, biblical, or ecclesial place.

More pertinent to the argument of this entire book: if Christians respond to the oppressive power of modern peoplehood by claiming to be an independent political entity as the people of God, we will not be able to offer substantive resistance to the racialized, voluntarist, friend-enemy difference that underlies modern political orders of peoplehood. And we will correspondingly remain internally divisive in the service of a false internal purity of identity. We will continue to play along with that violent political difference, which is precisely what does so much to make a great many people killable and many more exploitable, what raises international borders that protect some at the price of disappearing and exposing others, what orders society so that the bodies of some are the mammon machinery of others, and what makes community a place of rivalry rather than peacemaking.

So let us repent of pretending to decide who is "truly" the people of God and who is not, of a politics of constructing and policing mythological borders of peoplehood between ourselves and others who remember the God of Israel as their own. Such is a politics that involves disowning our sisters and brothers, as well as doing violence to others who are by extension supposedly "not us." Let us read the Bible more carefully, so as to tell the gospel as a story of the deepest solidarity rather than violent supersession. And let that story of God's love inform ways of mingling our flesh with those from whom our current borders divide us, be they territorial or deeper boundaries. The catholicity of Jesus is not a matter of "truthful" assertions from a safe distance, but the most self-implicating kind of political economic practice, a politics which itself opens our ears to hear the gospel as we have not before and to see Jesus as we have not before. Because the catholic way of Jesus is the politics of God's election of Israel that culminates in cross and resurrection, we should expect it to be more dangerous than we can anticipate, and at once a life of peculiar hope, a life of hospitality that the New Testament calls faith.

This is partly a life of conflict, of course, a life of disputes. But we cannot disown those with whom we have a dispute about how to be the people of the God of Israel, however wrong they may seem, for God has already claimed them as God's own, as is evident in their being part of the dispute. Let us not underestimate the fact that they contend with us in the name of that God and not some other. The Christian discipline of patience enjoined upon us by God's election of Israel as revealed in Messiah is to respond faithfully to the claims to be the people of God with which we are in fact presented, rather than preemptively excluding them (e.g., by overly objectifying or otherwise stabilizing the difference between us); it is to discourage their unfaithfulness and to encourage their faithfulness as we remain in peaceable, material, costly solidarity with them, even in opposing them. This is the catholicity of Jesus, in whose name and by whose light we are called to love as God loves, that is, patiently. It is at once the hope for the oneness of the people of God and the hope that that people embodies for the rest of the world. Such catholic patience with God's election is at the heart of the plea with which we began in chapter 1—that of Gamaliel, a Pharisee in the Sanhedrin, a teacher of the law, one honored by all the people: "I say to you, leave these men alone and release them. Because if this movement or this work be merely of human beings, it will be destroyed. But if it is of God, you will not be able to destroy them, and you may well find yourselves fighting against God" (Acts 5:38-39).

Selected Bibliography

Agamben, Giorgio. *The State of Exception*. Translated by Kevin Attell. Chicago: The University of Chicago Press, 2005.

_____. *The Time That Remains: A Commentary on the Letter to the Romans*. Translated by Patricia Daily. Stanford, CA: Stanford University Press, 2005.

Anderson, Benedict. *Imagined Communities: Reflections on the Origin and Spread of Nationalism*. London: Verso, 1983.

Bader-Saye, Scott. *Church and Israel after Christendom: The Politics of Election*. Eugene, OR: Wipf & Stock Publishers, 1999.

Balibar, Étienne. "Citizen Subject." In *Who Comes after the Subject?* edited by Eduardo Cadava, Peter Connor, and Jean-Luc Nancy, 33–57. New York: Routledge, 1991.

_____. "The Nation Form: History and Ideology." Translated by Chris Turner. In *Race, Nation, Class: Ambiguous Identities*, edited by Étienne Balibar and Immanuel Maurice Wallerstein, 86–106. London: Verso, 1991.

_____. "Racism and Nationalism." Translated by Chris Turner. In *Race, Nation, Class: Ambiguous Identities*, edited by Étienne Balibar and Immanuel Maurice Wallerstein, 37–67. London: Verso, 1991.

Barth, Karl. *Church Dogmatics*, edited by G. W. Bromiley and T. F. Torrance. 4 Vols. in 13 Parts. Edinburgh: T & T Clark, 1956-77.

_____. *The Church and the Political Problem of Our Day*. New York: Charles Scribner's Sons, 1939.

_____. *The Epistle to the Romans*. Translated by Edwyn C. Hoskyns. Oxford: Oxford University Press, 1933.

Barton, Stephen C. "The Gospel according to Matthew." In *The Cambridge Companion to the Gospels*, edited by Stephen C. Barton, 121–138. Cambridge: Cambridge University Press, 2006.

Batnitzky, Leora. *Idolatry and Representation: The Philosophy of Franz Rosenzweig Reconsidered*. Princeton: Princeton University Press, 2000.

Bauman, Zygmunt. *Intimations of Postmodernity*. London: Routledge, 1991.

Bell, David A. *The Cult of the Nation in France: Inventing Nationalism, 1680-1800*. Cambridge, MA: Harvard University Press, 2003.

Bercovitch, Sacvan. *The American Jeremiad*. Madison, WI: University of Wisconsin Press, 1978.

_____. *The Puritan Origins of the American Self*. New Haven: Yale University Press, 2011.

_____. *The Rites of Assent: Transformations in the Symbolic Construction of America*. New York: Routledge, 1993.

Berkhof, Hendrik. *Christ and the Powers*. Translated by John Howard Yoder. Scottdale, PA: Herald Press, 1977.

Bonhoeffer, Dietrich. *Christ the Center*. Translated by Edwin H. Robertson. San Francisco: Harper Collins, 1960, 1978.

_____. *The Cost of Discipleship*. Translated by R. H. Fuller. New York: Touchstone, 1995.

Boyarin, Daniel. *Border Lines: The Partition of Judaeo-Christianity*. Philadelphia: University of Pennsylvania Press, 2004.

Breen, T. H. "Ideology and Nationalism on the Eve of the American Revolution: Revisions Once More in Need of Revising." *The Journal of American History* 84, no. 1 (Jun. 1997): 13–39.

Bultmann, Rudolph. *Theology of the New Testament*. New York: Scribner, 1951.

Busch, Eberhard. *Unter dem Bogen des einen Bundes: Karl Barth und die Juden 1933-1945*. Neukirchen-Vluyn: Neukirchener, 1996.

Carter, Charles Edward, and Carol L. Meyers, eds. *Community, Identity, and Ideology: Social Science Approaches to the Hebrew Bible*. Winona Lake, IN: Eisenbrauns, 1996.

Carter, J. Kameron. *Race: A Theological Account*. Oxford: Oxford University Press, 2008.

Chatterjee, Partha. *The Nation and Its Fragments: Colonial and Postcolonial Histories*. Princeton: Princeton University Press, 1993.

Cohen, Jeremy. *Living Letters of the Law: Ideas of the Jew in Medieval Christianity*. Berkeley: University of California Press, 1999.

Cohen, Shaye J. D. *Beginnings of Jewishness: Boundaries, Varieties, Uncertainties*. Berkeley and Los Angeles: University of California Press, 1999.

_____. "The Significance of Yavneh: Pharisees, Rabbis, and the End of Jewish Sectarianism." *Hebrew Union College Annual* 55 (1984): 27–53.

Colley, Linda. *Britons: Forging the Nation 1707-1837*. New Haven: Yale University Press, 1992.

Columbus, Christopher. *The Four Voyages of Christopher Columbus*. Edited and translated by J. M. Cohen. London: Penguin Books, 1969.

Connor, William. *Ethno-Nationalism: The Quest for Understanding*. Princeton: Princeton University Press, 1994.

Crown, Alan David, ed. *The Samaritans*. Tübingen: Mohr Siebeck, 1989.

Dahl, Nils Alstrup. *Das Volk Gottes: Eine Untersuchung zum Kirchenbewusstsein des Urchristentums*. Oslo: I Kommisjon Jos Jacob Dybwad, 1941.

Davies, W. D., and Dale C. Allison Jr. *Matthew*. Vol. 2 of ICC. Edinburgh: T & T Clark, 1991.

Deutsch, Karl. *Nationalism and Social Communication*. 2nd ed. New York: MIT Press, 1966.

Dobkowski, Michael N. *The Tarnished Dream: The Basis of American Anti-Semitism.* Westport, CT: Greenwood Press, 1979.

Dunn, James D. G. *The Theology of Paul the Apostle.* Grand Rapids, MI: Wm. B. Eerdmans, 1998.

Feldman, Kiera. "The Romance of Birthright Israel." *The Nation* 293, no. 1 (July 4, 2011): 22–26.

Feldman, Louis H. *Jew and Gentile in the Ancient World: Attitudes and Interactions from Alexander to Justinian.* Princeton: Princeton University Press, 1993.

Fishman, Joshua. "Social Theory and Ethnography: Neglected Perspectives on Language and Ethnicity in Eastern Europe." In *Ethnic Conflict and Diversity in Eastern Europe*, edited by Peter Sugar, 69–99. Santa Barbara, California: ABC-Clio, 1980.

Ford, David F. *Self and Salvation: Being Transformed.* Cambridge: Cambridge University Press, 1999.

Foucault, Michel. *The History of Sexuality: An Introduction.* Translated by Robert Hurley. New York: Vintage Books, 1990.

France, R. T. *The Gospel of Matthew.* NICNT. Grand Rapids, MI: Eerdmans, 2007.

Frei, Hans W. *The Eclipse of Biblical Narrative: A Study in Eighteenth and Nineteenth Century Hermeneutics.* Chelsea, MI: Yale University, 1974.

Gellner, Ernest. *Thought and Change.* London: Weidenfeld and Nicolson, 1964.

Hall, Stuart. "Ethnicity: Identity and Difference," *Radical America* 23 (1989): 17-20.

_____, and Bram Gieben, eds. *Formations of Modernity.* Cambridge: Polity Press, 1992.

Harink, Douglas. *Paul among the Postliberals: Pauline Theology beyond Christendom and Modernity.* Grand Rapids, MI: Brazos, 2003.

Hengel, Martin. *Judaism and Hellenism: Studies in Their Encounter in Palestine During the Early Hellenistic Period.* Translated by John Bowden. Philadelphia: Fortress Press, 1981, 1974.

Herder, J. G. *Herder on Social and Political Culture: A Selection of Texts.* Translated and edited by F. M. Barnard. Cambridge: Cambridge University Press, 1969.

Heschel, Susannah. *The Aryan Jesus: Christian Theologians and the Bible in Nazi Germany.* Princeton: Princeton University Press, 2008.

Hill, Christopher. *Milton and the English Revolution.* London: Faber, 1977.

Hosking, Geoffrey A. *Russia: People and Empire, 1552-1917.* Cambridge, MA: Harvard University Press, 1997.

Howard, Thomas Albert. *Protestant Theology and the Making of the Modern German University.* Oxford: Oxford University Press, 2006.

Hunsinger, George. "Election and the Trinity: Twenty-five Theses on the Theology of Karl Barth." *Modern Theology* 24, no. 2 (April 2008): 179–198.

Kaminsky, Joel S. *Yet I Loved Jacob: Reclaiming the Biblical Concept of Election.* Nashville: Abingdon, 2007.

Kelley, Shawn. *Racializing Jesus: Race, Ideology, and the Formation of Modern Biblical Scholarship.* London: Routledge, 2002.

Klotz, Marcia. "The Weimar Republic: A Postcolonial State in a Still-Colonial World." In *Germany's Colonial Pasts,* edited by Eric Ames, Marcia Klotz, and Lora Wildenthal, 135–147. Lincoln: University of Nebraska Press, 2005.

Lehmann, Hartmut. "Pietism and Nationalism: The Relationship between Protestant Revivalism and National Renewal in 19th Century Germany." *Church History* 51 (1982): 39-53.

Levine, Amy-Jill. *The Social and Ethnic Dimensions of Matthean Salvation History.* Vol. 14 of Studies in the Bible and Early Christianity. Lewiston, New York: Mellen House, 1988.

_____. "'To All the Gentiles': A Jewish Perspective on the Great Commission." *Review and Expositor* 103, no. 1 (Winter 2006): 139–158.

Luz, Ulrich. *Matthew 1-7: A Commentary*. Translated by James E. Crouch. Minneapolis: Fortress Press, 2007.

Marcus, Joel. "Birkat Ha-Minim Revisited." *New Testament Studies* 55 (2009): 523-51.

Martyn, J. Louis. *History and Theology in the Fourth Gospel*. Louisville, KY: Westminster John Knox Press, 1968, 1979, 2003.

McCormack, Bruce. "Grace and Being: The Role of God's Gracious Election in Karl Barth's Theological Ontology." In *The Cambridge Companion to Karl Barth*, edited by John Webster, 92–110. Cambridge: Cambridge University Press, 2000.

Miller, Perry. *The Life of the Mind in America: From the Revolution to the Civil War*. New York: Harcourt, Brace & World, 1965.

Neusner, Jacob. *In the Aftermath of Catastrophe: Founding Judaism 70-640*. Quebec: McGill-Queen's University Press, 2009.

_____. *Making God's Word Work: A Guide to the Mishnah*. New York: The Continuum International Publishing Group, 2004.

_____. *Method and Meaning in Ancient Judaism*. Missoula: Scholars Press, 1979.

_____, Bruce Chilton and William Graham. *Three Faiths, One God: The Formative Faith and Practice of Judaism*. Boston: Brill, 2002.

_____, William Scott Green, and Eernst S. Frerichs, eds. *Judaism and Their Messiahs*. Cambridge: Cambridge University Press, 1987.

Novak, David. *The Election of Israel: The Idea of a Chosen People*. Cambridge: Cambridge University Press, 1995.

Painter, Nell Irvin. *The History of White People*. New York: W. W. Norton & Company, 2010.

Pease, Donald E. *The New American Exceptionalism*. Critical American Studies. Minneapolis: University of Minnesota Press, 2009.

Poliakov, Léon. *The History of Anti-Semitism, vol. III: From Voltaire to Wagner.* Translated by Miriam Kochan. Philadelphia: University of Pennsylvania Press, 1975, 2003.

Renan, Ernest. "What Is a Nation." Translated by Martin Thom. In *Nation and Narration,* edited by Homi K. Bhabha. London: Routledge, 1990.

Riff, Michael. "Nationalism." In *Dictionary of Modern Political Ideologies,* edited by M. A. Riff, 145–165. New York: St. Martin's Press, 1987.

Rosenzweig, Franz. *The Star of Redemption.* Translated by Barbara E. Galli. Madison, WI: University of Wisconsin Press, 2005.

Said, Edward W. *Orientalism.* New York: Vintage Books, 1979.

Sanders, E. P. *Paul and Palestinian Judaism: A Comparison of Patterns of Religion.* Philadelphia: Fortress Press, 1977.

Schama, Simon. *The Embarrassment of Riches: An Interpretation of Dutch Culture in the Golden Age.* New York: Random House, 1987.

Schmitt, Carl *The Concept of the Political: Expanded Edition.* Translated by George Schwab. Chicago: The University of Chicago Press, 2007.

_____. *Political Theology: Four Chapters on the Concept of Sovereignty.* Chicago: The University of Chicago Press, 1985.

Sechrest, Love L. *A Former Jew: Paul and the Dialectics of Race.* London: T & T Clark, 2009.

Sheehan, Jonathan. *The Enlightenment Bible: Translation, Scholarship, Culture.* Princeton: Princeton University Press, 2005.

Sim, David C. *The Gospel of Matthew and Christian Judaism: The History and Social Setting of the Matthean Community.* Studies in the New Testament and Its World. Edinburgh: T & T Clark, 1998.

Simon, Marcel. *Verus Israel: A Study of the Relations between Christians and Jews in the Roman Empire (AD 135-425).* Translated by H. McKeating. Oxford: Oxford University Press; Littman Library of Jewish Civilization, 1986.

Smith, Anthony D. *Chosen Peoples: Sacred Sources of National Identity*. Oxford: Oxford University Press, 2003.

Sonderegger, Katherine. *That Christ Was Born a Jew: Karl Barth's "Doctrine of Israel."* University Park, Pennsylvania: The Pennsylvania State University Press, 1992.

Soulen, Kendall. *The God of Israel and Christian Theology*. Minneapolis: Fortress Press, 1996.

Spruyt, Hendrik. *The Sovereign State and Its Competitors*. Princeton: Princeton University Press, 1994.

Stanton, Graham. *The Gospels and Jesus*. 2nd ed. Oxford: Oxford University Press, 2002.

_____. *A Gospel for a New People: Studies in Matthew*. Louisville, KY: Westminster John Knox Press, 1992.

Stille, Alexander. "Historians Trace an Unholy Alliance: Religion as the Root of Nationalist Feeling." *New York Times*, May 31, 2003, Online edition.

Strathmann, Hermann. "Laós in the New Testament." In *Theological Dictionary of the New Testament: Abridged in One Volume*, edited by Geoffrey W. Bromiley, 502. Grand Rapids, MI: Wm. B. Eerdmans, 1985.

Taubes, Jacob. *The Political Theology of Paul*. Translated by Dana Hollander. Stanford: Stanford University Press, 2004.

Thurman, Howard. *Jesus and the Disinherited*. New York: Abingdon-Cokesbury; Boston: Beacon, 1949, 1976, 1996.

Wellhausen, Julius. *Prolegomena to the History of Israel, with a reprint of the article "Israel" from the Encyclopedia Britannica*. Atlanta: Scholars Press, 1994.

Willitts, Joel. "Matthew's Messianic Shepherd-king: In Search of 'the Lost Sheep of the House of Israel.'" *Harvard Theological Studies* 63:1 (March 2007): 365-382.

Wright, N.T. *The Letter to the Romans*. Volume X of *The New Interpreter's Bible: A Commentary in Twelve Volumes*. Nashville: Abingdon Press, 2002.

_____. *The New Testament and the People of God*. Minneapolis: Fortress Press, 1992.

_____. *Paul and the Faithfulness of God*. Minneapolis: Fortress Press, 2013.

Wyschogrod, Michael. *The Body of Faith: God in the People of Israel*. Northvale, NJ: Jason Aronson, Inc., 1996, 1983.

_____. *The Body of Faith: Judaism as Corporeal Election*. New York: Seabury Press, 1983.

Yoder, John Howard. *Body Politics: Five Practices of the Christian Community before the Watching World*. Nashville, TN: Discipleship Resources, 1992.

_____. *Christian Attitudes to War, Peace, and Revolution*. Edited by Theodore J. Koontz and Andy Alexis-Baker.Grand Rapids, MI: Brazos Press, 2009.

_____. *The Christian Witness to the State*. 2nd ed. Scottdale, PA: Herald Press, 1964, 2002.

_____. *For the Nations: Essays Evangelical and Public*. Grand Rapids, MI: Wm. B. Eerdmans, 1997.

_____. *The Jewish-Christian Schism Revisited*. Edited by Michael G. Cartwright and Peter Ochs. Grand Rapids, MI: Wm. B. Eerdmans, 2003.

_____. *Nevertheless: Varieties and Shortcomings of Religious Pacifism*. Scottdale, PA: Herald Press, 1992.

_____. *The Original Revolution: Essays on Christian Pacifism*. Scottdale, PA: Herald Press, 1971.

_____. *The Politics of Jesus: vicit Agnus noster*. Rev. ed. Grand Rapids, MI: Wm. B. Eerdmans, 1972, 1994.

_____. *The Royal Priesthood: Essays Eschatological and Ecumenical*. Edited by Michael G. Cartwright. Scottdale, PA: Herald Press, 1998.

Zamora, Margarita. *Reading Columbus*. Berkeley: University of California Press, 1993.

Index

CPSIA information can be obtained at www.ICGtesting.com
Printed in the USA
LVOW07s2139150914

404125LV00004B/6/P